Medical Negligence

The Cranium, Spine and Nervous System

Edited by

John Garfield
MChir, FRCP, FRCS

C.J. Earl
MD, FRCP, FRCOphth

Blackwell
Science

Editorial Offices:
Osney Mead, Oxford OX2 0EL
25 John Street, London WC1N 2BL
23 Ainslie Place, Edinburgh EH3 6AJ
350 Main Street, Malden
MA 02148 5018, USA
54 University Street, Carlton
Victoria 3053, Australia
10, rue Casimir Delavigne
75006 Paris, France

Other Editorial Offices:

Blackwell Wissenschafts-Verlag GmbH
Kurfürstendamm 57
10707 Berlin, Germany

Blackwell Science KK
MG Kodenmacho Building
7–10 Kodenmacho Nihombashi
Chuo-ku, Tokyo 104, Japan

First published 1999

Set in 10/13 pt Palatino
by DP Photosetting, Aylesbury, Bucks
Printed and bound in Great Britain by
MPG Books Ltd, Bodmin, Cornwall

DISTRIBUTORS

Marston Book Services Ltd
PO Box 269
Abingdon
Oxford OX14 4YN
(*Orders:* Tel: 01235 465500
Fax: 01235 465555)

USA
Blackwell Science, Inc.
Commerce Place
350 Main Street
Malden, MA 02148 5018
(*Orders:* Tel: 800 759 6102
781 388 8250
Fax: 781 388 8255)

Canada
Login Brothers Book Company
324 Saulteaux Crescent
Winnipeg, Manitoba R3J 3T2
(*Orders:* Tel: 204 837 2987
Fax: 204 837 3116)

Australia
Blackwell Science Pty Ltd
54 University Street
Carlton, Victoria 3053
(*Orders:* Tel: 03 9347 0300
Fax: 03 9347 5001)

A catalogue record for this title is available from the British Library

ISBN 0–632–05183–3

Library of Congress
Cataloging-in-Publication Data
Medical negligence: the cranium, spine, and nervous system/edited by John Garfield, Christopher Earl.
p. cm.
Includes bibliographical references and index.
ISBN 0-632-05183-3
1. Neurological errors. 2. Neurologists–Malpractice–Great Britain.
3. Neurosurgeons–Malpractice–Great Britain.
I. Garfield, John, 1930– . II. Earl, Christopher.
RC346.3.M43 1999
616.8–dc21 99-17519
CIP

For further information on
Blackwell Science, visit our website:
www.blackwell-science.com

Contents

Contributors

John Garfield MChir, FRCP, FRCS Honorary Emeritus Consultant Neurosurgeon, Wessex Neurological Centre, Southampton University Hospitals NHS Trust.

C.J. Earl MD, FRCP, FRCOphth Honorary Consultant Physician, National Hospital for Neurology and Neurosurgery, Queen Square, Middlesex Hospital, Moorfields Eye Hospital, London.

John R. Bartlett MB, BChir, FRCS Consultant Neurosurgeon, King's College Hospital, London.

George Bonney MS, FRCS Formerly Orthopaedic Surgeon to the former St Mary's Hospital, Paddington, London.

Edward M. Brett MA, DM, FRCP, Hon FRCPCH Honorary Consultant Neurologist, Great Ormond Street Hospital for Children NHS Trust and former Consultant Physician, the National Hospital for Neurology and Neurosurgery, London.

Hugh Halle FRCGP General Practitioner.

Anthony D. Hockley MB, BS, FRCS Consultant Neurosurgeon, Birmingham Children's and Queen Elizabeth Hospitals, Birmingham.

R.A. Johnston MD, FRCS Consultant Neurosurgeon, Institute of Neurological Sciences and Queen Elizabeth National Spinal Injuries Unit, Glasgow.

B.E. Kendall FRCR, FRCP, FRCS Consultant Neuroradiologist, Royal Free Hospital, London, National Hospital for Neurology and Neurosurgery.

M.A.M.S. Leigh, Solicitor Senior Partner, Hempsons Solicitors.

Lindsay McLellan MA, MB, PhD, FRCP Professor of Rehabilitation, Rehabilitation Research Unit, University of Southampton.

David Markham FRCS Formerly Consultant Orthopaedic Surgeon, Manchester Royal Infirmary.

David Sumner TD, BSc, MB, FRCP, FRCP (Ed) Formerly Consultant Neurologist, St James's Hospital, Leeds.

Adrian Whitfield QC 3 Serjeants' Inn, London.

Introduction

In the UK and elsewhere, medical negligence litigation is increasing. Some of the increase is related to errors in practice which should never occur if simple rules of clinical management are followed, clinical information is accurately recorded, and there is appropriate communication with patients. These principles are applicable to all forms of medical practice, and have been the subject of many publications.

Neurologists and neurosurgeons do not figure frequently as defendants in medical negligence actions. Patients with neurological and neurosurgical disorders usually present, in the first place, to 'generalists', that is to doctors who are not specialists in, or who do not have special training in the clinical neurosciences. Such generalists include general practitioners, general physicians, general surgeons, orthopaedic surgeons and casualty officers.

Because many disorders of the nervous system are rare, the individual generalist is unlikely to acquire any considerable personal experience in this field. Since most medical practice depends upon personal experience and training, it might appear that the 'generalist' is at particular risk of making errors which lead to litigation. Two questions then arise: (1) What level of knowledge and experience in this very specialised field is required of the generalist? (2) Can simple general rules of management and setting of priorities make up for the lack of highly specialised knowledge and experience? In effect the two questions are also applicable to the specialist, especially in these days of increasing sub-specialisation within the clinical neurological sciences. These are questions which provoke great efforts of advocacy when issues of liability are being tried. As methods of neurological investigation become increasingly sophisticated, accurate and more widely available, both the generalist and the specialist may appear to become more liable to criticism for failing to be aware of, and to implement, such studies. This could be regarded as a race, *ad infinitum*, between available technical advances and individual knowledge and clinical experience. Fortunately, as the different sections of this book show, courts, at least in the UK, are aware of this dilemma and defendants will not be expected to have won the race at every stage of their professional careers.

Another reason for special consideration of the clinical neurological sciences is the nature and implications of neurological disability. Quite apart from its more emotive aspects, there are special difficulties in assessing the level of, and prognosis for, disability, particularly in cases involving children. In the context of litigation, financial quantification of damages may lead to very large settlements, not unlike those appropriate to birth injuries attributable to obstetric error. These may be a consequence of errors by the generalist as much as by the specialist. Hence as much legal attention is devoted to issues of causation as to those of liability; and negotiations and arguments in court over levels of damages may be very prolonged. Often they are a matter of opinion or even speculation from opposing experts, which, ideally, should be settled by reasonable compromise, a course which judges are likely to endorse.

In many cases allegations against generalists which do not appear to be of a neurological nature at first sight may lead to complex causation arguments when the patient is left with significant neurological disability. In those circumstances the generalist may be surprised and disturbed to find that in pursuing the causation aspects of a case, his actions are minutely examined in terms of their consequences for neurological function. Therefore there are sections of this book which deal with the assessment and quantification of neurological disability in general. There is a separate section dealing with the special problems arising in children.

This book is not intended to be yet another text on selected topics in neurology and neurosurgery, nor is it a catalogue of common diagnostic and management errors. Every clinician can expect to make mistakes in diagnosis and management which cannot be regarded as negligent. That does not diminish the importance of highlighting those errors which, in the experience of the authors, have led to legal action with allegations of medical negligence. Throughout the book the accent is upon those situations which have actually led to such actions where neurological aspects have played a central part in relation either to liability or to causation, or both. Therefore contributions have been invited from those who are known to have considerable personal experience in advising in medical negligence actions, and who have advised, at different times, plaintiffs and defendants. Since the expert's duty is to advise the court rather than plead a litigant's case – a duty which is easily overlooked and to which attention has been drawn in Court of Appeal judgments – it is to be expected that respected experts' advice will be sought by plaintiffs and defendants. For that reason we have asked our contributors to concentrate upon the simple errors which have led to medical negligence actions. It is the simple errors which are more likely to become clear from evidence given at trial. In the same way, the simpler points in reports will carry far greater weight than more complex arguments in lengthy experts' reports produced in support of one party's pleaded case.

Although neurological and neurosurgical disorders are the main subjects of this book, its object is to provide guidance for those in other disciplines, general or specialist, in which the nervous system and its skeletal adjuncts are involved. Inevitably some readers will disagree with opinions expressed by the contributors. We will be encouraged by such disagreements, which reflect continuing medical controversies, and which demand so much time and effort from lawyers and from the judiciary. It will also show that the book is not yet another soporific text in a specialty which is too often regarded as being beyond the generalist, who may be overcome by fear of the minutiae of neurology of which many are largely irrelevant to good medical practice.

John Garfield and Christopher Earl

Chapter 1

The Law

Adrian Whitfield QC

One hundred years, or even 25 years, ago the need for a book on the impact of the law on any branch of medicine would have seemed wholly unnecessary. The law barely troubled the lives of doctors, and 'medical law' was not a subject known to law students. Today, however, the law is a matter of growing concern to the former and of growing interest to the latter.

The type of litigation of which the medical profession is most aware is the claim for damages for professional negligence. It is notorious that the number and size of claims has grown, and it is worthwhile considering why this is so. In a recent article in the *Lancet* entitled 'Why do people sue doctors? A study of doctors and relatives taking legal action'[1] it was concluded that:

> 'the decision to take legal action was determined not only by the original injury, but also by insensitive handling and poor communication after the original incident. Where explanations were given, less than 15% were considered satisfactory. Four main themes emerged from the analysis of reasons for litigation: concern with standards of care – both patients and relatives wanted to prevent similar incidents in the future; the need for an explanation – to know how the injury happened and why; compensation – for actual losses, pain and suffering or to provide care in the future for an injured person; and accountability – a belief that the staff or organisation should have to account for their actions.
>
> 'Patients taking legal action wanted greater honesty, an appreciation of the severity of the trauma they had suffered, and assurances that lessons had been learnt from their experiences.'

Current trends show that the volume of such litigation is continuing to increase. For example, in 1998 the Medical Defence Union reported an annual increase of 15% in the number of claims: the Department of Health reported an annual increase of 20% in litigation costs. There are several reasons for this. First, the growing level of sophistication and success in medical treatment has raised patients' expectation of success, and thus added to the sense of grievance which is experienced when a good result is not achieved. Second, in the last few years the existence of organisations which support patients' rights, notably Action for Victims of Medical Accidents, has made it far easier for patients to get access to competent expert medical and legal advice. Third, there has been a growth in the number of skilled and committed lawyers trained in the presentation of claims on behalf of patients.

However, not all medical law is about suing doctors. Indeed, such claims, though highly publicised and disturbing to the practitioners involved, raise only the one issue of the right to compensation, and do not touch on a number of legal and ethical problems which affect medical practitioners. It has been said of medical law[2]:

> 'There are common issues which permeate all the problems which arise: respect for autonomy, consent, truth-telling, confidentiality, respect for personhood and persons, respect for dignity and respect for justice. All of these ethical issues run throughout the field. Until these common themes are recognised and reflected in legal thinking and analysis, a coherent approach to the emerging problems in medical law will be difficult. Thus, we see medical law as having some conceptual unity. The unifying legal theme is, to us, that of human rights. In our view, therefore, medical law is a subset of human rights law. This is what provides its intellectual coherence.'

Thus, in some legal bookshops the books about medical law are, correctly, placed on shelves marked 'Civil Liberties'.

Until comparatively recently, most ethical issues were decided, in private, by doctors themselves using good sense, experience and intraprofessional ethical standards. However, within the last ten years there has been increased resort to the courts for declaratory rulings about what, broadly, may be called 'treatment decisions', by which is meant decisions on such issues as whether to treat in the absence of consent, whether to treat for reasons which are not purely clinical (e.g. to sterilise for social or welfare reasons) and whether to withdraw treatment from the terminally ill. This trend is healthy in that it helps to demystify the ethics of the doctor–patient relationship and should promote greater confidence on both sides. The volume of this type of litigation is not increasing, because a body of principle has been established, but cases continue to go to court because the details are still being worked out on a case-to-case basis.

For all these reasons, the individual practitioner is becoming more and more likely to come into contact with the law. This may be because he or she is sued, or because a colleague or employer is sued and the doctor is needed as a witness, or (not uncommonly in neurology and neurosurgery) because a difficult ethical decision is thought to require the approval of a High Court judge and the protection of a declaratory judgment. In all these contexts, a doctor may have to give evidence of fact: alternatively, he or she may volunteer to give expert evidence to the court. It is the purpose of this chapter to give some very general guidance as to the problems which may be encountered by doctors in their contact with the law, preceded by a brief introduction (no more) to certain important legal concepts.

Consent to treatment: competent adults

There is a legal presumption that every adult has the mental capacity to consent to treatment, that is to say the ability to understand sufficiently the nature, purpose and effects of the treatment proposed and to make and communicate a decision on the matter in question. In considering the sufficiency or otherwise of the patient's capacity to understand, the court will consider not only whether the patient can comprehend and retain treatment information, but also whether he or she believes it and is capable of 'weighing it in the balance to arrive at choice' [*Re C* (Adult: Refusal of Treatment)][3]. In the case of such a 'competent adult', the importance of consent to treatment cannot be over-emphasised. In the famous words of an American judge [in *Schloendorff* v. Society of New York Hospital (1914)][4]:

> 'Every human being of adult years and sound mind has a right to determine what shall be done with his own body, and a surgeon who performs an operation without his patient's consent commits an assault.'

It is important to note that while mistaken belief that there has been consent is a defence to a criminal charge of assault, it is arguably no defence to a civil claim. Nor is it any defence that other doctors, however respectable, might have done the same, or that the treatment was good for the patient. A competent adult is perfectly entitled to refuse treatment which is in his or her best interest, even treatment required to save life, and can do so for reasons which are idiosyncratic, irrational or indeed non-existent. Thus, a 'competent adult' hunger striker can refuse food, a 'competent adult' woman in labour can refuse Caesarean section whatever the risks to herself and the fetus, and a 'competent adult' Jehovah's Witness can refuse a blood transfusion [*Home Secretary* v. *Robb* (1995); *Re MB* (1997); *Re T* (an Adult: Refusal of Treatment) (1993)]: provided they know what they are doing and appreciate the consequences, then nobody can override their wishes[5].

Moreover, it is to be noted that it is possible for a patient to place an anticipatory ban on treatment. A simple example is that of a card carried by a Jehovah's Witness, which may ban the transfusion of blood products even if later indicated from a medical point of view. During the 1970s, there emerged in the USA legislation designed to give effect to a 'living will', or anticipatory refusal by a patient to be treated in certain ways, should he or she later become incompetent. Subsequent developments led to legislation permitting the appointment of a 'health care proxy' by the creation of durable powers of attorney empowering an identified person to make health care decisions after the onset of incompetence. These two devices together became known as 'advance directives'. There is as yet no equivalent legislation in the UK, although the Law Commission[6] advocated statutory backing for 'advance refusals of treatment', and also for decision-taking by proxies in matters of personal welfare and health care by holders of 'continuing powers of attorney'. However, in certain circumstances, under the common law, advance directives barring identified forms of treatment do have legal effect. This is so if the patient (1) had capacity; (2) was aware of the nature, purpose and effect of the proposed procedure; (3) made the decision to refuse treatment freely; and (4) made a decision which was intended to apply to the circumstances in question. If the circumstances change, the advance directive may become inappropriate.

The law and practice is still developing. The following suggested draft has recently appeared in the *British Medical Journal*[7]:

Advance directive for health care
Name: . . . .
Address: . . . .
Hospital Unit Number: . . . .

It is my express wish that if I should develop:

(a) senile, severe degenerative brain disease (due to Alzheimer's disease, arterial disease, AIDS, or other agency) or
(b) serious brain damage resulting from accidental or other injury or illness or
(c) advanced or terminal malignant disease or
(d) severely incapacitating and progressive degenerative disease of the nerves or muscles

and have become mentally incompetent to express my opinion about accepting or declining life-sustaining treatment, and if two independent physicians conclude that, to the best of current medical knowledge, my condition is irreversible then the following points should be taken into consideration:

- In the event of a cardiac arrest, regardless of the cause, I should not be given cardiopulmonary resuscitation.
- Any separate illness – for example, pneumonia or a heart or kidney condition – that may threaten my life should not be given active treatment unless it appears to be causing me undue physical suffering.
- During such an advanced illness, if I should become unable to swallow food, fluid, or medication then these should not be given by any artificial means except to relieve obvious suffering.
- During such an illness, if my condition deteriorates without reversible cause, and as a result my behaviour becomes violent, noisy, or in other ways degrading, or if I appear to be suffering severe pain, then any such symptoms should be controlled with suitable drug treatment, regardless of the consequences on my physical health and my survival, within the extent of the law.

- Other requests: . . . .
  . . . .

The object of this directive is to minimise distress or indignity which I may suffer or create during an incurable illness, and to spare my medical advisers or relatives, or both, the burden of making difficult decisions on my behalf.

Signed: . . . .
Date: . . . .
Witness 1: . . . .
Witness 2: . . . .
Statement by one witness: I . . . . declare that in my opinion the above person . . . . is of sound mind.
Signed: . . . .
Date: . . . .

However, while the mere existence of a formal document is no guarantee of its validity or applicability, its absence does not mean that no effective advance refusal has been given. Indeed in the USA it is not uncommon for 'living wills' to be recorded on tape or video recordings. In the UK the practice is yet to be developed: guidance is to be found in the British Medical Association's (BMA) publications *Advanced Statements About Medical Treatment*[8], which lays down a number of general principles in the form of a Code of Practice with explanatory notes, and *BMA Views on Advance Statements*[9].

The fact that others may suffer from a patient's refusal to have treatment does not make that refusal ineffective. Social and family obligations do not override an individual patient's personal autonomy. A dramatic example comes from Pennsylvania [*McFall* v. *Shimp* (1978)][10]: a plaintiff suffered from aplastic anaemia, and the only compatible donor who could be found was his cousin. However, even though the plaintiff was dying the cousin refused to give a bone marrow transplant. This, said the court not surprisingly, was 'morally indefensible', but it refused to order the transplant, stating:

> 'for a society, which respects the rights of one individual, to sink its teeth into the jugular vein or neck of one of its members and suck from it sustenance for another member, is revolting to our hard-wrought concepts of jurisprudence. Forcible extraction of living body tissue causes revulsion to the judicial mind. Such would raise the spectre of the swastika and the Inquisition, reminiscent of the horrors this portends. This court makes no comment on the law regarding the plaintiff's rights in an action at law for damages, but has no alternative but to deny the requested equitable relief.'

Less dramatic, but of great importance, is the related principle that when a patient consents to specified treatment, that consent does not justify any other treatment. For example, consent to abortion does not justify sterilisation, and consent to operation on one ear does not justify an equivalent operation on the other ear.

However, more subtle difficulties arise in practice. There is a well known exception to the requirement of consent where emergencies arise and there is a need to act before it becomes practicable to communicate with the patient, and in such cases (which may arise when the patient is unconscious as a result of trauma or of anaesthetic) a doctor may, in the absence of an effective advance directive barring the proposed procedure, treat the patient in his or her best interests as a matter of necessity. The difficulty is in deciding what amounts to a necessity.

This is illustrated by two Canadian cases [*Marshall* v. *Curry* (1993); *Murray* v. *McMurchy* (1949)][11]. In one, a doctor discovered a grossly diseased testicle in the course of a hernia operation and, without waking the patient up to get consent, removed it, firstly because it was necessary for the hernia operation, and secondly because he judged it potentially gangrenous and thus a menace to the patient's life and health. The patient's claim against him was dismissed. However, in the other case a doctor doing a Caesarean section discovered fibroid tumours in the uterine wall and, being concerned about the hazards of a second pregnancy, tied the fallopian tubes: he was found liable. The distinction is that in the first case the extended treatment was considered to be 'necessary' in an emergency, but in the second case it was considered only to be convenient. The moral is that, emergencies apart, it is for the patient and not for any health care professional to decide what the treatment should be. This was recently driven home by a decision of the General Medical Council that a paediatric cardiologist who proceeded from a diagnostic catheterisation, for which he had consent, to a balloon dilatation catheterisation, for which he had no consent, in an attempt to retrieve a deformed stent was, although acting in what he believed was the patient's best interests, guilty of serious professional misconduct[12].

In such contexts it may be unwise for a doctor to place too much reliance on the consent form. To be valid, a consent does not have to be in writing: it may be oral, and it may be implied, for example by baring the skin to a needle. A consent form is not a necessity. By contrast, a signature on a consent form may not be sufficient to confer consent, either because its scope does not cover the proposed treatment or because the signature of the patient was a mere formality. What is required is careful counselling, understanding and clear agreement.

Consent to treatment: minors

Minors, that is to say those who are under 18 years of age, can be divided for the purposes of deciding upon their capacity to consent into three categories.

First, in relation to those over 16, section 8 of the Family Law Reform Act 1969 provides:

> '(i) The consent of a minor who has attained the age of 16 years to any surgical, medical or dental treatment which, in the absence of consent, would constitute a trespass to his person, shall be as effective as it would be if he were of full age; and where a minor has by virtue of this section given an effective consent to any treatment it shall not be necessary to obtain any consent for it from his parent or guardian;
>
> (ii) In this section "surgical, medical or dental treatment" includes any procedure undertaken for the purposes of diagnosis, and this section applies to any procedure (including, in particular, the administration of anaesthetic) which is ancillary to any treatment as it applies to that treatment.'

Second, minors under the age of 16 have the capacity to consent to medical treatment if, but only if, they are '*Gillick*[13] competent' [*Gillick* v. *West Norfolk and Wisbech Area Health Authority* (1986)], that is to say if they have achieved sufficient understanding and intelligence to enable them to understand fully what is proposed.

Third, in relation to children under the age of 16 who are not '*Gillick* competent' the decision whether to consent to treatment is that of those with parental responsibility.

Curiously, even where a minor has the age or '*Gillick*' capacity to consent to treatment, it has been said that he or she does not have the power, in refusing treatment, to override a consent to that treatment by somebody who has parental responsibility. Even if the child says 'No', a doctor may legally treat if the parent says 'Yes'. This legal oddity raises a number of ethical problems. Clearly, the doctor must take the child's refusal into account, for a parent's consent to treatment, like any other consent, can amount to no more than a justification for treatment, and can never impose an obligation to treat. Where, however, there is such a dispute between a child capable of giving consent and a parent as to whether there should be treatment and it is thought that such treatment is in the child's best interests, it may, in the absence of urgent necessity, be wise to obtain the guidance of the court as to what should be done, for it is now settled law that the court can override the refusal of any minor, competent or not, to accept medical treatment.

Lack of capacity to consent

Patients may lack capacity to consent, not only by reason of age but also by reason of lack of competence. Such incompetence is not the same as the status of being a patient under the Mental Health Act 1983, although the two may coincide. The subject of treatment for mental disorder under that Act is a complex one to which this chapter is not addressed. We are here concerned with inability to obtain consent to treatment other than that for mental disorder. Such inability may arise through accident, and be temporary; it may as a result of illness be intermittent, and it may also be lasting; in the case of a child too young to consent, the problem may be that no parent is available.

In all such cases, the principles are the same. First, although it is good practice to consult relations about proposed treatment for adults who cannot give a valid consent, the consent of any relation (other than one with parental responsibility for a child patient) has in fact no legal effect whatsoever. The justification for treating adult patients who cannot give a valid consent can only be that such treatment has not been countermanded by a valid advance directive, and is in the patient's 'best interests'. This elastic phrase is easier to invoke than to apply. However, it certainly does not imply that life must be preserved at all costs. The Law Commission[14] has made the following proposal:

> 'We recommend that in deciding what is in a person's best interests regard should be had to:
> (1) the ascertainable past and present wishes and feelings of the person concerned, and the factors that person would consider if able to do so;
> (2) the need to permit and encourage the person to participate, or to improve his or her ability to participate, as fully as possible in anything done for and any decision affecting him or her;
> (3) the views of other people whom it is appropriate and practicable to consult about the person's wishes and feelings and what would be in his or her best interests;
> (4) whether the purpose for which any action or decision is required can be as effectively achieved in a manner less restrictive of the person's freedom of action.'

Second, where the criterion for treatment is that it is in fact in the patient's best interests, it follows that treatment which is not, or has ceased to be, in the patient's best interests accordingly ceases to be lawful and has to be stopped. This principle has been most publicly and starkly illustrated in recent cases of patients in a persistent vegetative state (PVS). In most terminal cases it is for the responsible medical staff, no doubt after consultation with the patient's family, to decide whether treatment should be stopped, and if it is adjudged that it is in the patient's best interests to stop treatment then that can and should be done.

A special feature of a PVS case, however, may be that it is desired to cease nutrition and hydration, knowing that this will result in the death of the patient. A concern that arises from this is that such an act could be construed as unlawful homicide. However, this fear has been dispelled, and in the case of

Airedale NHS Trust v. *Bland*[15],which arose out of the Hillsborough football tragedy, it was decided that the withdrawal of life-saving treatment or care is an omission rather than an act; that causing death by omission is only criminal if there is a duty to do that which is omitted; and that as the irreversible condition of PVS was established, there was no duty to persist in treatment and care. As Lord Goff said:

> '... medical treatment may be provided for a number of different purposes. It may be provided, for example, as an aid to diagnosis: for the treatment of physical or mental illness; to alleviate pain or distress, or to make the patient's condition more tolerable. Such purposes may include prolonging the patient's life, for example, to enable him to survive during diagnosis and treatment. But for my part I cannot see that medical treatment is appropriate or requisite simply to prolong a patient's life, when such treatment has no therapeutic purpose of any kind, as where it is futile because the patient is unconscious and there is no prospect of any improvement in his condition.'

In this case, the House of Lords expressly endorsed as evidence of good medical practice a BMA discussion paper on PVS and, in particular, the four safeguards recommended in it. That paper has now been replaced by the BMA's *Guidelines on Treatment Decisions for Patients in Persistent Vegetative State*[16], which sets out, *inter alia*, recommendations which may be summarised as follows:

(1) Stimulation and rehabilitation should be available for patients suspected of being in a persistent vegetative state as soon as their condition is stabilised.
(2) Decisions to withdraw treatment should only be considered when the patient has been insentient for 12 months.
(3) The clinician making a persistent vegetative state diagnosis should seek views from two other doctors, one of whom should be a neurologist.
(4) In any case of doubt as to whether the patient's condition is irreversible, decisions about possible withdrawal of medical treatment must be deferred.
(5) A decision whether it is in the patient's best interests to consider treatment to prolong life will include a careful evaluation of the patient's diagnosis and prognosis, the anticipated benefits and burdens of that treatment, the patient's views if known (including those in any advance directive) and the views of people close to the patient.

In PVS and similar cases, applications should be made to the court before withdrawing nutrition and hydration. This is not because the court has the power to make lawful that which is unlawful, but because declarations by the court that a proposed course of action is lawful will set at rest the minds of those involved and, in practice, protect the health professionals from any risk of criminal prosecution. It is good practice, in such cases, for any application to the court to be made by the responsible National Health Service (NHS) body or hospital.

Actions for negligence

Most claims against doctors are not for assault, because one way or another patients usually consent to treatment or, if incapable of consent, are treated with a view to their best interests and thus are not assaulted. The overwhelming majority of patients who sue do so for negligent treatment or advice.

To succeed in establishing a claim in negligence a patient must establish three things: (1) that a duty of care was owed to him or her; (2) that the defendant was in breach of that duty; and (3) that the breach of duty caused the injury complained of, that is to say that it was as a result of that breach that the patient sustained injury which would otherwise have been avoided. Throughout, the 'burden of proof' is on the plaintiff. He or she must prove the case, not beyond reasonable doubt but on the balance of probability. It is not necessary to prove every detailed fact, but unless the court is satisfied that there was a breach of duty which caused injury the claim will fail.

Breach of duty: diagnosis and treatment

The first question to be decided upon is the type and level of duty owed by a doctor. Now no doctor guarantees a cure: the duty is to exercise reasonable care, no more, no less. What is reasonable is measured by three things. First, doctors are judged by their specialty: a neurologist is expected to show the skill of a neurologist and not of a neurosurgeon, and vice versa. Second, they are judged by grade and not by seniority: a registrar, for however long or short a time he or she has been in that post, is judged as a registrar and not as a consultant or as a senior house officer. If doctors have been asked to do something beyond their capacity and fail because of inexperience, the fault may be that of those who put them in such a position, but the doctors will be blamed personally only if they carried on doing what they knew or should have known was beyond their experience when they could have arranged for others more senior to undertake the task. Third, doctors are judged in the circumstances in which they find themselves. Thus, they are judged by not only what they ought to know but also by what they actually know. If, for example, a registrar happens to have specialist knowledge which most registrars do not, but fails to use it, he or she may be liable where other registrars possessed only of average knowledge would be excused.

Such, then, is the duty of care. Next to be considered is what sort of departure from it constitutes negligence. In England and Wales, the law appears to many to be peculiarly defensive of doctors on this point, allowing them what is called the *Bolam* defence [*Bolam* v. *Friern Hospital Management Committee* (1957)][17], both in cases about diagnosis and treatment and in cases about counselling and advising patients and obtaining their consent to treatment. The *Bolam* defence is generally understood as meaning that if there are 'two schools of thought', and that if a doctor follows one general and approved practice rather than another, then he or she is not negligent; and by extension it is sometimes believed that if a doctor can call evidence that other competent practitioners would have acted as he or she did in the same circumstances, then that is a cast-iron defence. The matter, however, is not quite so simple.

First, let us look at cases of diagnosis and treatment. In some cases there may be a clear divergence of medical practice, for example in the surgical approach to a particular operation site. This is a true case of 'two schools of thought', and here the law is quite clear. The case of *Bolam* says that a doctor

> 'is not guilty of negligence if he has acted in accordance with a practice accepted as proper by a responsible body of medical men skilled in that particular art... Putting it the other way round, a man is not negligent, if he is acting in accordance with such a practice, merely because there is a body of opinion who would take a contrary view. At the same time, that does not mean that a medical man can obstinately and pig-headedly carry on with the same old technique if it has been proved to be contrary to what is really substantially the whole of informed medical opinion.'

It is to be noted that the 'responsible body of medical men' against which the practice of the defendant doctor is being measured need not be large. The issue of negligence is not decided by counting heads. If even a small number of relevant specialists follow the defendant's practice, and if they are 'responsible', that will prevent the plaintiff from proving that the practice is negligent. The recent case of *De Freitas* v. *O'Brien*[18] illustrates this point. The defendant, an orthopaedic surgeon who specialised in spinal surgery, operated for suspected nerve root compression at the L4/5 level in the absence of unequivocal signs or symptoms or radiological evidence of compression. The trial judge found that there was a separate specialism of spinal surgeons, which on the evidence was small in number, comprising orthopaedic surgeons and neurosurgeons engaged wholly or mainly in spinal surgery whose expertise justified such an operation, and the Court of Appeal expressly rejected the plaintiff's argument that the practice was only defensible if it was upheld by a body of opinion which was substantial in the numerical sense.

More difficult is a second class of case, in which the doctor is not following an established school of thought but merely making a clinical decision in an individual case. Here *Bolam* says that:

> 'the test is the standard of the ordinary skilled man exercising and professing to have that special skill. A man need not possess the highest expert skill at the risk of being found negligent. It is well-established law that it is sufficient if he exercises the ordinary skill of an ordinary competent man exercising that particular art.'

In such a case, however, it may not be a defence merely to call other doctors to say they would have done the same thing as the defendant, if their reasoning does not stand up to analysis [*Bolitho* v. *City and Hackney Health Authority* (1998)][19]. Thus, in one case, where a doctor was said to be negligent for failing to change an antibiotic [*Hucks* v. *Cole* (1993)][20], that tactic failed and it was said that:

> 'despite the fact that the risk could have been avoided by adopting a course that was easy, efficient, and inexpensive, and which would have entailed only minimal chances of disadvantages to the patient, the evidence of the four defence experts to the effect that they and other responsible members of the medical profession would have taken the same risk in the same circumstances has naturally caused me to hesitate considerably on two points. Firstly, whether the failure of the defendant to turn over to penicillin treatment during the relevant period was unreasonable. On this, however, I was in the end fully satisfied that in the light of the admissions made by the defendant himself and by his witnesses - quite apart from Dr May's very cogent evidence - that failure to do this was not merely wrong but clearly unreasonable. The reasons given by the four experts do not to my mind stand up to analysis...
>
> 'Secondly, as to whether, in the light of such evidence as to what other responsible medical practitioners would have done, it can be said that even if the defendant's error was unreasonable, it was [not] negligence in relation to the position as regards practice at that particular date. On this second point it is to be noted that this is not apparently a case of "two schools of thought" ... it appears more to be a case of doctors who said in one form or another that they would have acted or might have acted in the same way as the defendant did, for reasons which on examination do not really stand up to analysis.'

There is a third class of case in which a doctor departs from previously established practice because he or she is trying a new technique. In such a situation, the doctor may well be quite unable to call others who could say that they would have done the same thing. It does not, however, follow that the doctor is negligent; such a conclusion would stifle medical progress. In such circumstances the burden of proof will still be on the patient to prove negligence, but in practice the doctor will have to marshal the defence carefully by demonstrating the reasoning, research and planning leading up to the procedure.

Finally, there is a fourth class of case, in which the impugned act or omission happens in a medical context, but does not really raise a question of professional skill at all. An example of such a case would be where an important record was lost, or samples or slides mixed up. It does no good for the doctor or NHS body or hospital to establish that others might have done the same thing or that such things can occur even in the best regulated institutions; the mistake is one of incompetence and is indefensible.

Breach of duty: 'informed consent', advice and counselling

A patient may consent to treatment after and as a result of bad counselling, but that does not make the treatment an assault. A claim that a patient has been assaulted can only be made by one capable of giving consent if there was no valid consent at all, or by a patient incapable of giving consent if the treatment was not in his or her best interests. All other cases about bad counselling, or lack of 'informed consent' as it has been called, must be framed in negligence.

The phrase 'informed consent' is not of UK origin. It denotes a concept found in various forms in the law of certain American States and in Canada. A landmark case was that of the US Court of Appeals, District of Columbia, called *Canterbury* v. *Spence*[21], and an attempt was made to introduce the doctrine into English law in the case of *Sidaway* v. *Board of Governors of the Royal Bethlem Hospital*[22].

In *Sidaway*, Lord Scarman summarised the *Canterbury* principle as follows:

> 'In *Canterbury* v. *Spence* the court enunciated four propositions. (1) The root premise is the concept that every human being of adult years and of sound mind has a right to determine what shall be done with his own body. (2) The consent is the informed exercise of a choice, and that entails an opportunity to evaluate knowledgeably the options available and the risks attendant on each. (3) The doctor must, therefore, disclose all "material risks"; what risks are "material" is determined by the "prudent patient" test, which was formulated by the court (464 F 2d 772 at 787):
>
> (a) risk is ... material when a reasonable person, in what the physician knows or should know to be the patient's position, would be likely to attach significance to the risk or cluster of risks in deciding whether or not to forgo the proposed therapy.
>
> (4) The doctor, however, has what the court called a "therapeutic privilege". This exception is that a reasonable medical assessment of the patient would

have indicated to the doctor that disclosure would have posed a serious threat of psychological detriment to the patient.'

The facts of *Sidaway* were straightforward. Mrs Sidaway, who was aged 63, had arm and shoulder pain and was shown on the myelogram to have a partial block at the C4/5 disc space, a posterior ridge and a narrowed subarachnoid space in that area. The consultant neurosurgeon, Mr Murray Falconer, diagnosed pressure on a nerve root and decided on laminectomy of the fourth cervical vertebra and facetectomy. The judge found that the operation carried the risk of damage to the nerve root and the spinal cord in all of 1–2%, but that the risk of damage to the spinal cord alone was less. Before the operation, Mrs Sidaway had been warned of the danger to the nerve root, but not of that to the spinal cord. Unhappily, though the operation was skilfully carried out, it was the latter which materialised. It was her case that had she been warned of the risk of damage to the spinal cord she would not have consented to the operation.

The defence was straightforward. It established by all the expert evidence that in refraining from a full warning the medical team was merely following a practice which, at the time of the operation, would have been followed by a responsible body of skilled and experienced neurosurgeons, and argued that the *Bolam* doctrine, that is to say the criterion of the 'reasonable doctor', rather than the *Canterbury* or 'informed consent' criterion of the views of the 'prudent patient', should apply to cases of advice and counselling. By a majority, the House of Lords agreed, and thus the doctrine of 'informed consent' in its full blown transatlantic sense is not part of the law of England and Wales.

Nevertheless, this decision has caused continuing controversy. Although many of the excesses of the 'informed consent' doctrine have been curbed by state legislature in the USA, English law stands alone among common law jurisdictions in placing so firm a reliance on *Bolam* in counselling cases. It is true that in *Sidaway* Lord Bridge allowed of an exception:

'I do not see that this [*Bolam*] approach involves the necessity "to hand over to the medical profession the entire question of the scope of the duty of disclosure, including the question whether there has been a breach of that duty." Of course, if there is a conflict of evidence as to whether a responsible body of medical opinion approves of non-disclosure in a particular case, the judge will have to resolve that conflict. But even in a case where, as here, no expert witness in the relevant medical field condemns the non-disclosure as being in conflict with accepted and responsible medical practice, I am of opinion that the judge might in certain circumstances come to the conclusion that disclosure of a particular risk was so obviously necessary to an informed choice on the part of the patient that no reasonably prudent medical man would fail to make it. The kind of case I have in mind would be an operation

> involving a substantial risk of grave adverse consequences, as, for example, the ten per cent risk of a stroke from the operation which was the subject of the Canadian case of *Reibl* v. *Hughes*, 114 DLR (3d) 1. In such a case, in the absence of some cogent clinical reason why the patient should not be informed a doctor, recognising and respecting his patient's right of decision, could hardly fail to appreciate the necessity for an appropriate warning.

However, it is the principle itself that is being questioned: thus, Lord Mustill said in *Airedale NHS Trust* v. *Bland*:

> 'I accept without difficulty that this [*Bolam*] principle applies to the ascertainment of the medical raw material such as diagnosis, prognosis and appraisal of the patient's cognitive functions. Beyond this point, however, it may be said that the decision is ethical, not medical, and that there is no reason in logic why on such a decision the opinions of doctors should be decisive.'

In consequence, and increasingly, one observes the tendency of trial judges to conclude, as one found recently [*Smith* v. *Tunbridge Wells Health Authority* (1994)][23]:

> 'although some surgeons may not have been warning patients similar in situation to the plaintiff of the risk ... that omission was neither reasonable nor responsible.'

The moral is clear. The law is catching up with good medical practice, which is to give as full an explanation, including accurate answers to questions, as the individual patient can take in without positive harm resulting from such an explanation.

Causation: diagnosis and treatment

The formulation of the test for causation is simple: has the patient established on the balance of probabilities that the breach of duty proved caused or materially contributed to the injury complained of? The simplicity of that formulation, however, conceals difficulties in practice, not least in the fields of neurology and neurosurgery.

Of course, if the patient establishes that, but for the negligence, he or she would not have sustained the injury complained of at all, then no difficulty arises: causation is established. Moreover, this 'but for' test can be satisfied in two ways, either by showing that the negligence was the sole cause of the injury or by showing that, although there were other adverse factors operating, it was the negligence which tipped the balance and brought about an injury which would not otherwise have occurred – in other words, that the negligence was the straw which broke the camel's back. In each case, the negligence can be said to have made a 'material contribution' to the occurrence of the injury, and no problem arises.

Problems do, however, arise in cases where plaintiffs can point to negligently missed opportunities to treat, but cannot prove what would have happened if the opportunities had not been missed. Here the court's solution, if not logical, is just. Plaintiffs will succeed, even if they cannot show what *would* have happened, if they can show that what *should* have happened on the occasion of the missed opportunities would have produced a better result[24].

Other situations may be even more troublesome. First, it may be the case that a plaintiff has to concede that the natural course of a pre-existing condition would have resulted in a disability of some sort, and can contend only that the negligence aggravated that disability. Here the difficulties are those of proof and quantification. An award of damages for the aggravation of disability can only be made if there is evidence which enables the court to identify and quantify the degree of aggravation [*Tahir* v. *Havering Health Authority* (1998)][25].

Second, not infrequently it is the case that a plaintiff has difficulty in pointing to particular causative features in his or her own case, and has to rely on general propositions or statistics as demonstrating a causal link between negligence and injury. For example, there may be a negligent delay in the diagnosis of a brain tumour, and at the time of the eventual operation the tumour may be untreatable. The patient may well be able to persuade a court that, as a general proposition, the delay has worsened the chance of a successful outcome, but that is only a step on the way to, and falls short of, proof that the delay actually caused injury. Similarly reliance on statistics, if such exist, showing the growth rates of the tumour and any correlation between the stage of diagnosis and particular outcomes may be useful and persuasive evidence, but not necessarily determinative. This is because statistics are about groups of patients, and proof of causation is about the particular patient in question. It is not enough for a patient, by reference to statistics, to show that most people with the same condition, if treated non-negligently, would have had a better outcome. It is only if these statistics can be, as it were, personalised to the patient, by showing that in the absence of negligence he or she would probably have fallen into the group which did well, that an inference of causation can logically be drawn from them.

Faced with such difficulties of proof, patients have relied on two lines of argument. First, it has been suggested that there can be compensation not only for an injury but also for a lost chance of recovery. In the leading case of *Hotson* v. *East Berkshire Area Health Authority*[26], a boy who fell from a tree fractured his left femoral epiphysis, which, as a result of negligence, was diagnosed and treated later than it should have been. He later developed avascular necrosis and consequent long-term disability. The judge found as a fact that, even if properly treated, there was a 75% risk that he would have suffered the same adverse consequences, that the negligence had deprived him of a 25% chance of avoiding those consequences, and that accordingly he was entitled to damages for loss of that 25% chance, which was quantified at 25% of the full value of what would have been compensation for the full disability. In other words, he awarded damages for loss of a chance. This decision, initially supported by the Court of Appeal, was reversed by the House of Lords in speeches which, while not completely excluding claims for loss of a chance in other contexts, effectively ruled them out in medical negligence cases.

The second line of argument has been more successful. It has been to encourage in judges what one Law Lord, in a further leading case on causation [*Wilsher* v. *Essex Area Health Authority* (1988)][27] called 'a robust and pragmatic approach to the undisputed primary facts of the case.' Where negligence has, on the evidence, substantially increased the risk of a bad outcome, it is open to judges to draw an inference of causation. It used to be thought that there was a reluctance among judges, when negligence was proved or admitted, to reject the claim on the grounds that causation had not been proved, as if such a decision was somehow unfairly favourable to the negligent defendant. Such reluctance is not apparent today, as judges are increasingly impressed by the difficulty of applying uninstructed common sense to medical problems under the banner of 'robustness'. However, where the evidence shows that negligence has substantially increased the risk of a particular injury, it is open to them to draw an inference that, in the particular case, the negligence did cause that injury.

One further issue requires discussion, namely that of the unco-operative patient. It is not unheard of for patients to refuse to co-operate with the treatment, by failing to respond to signs of which they have been warned and of which they are aware, by failing to attend for investigation or by not taking up the treatment offered. Such lack of co-operation may contribute to a bad outcome, and in extreme cases can be said to amount to negligence by a patient in failing to take reasonable care for his or her own health. Suffice it to say that it is extremely difficult for those acting for a negligent doctor to persuade a court that a patient, whose non-compliance with a medical regime is frequently a function of fear of a real or imagined condition, was actually negligent. The plea is not often raised, and it is even more rarely successful.

Causation: 'informed consent' advice and counselling

Where it has been established that, following negligent advice and counselling, a patient has undergone treatment and has suffered as a result, the question still remains as to whether the negligence can be said to have caused the injury complained of. To succeed, the plaintiff must prove not only '*post hoc*' but also '*propter hoc*', in other words, that, but for the negligent advice and counselling, he or she would not have agreed to or undergone the damaging treatment. In England and Wales a test of what, hypothetically, the plaintiff would have decided to do, given proper advice, is decided not objectively but subjectively. In other words, the test is not what 'the reasonable patient' would have decided in the circumstances, but what the individual patient would have decided. His or her word that the negligent advice was determinative of treatment is, however, by no means necessarily accepted by judges, who bear in mind what is reasonable in the objective sense and are alert to the dangers of retrospection, self-deception and self-serving statements.

This blending of objective consideration with the subjective test is illustrated in a neurosurgical context in a recent decision about an operation to drain a cyst in the cervical spinal cord [*Smith* v. *Barking, Havering and Brentwood Health Authority* (1994)][28]. Both sides agreed that if the operation had not been done the patient would have been tetraplegic in nine months, and that she should have been given, but was not given, preoperative warning about the risks of the operation itself. In the event the operation was unsuccessful, and the plaintiff did develop immediate and permanent tetraplegia. On the issue of causation the judge said:

> 'the question must be: if this plaintiff had been given the advice that she should have been given, would she have decided to undergo the operation or not?
>
> 'However, there is a peculiar difficulty involved in this sort of case – not least for the plaintiff herself – in giving, after the adverse outcome of the operation is known, reliable answers as to what she would have decided before the operation had she been given proper advice as to the risks inherent in it. Accordingly, it would, in my judgment, be right in the ordinary case to give particular weight to the objective assessment. If everything points to the fact that a reasonable plaintiff, properly informed, would have assented to the operation, the assertion from the witness box, made after the adverse outcome is known, in a wholly artificial situation and in the knowledge that the outcome of the case depends upon that assertion being maintained, does not carry great weight unless there are extraneous or additional factors to substantiate it. By extraneous or additional factors I mean, and I am not doing more than giving examples, religious or some other firmly-held convictions; particular social or domestic considerations justifying a decision not in accordance with what, objectively, seems the right one; assertions in the immediate aftermath of the operation made in a context other than that of a possible claim for damages; in other words, some particular factor which suggests that the plaintiff had grounds for not doing what a reasonable person in her situation might be expected to have done.'

He then analysed the advice which should have been given, held that it should have included:

> 'a clear indication that the surgeon, weighing all the considerations as best he could, had reached the view that an operation was in her best interests'

and concluded:

> 'looking at the matter objectively, I cannot escape the conclusion that these factors pointed very strongly towards agreeing to have the operation. Reflection on what she was told would have led a reasonable patient to say to herself: "Well, it seems I'm going to be paralysed anyway in a very short time. This operation gives me a reasonable chance of avoiding that condition perhaps for a few years. True, there is a real risk that the operation will not be successful and I'll then be paralysed even sooner, but the possible benefits clearly considerably outweigh the possible detriment and the chance is one well worth taking."
>
> 'In the light of these conclusions I ask myself what the plaintiff would have decided, had she been given advice along the lines I have indicated. For reasons already foreshadowed in this judgment I unhesitatingly conclude that the strong probability is that the plaintiff would have agreed to have the operation.'

Damages

The assessment of damages is somewhat technical, and only the main principles are here summarised.

First, there is always an award for what is called 'pain, suffering and loss of amenity', that is to say for the injury or disability itself rather than for its financial consequences. Such an award is modest. Even for brain damage resulting in massive intellectual and physical impairment, the award is most unlikely to exceed £130,000, and increases in the future will not exceed those of inflation.

Second, there are 'special damages', which represent the financial loss and expense incurred before trial by the plaintiff, and which will include compensation for family members who have provided care.

Third, 'general damages' are awarded for future loss and expense, and it is these which, in large claims, make up the bulk of the award. The various items of loss and expense consequent on the injury are calculated without regard to the risk of future inflation, on the basis of the rates of loss or expense calculated as at the date of trial: these are called the 'multiplicand'. Each multiplicand is then multiplied by a factor, called the 'multiplier', which is intended to generate a sum which will itself, out of capital and income, produce enough for each actual future year of loss or need. The award is thus discounted for the accelerated receipt of the amount required to compensate for loss and needs in future years.

This process of discounting, and the choice of multiplier, depends on the interest rate which it is assumed will be obtained on the investment of damages. At the time of writing, the law assumes that the sum awarded by way of damages will be invested so as to generate a net rate of return of 3% [*Page* v. *Sheerness Steel Company Ltd* (1998)][29]. To take an example: there is an annual need of £1,000 for each of the next 20 years. The sum which, if invested at a net rate of 3% compound, will in fact produce £1,000 for each of the next 20 years is £14,880. Thus, arithmetically the 'multiplier' for a span of 20 years is 14.88. Therefore, the court will apply a 'multiplier' of 14.88 to each 'multiplicand' required over the next 20 years.

There is, however, potential injustice in the system. First, patients may have to wait years before getting any award. Second, the 'once for all' system of awarding damages by way of one lump sum means that the court is really trying to assess the future, which is in many cases unknowable. Several devices for mitigating these difficulties have been developed.

First, where a defendant has admitted liability or a plaintiff has obtained a judgment for damages to be assessed, or where it appears before trial that a plaintiff will obtain substantial damages against a defendant, the court has the power to make an order for an 'interim payment' representing a reasonable proportion of the damages which are likely to be recovered by the plaintiff. This means that in a strong case the plaintiff can get his or her hands on some money pending the eventual trial. Such applications are relatively common.

Second, there is a system for awarding 'provisional damages' in cases where it is established that at some time in the future the injured person may, as a result of the negligence, eventually develop some serious disease or suffer some serious deterioration in his or her physical or mental condition. This provision allows a patient who may or may not get worse as a result of the negligence to have 'two bites at the cherry': in other words, the patient will initially get damages assessed on the assumption that the serious disease or deterioration will not occur, coupled with a right to apply for further damages at a future date if the disease or deterioration occurs. The 'provisional damage' system has been in existence for a decade, but it has to be said that it is not frequently invoked. In most cases, a reasonable prognosis can be made of the patient's condition, and the probability is that both sides usually want to get the action over and done with.

The third development is an alternative to the lump sum payment known as a 'structured settlement'. This is an agreement made between the plaintiff and defendant whereby the defendant or the insurer either applies part of the damages to purchasing annuities (usually index-linked), paying the equivalent of each annuity to the plaintiff, or alternatively (and this is currently done by the NHS Litigation Authority in many cases) withholds part of the damages and in return agrees to pay the plaintiff index-linked annual sums for life. Such an arrangement cannot be ordered by a court, but, particularly when returns on annuities are good, has considerable attraction to both sides. Invariably, only part of the award is applied to a structured settlement, and the balance held and invested in the normal way as a 'contingency fund'. For a plaintiff, the advantage is that the stream of payments will last for the whole of his or her lifetime and that, if the agreements are in a form approved by the Inland Revenue, they are received and retained without deduction of tax (in contrast to income from ordinary damages awards, which is taxable in the plaintiff's hands). The principal disadvantage is that once an agreement for a structured settlement has been made, it cannot be altered, and adverse changes in circumstances can only be met by resort to the contingency fund.

The doctor as expert witness

Often it is the case that a doctor is required to attend court as a witness of fact. There the duty is plain: the doctor simply has to answer questions as clearly and accurately as possible. Far more difficult, however, is the role of a doctor when asked to advise and appear as an expert witness. When so instructed, he or she must address a number of questions.

(1) Has he or she any connection with any party? If so, independent expert advice becomes impossible.
(2) Is the doctor prepared to read every word of the medical notes, research the literature and attend conferences with counsel and solicitors?
(3) Is he or she prepared if necessary to attend court, give evidence and be cross-examined?
(4) Is the case, or the aspect of the case upon which advice is sought, truly within the doctor's specialty as a practitioner?
(5) If asked to advise on liability, does he or she have relevant experience contemporary with the events under investigation?
(6) If asked to advise on causation, is the doctor's knowledge of any relevant learning and literature up-to-date or capable of being brought up-to-date?

If the doctor has doubts on any of these points, he or she should, before accepting instructions, discuss them with the solicitor, to avoid potential future embarrassment which may well damage the litigant's chances of success. Moreover, if it appears that the case demands the attention of a different or additional specialist (for example, a neuroradiologist or a neuropathologist in a puzzling case of tetraplegia) then the doctor should say so at the outset.

A failure to observe some of these precautions led, in a recent decision, to the following strictures from a judge [*Scott* v. *Bloomsbury Health Authority* (1990)][30]:

> 'Finally although Mr X described himself, no doubt correctly, as consultant surgeon to the Y Hospital, senior examiner in surgery at the University of London and a member of the Court of Examiners at the Royal College of Surgeons of England, he became a consultant over 40 years ago, retired from active practice as a NHS consultant 14 years ago and has not sat on an examination board for nine years. He is now a very old man. He was very free with his allegations of professional negligence against a number of dedicated doctors and surgeons, all of which have been shown to be without foundation. These allegations were in my judgment founded on a superficial reading of the relevant notes and records and a totally inadequate appreciation of matters which were well known to those who have up to date responsibility for the day to day care of patients suffering from the long term effects of spinal injuries but which were unknown to him. The plaintiff's case was critically dependant on Mr X's uncorroborated assertion that there was a bone growing backwards into his spinal canal at the fracture site for which there was not, in my judgment, a shred of reliable evidence. At no time did he cause any effective request to be made to enable him to see the X-ray on whose report he placed so much unjustified reliance, and I saw no indication that he had read Mr Z's operation note before he entered the witness box.
>
> 'In my judgment the Legal Aid Board should review this judgment carefully in order to see what steps can be taken, perhaps in consultation with the General Medical Council and the Royal Colleges, to prevent complex claims from being supported in future at public expense on the uncorroborated evidence of a consultant who has retired from practice so long ago.'

Once an expert has accepted instructions, his or her duties are twofold. First, the expert must provide independent objective advice to the litigant on whose behalf instructions are given. In the initial stages of the case the duty of care is owed to that litigant, and if the claim is lost or identifiably weakened as a result of negligent advice the expert may be liable in damages. However, once the pre-trial work upon which the expert is engaged becomes so connected with the general running of the case that it can be described as a preliminary decision affecting the way the case is to be conducted, then there is a shift in the emphasis of the expert's responsibilities: he or she becomes immune from litigation by a discontented client, because the duty is now owed to the court. The difficulty is in deciding where to draw the line beyond which liability to the client ceases; in a recent case it was said [*Palmer* v. *Durnford Ford* (1992)][31]:

> 'The immunity would only extend to what could fairly be said to be preliminary to his giving evidence in court, judged perhaps by the principal

purpose for which the work was done. So the production or approval of a report for the purposes of disclosure to the other side would be immune but work done for the principal purpose of advising the client would not. Each case would depend on its own facts, with the court concerned to protect the expert from liability for the evidence which he gave in court and the work principally and proximately leading thereto.'

The maintenance of objectivity by an expert is surprisingly difficult. Ideally, an expert should be equally prepared to give advice and evidence both for plaintiffs and defendants, as this not only helps that expert to maintain personal objectivity but also dispels the aura of bias which, no doubt sometimes unfairly, may surround those who have decided, or appear to have decided, to give expert evidence only for one side or another, and thus appear to be campaigners.

However, maintenance of objectivity is a more complex problem than mere willingness to act for either side. The expert forms an initial point of view and, as litigation progresses, will on balance find it easier to adhere to that point of view than to depart from it, even in the face of fresh evidence. Also, the importance of an expert opinion is more than purely academic. A change of opinion may not only involve 'loss of face', but it may also engender a feeling of 'letting the side down'. All these pressures, coupled with a growing feeling that the expert is part of a team which wants to win, can and do affect even the most detached of professionals. Objectivity is therefore made easier by very careful early analysis.

The expert's first task is usually the preparation of a preliminary report in writing. His or her duties and functions from this point onwards have been defined in the High Court as follows [*The 'Ikarian Reefer'* (1993)][32]:

'(1) Expert evidence presented to the court should be and should be seen to be the independent product of the expert uninfluenced as to form or content by the exigencies of litigation.

(2) An expert witness should provide independent assistance to the court by way of objective unbiased opinion in relation to matters within his expertise. An expert witness in the High Court should never assume the role of advocate.

(3) An expert witness should state the facts or assumptions on which his opinion is based. He should not omit to consider material facts which detract from his concluded opinion.

(4) An expert witness should make it clear when a particular question or issue falls outside his area of expertise.

(5) If an expert's opinion is not properly researched because he considers

that insufficient data is available, then this must be stated with an indication that the opinion is no more than a provisional one.

(6) If after exchange of reports an expert witness changes his view on a material matter ... such change of view should be communicated to the other side without delay and when appropriate to the court.

(7) Where expert evidence refers to photographs, plans, calculations ... or other similar documents, these must be provided to the opposite party at the same time as the exchange of reports.'

Experts should also make it clear in their reports (if it be the case) that although they would themselves have adopted different practices or approaches they accept that the defendant's was one which was acceptable as proper by a responsible body of practitioners in the relevant field [*Sharpe* v. *Southend Health Authority* (1997)].[33]

As a guide, the expert report should conform to the following criteria:

- It should set out his or her qualifications and expertise: this should be supplemented by a curriculum vitae, forming an appendix to the report.
- The report should identify the factual sources relied upon, i.e. the medical notes, witness statements, examinations and other factual material.
- In setting out the facts and assumptions upon which his or her opinion is based, the expert should clearly distinguish between the two: in the case of assumptions, he or she should state their basis (for example, that an inference can be drawn from a striking omission in the clinical notes).
- The issues and questions to be addressed should be set out, and the report should make clear which issues or questions are outside the expert's particular expertise.
- It is frequently most helpful to explain the anatomy with illustrations or diagrams.
- The report should set out the expert's opinion on each question or issue, supporting it by reference to the facts and assumptions earlier referred to and dealing with material facts which are inconsistent with the conclusion.
- Reference should be made to any supporting learning or literature. If these are considerable, references to literature and citations of text relied upon should be set out in the appendices.
- If the opinion expressed is only provisional (for example, because insufficient information is available) the report should say so, and identify what further investigations are required.

The use of literature requires some thought. It is not uncommon for an expert to be cross-examined upon passages in his or her own writings which conflict with views expressed in the report. Changes of view may be justifiable, but the expert must be prepared to justify them in the witness box. Quite frequently experts refer only to selected passages in literature, only to be reminded when they are in the witness box of other passages from the same work which contradict their views, perhaps on different aspects of the case. Literature should be used for illumination rather than merely for support.

If the preliminary expert report is supportive, it is usual for the expert to have a meeting with solicitors or a conference with a barrister. This may or may not precede the exchange of the statements of the witnesses of fact on either side; such statements may well cast a great deal of light on the case by revealing what the notes do not reveal, or by qualifying or explaining aspects not earlier understood.

If the case is to proceed further, the reports of experts on both sides will be put in a final form, that is to say the form in which they will be disclosed to the other side and upon which the expert will be cross-examined, should the case come to court. They should, therefore, be as factually accurate as possible and avoid mis-statement or exaggeration of opinion. It is important that, whatever concern the lawyers may have expressed in discussion, the report is the expert's own.

> 'While some degree of consultation between experts and legal advisers is entirely proper, it is necessary that expert evidence presented to the court should be, and should seem to be, the independent product of the expert, uninfluenced as to form or content by the exigencies of litigation [*Whitehouse* v. *Jordan* (1981)][34].'

It is perfectly proper for the lawyers to direct the expert as to the issues which he or she should discuss, but it is the expert and not the lawyer who takes responsibility in court for what is said about those issues.

It should also be noted that the courts are increasingly trying to ensure that experts should finally identify the literature upon which they wish to rely by the time the final reports are disclosed. Too frequently, learned articles are produced at the last moment, even after the trial has begun, leaving inadequate time for analysis. Thus, it is not unusual for a court, during the preparatory stages of litigation, to make an order with the following effect:

> 'If any witness giving expert evidence proposes to rely in evidence at trial on any textbook, article or other published item of any such unpublished work, a list of such references and copies of the text should be disclosed by simultaneous mutual exchange with the report of that witness.'

Occasionally, the court orders, or the parties agree, that there should be a 'without prejudice' meeting of experts on opposing sides of the case. A meeting or discussion is said to be 'without prejudice' if its contents are off the record in the sense that, in the absence of agreement, they are not thereafter to be used in the litigation or referred to in court. The purpose of such a meeting is to try and limit and define the areas of real disagreement between experts, with the view to compromising the case or, should that be impossible, shortening the hearing. The guidelines will usually be drawn up in advance by the lawyers on each side, and the intention is that, following the meeting, the experts prepare a joint statement setting out what is and what is not agreed.

If the case is not settled and does go to court, the expert's evidence will fall into three parts. First, there is examination in chief, when the lawyer for the side which instructs the expert presents the evidence, usually by reference to the disclosed report. Cross-examination follows, and at this point the expert's views are tested by the opposing lawyer. Finally, he or she may be re-examined by the lawyer who has called the expert in the first place, so that he or she may be invited to clear up any difficulties or ambiguities which remain unresolved by the cross-examination. It is only in cross-examination that the expert should be asked 'leading questions', that is to say questions which suggest the answer.

Particularly in neurological and neurosurgical cases, where the facts can be difficult, the experts must at all times recall that the subject matter of the case is new to the judge, who may have no medical knowledge whatsoever and requires a clear and detailed explanation of the anatomy and physiology. It is easy to forget that, while the lawyers have, through extensive reading and discussion in conference, come to understand the case reasonably well, the judge has had no such opportunity and, while doing his or her best to repress the understandable temptation to ask questions, nevertheless needs all the help he or she can get.

All evidence proceeds by question and answer, and it is wise for the expert to assume that, however naive the questions may appear to be, they could well have been chosen and framed for a particular reason. Questions should therefore accordingly be given a careful answer, and not used as an excuse for an exegesis of the case generally, still less as a platform for advocacy. It is a slow process, but as the Irish advocate John Philpot Curran once said, answering a Lord Chancellor who interrupted him:

> 'I am aware, my Lord, that the truth is to be sought only by a slow and painful process. I also know that error is in its nature flippant and compendious. It hops with airy and fastidious levity over proofs and arguments, and perches on assertion, which it calls conclusion.'

It is easy for the expert to forget that, in court, it is the apparently naive question which is frequently telling, because it may test assumptions underlying an opinion which the expert has taken for granted without analysis for many years and which may be outdated, irrelevant, plainly wrong or simply so much part of the expert's intellectual framework that he or she has forgotten how to justify them.

The following extract from a judgment illustrates the process by which a judge constantly evaluates an expert witness during his or her evidence [*Loveday* v. *Renton* (1990)][35]:

> 'This involves an examination of the reasons given for his opinions and the extent to which they are supported by the evidence. The judge also has to decide what weight to attach to a witness's opinion by examining the internal consistency and logic of his evidence; the care with which he has considered the subject and presented his evidence; his precision and accuracy of thought as demonstrated by his answers; how he responds to searching and informed cross-examination and in particular the extent to which a witness faces up to and accepts the logic of a proposition put in cross-examination or is prepared to concede points that are seen to be correct; the extent to which a witness has conceived an opinion and is reluctant to re-examine it in the light of later evidence, or demonstrates a flexibility of mind which may involve changing or modifying opinions held; whether or not a witness is biased or lacks independence.'

The future

The likely future growth of medical litigation, particularly in cases of negligence, increases the chances of the neurologist or neurosurgeon becoming involved in court work. Meanwhile, efforts are being made to curb its growth.

There have been recent changes in the criteria for eligibility for legal aid, decreasing the number entitled to it, and because litigation, not least medical litigation, is expensive this in theory should at least have slowed down the rate of growth; but there is no sign that this has yet happened.

The government, however, is now considering abolishing legal aid for medical negligence cases altogether, leaving litigants to fund their cases out of their own pockets, through insurance cover or by 'no win, no fee' agreements with lawyers. It is anticipated that these changes, if they come about, would severely limit the number of medical negligence cases, because it is extremely difficult to predict the outcome of a medical negligence action at an early stage, and lawyers will be reluctant to enter a 'no win, no fee' agreement unless the chances look good from the outset.

However, while there are increasing cost restraints on traditional litigation in the courts, other methods of resolving disputes are under consideration. It is to be hoped that sooner or later a popular and effective system of resolving medical negligence cases by mediation can be devised. Also, a committee under Lord Woolf is at present considering radical changes in the nature of litigation itself, with a view to making it cheaper, quicker, more available and more user-friendly. It is premature to predict the outcome, but in public consultation there has been discussion of two proposals which require special mention. First, it has been suggested that in cases of lower value it might be advantageous for there to be a single expert appointed by the court rather than experts for each side; it has to be said, however, that it is difficult to see how such a system would work in any substantial medical case. A second suggestion is that efforts should be made to increase the effectiveness of pre-trial meetings between experts.

At this stage, all that can safely be said is that all the proposed changes are likely to place greater demands upon the objectivity of experts and therefore increase their importance. Clearly, no expert's fee will be 'contingent' on the result of a case: he or she will be paid, win or lose. However, 'no win, no fee' cases will require very careful and thorough advice from an expert at an early stage. A court-appointed expert would effectively act as a sort of judge, and could in no way be partisan. To the extent that pre-trial meetings become more effective, this can only be because experts are prepared to see, and to concede, points of view different from their own and weaknesses in their case. Such an attitude must, in the long run, be of advantage to everyone concerned in litigation except (and, quite rightly, nobody minds about this) the lawyers.

References

1. Vincent, C., Young, M. and Phillips, A. (1994) Why do people sue doctors? A study of patients and relatives taking legal action. *Lancet* **353**, 1609–13.
2. Kennedy, I. and Grubb, A. (1994) *Medical Law, Text with Materials*, 2nd edn, p. 3. Butterworths, London.
3. *Re C* (Adult: Refusal of Treatment) [1994] 1 WLR 290.
4. *per* Cardozo J in *Schloendorff* v. *Society of New York Hospital* (1914) 211 NY 125.
5. *Home Secretary* v. *Robb* [1995] 1 FLR 412 (hunger striker)
   Re MB [1997] 8 Med LR 217 (Caesarean section)
   Re T (an Adult: Refusal of Treatment) [1993] Fam 95 (Jehovah's Witnesses).
6. Law Commission Report: 'Mental Incapacity': Law Com No. 231. The Lord Chancellor's Department has now issued a consultation paper on these proposals: 'Who decides? Making decisions on behalf of Mentally Handicapped Adults', Cm. 3803, December 1992.
7. Robertson, G.S. (1995) Making an advance directive. *British Medical Journal* **310**, 236.
8. British Medical Association (1995) *Advanced Statements About Medical Treatment*. BMJ Publishing Group, London.
9. British Medical Association (1995) *BMA Views on Advance Statements*. BMJ Publishing Group, London.
10. *McFall* v. *Shimp* (1978) 10 Pa D&C 3d 90.
11. *Marshall* v. *Curry* (1933) 3 DLR 260; *Murray* v. *McMurchy* (1949) 2 DLR 442.
12. Dyer, C. (1998) Consultant suspended for not getting consent for cardiac procedure. *British Medical Journal* **316**, 955.
13. *Gillick* v. *West Norfolk and Wisbech Area Health Authority* [1986] AC 112.

14. *Gillick* v. *West Norfolk and Wisbech Area Health Authority supra*, note 7.
15. See in particular *Airedale NHS Trust* v. *Bland* [1993] AC 789.
16. British Medical Association (1996) *Guidelines on Treatment Decisions for Patients in Persistent Vegetative State*, July 1993, revised June 1996. BMJ Publishing Group, London.
17. *Bolam* v. *Friern Hospital Management Committee* [1957] 1 WLR 582 (the leading case on the standard of care expected of doctors).
18. *De Freitas* v. *O'Brien and Another* [1993] 4 Med LR 281; *The Times* 16 February 1995.
19. See *Bolitho* v. *City and Hackney Health Authority* [1998] AC 232.
20. *Hucks* v. *Cole* [1993] 4 Med LR 393, at 398 *per* Lord Justice Sachs.
21. *Canterbury* v. *Spence* (DC 1972) 464 F 2d 772.
22. *Sidaway* v. *Board of Governors of the Royal Bethlem Hospital* [1985] AC 871.
23. *Smith* v. *Tunbridge Wells Health Authority* [1994] 5 Med LR 321, at 339 *per* Mr Justice Morland.
24. See *Bolitho* v. *City and Hackney Health Authority*, *supra* n. 18.
25. *Tahir* v. *Havering Health Authority* [1998] Lloyd's Rep Med 104.
26. *Hotson* v. *East Berkshire Area Health Authority* [1987] AC 750.
27. *Wilsher* v. *Essex Area Health Authority* [1988] AC 1074, at 1090 D *per* Lord Bridge.
28. *Smith* v. *Barking, Havering and Brentwood Health Authority* [1994] 5 Med LR 285, *per* Hutchison J.
29. *Page* v. *Sheerness Steel Company Ltd*, House of Lords, 16 July 1998.
30. *Scott* v. *Bloomsbury Health Authority* [1990] 1 Med LR 214.
31. *Palmer* v. *Durnford Ford* [1992] 1 QB 483.
32. *The 'Ikarian Reefer'* [1993] 2 Lloyd's Rep 68.
33. *Sharpe* v. *Southend Health Authority* [1997] 8 Med LR 299.
34. *Whitehouse* v. *Jordan* [1981] 1 WLR 246, at 256–7 *per* Lord Wilberforce.
35. *Loveday* v. *Renton* [1990] 1 Med LR 177, *per* Stuart-Smith LJ.

Chapter 2
Avoiding Litigation

John Garfield

Introduction

This chapter considers general points of particular importance in neurology and neurosurgery which may give rise to litigation. Where applicable to the wider field of medicine and surgery, some of these points are covered in the sections by lawyers. As discussed in the introduction, the level of knowledge and expertise - loosely and often wrongly equated with competence - is particularly germane to neurology and neurosurgery, and is addressed here in a general way. The term neurology is used synonomously with neurosurgery in describing clinical situations.

The neurological history

Although it may be claimed that the detail of, and the way of obtaining, a history of neurological disease calls for considerable expertise and experience, this is not so in relation to the relatively limited number of symptoms that should alert the doctor to the possibility of a diagnosis which might call for action. This is not to deny that there are difficulties which may be diagnostically misleading, but these are rare. Litigation is more likely to follow the failure to elicit simple symptoms, rather than the complex and poorly described. The patient, as plaintiff, will probably have a clear and often substantiated recollection of the symptoms which proved to be consistent with the evolution of a disorder. Examples of cardinal neurological symptoms which are difficult to discard later are: headache; vomiting; failing visual acuity; weakness of the lower limbs; and impaired bladder control (Table 2.1). These are discussed later in the relevant sections of this book, with some of the difficulties of assessment of, for example, headache as a symptom of raised intracranial pressure. Nevertheless, it is the very simplicity of the symptoms which often makes it difficult to defend the practitioner on

Table 2.1 Neurological history: potentially negligent errors.

Symptom	Cause	Diagnostic error
Headache		
Mode of onset Severity Duration Recurrence	Subarachnoid haemorrhage due to aneurysm/angioma Raised intracranial pressure	Migraine 'Tension'
Vomiting		
Recurrent	Raised intracranial pressure Posterior fossa tumour	Migraine
Persistent	Subarachnoid haemorrhage	
Reduced visual acuity	Raised intracranial pressure Chiasmal/optic nerve compression Glaucoma	Refractory error Cataract
Reduced hearing	Acoustic schwannoma	Wax Barotrauma Ménière's Ageing
Dysuria/retention/ incontinence	Spinal cord/cauda equina compression	Prostatism
Lower limb weakness	Spinal cord/cauda equina compression	'Arthritis'

grounds of a justifiable lack of knowledge of disorders which occur infrequently.

Inaccuracy is usually a consequence of failing to address a problem in a simple and logical manner. The mode of onset of cardinal symptoms, crucial for diagnosis, is often not sought. Clearly, the depth and detail of the neurological history will depend upon the circumstances of the consultation; the general practitioner (GP) is hardly comparable to the consultant neurologist. But pressure of time, or an unco-operative patient or relatives, may not be enough to explain defects in simple history-taking.

Equally important is the failure to consider the differential diagnosis, and priorities for management on the basis of the history alone, even if the neurological examination does not reveal any supporting abnormal physical signs. One example of this is the absence of papilloedema, which never excludes the presence of raised intracranial pressure; in fact, papilloedema is present in only 30% of patients prior to neurosurgery for an intracranial space-occupying lesion. Although this is specialist knowledge, it does not diminish the onus on the GP to form a view on management on the basis of the history, and not to be deflected by an apparently normal physical examination.

How the history is recorded may make or mar a successful defence on liability, as well as having obvious implications for clinical management, especially by other practitioners who may have to rely on those recordings at a later consultation. Again the circumstances of the consultation will influence the type of record employed; but necessary brevity is no reason for omission of essential information, be it in single words, hieroglyphics or the usual dictated and typed hospital out-patient letter. Recording of 'negatives' is always a matter of debate; but if all essential positive points are recorded, courts are more likely to accept that the absence of lengthy lists of complex neurological symptoms is not of any importance. The hallowed tradition of recording the history in the patient's own words is often inadequate in neurology. Thus, vision may be described by patients as 'blurred', 'double', 'misty', etc. The practitioner's record must provide evidence that the symptom was explored by questioning, so that reduced visual acuity, or diplopia, if recorded, will make it clear, often in retrospect, that there were or were not grounds for the patient's urgent referral to the appropriate department.

The practitioner's next step will depend upon his or her awareness of the symptoms of neurological conditions that do call for referral. They are usually those of which a final year medical student should be aware. Although it is mainly to GPs that these strictures apply, they are also relevant in hospital practice when generalists - medical or surgical - are seeking advice and help from neurologists or neurosurgeons. Failure to elicit or transmit the cardinal symptoms may lead to indefensible errors in management, none more so than in patients with head injuries.

In acute medical and surgical conditions, the *telephone* is rightly the essential method of communication between the district general hospital and the specialised neurosurgical or neurological department. The gathering of the essential information, its clear description and communication, and its interpretation by the member of the neurosurgical team receiving the call require considerable experience and verbal ability. Furthermore, the specialist may need to seek further information, the importance of which is not recognised by the caller. Serious errors have occurred, particularly in the management of patients with head injuries, when at the district general hospital a relatively junior member of the team (e.g. pre-registration house surgeon or inexperienced senior house officer) had been deputed to telephone the neurosurgical department. Errors have also occurred because junior members of the district general hospital team have, on their own initiative, and quite inappropriately, approached a neurosurgical department, when the apparent deterioration in the patient's level of consciousness was in fact due to intrathoracic injury, from which the patient died *en route* to the neurosurgical department. Other errors have occurred when relatively inexperienced members of a neurosurgical team have received telephone calls and have not made sufficient enquiries to establish the need to transfer the patient to that department; or to establish that it would have been more appropriate, and more important, to determine that the patient should not be transferred at all, but that life-saving measures should and could have been taken in the district general hospital.

The neurological examination

In many respects this gives rise to great difficulty, and even fear, as does the neurological history, largely unnecessarily. The *essential* parts of the neurological examination are few, and do not require great expertise. Furthermore, if an abnormal physical sign is of importance, there is usually little doubt that it is present. Doubt usually means that the finding can be dismissed at that stage, and management can proceed on the basis that the observation was normal. It is curious how the generalist is often more attentive to, and perplexed by, the minutiae of the neurological examination than is the neurologist. The neurologist is often happy to rely upon a few simple and essential observations, and to dismiss the equivocal signs as irrelevant. The corollary for the generalist and the specialist is to place great reliance upon the neurological history and its accurate recordings. Quite apart from the importance of physical signs in the management of patients, the contemporaneously recorded statement is more likely to impress a court than equivocal statements. Thus, for example, the simple statement that the optic fundi were normal is likely to be more impressive than recordings such as early papilloedema, or slight blurring of the disc margins. The expert witness should be able to advise the court that papilloedema may well be absent in the relevant circumstances, and that seeing the optic discs, for example in children and unco-operative adults, may be very difficult. Therefore to record that the optic discs could not be seen is as acceptable as it is to record the findings as normal, rather than as equivocal. These comments will ring true as contemporaneous notes, and will withstand cross-examination in court.

Although the *neurological examination* will be influenced by the history, the essential points are usually sufficient, and are as follows:

- Level of consciousness and cerebration
- Visual acuity, visual fields and optic fundi
- Pupils and external ocular movements
- Hearing
- Upper limbs: power, crude sensation (e.g. appreciation of pinprick) and tendon reflexes
- Trunk: simple sensory testing to detect a sensory level, and palpation and percussion to detect an enlarged bladder
- Lower limbs: power, crude sensation, tendon reflexes and plantar responses

The specialist neurologist to whom a patient is referred with a problem that is beyond the remit of a GP or general physician will employ more extensive and perhaps more refined techniques of clinical neurological examination. But even the neurologist and the neurosurgeon rely upon the basic methods of examination in deciding whether any serious condition is present, and particularly whether urgent investigation or action is required. Rather than belittling the simpler methods of examination, the specialist will acknowledge their importance, and the court will look unfavourably upon any failure to carry them out.

Much of this is considered in the sections dealing with specific conditions, such as the importance of accurate assessment and recording of the level of consciousness and pupillary size and reactions in the management of head injuries, and the importance of sensory levels and palpation of the bladder and lower limb power in the diagnosis of spinal cord or cauda equina compression.

Two special senses deserve mention. *Visual symptoms* are amongst the most important in neurology, and the loss of visual acuity is one of the most sinister; yet it is unusual for the generalist to assess and record, however crudely, visual acuity. The belief that the measurement of acuity requires special charts or even instrumentation is entirely mistaken. The print in a newspaper will suffice, noting that for neurological purposes it is the corrected acuity which is all-important. Negligence can hardly be denied without some simple recorded observation.

Similarly, with *hearing*, it is unusual for any assessment to be made by the generalist, or even by the specialist. Although acoustic schwannomas are rare, a failure to assess and record the early stages of hearing loss, or the ascription of hearing loss incorrectly to wax in the external auditory meatus, may be responsible for a delay in diagnosis, with consequent grave neurological disability, and an indefensible negligence action.

The neurological examination of the trunk and limbs can be relatively simple. The assessment of power does not usually demand testing of each muscle group separately. Weakness is soon apparent in the outstretched upper limbs, and in the lower limbs, when raised from the horizontal either against gravity or against added resistance. The plantar responses, to which much unnecessary attention is paid, are not unlike the optic fundi and papilloedema; an equivocal response may be irrelevant, and an extensor response is far less important than the other signs of an intracranial or spinal lesion, and a flexor response never excludes any lesion.

These points are not simply the tricks of the trade in neurology. They are of importance to the generalist, and it is very difficult to sustain a successful defence on the grounds that these simple clinical observations were beyond the level of competence expected of a particular practitioner. Furthermore, the essential parts of the examination are not time-consuming, in the circumstances of either general practice or in an accident and emergency department. Some potentially negligent errors of neurological examination are shown in Table 2.2.

Table 2.2 Neurological examination: potentially negligent errors.

Error	Remediable condition
Defective observation and recording of level of consciousness	Raised intracranial pressure Head injury Meningitis
Failure to elicit neck stiffness	Subarachnoid haemorrhage Meningitis
Failure to assess and record visual acuity	Optic chiasm/nerve compression Raised intracranial pressure
Failure to examine fundi	Raised intracranial pressure
Failure to assess hearing	Acoustic schwannoma
Failure to assess perineal sensation	Cauda equina compression
Failure to observe lower limb weakness	Spinal cord compression

Priorities in diagnosis

Neurological differential diagnosis has at times been regarded as a relaxed intellectual exercise, only to be undertaken by the most astute of clinicians with unlimited time to spare; the exercise might be thought to have little effect upon the outcome of the neurological disease. Fortunately those days have passed. More importantly, the generalist is now aware that a number of conditions are amenable to treatment or relief by neurosurgical or medical means, and that some of these need more – and some less – urgent treatment for a successful outcome. Therefore within certain parameters, including time, avoidable and unavoidable morbidity and mortality can generally be defined. Sometimes these may become the subject of legal argument, especially on issues of causation and level of damages, but usually there is little dispute, especially over mortality. Thus it would be difficult to deny that indefensible errors which were responsible for a failure to diagnose a removable benign intracranial tumour had resulted in an avoidable death. Even more obvious is the result of a failure to diagnose and treat bacterial meningitis.

It is possible, therefore, to formulate a relatively short list of clinical diagnoses which, once made, or even considered, should immediately take precedence in management over other, albeit more common, diagnoses. The factor of potential remediability is more important than that of diagnostic probability.

This concept is not peculiar to neurology, but the failure to recognise and set those diagnostic management priorities is one of the primary causes of negligence actions. This can cause defendants and experts considerable discomfort when cross-examined during trial. In hospital practice, the correct setting of priorities is most easily discerned from the entries at the end of the admission notes, and particularly the order of the differential diagnoses. Sadly such essential statements are often lacking; instead there may be a list of proposed investigations, whose very order reveals that the clinician had not attempted any setting of management priorities in the light of any remediable conditions, and especially those needing urgent action.

The *priority list* will become evident from other sections in this book which deal with the different conditions. Here it will suffice to repeat the main headings, most of which will already be familiar to generalists and specialists; but medico-legal practice suggests that its repetition may not be amiss.

- Intracranial space-occupying lesions with raised intracranial pressure or increasing intracranial pressure
- Failing visual acuity due to optic nerve or chiasmal compression, or to rising intracranial pressure, or to cranial arteritis
- Pyogenic meningitis, acute or chronic
- Tetanus
- Subarachnoid haemorrhage due to intracranial aneurysm
- Loss of hearing
- Embolic strokes
- Transient cerebral ischaemia
- Spinal cord compression
- Cauda equina compression

Clinical notes

In all fields of medicine the contemporaneous clinical notes are essential for good management; and they are the single most important piece of evidence upon which the defence in medical negligence actions will rely. This is well-known, and advice on the quality and clarity of notes is abundant, and is referred to elsewhere. There are only a few particular points which have special importance for neurological and neurosurgical conditions. Because the clinical condition may change rapidly, it is essential that *sequential or continuation notes* are made, at least whenever a change occurs. In addition, the writer of the notes should be identifiable, not simply because of the possibility of litigation at a later date, but more to assess the importance or reliability of the observations depending upon the observer's status. A changing clinical situation often requires frequent decisions; those decisions merit a note, however brief. Thereby the decisions taken at a certain moment can be viewed later, if necessary, in the light of the contemporaneous circumstances, rather than purely retrospectively in the light of later events.

Nursing records

Not infrequently when reviewing case records, the contemporaneous nursing records give a clearer account of the patient's condition at a particular time than do the medical notes; and there may be considerable discrepancies between the two. This is not peculiar to neurology and neurosurgery, but in these specialties there is the additional factor of the expertise of the nursing staff and their special training in neurological observations. The contemporaneous use and inspection of the nursing records by the medical staff, and even of the observation charts, which are usually kept assiduously, is often inadequate. Unfortunately, the nursing records and observations charts may be seen later after mishaps, when it is found that the records clearly showed a change which should have prompted medical or surgical action. Perhaps too much reliance was placed on the brief spoken comments at the time. Much would depend upon the nurses' experience. Conversely, the verbal comments of an experienced neurosurgical ward sister to the medical staff may not have been afforded sufficient weight, simply because the charts appeared to be satisfactory.

This inevitably raises questions about the type of neurological observation charts used. In non-neurological departments, the introduction of the Glasgow coma charts has been of great benefit; but they are not ideal for all forms of neurological disorder. It is not easy to record the milder changes of cerebration, nor the changes in lower limbs in incipient spinal cord compression. Therefore, at least in specialist departments, the traditional descriptive methods are still of value, even when used in conjunction with the coma charts.

Errors of investigation

Errors in simple clinical diagnosis which depend upon the history and physical examination are responsible for the majority of medical negligence actions, especially those which cannot be successfully defended. The move towards investigation - ever more complex and technically demanding - and away from assiduous clinical assessment, together with the increasing availability of investigations, has increased the scope for errors by doctors who may be less, rather than more, familiar with their use and interpretation.

The place of specific investigations, their misuse, and errors of interpretation which may lead to actions for medical negligence is discussed in the chapters on the relevant conditions. Here attention is drawn to some general points relevant to investigating patients with potentially remediable conditions. Errors which may lead to allegations of negligence include:

- Failure to request an essential investigation, e.g. radiographs of the cervical spine and chest in trauma.

- Failure to interpret correctly the results of an essential investigation, e.g. skull radiograph, cerebrospinal fluid.
- Requesting an investigation which is irrelevant, and which may deter the clinician from requesting the appropriate and essential investigation, e.g. electroencephalogram (EEG) in raised intracranial pressure.
- Critical time being lost by requesting an investigation, instead of referring a patient urgently for neurosurgical management, e.g. computerised tomography (CT) scan in head injury.
- A negative investigation which deflects the clinician from pursuing a correct clinical diagnosis, e.g. CT scan in subarachnoid haemorrhage; EEG in epilepsy.
- The availability and use of specialised investigations by clinicians who are not familiar with the limitations of, and the correct indications for, those investigations.

Communication and consent for operation

In recent years there has been an increasing awareness of the importance of communication with patients and relatives as an essential part of management, and as a way of avoiding litigation. This is particularly relevant in neurological conditions, and even more so in neurosurgical, where the complexities and uncertainties of diagnosis, natural history and outcome, following medical or surgical treatment, engender anxiety in patients and relatives. Those complexities may well be no less troublesome to the doctor. Discussion, therefore, has a very particular place in neurological disease, but such discussions may well be futile if the practitioner is inexperienced. This may be largely a matter of organisation at a senior level, but often goes by default. Rightly, nursing staff may try to help, but on occasions that will add to the confusion and anxiety which can be the primary stimulus to litigation later.

Consent for operation is an important topic which has stimulated much legal and medical thought; there are judgments which now have an established place, and the medical defence organisations have published guidances. The nature of neurological disease, and the results of neurosurgery, are such that consent for operation is open to considerable debate over the evaluation and enumeration of the risks of surgery, and the extent to which it is right to burden the patient with information which, although factually correct, may cause great anxiety. There is a fine line to be drawn between the information required to satisfy the term 'informed consent', and information which can so easily deter a patient from an operation which, by medical criteria, will bring great benefit. Fortunately, in the English jurisdiction, the courts have accepted that this is a matter for the doctors concerned, but it is one that the court may examine. So far, and rightly so, there is not a defined level of risk, or incidence of a complication, above which it is obligatory to inform the patient of that complication, or of any relevant figures. In discussion the neurosurgeon has to balance the incidence of a complication against its possible severity, a balance that may be difficult. Choice of words is all-important, and therefore this should never be left to an inexperienced member of the team. Be it in the in-patient or out-patient notes, or simply on the usual consent form, there should be a record that the patient was informed about the operation by a doctor of sufficient seniority, and with sufficient experience of that particular operation. For medico-legal purposes, it is not required that a note is made of the specific complications of which the patient has been informed; but a phrase such as 'The implications of the operation have been discussed with the patient and the relatives' is wise, particularly when a neurosurgeon advised an operation on a patient who has not been under his or her care previously.

Delegation and supervision

These are difficult matters which, in surgery, may well demand greater circumspection and experience than the actual performance of the operation by the senior surgeon responsible for the patient's care. It is equally important in clinical medicine, especially when important decisions have to be taken urgently soon after admission. For the reasons set out above on priorities in diagnosis, early decisions may have to be delegated to less senior members of the team, but this is only acceptable if the delegator, usually the consultant, is satisfied of the competence and experience of the member of the team involved. The review of that competence following a medical mishap may well go back to the process of appointment of the doctor concerned, which, again, can devolve upon the delegator. In neurosurgery particularly, the risks of complications is such that even with the so-called less dangerous procedures, for example in the lumbar spine, senior help should always be available within the same hospital. That is not always the case, and this has undoubtedly contributed to litigation. The same can be said of direct operative supervision.

Out-patient consultations in neurosurgery and neurology present particular problems for delegation and supervision, because often the patients have been referred by consultants in other specialties. The patients will soon gauge the seniority and expertise of the doctor in the out-patient clinic, and often will already know that they have been referred to a particular neurological or neurosurgical consultant. If there has been inadequate care in delegation and supervision, a disappointed or disgruntled patient may well be moved to consider litigation if the outcome was poorer than had been hoped for, or expected.

Shared responsibility

In acute neurosurgery and neurology there is frequently the need to involve other specialists. This is most common with intensive care, paediatrics, otological surgery and interventional neuroradiology. If the areas of responsibility, or ultimate overall responsibility, are not defined, patients can easily fall between two or more stools; this has been a cause for litigation. Pressures of other work may tempt the neurosurgical team to leave too much to the intensive care team, and the patient, or more likely the relatives, will become aware of this. The relatives may become confused by explanations given, in perfectly good faith, by medical and nursing staff drawn into a situation with which they may not be entirely familiar.

The development of interventional radiology, and specifically endovascular embolisation for intracranial and spinal vascular lesions, has given rise to litigation. This is covered in the appropriate section of the book. Shared, and ill-defined, responsibility for obtaining informed consent, and for the care of patients should ischaemic complications occur, are prime examples of medical failures which can encourage litigation and make the defence of negligence actions difficult. The radiologist's responsibilities may not become apparent until a major complication occurs. Knowing the risks of the procedure, it is the radiologist's responsibility to decline to perform a procedure unless he or she is certain that appropriate facilities are readily available to deal with the patient who suffers an ischaemic complication. Radiologists may be tempted to embark on procedures in private hospitals where there is neither neurological and neurosurgical expertise nor a neurologically orientated intensive care unit. Fully informed consent requires the referring clinician to be familiar with the radiological technique, the risks, and the particular radiologist's expertise; the patient must understand the reason for the referral. The radiologist must also discuss the procedure with the patient, because the ultimate responsibility for any untoward events rests with the radiologist.

Conclusion

None of the measures which can go some way to avoiding litigation demand extraordinary knowledge by generalists, or for that matter by specialists, including neurologists and neurosurgeons. But they do demand clarity and discipline of thought, concern for organisation, and attention to simple, but not complex, detail. Within the neurological clinical sciences, training of neurologists should ensure a familiarity with the management of the common urgent neurosurgical situations, and neurosurgeons must acquire a reasonable grasp of neurology and general medicine.

Despite the overloading of the undergraduate curriculum, the final year medical student should be made aware of most of the points discussed in this chapter. Even more importantly the pre-registration medical house officer should have appropriate instruction. Without this it is unlikely that most GPs will acquire the essential knowledge to avoid errors that will have dire consequences. Despite the general view that neurology is a hospital-based specialty, the records of the medical defence organisations reveal that errors by GPs are important and costly. Those who consider that attempts to prevent litigation are no more than 'defensive medicine' should be reminded that the prime objective is to raise standards of care. The medical profession's reputation would not be enhanced if the public believed that the primary purpose of raising standards of medical care was to prevent litigation.

Chapter 3

Assessment and Quantification of Neurological Disability

Lindsay McLellan

The purpose of assessing neurological disability is to define the extent of damage to the nervous system, its cause and its impact upon the subject's lifestyle. A rehabilitation assessment attempts to predict the subject's capacity to improve and suggest strategies for change both in the subject and in the environment so as to optimise function in the future.

The future course of events will be determined partly by the age of the patient, by the nature of the cause of the disability and, to some extent, by the lifestyle that is anticipated for the future. While the cause and extent of neurological disability can be defined reasonably precisely in a standardised way for every subject, the impact that this has on function and on lifestyle depends upon factors that are individual to the subject and reflect his or her previous attributes and experiences.

This chapter highlights the aspects of neurological disease and impairment that have the most impact upon the daily function of the disabled person. This section introduces some general principles relating to the practical impact of neurological disease and how this impact can be categorised. 'Assessment of neurological disability and handicap from history and observation' summarises some common domains of neurological impairments, drawing attention to the often oblique and indirect ways in which impairments can affect performance. This relates particularly to cognitive impairments, the effects of which are frequently underestimated in clinical practice and probably in medico-legal practice as well. 'Measuring disabilities and needs' summarises the range of daily living functions that are basic to personal independence and which are often the focus of attention during the hospital in-patient phase of rehabilitation following an illness or injury. They include key elements to be covered in long-term care for people with static or deteriorating conditions, and also in the rehabilitation of young people with congenital disabilities who have reached the stage of life where they wish to establish themselves as independent adults. 'Basic list of functions' (see Table 3.1) summarises the main domains of handicap and suggests how they could be approached in the formulation of medico-legal reports. 'Assessment of rehabilitation potential and rehabilitation needs' considers the role of rehabilitation, how a person's rehabilitation potential is assessed, and how the effectiveness of a rehabilitation plan or programme can be judged.

Should formal scales be used?

Formal scaling systems for disability are useful for surveys and research purposes and some examples are given in the appendix. However, they are rarely precise enough to define the situation for an individual without the addition of less formalised observations and 'clinical judgements'. This is particularly true for future prognosis and for assessing the likely impact of a rehabilitation programme, where the psychological attributes and personality of the subject may have a profound effect upon the impact that a particular degree of neurological impairment will have upon the subject's eventual performance.

Some basic definitions

The World Health Organisation has suggested that the effects of disabling conditions can be considered at three levels. *Impairment* is the loss of a part or function – for example, the loss of a leg, or of the capacity to move a leg. *Disability* is the inability to perform a function to a level or in a manner that is considered normal for a human being. To continue the same example, a person who has lost the use of a leg may, in consequence, have the disability of being unable to climb stairs or to walk at normal speed. *Handicap* is the restriction of the social role associated with disability, taking into account the other personal environmental and cultural factors of the subject. Thus someone with one leg can no longer work as a labourer on a building site, though his or her capacity to work as a telephonist would be little affected. Handicap, therefore, covers the degree of mismatch between a person's capacities and his or her desired social role. The factors that contribute to handicap are not only the disability of the subject, but the nature of the environment in which he or she has to operate – including the behaviour of the other people in that environment. In considering whether an impairment (such as damage to a particular part of the brain) is likely to cause handicap or not, it is therefore necessary to consider carefully other coexisting impairments and disabilities and the nature of the environment in which the subject lives or wishes to live. Handicap must be considered in relation to the social role that the subject wishes to have in that environment.

Objective of assessment: prognosis

It is important to consider the subject's situation prior to the illness or injury and to compare it with the current situation, in order to establish a trajectory from which to judge the probable course of future events. Even for the basic medical condition, this is often a difficult matter, because there are very few good longitudinal studies of disabilities from various causes that can establish risk with any degree of certainty. Studies that are available, such as in spinal cord injury, are inevitably 20 to 30 years out of date because people dying today from the effects of an injury acquired 20 years ago did not have the advantage, in the early years after the injury, of the advances in medical treatment that are present today, let alone the further advantages that are likely to accrue from research in the future. In addition, predicting the future for an individual is different from predicting mean outcomes for a group, because there are likely to be particular characteristics of the individual that make it inappropriate to base the prognosis for that individual on the average outcome derived from studies of a group. Some people are going to do better than average and some are going to do worse. Just as in clinical practice, a more accurate individual prognosis will be given by a skilled practitioner than by an unskilled one, so in medico-legal work a practitioner who has experience in following up individuals over a period of time is likely to be in a better position to assess whether a particular subject is likely to do better or worse than average, in the light of the level of disability and the other circumstances of the case.

Location of damage in the nervous system: implications for function

The brain and spinal cord constitute the central nervous system. Consciousness is believed to rise within the cortex or outer layer of brain tissue for the cerebral hemispheres. Neural pathways pass from here through the brain stem, which is deeply placed and in the midline near the base of the skull. From here the pathways pass to the spinal cord. In order to cause muscles to move and the various other bodily functions to occur, *peripheral* nerves pass into the limbs, transmitting information from the brain to the limbs and also in the reverse direction, from receptors in the limbs to the brain. Nerves leave the spinal cord in a series of roots, a pair of roots emerging on each side of the body between each vertebra and combining in various ways to form peripheral nerves.

The standard neurological examination and assessment is designed to define the time course of the patient's symptoms and signs, and the location in the nervous system of the lesions that are responsible for them. Together with factors such as the age of the patient and the circumstances in which his or her symptoms started, it is often possible to make a clinical diagnosis of the cause and extent of damage. This may be supported, if necessary, by investigations to define precise areas and patterns of damage.

Can brain scans predict function?

One of the difficulties in assessing the impact of brain trauma upon function is that the neurones which provide the basic functions of the nervous system are microscopically small and cannot be individually recognised by imaging techniques. The situation may be likened to an aerial photograph of a town after an earthquake. From the air, some areas of the town will show obvious damage while others may appear unscathed. However, at ground level, there may be some retained services and survivors in the obviously damaged areas and considerable impairment of activity in the apparently undamaged ones. Thus, radiological techniques such as brain scans may be a useful adjunct to a careful clinical assessment and examination, but they can never be a substitute for it. Current X-ray and scanning techniques cannot give precise information as to how a particular area of the brain is functioning. Only a clinical assessment can do this.

Importance of the clinical history

The most important part of a neurological assessment is the history, because this should contain the experiences of the subject and helps to define the relationship between an episode or injury and the subsequent changes in function. At the same time, the psychological and emotional effects of the condition upon the subject can be assessed. Sometimes it is clear from the way in which subjects communicate or the content of what they say that there is impairment of cognitive function. In all such cases, the testimony of someone who knows the patient well and is in daily contact with him or her is of vital importance, because the subject may forget or misinterpret events and therefore give a misleading account of them. A further difficulty arises in subjects who elaborate or fabricate elements of their account, when it is necessary to look for internal consistencies in the history and in the relationship between the history and the findings on examination, supplemented, if possible, by independent reports from other people.

Assessment of neurological disability and handicap from history and observation

It is important to categorise the following domains of function:

(1) Arousal and awareness

As someone recovers consciousness, he or she may start to make movements either spontaneously or in response to stimuli such as touch or the sound of his or her name. Certain responses are reflexes mediated by the nervous system without involving consciousness (for example, tendon reflexes or cough reflexes). A degree of awareness may be inferred if the subject's eyes are open and consistently follow people moving round the room. However, full awareness, for example of an individual situation and its implications, requires a much higher level of cognitive function. In the absence of effective communication (see below), the degree of awareness has to be inferred by careful observation of the subject's response to events and an apparent wish to communicate. The term *arousal* refers to whether the person appears to be awake and to be experiencing some kind of conscious activity. The term *awareness* relates to the content of consciousness as well as to the degree of arousal.

(2) *Communication*

The usual means of communication is through a combination of speech, facial expression and gesture ('body language'). The effectiveness of communication, especially with strangers, is impaired if any of these modalities is compromised.

Speech involves (1) the generation of words; and (2) the production of sound through co-ordinated movements of the lips, tongue, jaw, palate, larynx and respiratory muscles. Failure to co-ordinate movement properly produces speech that is slurred, soft or slow and lacking in the usual inflection. This can pose a serious communication barrier in some circumstances (for example, when at work or talking to strangers) but does not, of course, affect reading and writing and may be a much less troublesome barrier when communicating with close relatives and friends. If the generation of words is impaired (a condition termed 'expressive dysphasia') then writing and spoken speech are both likely to be affected. If the dysphasia is severe, it may be very difficult to assess the content of consciousness or the presence of other cognitive impairments.

Not infrequently, the capacity to understand speech is less impaired than the capacity to generate speech or, in more technical language, receptive dysphasia is often less severe than expressive dysphasia. Thus some individuals may be able to understand language better than they can express it – similar to the ability to understand a foreign language better than one can speak it. More subtle impairments are referred to as 'high-level language disorders' and are characterised by slowness and errors in the interpretation of language and in conversation, leading to difficulty in participating in conversations at normal speed, especially when more than one person is participating in the conversation or there is a potentially distracting background noise.

People who are severely dysphasic are often unable to use formal gestures or sign language. Facial expressions and simple gestures may be the only means of conversational communication open to them. Feelings and mood may be expressed visually by those who are able to draw or paint, and musically by those with retained senses of pitch and rhythm. Art and music therapy may be valuable in establishing ways and opportunities for expressing emotions, the therapist's contribution being a combined one of stimulation, guidance and interpretation.

Detailed and formal assessment of communication ability is part of the work of the speech and language therapist. Coexisting impairments of vision, hearing or cognition (see below) often contribute to poor communication.

(3) *Vision and hearing*

Vision: Vision is assessed in terms of the boundaries of the field of vision and by the acuity of vision in each eye. Acuity relates to the ability to perceive small objects and detail. It can be impaired by damage to the eye itself, to the optic pathways in the brain and also to disturbance of the co-ordination of eye movements by the brain stem. In the latter case, blurring of vision is caused by the fact that the two eyes are not pointing precisely at the same target so that the brain receives two images which cannot be precisely matched. In such circumstances, covering one eye will immediately 'improve' the apparent acuity of the other.

When one cerebral hemisphere of the brain is damaged, a loss of up to half the opposite visual field in *both* eyes (a 'homonymous hemianopia') may result. The subject with left homonymous hemianopia will see objects that he or she is looking directly at, but will have no vision at all to the left of the fixation point from top to bottom of his or her visual field. This may be associated with a separate difficulty, namely a lack of awareness that the deficit exists. Such subjects are at risk of injury by bumping into doorways on their 'blind' side, stumbling at corners, for example on stairs, bumping into furniture or people, or burning themselves on a cooker. This deficit ('lack of awareness' or 'neglect') causes particular difficulties when crossing roads and is an absolute barrier to driving a car or riding a bicycle. It also impedes rehabilitation because the patient may have great difficulty in recognising that the problem exists.

Hearing: People with normal hearing in one ear can often continue a conversation normally, even if the other ear is totally deaf. They will, however, have difficulty in identifying the source of the sound and thus be unable to filter a conversation from background noise. Mild deafness in both ears is usually more disabling than total deafness in one.

(4) *The senses of touch, smell and balance*

Touch: The sense of touch has a number of modalities that include the ability to detect movement, texture, temperature and painful stimuli such as a pinprick or thumb squeeze. The use of the hands for dexterous tasks, the ability to move about safely in the dark, the ability to avoid damage to tissues that are being pressed upon (for example, the weight of the body on the buttocks while sitting, or chafing from ill-fitting footwear) and the ability to avoid being accidentally burned or cut all depend upon intact sensation. People with impaired sensation in the lips, hands, genitalia or other 'erogenous zones' often experience a diminution of their ability to enjoy sexual activity and to obtain an orgasm.

Smell: The sense of smell contributes to one's sense of the taste of food. If the sense of smell is impaired, food may taste insipid unless it is spiced so strongly with salt, chilli or curry that no one else in the family can eat it. The ability to detect fire or toxic fumes is lost, and particular care must be taken to install full fire alarm systems in the patient's house. Toxic chemicals must be stored safely and systematic strategies of ventilation used when undertaking activities such as interior decorating or spraying.

Balance: The sense of balance is a very complex entity. It involves integrating the input from vision, hearing, the semicircular canals and otolith of the inner ear on both sides, and muscle and joint receptors in the neck. An impaired sense of balance affects people's ability to move and, in particular, to change head position suddenly without feeling dizzy, unsteady and nauseated. It thus affects mobility and nearly all forms of social integration.

Perception: Even when the basic mechanisms of touch, vision or hearing are intact, cognitive perceptual problems may impair a subject's ability to make sense of what he or she touches, sees or hears. Thus a patient with impaired visual perception may see objects clearly but have difficulty in identifying them, in assigning them into a category according to their shape, or in distinguishing foreground from background. This could cause problems with mobility, for example when traversing stairs or patterned carpets. Difficulties in recognising spatial relationships may impair a person's ability to dress because he or she cannot work out how to lay out his or her clothes. The subject may become lost even in his or her own house through lack of appreciation of the spatial relationships between the different rooms. One architect recovering from a head injury whose non-dominant parietal lobe had been damaged appeared normal in terms of social function, physical independence and vision; yet when he travelled to visit his old home in London, he was unable to find or recognise the building, and his draft design for an office block included a basement area with skylights placed in the centre of the ceiling.

(5) Movement

Movement depends upon the following:

(1) The range of movement physically possible at the various joints. Contractures, deformities and pain can affect this.

(2) The strength of voluntary power. This is reduced by damage to motor pathways and disease or lack of fitness of the muscles themselves.
(3) The ability to co-ordinate movement precisely. This is affected by damage to motor pathways (including cerebellar pathways and basal ganglia of the brain, and the presence of spasticity). Co-ordination is also impaired where there is a severe loss of touch and position sensation in the limbs.

Inco-ordination of fine dextrous movement affects the ability to undertake fine or skilled tasks, such as using tools or - on a more mundane level - doing up buttons. Loss of co-ordination in the proximal muscles (e.g. around shoulders or hips) means that the limb cannot be held in a stable position even if manual dexterity is unimpaired. Loss of control of the muscles of the trunk may make it impossible to stand or walk.

Immobility may lead to many undesirable consequences in the longer term, including demineralisation of the spine, an increased risk of calculi or stones in the renal tracts and bladder, deep vein thrombosis, deformities and pressure sores.

(6) Control of the bowel and bladder

Control basically consists of (1) allowing the bowel or bladder to become full, with an awareness that it is full, without involuntary leaking of the contents; (2) emptying the bowel or bladder to order. If either function is impaired there is a risk of incontinence and of damage, especially to the urinary tracts, and this may eventually influence general health and life expectancy. The person must also have the other physical functions needed to get to a toilet or to use it; if this is not possible, there will be a need either for personal assistance or for various forms of equipment. The nature of the diet and the timing of the intake of food and drink can influence the level of continence experienced. Incontinence itself increases the risk of pressure sores and infection, as well as leading to some social handicap.

(7) Sexual function

There is, of course, much more to sexual function than the act of intercourse itself. The libido of the patient may be reduced by the psychological experience of illness, depression, and by changes in the partner's behaviour. It can also be reduced, or in some cases increased, by damage to the frontal lobes and associated deep structures of the forebrain. Lack of sensation (see above) may impair the pleasure experienced during physical lovemaking. Damage to the spinal cord may seriously impair the capacity of males to achieve erection or ejaculation and the capacity of males or females to experience orgasm.

(8) Cognition

Cognition covers a number of domains of mental function, notably knowing, understanding, learning, perceiving (see above), attending, remembering, judging and thinking. Cognition may be very significantly impaired in people with lesions of the frontal and temporal lobes of the brain, and other areas of cerebral cortex, who have no observable physical defect and may appear unimpaired on superficial conversation. After a head injury, the presence and effects of cognitive impairment are often a cause of dispute in medico-legal cases because of an apparent discrepancy between the patient's physical abilities and his or her continuing incapacity when faced with real-life situations.

An important general point here is that, although formal cognitive assessment by a neuropsychologist is nearly always essential, the overall impact in real life of a collection of cognitive impairments is often greater than would be anticipated from the degree of impairment measured in relation to each modality alone. In particular, lawyers may pay undue attention to the significance of measures of intelligence. There are many instances of individuals with an intelligence quotient (IQ) of 120 or more who are unable to boil an egg safely, let alone live independently or work, because of the interacting effects of other cognitive impairments. Substantial disability and handicap may result from cognitive impairment, illustrated by impairments of *function* (as given in the subject's history) that may result. Such evidence must be actively sought in the subject's history.

Memory: Impairment of day-to-day memory affects nearly all aspects of activity. Names, faces, appointments, confidences, plans, commitments and instructions may all be forgotten. The capacity to learn may be seriously affected, although it may still be possible to acquire new skills and knowledge through a process termed 'procedural learning'. By many repetitions, the subject acquires a skill without being able to recall ever having practised it. Recent research has established that procedural learning in people who are amnesic (unable to remember) depends also upon the avoidance of errors. An amnesic subject who attempts a task and intuitively makes an error is unable to remember that it *was* an error. Each time the same choice is presented, the subject therefore makes the same mistake but with increasing confidence, as a result of procedural learning. Learning situations have to be tightly controlled to ensure that subjects are prevented from consolidating their intuitive errors. This requirement runs counter to current educational practice for people with unimpaired memory. If therapy or training has been given which has failed to recognise this problem, the patient's history and previous response to therapy may give an unduly pessimistic impression of the capacity for future change.

Decision-making and planning: the 'dysexecutive syndrome': In order to undertake a daily activity like preparing a meal, a subject has to be able to hold in the mind the overall objective of the exercise and the sequencing of the various tasks that have to be done to carry it out. This is likely to require frequent decisions, such as where to look for the fresh milk, how long it will take to peel potatoes, and whether it will be necessary to use a utensil more than once. Faced with a formal psychological test of intelligence, where everything is laid out in order and a logical pathway has to be followed, a subject with a dysexecutive syndrome might score well. However, as soon as a series of real-life practical decisions have to be made in an appropriate sequence in the *absence* of the kind of structure provided by a psychological test battery, mistakes and misjudgements abound. The first course of the meal may be fully prepared before the table has been laid or any of the other courses started. Alternatively, all the subtasks are attempted concurrently, and become inextricably muddled. After two hours the kitchen is in chaos, the various courses are all in different stages of disarray, while the subject is despondent, frustrated and unable to grasp why cooking has become so difficult. This inability to solve problems is often accompanied by a lack of the ability to take clear decisions or to initiate a course of activity without prompting from others.

Behaviour: Normal social behaviour requires good planning, judgement and memory, effective verbal and non-verbal communication, and an ability to maintain an adult level of control over one's feelings. The disorders summarised above can rapidly lead to repeated episodes of frustration and embarrassment for the subject. If to this is added a lack of ability to appreciate someone else's point of view and an impaired control over the build-up of powerful feelings (common in deep frontal lobe lesions) then it is easy to see why outbursts of verbal or physical anger commonly occur. Frontal lobe lesions do not always 'disinhibit' behaviour. Some subjects, by contrast, become apathetic, meandering aimlessly through their day without achieving anything or expressing any more than mild intermittent frustration.

These difficulties can have a profound effect on people's capacity to live independently without someone to monitor and prompt them in ways that help them to achieve daily tasks, avoid emotional outbursts and maintain their social contacts.

Many families learn intuitively how to help the disabled person do this. Unfortunately many do not, and if patterns of mutual frustration and rejection become established (or accentuated, for they may have been present to some degree prior to the illness or injury) the subject risks becoming increasingly isolated and facing ever more difficult and unfavourable social situations with which he or she cannot deal effectively. Recent evidence suggests that a substantial proportion of the incidence of physical violence shown by head-injured people returning home could have been prevented by effective training and education of the subject and family during the hospital phase of treatment. The history needs to pay careful attention to any instances of aggressive or disinhibited behaviour, to record the antecedents or circumstances leading up to emotional outbursts, and ways in which families and others respond to them.

Attention and flexibility of thinking: These are actually separate functions, but both depend upon the frontal lobes of the brain. Attention is the ability to focus concentration on an object or activity and to respond (or not respond) appropriately to distractions. 'Over-focused' behaviour may manifest in excessive talkativeness and repetitiveness, inflexibility of thinking and decision-making and a tendency to concrete rather than abstract patterns of thinking and analysis. People who are excessively distractible repeatedly lose track of conversation and other activities, especially in environments that are noisy or where they are engaged in conversation involving more than one other person.

(9) *Stamina, fatigue, pain and mood*

Stamina and fatigue are of considerable importance in judging a person's capacity for daily life activities. In people with cognitive impairment, especially in the first year to 18 months after moderately severe head injury, performance may fall off dramatically when the subject becomes tired. Physical performance may also be affected so that the person's speech becomes more slurred or movements become weaker and more clumsy. The underlying mechanisms for these well-recognised phenomena are not understood. The only solution is for the person to rest and allow these capacities to recover. This is the principle reason for advising a staged and gradual return to work for people recovering from severe brain injuries.

A lack of physical stamina may, of course, reflect a lack of physical fitness as well as the impact of brain injury.

States of chronic pain, and depression, often impair physical and mental stamina. It is important to assess a person's mood and to take chronic or frequent pain into account when determining a subject's probable capacities, especially for prolonged periods of work or physical activity. Sometimes excessive fatigue can be linked with a lack of sleep or loss of weight, or to the sedative side-effects of drugs. Many drugs used in neurological conditions, such as spasticity, cramps, voluntary movements and epilepsy, may accentuate fatigue.

(10) *Paroxysmal symptoms: epilepsy*

The commonest paroxysmal neurological symptom is epilepsy. Epilepsy usually leads to the taking of anticonvulsant drugs to reduce the severity and frequency of attacks; all these drugs potentially have side-effects. The side-effects of certain drugs such as phenytoin upon cognitive function are often underestimated, and many patients even today are discharged from neurosurgical units taking phenytoin in doses that impair cognitive function. Any subject experiencing side-effects from medication should be reviewed by a neurologist.

Nocturnal seizures or those that are preceded by an aura in which the patient can take evasive action are less disabling than seizures that occur without warning. Minor attacks are less disabling than generalised convulsions. The occurrence of any attack will preclude the patient for life from driving a public service vehicle or aeroplane. Once a patient has established a pattern of having attacks only while asleep, or as had no attacks over a two-year period, current UK law permits the resumption of driving on a standard car licence. Further attacks lead to suspension of the licence for at least 12 months. Unsupervised swimming and climbing activities are inadvisable.

The transition from childhood to adulthood may be difficult because of the need for the young adult to assume responsibility for his or her own life and anticonvulsant treatment, and to choose which risks to take. Parents who have given protection for many years often find it difficult to watch their offspring taking risks and running into potentially avoidable difficulties.

Much of the handicap associated with epilepsy is not so much due to the practical effects of the disorder as to prejudice among employers and the public at large. The teaching profession and the armed forces pose barriers that are probably unnecessarily high. The National Health Service (NHS) itself has a disappointingly poor record of employing people with epilepsy, especially in the light of the opportunities provided by the recent expansion of administrative posts in the service. Regrettable though such prejudices are, their impact upon social integration and employment is very real and must be given a corresponding emphasis in medico-legal settlements.

(11) Persisting coma and minimally responsive states

After severe and widespread injury to the cerebral hemispheres of the brain, spontaneous opening of the eyes and apparent 'sleeping and waking cycles' may gradually become established whether or not there is any evidence of conscious awareness or of response (other than reflex response) to the environment. Such patients are regarded as still being in coma with the potential for some recovery of awareness, but the likelihood of such recovery declines progressively with time. If 12 months after the injury there is still no evidence of awareness, the term 'persistent vegetative state' is used, and at this point the relatives of the patient (and others involved in his or her care) may seek a court ruling for the withdrawal of nutrition and/or ventilatory assistance, which would result in the death of the patient. Such a decision depends upon evidence collected *over a continuous period of observation of several weeks by an experienced ward team.* A single assessment of an hour or two by an experienced professional is not sufficient to establish that this point has been reached, because of the possibility of infrequent 'islands' of awareness occurring between long periods of unawareness and unresponsiveness.

This situation must be distinguished from the 'locked-in syndrome', an infrequent occurrence in which full awareness (with cognitive functions ranging from normal to substantially impaired) is present but the patient cannot signal this except by tiny movements, because of focal damage to structures in the brain stem that relay stimuli from the brain to the nerves serving the muscles of the body. Movement or blinking of the eye may be the only means by which such a subject can communicate awareness to other people. Such movements can be misinterpreted as reflex in origin by staff who are not specifically trained in the process of neurological assessment.

Sometimes even expert observers find it difficult to agree on whether there is a complete lack of awareness or not. Two sets of guidelines exist to help define the situation, and attempts are currently being made to redraft these to avoid any ambiguity in interpretation. They are:

(1) The Permanent Vegetative State. Review by a Working Party convened by the Royal College of Physicians of London, 1996.
(2) International Working Party Report on the Vegetative State. London: Royal Hospital for Neurodisability, Putney, 1996.

Measuring disabilities and needs

The activities that form the basis of most hospital rehabilitation programmes are grouped around the basic daily living functions required for personal independence. A number of formal validated outcome measures such as the Barthel scale, the Functional Independence Measure (FIM) and the Frenchay Activities Index (FAI) are used for audit and research purposes. In the author's opinion, they are of very limited value in assessing the impact of disabling conditions for medico-legal purposes. Many daily living scales (such as the Barthel Scale and the FIM) are not so much disability scales as dependency scales, because they are scored according to the level of assistance a subject needs to perform each of the basic activities. They progress from low levels of assistance such as set-up and verbal prompting, through the use of equipment and intermittent physical help from another person, to the most severe category of dependency where the help of two other people is always needed in order to achieve a function.

While dependency may be a helpful if indirect way of scoring disability, the reason for wishing to measure it is usually to establish a patient's *current and unmet needs*. A health need is defined as an item or service that would confer a health gain if made available to the patient. Care needs and rehabilitation needs can be defined similarly. This is not the place to enter the current fiscal debate in the UK as to the precise boundary between a health need, a rehabilitation need and a care need; it is assumed that all three will be relevant to medico-legal assessment and can therefore be considered together.

Assessment of a disabled person's current performance should include a representative daily plan in which the nature of his or her needs and the duration of any service provided is timetabled. Weekends and weekdays may be different because of different levels of activity undertaken and different patterns of support being available. Examples of such timetables are given below.

In general, activities to be included in such a timetable will involve both maintenance of comfort and state of health, and the prevention of complications associated with disability, such as the occurrence of pressure sores, respiratory infections, deformities (contractures) and psychological problems such as depression. At a higher functional level (handicap), it would be necessary to consider maintenance of social contacts and social role, and an acceptable quality of life without unwanted social isolation, boredom and lack of personal development.

Basic list of functions

The important items are tabulated in Table 3.1.

Table 3.1

(a) Basic self care

Item	Immediate objective	Prevention objective	Examples of possible relevant needs
Ability to change position in chair and bed	Comfort	Pressure sores and deformity Deep vein thrombosis and embolism	Electric bed, grab handles, physiotherapy, nursing or other care assistance
Washing and bathing, grooming, shaving	Hygiene and comfort, self-esteem	Infections, social isolation, depression	Adapted washing, bathing and showering facilities Personal assistance
Dressing and undressing	To leave bed and house	Social isolation	Training in techniques Personal assistance
Transferring between bed, chair, wheelchair and toilet or commode	Comfort, basic mobility and independence about the house	Pressure sores, deformity, lack of physical fitness, accidental injury	Adapted toilet, transferring equipment, relocated toilet, physiotherapy, antispastic therapy, personal assistance

Contd

Table 3.1 *Contd*

Item	Immediate objective	Prevention objective	Examples of possible relevant needs
Eating food and drink Selection of appropriate diet	Maintain nutrition Participate in pleasant social activity	Social isolation, incontinence	Special selection and preparation of food Assistance with feeding Feeding equipment; gastrostomy and associated equipment
Preparing meals	Maintain nutrition, choice and independence	Undue gain or loss of weight Social isolation	Adaptations in kitchen, special equipment and training in its use, meals on wheels, home help
Emptying bowel and bladder, use of toilet	Comfort	Pressure sores, infections, damage to kidney Restriction of social activities	Medical treatment of disorders of elimination, treatment of infections, use of self-catheterisation or specialised equipment
Communication	Maintain social contacts and role, self-expression	Social isolation, unmet needs not identified, depression	Technical aids to augment speech and writing, training in sign language, equipment for alarm systems Telephones and environmental control
Mobility indoors	Maintain fitness and independence	Restricted lifestyle, accidental injury	Wheelchairs, physiotherapy, adaptations to environment
Housework and home maintenance	Maintain comfortable and socially appropriate environment		Specialised equipment Modification of environment Help from other people

Contd

Table 3.1 *Contd*

(b) Higher levels of function (handicap)

Item	Immediate objective	Prevention objective	Examples of relevant needs
Outdoor mobility	Independence and maintenance of social, recreational and employment activities	Lack of fitness, social isolation, restricted lifestyle	Outdoor–indoor wheelchairs, adapted external environment Specialised car or van Public transport Adapted car Personal assistance
Pre-employment training or retraining including further education	Re-establish social role Help to identify future life plan	Poverty, social isolation, depression, loss of self-esteem	Local assessment and training services dealing with social, cognitive and physical skills Transportation to and at training venues with access to facilitate which formal employment assessment and training may be adopted
Leisure and formal recreational activities	Re-establish social role Help to identify future life plan Personal development	Poverty, social isolation, depression, loss of self-esteem	Local assessment and training services dealing with social, cognitive and physical skills Transportation to and at training venues with access to facilitate which formal employment assessment and training may be adopted
Social contacts with family and others	Maintain and develop personal relationships and contacts	Poverty, social isolation, depression, loss of self-esteem Stress on close personal relationships, especially carers	Good communication systems, regular social contacts, transport and appropriate travel systems, appropriate environments in which to meet 'respite' care Holidays

These tables introduce some of the components that are likely to be included in subjects' timetables and in their inventories of need. It is clear that the precise selection of needs depends upon a detailed assessment of what the problem is, rather than simply an assessment of disability. For example, the disability of incontinence of urine *could* give rise, in different cases, to a number of alternative needs:

- Help of another person to get to the toilet
- Training in the use of self-catheterisation
- Medical re-assessment
- Provision of a downstairs toilet or commode
- Adaptation of clothing and equipment to assist transfers.

Only a specific assessment on an individual basis could establish which of these possibilities the individual actually needs. This cannot be predicted or deduced from measuring the disability itself.

Home with support, or institution?

One of the most contentious areas of assessment involves the question of whether a disabled individual can live safely alone. Related to this is whether a severely disabled individual would be better off in a flat or house with attendant support, or in an institution.

It is often difficult for disabled teenagers to make the transition to adult independence. Non-disabled teenagers may not always wash regularly. They may show social indiscretions, keep very messy bedrooms and take foolish physical risks when they go out. No one would suggest, however, that on these grounds they should spend the rest of their lives under the supervision of a nurse or occupational therapist, or live permanently in an institution. Non-disabled teenagers can experiment and acquire independence gradually and relatively informally by staying with friends, trying out life in a flat and then returning home again for a while before trying again. This pattern of events is rarely seen as appropriate for disabled teenagers – or for medico-legal reports – because it is all so inconvenient for the planners, carers and others who may need to be involved.

In general, the process of establishing independence is likely to take longer for disabled teenagers, partly because of their disability (especially if there is some cognitive impairment), partly because parents find it harder to let go, and because of the logistics of setting up appropriate and flexible support. It may not be realistic to expect newly disabled young people to establish themselves independently in the community *and* to retrain for employment at the same time. It is often easier to succeed if accommodation and social independence is established first, and efforts are them made to establish the person in employment, although this order of events is not invariable.

Most people prefer not to live in an institution. The advantage of a good institution is that an appropriate range of resources is available without their having to be organised by the person or by a case manager and without taking over the lives of other family members. Social and recreational activities and opportunities for the development of close personal relationships with peers may be more frequent and varied. Some institutions are, in reality, more like retreats or small communities of their own, and have daily contact with the community at large built into their structure and function. They may be particularly helpful for people with marked cognitive impairment that affects their ability to make their own decisions and to form friendships.

The advantage of living in a more standard domestic setting is that the occupant has greater autonomy in deciding what to *do* and what to take responsibility for. Most people *do* prefer to live in their own homes and usually manage to do this by building up, over a period of a year or two, links with individuals in the local community whom they 'get on with' and who can provide, perhaps on a rota basis, the kind of support that is needed.

In arriving at a decision, it is very important to assess the needs of the family as well as the needs of the disabled person. Some families will still be in a stage of shock and psychological denial and may insist on taking on commitments that are self-evidently (to other people!) unrealistic in the longer term. It is essential to build in to any plan contingency arrangements for what should happen if the parents or other informal carers become temporarily or permanently incapacitated.

Assessment of rehabilitation potential and rehabilitation needs

There are no generally accepted instruments or inventories for measuring rehabilitation potential or rehabilitation needs. One approach to this problem is the Edinburgh Rehabilitation Status Scale (Affleck *et al.*, 1988). Rehabilitation potential depends upon the following factors:

(1) *Biological factors:* The cause and nature of the disability and the natural history of the cause. For example, it is known that significant improvement can continue to occur after moderate or severe brain injury for three to five years, or longer in some cases. By contrast, the time period for biological recovery after a stroke is usually regarded as around six months, possibly extending in some cases to 12 months. After *complete* physical transection of the spinal cord, there is little likelihood of biological recovery after the initial stabilisation phase.

(2) *Personal assets and weaknesses:* People who are well-educated, have a problem-solving approach to life and are used to decision-making and

success, who are financially well off, well-supported socially and who have a defined belief system or religion from which they can draw support have greater rehabilitation potential than those who do not have such assets. A previous history of dependence upon drugs or alcohol, or of marked antisocial behaviour and a string of broken relationships, are adverse prospective factors for successful rehabilitation.

(3) *Lifestyle ambitions:* Rehabilitation is a process of active change by which a disabled person acquires the skills and knowledge needed for optimal function and the avoidance of complications. This is possible only in so far as the objectives are firmly espoused by the disabled person. For example, it may be potentially possible, on the basis of two hours of physiotherapy a day, for someone to retain the ability to walk albeit slowly and for short distances. But he or she may prefer to spend these two hours in other ways and to use a wheelchair for getting about. Similarly, it may be possible to teach someone to dress him- or herself by dint of great effort, regular training and the use of modified clothing, even though it takes 50 minutes for him or her to do so. But the subject may prefer to be dressed by someone else in ten minutes, allowing him- or herself to start the day 40 minutes earlier in a more refreshed condition.

The context of such functions is the lifestyle and social role the person wishes to have. The identification of possible employment and specific leisure activities inevitably depend upon what the person wants, not simply what might be possible. Some people from ethnic minorities often perceive the future in more restrictive terms and there is a danger that in these circumstances the potential for rehabilitation is not realised.

(4) *Capacity for learning and for change in function:* This is the most difficult component to assess. It is always helpful to look back on the pattern of behaviour and change that the subject has displayed since the injury, and indeed before that. Particular difficulties arise when the person is still in a state of shock or psychological denial and thus unable to make a realistic assessment of future options. Once this phase has been worked through, the subject may be able to make progress. His or her previous personality and responses to adversity are more helpful pointers to the future.

(5) *How much therapy and what sort of therapy is it justifiable to prescribe?* People with complex disabilities may need help from a number of different professions including (in alphabetical order) the arts-based therapies, clinical psychology, medicine, nursing, occupational therapy, physiotherapy, rehabilitation engineering, speech and language therapy and social work. Professionals used to working as members of a multiprofessional team have the advantage of the experience of weekly discussions with their colleagues about their patients' general progress across the range of disabilities and

treatments involved. There is often a tension between those working in statutory service teams who may have a lot of experience of what to do with inadequate resources across the range of disabilities, and those working as independent private practitioners who lack regular peer support and involvement in clinical audit, and who may acquiesce rather uncritically in long periods of regular monotherapy without any formal objectives or monitoring of outcome. Such tensions and disagreements are probably inevitable until scientific research has caught up with current practice.

Example of a timetable

Fig. 3.1 shows an example of a weekday timetable for a young man aged 20 recovering from a severe brain injury received two years earlier. He is living in his parents' home. No distinction is made between health, social and rehabilitation activities and needs.

From this timetable, the nature and frequency of assistance can be plotted. The table leaves open the question of whether constant supervision and the presence of someone in the house is required. For people whose behaviour is unpredictable and who wander, it is helpful to assess the longest time for which they can safely be left alone in the house. Allowance needs to be made for over-anxiety, and lack of the ability to 'let go' and permit reasonable risks, on the part of informal carers.

Conclusion

The assessment of disability requires an understanding of the impact that different impairments of behaviour, cognition and physical function have on a person's capacity for independence and for the fulfilment of a full social role. Combinations of cognitive and physical impairment are much more disabling than might be expected from the impact of either type of impairment alone.

It is important to distinguish between performance on formalised tests and performance in real life situations, where factors such as distractability, lack of initiation and decision-making, lack of judgement and fatigue may cause fluctuations in performance. Very often the purpose of an assessment is to identify the individual's *needs* for health and social care and rehabilitation – including the provision of assistance, therapy, equipment, training in its use, and changes to the environment.

A careful history supplemented by evidence from others who know the individual well is vital in establishing the context in which disability is likely to be expressed, and in making a realistic estimate of future prospects. It must cover not only basic daily living function at home, but all other reasonable recreational and social activities, education and employment.

Time (24-hour clock)		Activity	Duration	Assistance needed and comments
02.00		Rearrange position in bed	5 min	Parent
04.30		Rearrange position in bed Go to toilet	15 min	Parent
07.00		Wake up Cup of tea	15 min	Parent
07.30		Shower, toilet and dress	45 min	Care attendant (adapted shower room and toilet)
08.30		Breakfast	45 min	Parent prepares meal
09.30	M, W	Physiotherapy	1 hour	Physiotherapist and equipment
	T, Th	Picked up to attend 'Headway'	6 hours	Day centre staff and facilities
	F	Shopping	3 hours	Mother, sometimes grandparent or neighbour
12.30		Watch television	30 min	
13.00		Lunch	45 min	Parent prepares meal
13.45		Toilet	15 min	Helped by parent
14.00	W	Picked up for life skills class at local education college	3 hours	
	M. F	Rest period		
15.00	M, F	Taken for walk	2 hours	Parent, friend or neighbour
17.00		Tea Toilet	45 min 15 min	Parent Parent
17.45		Television		
19.00		Supper	30–45 min	Parent
19.30	Th	Social club		
22.00		Wash, toilet, undress, bed	45 min	Parent

Fig. 3.1 Specimen weekday timetable. Male aged 20 recovering from severe traumatic brain injury living at his parents' home.

LEGAL COMMENTARY

M.A.M.S. Leigh

The depth of the gulf which divides medicine from the law comes across clearly from Lindsay McLellan's chapter. Truly for the doctor the devil is in the detail: just as similar accidents will provoke different physical insults, similar insults will provoke different bodily lesions; similar lesions will provoke different sorts of physical impairment; similar levels of physical impairment will cause different sorts of physical disability; similar sorts of disability will cause radically varying levels of handicap; similar levels of physical handicap will lead to varying levels of recovery; similar levels of recovery will lead to a wide variety of levels of financial compensation.

The lawyer needs to translate a complex set of data into a simple fact, a sum of money. A simple label such as cerebral palsy, paraplegia or deafness does not enable the lawyer to quantify the claim. We need a more sensitive description by the doctor of precisely what the individual patient can do and what they cannot do, and how this relates to their chosen or pre-existing walk of life. In most cases involving profound injury, by far the most expensive head of damage is the cost of care. Yet not all victims of similar injuries will need or want the same degree of care. A further problem arises from the fact that the lawyer is having to deal with a shifting picture. The effects of organic recovery from an injury, or training to mitigate the consequences of a given aspect of disability and, in the case of younger patients, of ordinary maturation, all have to be taken into account.

The doctor is certainly better placed than the lawyer to predict how a given patient's lesion will evolve, but in many cases the skills required also have more in common with those of the soothsayer than the medical practitioner. The picture may be modified in a radical fashion by social adjustments, the arrival and departure of other people in the victim's life, the effect of other illness, or social changes such as rising unemployment in the area where the victim lives. The doctor is certainly better placed from experience to predict how ordinary maturation and training will be likely to affect a patient's recovery than a lawyer. The doctor may be better placed to predict the likely impact of future medical developments than a lawyer, but there are wide areas of assessment which have to be made by the judge on the basis of a paucity of evidence.

Just as the patient's practical disability is only crudely predicted by the severity of the original accident, so the compensaion will be a crude expression in financial terms of the disability. Thus it happens that the layman may be affronted by the way in which very different levels of disability provoke surprisingly similar awards. The layman may also be offended by the low level of awards in some cases and, perhaps increasingly, by the unexpectedly high level of awards in others.

The law still insists in lump sums being awarded in the vast majority of cases. This means that the victim's need has to be assessed at a fixed point in time. There is, in financial terms, a counter-incentive to recovery until the award has been fixed and this is perceived as being particularly strong during the process of litigation. There may be no dishonesty involved where a patient seems to be making less vigorous attempts to help themselves than might be expected in a case where they did not have a defendant.

There are several ways in which the law permits the lump sum system to be modified. The first is the ability of the court to order interim payments to meet the plaintiff's needs until their damages have been finally assessed. Defendants feel ambivalent about agreeing to large interim awards: on the one hand they are usually ready, willing and able to do whatever can be done to compensate patients for the damage which they have sustained. At the same time, if the interim award is expended on capital items or the institution of an extravagant regime of care before it has been proved to be reasonable, it will inevitably tend to pre-empt decisions which the judge has to take. The judge will be reluctant to order that a large house be sold once a plaintiff is settled in it, even though it cannot be proved to be reasonable for the plaintiff's own needs and seems to be an extravagant way of housing the plaintiff's family.

The second inroad into the lump sum system is the ability of the court to make a provisional award. This enables the court to make an award based on the plaintiff's present condition, but to recognise the danger that the plaintiff will suffer some specific serious deterioration in his physical or mental condition. If the patient subsequently suffers that deterioration then he may return to the court for a further award. The disadvantage of this award from a defendant's point of view is that it makes it impossible to 'close the book' on an episode. From a plaintiff's point of view it also has the disadvantage of further minimising the incentive to complete recovery. In practice, very few provisional awards have been made since the system was introduced in July 1985.

Third, the court is empowered to make an award for periodical payments. This deals with the danger that a plaintiff who needs the money to live on will overspend in the early years or invest rashly. It also pre-empts the argument in *Thomas* v. *Brighton Health Authority* which has led to such inflation in awards. Few if any awards of periodical payments have been made since the Damages Act came into force in September 1996.

Finally, since 1989, it has been possible for courts to make an award of a structured settlement. Like an award of periodical payments, this has the advantage that the plaintiff receives a stream of awards of damages which are tax free, unlike the earnings that the plaintiff will make from an invested lump sum. Usually, structured settlements payable by insurance companies will be financed as a result of the defendant purchasing an annuity from one of the life offices, and the annuity payable will be that which will be available routinely in the market. However, where the NHS is a defendant it is likely that the structured settlement will be self-funded. Because structured settlements, like periodical payment awards, do not vary the amount which is to be paid, merely the way in which the sum will be delivered, they do not interfere with the patient's recovery.

Commentary reference

1. *Thomas* v. *Brighton Health Authority* (1998) 43 BMLR 99.

Reference

Affleck, J.W. *et al.* (1988) Rehabilitation status: a measure of medicosocial dysfunction. *Lancet* **1**, 230–33.

Chapter 4

General Practice

Hugh Halle

Introduction

In the UK the general practitioner (GP) is the doctor to whom patients initially present their symptoms. Some patients bypass the GP and attend an accident and emergency department for reasons which are often unclear and frequently spurious. The term primary care physician (PCP) encompasses GPs and doctors staffing accident and emergency departments.

The PCP daily walks the tightrope of having to differentiate on clinical evidence and in the absence of full investigations those patients who may be safely treated at home from those who need referral for secondary care. These difficult judgements are based on knowledge, experience and instinct. With experience, the PCP develops a sixth sense that enables him or her to suspect that the patient's symptoms and signs indicate a condition that requires diagnostic and therapeutic skills greater than the PCP can offer.

Judgements based on this evidence cannot be correct on every occasion. The public has been led to expect standards of practice that cannot be achieved. As a result dissatisfaction becomes inevitable. Litigation has to be accepted as an unavoidable hazard of general medical practice.

This chapter gives an account of legal actions raised against GPs in the field of neurology and neurosurgery, and makes recommendations as to how they may be avoided or successfully defended if they are not well-founded.

General considerations

Emergency calls

A patient may suffer harm and litigation will ensue if the GP has deferred an urgent request to visit a patient who is found to suffer from an acute neurological condition such as meningitis. Requests for a home visit during a fully booked consulting session pose a difficult problem. The response most likely to come to mind is to pay the visit at the end of the session. It requires courage and determination to walk out on a waiting room filling up with disgruntled patients, who have little sympathy with the fellow patient allegedly acutely ill and are concerned only with their own convenience and complain bitterly about being kept waiting. Moreover, the doctor's experience is that the great majority of acute emergency calls turn out to be for relatively trivial illnesses. The doctor should keep in mind the years of hassle that may be faced if he or she ignores the request for an urgent visit to a patient complaining of, *inter alia*:

- a high temperature with a rash
- severe backache radiating down both lower limbs
- sudden onset of an unaccustomed headache.

The history

It is generally more rewarding to spend time on obtaining a good history of the patient's complaint than to attempt to perform a meticulous examination of the central nervous system (CNS). Having taken a history, the GP should be in a position to form a view of the likely diagnosis or differential diagnosis. Important points to elicit in the history are:

(1) (a) Is the patient (often a child) fully conscious and mentally his or her normal self?
 (b) Does the patient interact normally with members of his or her family?
 (c) Has the patient shivered or perhaps had a fit?
 (d) Has the patient vomited? If so, how often?
 (e) Does he or she have a rash?
(2) If the patient complains of headache, did the headache strike the patient suddenly or did it develop over some hours?
(3) (a) Has there been any disturbance of micturition?
 (b) Is there any numbness in the perineal area?

Medical records

In the absence of relevant records it is unlikely that a successful defence to an action can be mounted. It is not necessary to write long screeds. Single words may carry significant meaning and the severity of the symptoms can be denoted by plus signs, for example 'vomiting++'. The absence of cardinal symptoms such as headache or vomiting should be recorded. It is adequate to do so in an abbreviated form, for example '°V' to indicate no vomiting. The state of consciousness should be noted; two words, 'fully conscious' or 'wide awake', are often enough. 'Fits' or 'no fits' takes a few seconds to write, and may become vital evidence in court.

Many GPs are reluctant to record negative observations; this may greatly hinder any later defence. However, in general practice there has to be a limit to the recording of negative findings. If a febrile child has no rash, it is the author's view that useful though such a record may be forensically, a GP has not failed in his or her duty of care to the patient if he or she fails to record it. However, in such a patient it is mandatory to test and record neck stiffness and assess and record the child's state of consciousness.

If a practitioner records 'CNS✓', he or she must be able to describe his or her routine neurological examination.

The examination

If the diagnosis remains wholly obscure after the history has been taken, it is unlikely that it will be revealed by a detailed neurological examination; few GPs have the time or the skill to carry one out.

A note of the temperature, pulse and blood pressure assist in a defence should it become necessary. Its absence denotes to a judge a lack of care. A look at the pupils followed by recording 'PERL' (pupils equal and react to light) takes little time. A GP should try to inspect the optic fundi and record the presence or absence of papilloedema. If fundoscopy is unsuccessful, 'fundi not seen' should be recorded; failure to see the ocular fundi cannot be regarded as evidence of lack of skill or care.

An assessment of muscular power in the main muscle groups of the limbs should be made. Sensation may be assessed by asking the patient whether he or she can distinguish between the examiner's light touch and the prick of a pin, and between the warmth of the examiner's hands and the cold chest-piece of a stethoscope. Vibration sense at the bony points of the ankles and wrists can be quickly assessed. In particular circumstances, attention may need to be given to specific areas of examination, for example in a patient with bilateral sciatica sensation in the perineum must be tested (see Chapter 7, part II).

The major tendon reflexes in the limbs and the plantar responses should be elicited and the findings recorded. It takes little time to record 'muscular power, sensation and reflexes normal', and may determine the outcome of a legal action.

Continuity of care

The importance of adequate medical records has already been mentioned. In large practices, a patient may be seen by several doctors in the course of an illness and adequate records become an essential part of competent practice. Plaintiffs frequently aver that a failure to make a correct diagnosis was a consequence of their being seen by a succession of doctors who failed to communicate with each other the result being a lack of continuity of care and a great increase in liability to diagnostic errors.

It is usual and accepted practice to instruct patients or their relatives to inform or recall the doctor if the symptoms do not subside and the expected improvement does not occur; otherwise the visiting/appointments lists would become unmanageable. However, the courts will not accept this practice if the doctor has in mind or should have in mind the possibility of a serious and treatable condition. If the cause of a headache is uncertain, as it often is, or a backache is unusually severe or in an unusual location, it is advisable to give the patient a definite follow-up appointment; exactly when will depend wholly on circumstances. Sometimes the patient should be seen again on the following day, other patients need to be reviewed after a longer interval.

Deputies

In the course of an illness, the patient may be seen by a deputy who has to visit and assess him or her without having any previous medical records. This is a difficult task, often performed in the middle of the night and under time constraint. However, essentials of the history and the findings on examination should be recorded at the time or soon afterwards. Notes need not be long but will be invaluable in the defence of a legal action.

It is the deputy's primary duty to exclude an acute emergency requiring hospital admission. However, the deputy must ensure that he or she makes appropriate arrangements for the follow-up of the patient by his or her own doctor.

Attendance at accident and emergency departments

At the onset of an acute illness or in the course of a chronic one, a patient may refer him- or herself to an accident and emergency department, and be sent home. The patient subsequently consults his or her GP who, in the event of a legal action, pleads that he or she was reassured by the hospital's assessment. The plaintiff's expert will aver that a GP should have known that although a consultant is now in overall charge of most accident and emergency departments in the UK, he or she cannot see every patient. Many patients are seen in accident and emergency departments by doctors much less experienced than a principal in general practice.

A defence pleading that the patient had been assessed by a hospital doctor and that this reassured the GP is likely to fail if the GP had not put him- or herself in a position to make his or her own assessment of the patient's condition.

Hospital referral

When a GP is uncertain of the diagnosis in an acutely ill patient, it is considered good practice to revisit the patient later in the day. However, in acute neurological conditions time may be vitally important, and the doctor will be wise to admit the patient to hospital or seek an immediate second opinion. The GP lacks the essential tools to establish a firm diagnosis. If on returning home the doctor lies awake in bed wondering whether he or she acted correctly in keeping a patient at home, the answer is that he or she has acted incorrectly. It is no part of the GP's burden to be unnecessarily stressed and worried. It is the consultant's duty, assisted by the facilities available to him or her and with his or her expert knowledge to relieve the GP of the burden of anxiety about the patient. If the consultant finds nothing seriously wrong, the patient will be returned to the care of the GP. No harm has been done.

Patients complaining of less acute symptoms present an even greater problem. The GP is aware that if the neurologist is overburdened with unnecessary referrals, the waiting list, often very long, will become impossible to manage and the referral system will grind to a halt. Some 90% of patients are successfully treated at home by their GPs. An action for negligence based on delay in referral can be defended by pointing out the GP's difficulty in determining the appropriate time for referral. This defence becomes progressively more difficult the longer the symptoms have lasted. For example, in the absence of vomiting and abnormal physical signs, it could be regarded as reasonable to treat a patient with intermittent headaches at home for about three months. In court, the plaintiff who was found later to have a space-occupying lesion will allege that the pain was excruciating, and the judge will have sympathy with his or her plight. The plaintiff's expert will aver that early referral was indicated. If the GP has failed to refer the patient in a period of time considered reasonable by a judge, the defence will fail. The GP gains nothing and risks years of worry and anxiety about an impending court action by delay in seeking a second opinion.

In the UK, the waiting time for neurological appointments may be many weeks or months. The difficulty the GP faces is that until the appropriate investigations have been performed, he or she does not know whether the patient's headache or backache warrants urgent referral. If the GP cries wolf too often, the hospital staff will view his or her future requests for an urgent appointment with suspicion. There is no complete answer to this problem. It is only too easy with hindsight to conclude that management was defective. Errors of judgement are unavoidable. However, if the GP is concerned that the patient may suffer from a condition whose successful treatment will be adversely affected by delay, he or she should pick up the telephone and discuss the matter with a member of the neurological staff, and insist that the patient be assessed not later than at the next out-patient clinic.

Specific causes of negligence actions against general practitioners

Meningitis

Bacterial meningitis presents in two ways: the onset is insidious, developing over a period of up to one week, or it is acute, sometimes fulminant. A child may be well in the morning and die of meningococcal septicaemia on the same day. Are there any clues which may assist the doctor in suspecting bacterial meningitis in the early non-specific stage? To answer this question, the author has reviewed 50 cases that led to complaints or litigation. Five of these patients suffered from tuberculous meningitis. The onset of this condition is usually very insidious, over weeks rather than days, and is more common in patients of some ethnic groups, with a higher incidence among Asian populations.

The following symptoms may alert the doctor to the possible diagnosis of bacterial meningitis.

Impaired consciousness

Although an infant/child with a high temperature from any cause is listless and subdued in his or her reactions, drowsiness, a vacant expression and staring eyes indicate impaired consciousness. A statement by the mother that her infant doesn't appear to recognise her should be regarded as a sign of impaired consciousness. Unusual behaviour such as biting fingers or pulling hairs may be of serious significance.

A drowsy, unresponsive child should be admitted to hospital.

Convulsions

In infancy and childhood, the commonest cause of a fit is a febrile convulsion. The diagnosis of a febrile fit must be based on the following criteria (Illingworth, 1988):

(1) Febrile convulsions are definitely unusual before the age of six months, and they should not be diagnosed after the age of five years.
(2) They only occur with a rapid rise of temperature, and there must be a history of the child having been off colour and probably off his or her food for a few hours before the fit occurred.
(3) Fits occurring more than 12 hours after the onset of an illness are almost certainly not febrile convulsions.
(4) The fits should not last more than ten minutes.
(5) They should be general and not focal.

(6) There must be no history of fits without a precipitating infection.
(7) There is normally only one fit with the rapid rise of temperature.
(8) There must not be residual weakness of a limb (Todd's paralysis) after a fit.

Even if all the above criteria are fulfilled, it is the author's practice and advice to admit all children presenting with a first fit to hospital. The diagnosis of bacterial meningitis cannot be excluded clinically. If an experienced paediatrician decides to send the patient home, no harm results, but this is a responsibility which the GP should not take on him- or herself. It is no part of the GP's duty to bear the stress and anxiety of caring for a child at home who has suffered a first fit.

Vomiting

This is an extremely common symptom, particularly in infants and children. It usually subsides on appropriate management with fluids within 48 hours. If an infant or child continues to vomit after this period of time and is unwell, the PCP should consider seeking a further opinion, since vomiting may be a symptom of serious neurological disease.

Rash

In the developing stage of meningococcal septicaemia, the rash may consist of pink or red macules. The typical purpuric rash of 'spotted fever' appears later. The early macules are non-specific and are commonly seen in many viral infections. Infants and children with such infections are usually only mildly ill. Measles is an exception but is preceded by symptoms of an upper respiratory tract infection of three to four days' duration, and the diagnosis usually presents no difficulty.

An ill patient with a non-specific rash should alert the doctor to the possible diagnosis of meningococcal meningitis.

Neck stiffness

This sign is often absent in babies, infants and young children. Its absence should not persuade the attending doctor that bacterial meningitis is an unlikely diagnosis.

If the mother of an ill child thinks she has observed impaired neck movements and the doctor finds resistance on flexing the neck, he or she should not ponder the possibility that the resistance may be voluntary. Hospital admission is indicated.

Kernig's sign

This is not a helpful sign in infants and young children. Older children may be asked to sit up in bed or on the couch and attempt to kiss their flexed knees. If they can do this easily, meningeal irritation is unlikely to be present.

Photophobia

This is an uncommon early symptom, but when it is present it strongly suggests the diagnosis of meningitis.

Temperature

This may be normal. The presence or absence of a raised temperature is of no help in the diagnosis of bacterial meningitis.

The fulminating case of meningococcal septicaemia is virtually undiagnosable in time to prevent a fatal outcome.

Some patients with an illness whose onset is less acute pose such a difficult diagnostic problem that judgements made by careful and experienced doctors will be found to have been erroneous. Such errors may have the disastrous consequences of death or severe permanent disability, but do not necessarily indicate a breach of the duty of care by the doctor. The courts will submit the doctor's records of his or her examination and findings to detailed scrutiny, and the defence will be greatly assisted by good notes, including negative findings.

Intracranial space-occupying lesions

Headache is one of the commonest symptoms presented to a GP. The pain is frequently caused by nervous stress and anxiety. Migraine is a common condition and is often the cause of incapacitating headaches. Rarely, headache is a symptom of an intracranial space-occupying lesion. A GP may only see two or three patients with such a lesion in a lifetime of practice. He or she has the difficult task of picking out from the many patients who present with headaches the one patient who has a serious underlying condition. Are there any clues that may assist in this diagnostic exercise?

Tension headache often persists throughout the day and is not relieved by simple analgesics such as paracetamol or aspirin. Headaches associated with raised intracranial pressure may awaken the patient in the early hours or are present on waking; they tend to improve as the day goes on and are relieved, when not too severe, by analgesics. Tension headaches are not accompanied by vomiting. If the patient complains of vomiting in addition to headaches, the diagnosis is likely to be migraine or a space-occupying lesion. Migraine sufferers frequently do not exhibit the pattern of classical migraine: namely, visual prodromata followed by unilateral headache and vomiting. The pain may be experienced in both sides of the head or in the occiput. Sometimes numbness in the face or limbs on one side, aphasia, photophobia and hemiplegia may occur in migraine. It follows that the differential diagnosis between migraine and a space-occupying lesion may present great difficulty. Unless the symptoms are those of classical migraine and respond to appropriate treatment, and there is a past history of the condition, it is advisable to refer any patient complaining of persistent headache and vomiting for investigations. Most intracranial tumours can be excluded readily by computerised tomography (CT) scanning. Sometimes associated symptoms are important; for example, a patient complaining of unilateral deafness, with or without headaches and with a normal ear on otoscopic examination, should be referred for further study as he or she may have an acoustic Schwannoma.

An examination of the central nervous system is advisable but is unlikely to reveal abnormal signs until a late stage. The optic fundi should be examined as the finding of papilloedema demands urgent referral. However, the absence of papilloedema must not be thought to rule out the possibility of an underlying space-occupying lesion, as it may be a late sign.

Intracranial abscess

A patient suffering from chronic suppurative otitis media who complains of pain around the ear and/or the head should be suspected of suffering from an intracranial extension of the infection. If vomiting is also present, urgent referral is indicated.

Infection in the frontal sinus may extend and lead to an intracranial abscess. If a patient with pain and tenderness over the frontal sinus complains of vomiting or shows even minimal impairment of memory, the diagnosis of a cerebral abscess must be excluded. The author once saw a patient on a Monday morning who complained of pain over the frontal sinus of several days' duration. The patient was an ardent football fan who had watched a match on Saturday, as was his invariable practice. When asked the score, he could not remember it. He had a cerebral abscess.

Cerebrovascular accidents

Subarachnoid haemorrhage

Patients who survive a first subarachnoid haemorrhage may succumb to a further bleed which surgical intervention might have prevented. Diagnosis of the initial bleed is therefore important. A patient complaining of the sudden onset of severe pain in the head or neck, especially (but not necessarily) if the pain is accompanied by vomiting, should be suspected of having suffered a subarachnoid haemorrhage until proven otherwise. A past history of headache or migraine may make the diagnosis difficult, but the essential clinical clue is the sudden acute onset of the pain.

Migraine is a common condition and it is not surprising that it is often the erroneous diagnosis that has been made in patients with subarachnoid haemorrhage who have sought redress in the courts. A first attack of migraine after the age of 40 is so unlikely that a PCP should seek immediate confirmation of the diagnosis from a consultant. Between the ages of 30 and 40, the diagnosis of a first attack of migraine should only be made by a GP after a most careful consideration with the possibility of subarachnoid haemorrhage in mind. The absence of any signs of meningeal irritation should be fully recorded, although their absence does not exclude the diagnosis of a small but highly significant subarachnoid bleed.

Stroke

Hypertension: Hypertension is a substantial risk factor in the development of a stroke. It is accepted teaching that effective blood pressure control by treatment with appropriate drugs lowers the risk considerably. It follows that failure by the practitioner to attempt to lower a patient's raised blood pressure and to ensure that it stays at an acceptable level constitutes negligent management.

The upper limit of acceptable blood pressure is arguable. A level above 150 mmHg systolic and 95 mmHg diastolic determined on three occasions after a period of five minutes' rest on a couch should lead to investigations with a view to finding a possible cause, and to determining whether any complications such as renal impairment are present. Baseline investigations such as a full blood count, sedimentation rate, urine, blood urea and electrolytes, chest X-ray, electrocardiogram (ECG) and perhaps ultrasound examination of the kidneys may be undertaken by a PCP. If these prove negative and the patient is aged 50 or over, the doctor may reasonably decide to institute treatment. Initially non-pharmacological measures may be tried: cessation of smoking, weight reduction, reduced alcohol consumption, increased exercise, and avoidance of excessive salt intake. If these measures fail, first-line therapy drugs should be prescribed. If the response to treatment is inadequate, the advice of a consultant should be sought.

It is advisable to refer patients younger than 50 years of age to a consultant for full investigation prior to instituting treatment.

Oral contraceptives: There is evidence that the contraceptive pill may predispose the patient to a stroke. This evidence largely relates to preparations containing 50 μg of oestrogen. There is doubt as to whether there is an increased risk of stroke associated with an oestrogen content of 30 μg.

There is no good evidence that if other risk factors for thrombosis are present, such as hypertension, diabetes or smoking, there is an interaction with oral contraceptive medication so as to potentiate the increase in risk expected from either factor alone. However, this view may be challenged in a court of law, and great caution is therefore advisable in prescribing the oral contraceptive pill for patients with known risk factors. These are listed in the *Handbook of Contraceptive Practice* issued to GPs in the UK:

- Age of 40 years (35 for smokers)
- Cigarette smoking
- Obesity
- Diabetes mellitus
- Hypertension
- Familial hyperlipidaemia

The blood pressure level above which oral contraceptives should not be prescribed is debatable, but caution is indicated if it exceeds 130/90 at rest.

Some patients assert that no other method of contraception is acceptable to them. Every woman has to be judged individually. It should be borne in mind that normal pregnancy poses a greater risk of thromboembolic complications than does an oral contraceptive drug.

Transient ischaemic attacks: The risk of stroke in these patients is seven times that of the general population. It is therefore advisable to try to reduce this risk even if there has only been one attack. The patient must be advised to stop smoking, reduce excessive weight and take exercise. If it is raised, the diastolic blood pressure should be gradually lowered to about 100 mmHg. The blood cholesterol should be checked. If it is raised, dietary advice should be given. If after a period of about three months of appropriate dieting, the cholesterol level remains above an acceptable level (6.5 mmol/l), treatment with a statin is indicated. Aspirin in a dose of 75–150 mg should be prescribed unless there is a history of peptic ulceration. This drug should be given as soon as the diagnosis is made. Failure to do so may be regarded as poor management.

Episodes of transient disturbance of cerebral function may be due to atrial fibrillation with recurrent emboli. Anticoagulant therapy is indicated.

Another cause may be a surgically remediable lesion in a carotid artery.

The absence of a bruit over the carotid arteries does not exclude significant pathology in these arteries. Therefore, following the prescription of aspirin, it is advisable to refer a patient who has suffered a transient ischaemic attack to a specialist.

Anticoagulant therapy: A GP will have amongst his or her patients a considerable number who have been prescribed this treatment. It is a potentially hazardous form of treatment since bleeding may occur into the brain or spinal cord with disastrous consequences. Therefore, the practitioner must ensure that the treatment is carefully monitored at appropriate intervals. Many drugs interact with warfarin and increase its anticoagulant effect. The concomitant prescription of a non-steroidal anti-inflammatory drug has led to many legal actions. It is essential that the doctor consults the literature (the British National Formulary in the UK) before prescribing any additional drug to a patient being treated with warfarin.

Head injuries

Following a head injury, patients are discharged from accident and emergency departments with instructions to consult their doctor if a headache increases in severity, if they become unduly drowsy or start to vomit. Drowsiness is difficult to assess as the patient may be understandably fatigued or under the influence of a soporific drug, usually alcohol. If the GP is called out to such a patient, it is advisable to err on the side of safety and send him or her back to hospital.

The 'lucid interval' before a patient with a developing intracranial haematoma lapses into deepening coma is well-known. It is less well-known that an elderly patient who becomes increasingly confused over a matter of days may have had a fall which he or she has forgotten or considered insignificant, and a slowly expanding subdural haematoma may be the cause of the confusional state. This diagnosis should be considered in any patient complaining of symptoms compatible with increasing intracranial pressure following a head injury.

The spine

Central disc prolapse

The common cause of pain in the lower back radiating down one leg – unilateral sciatica – is a lateral disc prolapse. Most such cases are managed successfully at home by GPs. Acute onset of bilateral sciatic pain or pain alternating from one side to the other is probably caused by a central disc prolapse. Provided the patient has no other significant symptoms or signs (see below), this condition may be treated at home by bedrest. Most patients will respond to this management. However, there is an ever-present danger that the prolapsed central disc will protrude further into the spinal canal and press on the nerve roots in the cauda equina supplying the sphincters and subserving sexual function.

The symptoms and signs that should alert the PCP to this rare but devastating condition are:

(1) any sphincter disturbance;
(2) impaired sensation in the saddle area or the perineum.

Irrecoverable damage to the sphincters and to sexual function may occur if treatment is delayed. The prognosis is much better if surgery is performed at the onset of urinary symptoms before retention has set in. The patient may complain that he or she is uncertain of the need to void urine, has difficulty in starting micturition or experiences dribbling. These symptoms may precede the onset of saddle anaesthesia. Neurological examination of the perineum may be normal at this stage and anal sphincter control intact. The examining doctor must not be misled by these normal findings into concluding that the cauda equina is not in danger of sustaining permanent damage. In the presence of any disturbance of micturition, immediate hospital admission is mandatory. This subject is dealt with further in Chapter 7.

Osteomyelitis of the spine and extradural abscess

Backache is one of the most common complaints presented to the GP; only very rarely is it caused by a serious underlying lesion such as infection of a body of a vertebra. This may lead to abscess formation and paraplegia which, once it has occurred, may be irreversible.

Tuberculosis of the spine occurs in all ethnic groups but is more common in the Asian population. A complaint of backache in such a patient, particularly in a recently arrived immigrant, should lead to early baseline investigations such as radiograph and erythrocyte sedimentation rate (ESR).

As osteomyelitis of the spine responds to appropriate treatment, failure to diagnose it before the onset of paraplegia is of vital importance. The following management of patients with backache is suggested:

(1) Although abnormal signs are rarely found, it is necessary to ask patients to remove their clothes so that the spinal column can be fully inspected, palpated, and movements observed. Localised tenderness may indicate a serious underlying lesion.
(2) The site of the pain is important. Benign musculoskeletal disorders cause pain most frequently in the lumbar spine. Pain in the thoracic spine should be viewed with caution and investigated if it does not resolve rapidly; particularly sinister in its possible implications is pain referred to the anterior part of the trunk.
(3) A patient who has no previous history of backache should be referred for radiography and simple blood tests (blood count and sedimentation rate) if the symptoms have not improved in approximately two weeks, and earlier if the symptoms appear to progress during this period.

Summary

In the author's experience, legal actions against PCPs most commonly allege delay in the diagnosis of

(1) Meningitis
(2) Subarachnoid haemorrhage
(3) Central disc prolapse

With regard to a great many claims, I have no doubt that 'there but for the grace of God go I'. The usual reason claims are considered indefensible or are lost in court is failure to take and record an adequate history and carry out a simple examination.

LEGAL COMMENTARY

M.A.M.S. Leigh

Hugh Halle describes a picture which is readily familiar to those who have seen GPs under fire in the courts. One often feels that general practice is not like other areas of medicine and its practitioners often struggle to convey to judges their need to tolerate a margin of uncertainty. Just as most of us tolerate vague aches and pains for a period without having any clear idea as to their cause before presenting ourselves to our GPs, so GPs often seek to satisfy themselves that there is nothing sinister in circumstances where they cannot reach a clear diagnosis.

In cases involving children, we regularly see cases where the doctor has been well aware that there was something not quite 'right' about a baby, but nevertheless has been equally confident that there was nothing very sinister either. Often it is the doctor's own conscientious devotion to the patient which leads to a desire to keep the child at home for what proves fatally to be too long. In such cases the law finds it very hard to judge the doctor fairly. Usually it is accepted on all sides that the signs of abnormality were subtle and unconvincing; also that the risk of the sinister pathology was so rare that the GP would meet it no more than once in an average career. In these cases the doctor's own personality is crucially important. The doctor who strikes the court as conscientious, cautious and concerned is much more likely to be acquitted than an equally able colleague who is flamboyant, decisive or prone to concentrate on a holistic attitude to medicine which may overlook clear signs which, in the words of the *Bolam* doctrine [*Bolam* v. *Friern Hospital Management Committee* (1957)][1], any reasonable doctor in his or her position would have recognised. In these cases truly it is the doctor himself or herself who is on trial rather than any specific action.

The clinical notes are vital in all these actions for two reasons. First, because they provide the factual substratum on which the court has to work. The doctor who can demonstrate on the basis of a contemporary note that the patient's temperature was normal or that there was no neck stiffness has an immense advantage over the doctor who can only assert these things on the basis of memory. It is usually the doctor's case that the consultation was not particularly memorable. Second, it is extremely important to have good notes because these are the visible face of the clinical treatment. If the notes are untidy, inadequate or absent the plaintiff's advocate will have a fair basis for inviting the judge to draw analogous inferences about the quality of the clinical treatment which was given.

At quite another extreme are the cases where the doctors should have recognised an acute emergency on the basis of signs which were very probably there if the doctor had thought to look. Lower back pain is a common condition and those of us who do not need orthopaedics or neurosurgical treatment need GPs who will reassure us and tell us to go back to work. But we need them also to recognise acute central prolapsed intravertebral discs. Frequently these conditions do present to GPs when there is nothing very much wrong or it is too late for the doctor's negligence to cause any damage. In judging these cases, again the courts depend almost entirely on the clinical notes. Did the pain radiate below the knee on one side or both? Were the lower limb reflexes elicited? Was the patient displaying the signs of a sensory level? Truly in this area doctors' skills are for their patients but their notes are for themselves.

As Hugh Halle says, the third most common cause of neurological disaster in general practice is subarachnoid haemorrhage. We do seem to see quite a lot of cases in which a patient begins with a sudden sharp headache which is often not presented to the GP for a number of days, as a result of which the doctor is beguiled into under-reacting to a subacute state of affairs as the patient under-reacted to the original onset.

Characteristically these cases present considerable difficulties of causation, because it is by no means clear that there ever was a window of opportunity in which the patient would have been likely to receive the surgical treatment which was necessary to forestall a second bleed.

Fortunately disasters involving the contraceptive pill are very rare. A recent case which went to the Court of Appeal was *Vadera* v. *Shaw* (1998).[2] The evidence which was considered by the court strongly suggested that the other risk factors mentioned by Hugh Halle such as hypertension, age or smoking are independent of the risk associated with the pill. Furthermore, the available research – and the court considered more than 120 papers on the subject – suggested that the relative risk associated with the pill was statistically insignificant. Finally, because the risk was less than double, even if it had been statistically significant on the balance of probabilities, the court would have been driven to find that in any individual case a stroke was more likely to be a result of the background risk than the relative risk associated with the pill itself; again this is irrespective of age, weight, blood pressure or smoking status. These figures only relate to the risk of stroke, not pulmonary embolus.

It is probably fair to say that general practice cases before the courts depend far more on the findings of fact than most others. The role of the expert witness is very often to help the judge to put himself or herself in the room with the doctor and patient and to understand how the doctor is likely to have behaved or should have behaved. Thus there is frequently no mention of the *Bolam* test, it being agreed that the findings of negligence depend upon the finding of fact.

Commentary references

1. *Bolam* v. *Friern Hospital Management Committtee* [1957] 1 WLR 582.
2. *Vadera* v. *Shaw* (1998) (unreported).

Reference

Illingworth, R.S. (1988) *Common Symptoms of Disease in Children*, 9th edn. Blackwell Science, Oxford.

Chapter 5

Head Injury

John Garfield

Introduction

As indicated in Chapter 2, the errors in the management of head injuries which lead to litigation are almost invariably caused by a failure to follow simple principles, and are not due to ignorance of detailed neurology or neurosurgery. In the UK, the majority of adults who have sustained a head injury are assessed by and cared for by general practitioners (GPs), or in accident and emergency departments, and by orthopaedic and general surgeons. Therefore, simple principles of management should not be beyond the capabilities of these practitioners; they are capabilities which courts will certainly expect.

Basic management comprises accurate clinical assessment, accurate sequential observations and accurate unambiguous recording of those observations. That should be allied to an organisation which ensures that the recorded observations come to the notice of the responsible medical staff, who are of sufficient seniority and experience to take decisions rapidly whenever the situation demands. When medical negligence actions arise, at least one of these requirements has not been met. Since each is in itself relatively simple, a defence on liability may be very difficult; even if a strong defence on causation may be mounted, it is much diminished by weakness on liability.

Causation arguments are often centred upon the intracranial pathology present at particular stages in the evolution of the pathology. The evidence for the pathology may be clinical, radiological or surgical. To this should be added autopsy evidence in cases in which causation arguments often involve speculation in correlating a likely disability with the pathology, had the patient survived. This is a very difficult field, in which experts may express widely differing and honestly held views based upon surgical and neuropathological experience. It is unfortunate if such differences cannot be settled by 'without prejudice' meetings of experts; in any event, judges are likely to prefer compromises, particularly in deciding the level of damages.

General problems

History of injury

This may be difficult to establish from the patient; but relatives, witnesses and ambulance personnel may provide information which is essential if the circumstances and the *potential severity* of the injury are to be assessed. Since the incidence of complications of a head injury, such as intracranial haematoma, is generally related to the severity of the injury, such information may well influence decisions concerning admission to hospital, skull radiology and computerised tomography (CT) scanning, and the frequency and extent of sequential observations. The failure to take advantage of available sources of information may be difficult to defend, especially if a plaintiff can establish that this led to errors in management which were responsible in whole or in part for the damage suffered. Sources of information which may be disregarded at the time of the patient's admission, but which are examined meticulously at a later date in the course of litigation include:

(1) *Ambulance service records*
These record the circumstances of an accident and the patient's condition when first seen. In general the standard of observation by ambulance staff is high, and reflects training in which the observation of a patient following a head injury now plays a major part. In the accident and emergency scenario, it may or may not be possible for the medical staff to talk to the ambulance team; but their contemporaneous records are available with the patient in the department. Even if the information has been passed verbally to the nursing staff, that information may not necessarily be entered on the first reception note sheet, nor entered in the contemporaneous nursing records. (See Fig. 5.1 and accompanying description.)

(2) *Relatives and friends*
The turmoil of a busy accident and emergency department is rarely conducive to interviewing relatives and friends in order to clarify the circumstances of the injury and the patient's condition immediately following the injury. Relatives are distressed; doctors are often rushed and occupied with the necessary first steps in resuscitation and assessment; and the nursing staff rightly see their main role as the immediate care of the patient and the comfort of relatives. Therefore it is not surprising that careful fact-finding takes a secondary place in this scene of great, often frantic, medical activity. For a relative the circumstances of an injury will be burned permanently upon his or her memory.

Crew	Station		
Date	Call Time 06·30	Serial No.	Patients GP........
Location ROAD SIDE A.. EAST BOUND	Arrival Time 06·40	Surname	Forename ☑ M ☐ F
	Depart Time 06·45	Age 37	Address
Hospital	Arrival Time 07·05	DOB	

Type of Incident RTA ☑ Home ☐ Works ☐ Organised Sport ☐ Leisure ☐ Sudden Illness ☐ Other (specify) ☐

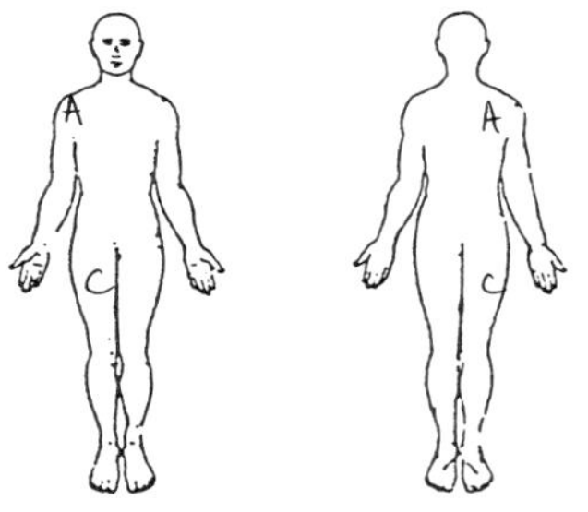

INJURIES
C Closed Fracture
O Open Fracture
B Burn (shade area)
L Laceration
P Pain (shade area)
F Foreign Body
A Abrasion

ACTION TAKEN - INITIAL OF PERSON TREATING

		Dose/Volume	Time
IV Fluids	☐ Cannulation		
	☐ Sodium Chloride		
	☐ Haemaccel/Gelofusine		
Other (specify)	☐		
Analgesia/ Drugs (specify)	☐ Entonox		
	☐ Adrenaline		
	☐ Lignocaine		
	☐ Atropine		
	☐ Salbutamol		
	☐ Sodium Chloride		
	☐ Glucagon		
	☐ GTN Spray		
	☐ Diazepam		
Other			

Cardiac Arrest ☐ ECM ☐ ECG Monitoring
☐ Defib. J
Public CPR ☐ J
Alive at Hospital Y ☐ N ☐ J

Airway ☑ Airway ☐ Oxygen ☐ Suction
☐ Ventilated ☐ Intubated

Splints ☐ Cx Collar ☐ Spinal ☐ Box
☐ Frac Straps ☑ Inflatable ☐ Traction
☐ Triangular ☐ Vacuum

OBSERVATIONS			Time 1) 06·40	2) 06·45	3)
Appearance	Normal		☐	☐	☐
	Pallid		☑	☐	☐
	Cyanosed		☐	☐	☐
Blood Loss	None		☐	☐	☐
	Slight		☑	☐	☐
	Moderate		☐	☐	☐
	Severe		☐	☐	☐
Blood Pressure	systolic / diastolic		100/60		
Pulse Rate			140		
Respiratory Rate			20		
CNS Eye Opening	Fitting		☐	☐	☐
	Spontaneous	4	☐	☐	☐
	To voice	3	☑	☐	☐
	To pain	2	☐	☐	☐
	Nil	1	☐	☐	☐
Best Verbal Response	Orientated	5	☐	☐	☐
	Confused	4	☑	☐	☐
	Inappropriate	3	☐	☐	☐
	Incomprehensible	2	☐	☐	☐
	Nil	1	☐	☐	☐
Motor Response	Obeys commands	6	☑	☐	☐
	Localises pain	5	☐	☐	☐
	Withdrawal (pain)	4	☐	☐	☐
	Flexion (pain)	3	☐	☐	☐
	Extension (pain)	2	☐	☐	☐
	Nil	1	☐	☐	☐
Total Glasgow Coma Scale Score			12		
Pupils	React Right	(√ or X)	☑	☐	☐
	React Left		☑	☐	☐
Constricted = 1, Normal = 2, Dilated = 3		Size R	2		
		L	2		
Capillary Refil	Normal		☑	☐	☐
	Delayed		☐	☐	☐
	None		☐	☐	☐

	4	3	2	1	0
Systolic BP	89	76 - 89	50 - 75	1 - 49	0
Resp. Rate	10 - 29	29	6 - 9	1 - 5	0
Glasgow comma scale	13 - 15	9 - 12	6 - 8	4 - 5	3

TOTAL REVISED TRAUMA SCORE 3

Additional Comments: FOUND NEXT TO MOTOR CYCLE WHICH HAD CRASHED INTO TREE. NO OTHER VEHICLE. HELMET ON ROAD.

Dr. at scene Name:

Essential data relating to the history of a head injury, a lack of which may contribute to indefensible actions for medical negligence include:

- Level of consciousness when first observed after injury, and ability to speak at some stage after injury, and therefore failure to recognise later deterioration.
- The position of the patient when found following trauma, therefore respiratory obstruction or inhalation may be unnoticed.
- The pupillary size soon after injury, therefore failure to recognise later dilatation as an indication of a lateralised supratentorial space-occupying lesion.
- The factor of speed in trauma, therefore failure to assess the risk of major intracranial and other injury.
- Inaccurate assessment of alcohol consumption prior to injury, therefore the level of consciousness may be too readily ascribed to alcohol.
- Inaccurate localisation of trauma to the head and the area of external bruising or laceration, therefore failure to assess the risk of an extradural haematoma leading to delay in evacuation, especially if CT scanning is not available.

Police custody

In a number of cases, difficulties in medical assessment and uncertainties over the responsibility of police officers have led to allegations of medical negligence. The 'Saturday night' scenario is well-known to police officers and casualty officers; and it is usual for a number of 'clients' of either service to appear with trauma to the head, whether it be self-inflicted, or due to more or less good-natured altercations. Alcohol is commonly implicated.

The *police surgeon* may be placed in an unenviable position. He or she will be only too aware that the local accident and emergency department, despite its

---

Fig. 5.1 Ambulance patient report form.

This example of an ambulance service report form shows that very comprehensive and valuable information can be immediately available to nursing and medical staff on arrival at the hospital. The timing of the call to the ambulance service, and of the arrival at the accident, in conjunction with the initial observations and especially the level of consciousness, may be crucial information in the light of the subsequent course and any deterioration. To fail to note these important entries has led to errors in management with serious consequences. Disregard of such clear data will be viewed unfavourably by a court.

Thus in the example shown, the patient was noted to have a total Glasgow coma scale score of 12 when the ambulance arrived at the scene of the accident. If the patient had developed an acute extradural haematoma causing rapid deterioration in level of consciousness soon after 06.45, the failure to take full notice of the information on the ambulance report form could lead to the failure to diagnose the lesion. It might be assumed, erroneously, that the patient had been unconscious from the time of the accident or at least from the time the ambulance arrived to collect the patient.

obligations, will not welcome a stream of unco-operative and disruptive patients who bring additional and usually unnecessary work to nurses already hard-pressed, often in an understaffed department; as might be the radiographers who are alone on duty and may have to examine patients without a nurse being present. The police officers may also be heavily occupied supervising the night's visitors; staffing is unlikely to be generous, and for one or more officers to leave the police station to accompany one of their charges to hospital adds to their burden. The police officers may sometimes be placed in a difficult position by a doctor who is reluctant to provide a 'fit to be detained' certificate.

This is the background to the police surgeon's position when faced with a detainee who may or may not have sustained a head injury, and who may or may not show the additional effects of alcohol. In these circumstances the assessment of a detainee may be particularly difficult, and a lack of co-operation may be ascribed quite understandably to belligerence and/or alcohol. The evidence for head trauma may be slight, usually there are no witnesses to the incident, and to be found lying on the pavement may be habitual for some members of the population. Unfortunately the clinical state may be what was once termed 'cerebral irritation' but which is now better recognised as an early stage in the development of raised intracranial pressure.

It is very difficult to define the degree of thoroughness of assessment expected of a police surgeon; it is not reasonable to equate it with that required of a casualty officer, or of a ward doctor admitting the patient. Unlike the GP, the police surgeon will not have the assistance of a family who might care for, and observe, a person who cannot yet be described as a patient. Even if the police surgeon is satisfied that the subject is fit to be detained, the extent to which he or she can rely upon police officers for later and sequential observations is equally problematic. It can be, and has been, argued that if the doctor requests police officers to observe the detainee every hour during the night, the doctor is depending upon a facility which is rightly in the province of a hospital nurse. These are dilemmas which have been at the root of medical negligence actions against police surgeons; and they have also led to disputes on apportionment between those indemnifying doctors and those indemnifying police officers. They are not solved easily, each party claiming reliance upon an accepted responsibility of the other.

To this may be added criticism of the accident and emergency department when the patient does reach hospital, especially if later there are allegations over any delay in referring the patient to a neurosurgical department. With such a complex train of events, apportionment becomes inextricably linked with causation arguments at each stage in the development of the patient's condition. Thus, what started as an apparently straightforward criticism of a police surgeon, which may or may not be refuted, progresses to tortuous and highly contentious considerations of neuropathology and neurosurgery.

There is no better example of a mundane beginning to a case leading to a highly specialised and sometimes obscure argument which is best kept out of court. It is even more unfortunate if specialists such as neurosurgeons and neuropathologists are allowed to express opinions about the action of police surgeons, instead of confining themselves to causation issues.

Alcohol

Of all the extracranial factors which lead to errors resulting in litigation, alcohol is one of the most common. It obscures the circumstances of injury; it increases the risks of intracranial haematoma, especially in the habitual drinker; it causes falls whose force of impact is greater because the usual protective reflexes are impaired; and the beer-filled stomach produces copious vomitus which is inhaled, obstructs respiration and precipitates severe brain swelling. Above all, alcohol prevents accurate assessment of the level of consciousness and neurological deficit through lack of co-operation and often through aggressive behaviour; and differentiation between the effects of alcohol and the effects of the head injury may be exceedingly difficult, the one compounding the other.

The police surgeon's predicament has been described. The GP is rarely placed in this situation, but the casualty officer frequently is. The easiest, and in some ways safest, way out is to admit all patients showing what are probably the effects of alcohol and who have sustained a head injury, but who lack any of the other or usual indications for admission. Whether the average casualty observation ward – if such a thing exists – or the busy general surgical ward can accept and cope with a number of such admissions is a consideration which inevitably influences the casualty officer's decision. Sadly such considerations carry little weight in court; it is all too easy for experts, often of a seniority far removed from the realities of a busy casualty department, to criticise juniors working in conditions with which all doctors, but not all judges, are familiar.

The habitual drinker with cortical and cerebral atrophy, and therefore a potentially larger subdural space, is more prone to acute sub-acute and chronic, subdural haematoma. To this may be added defects in clotting factors due to liver damage. The habitual drinker may be well-known to the staff of an accident and emergency department, who have often either seen him or her recover from the drunken stupor or have sent him or her away with a diagnosis of drunkenness rather than head injury; and generally the subject has not come to any harm. To this can be added the habitual drinker's familiarity to the local police officers, who may not be averse to a social visit to the accident and emergency department before departing with a belligerent customer. Thus, there is every encouragement for the casualty officer to regard alcohol rather than a head injury as the patient's condition, and to disregard the risks of intracranial complications which are increased by alcohol.

Communications

The great variation in linguistic communication in the UK today poses particular problems in dealing with patients who have sustained a head injury. In the absence of any witnesses to the injury and to the circumstances, it may be difficult to assess the accuracy or reliability of the patient's account, even if the level of consciousness appears to be normal. The safest course is to admit the patient for observation, advice which is more easily given than followed owing to the constraints of much hospital practice.

But beyond this there may be linguistic difficulties on both sides. The doctor and, for that matter, the patient and the relatives must be cautious that linguistic, racial and cultural differences do not engender a sense of opposition in either party, which can certainly jeopardise a fully objective assessment of the patient's clinical problem. It would be dishonest to deny that these factors can have a significant effect, particularly in the unhappy environment of a busy accident and emergency department. Thus errors in management, which lead later to litigation, may arise, or be aggravated, in this way. A defence on grounds of linguistic difficulty may not be sufficient, when time and sympathy could have solved the problem. This may be a counsel of perfection, which does not recognise the realities of an understaffed busy department; but courts have a tendency to expect such ideal behaviour, unless experts can convince them otherwise, which is not an attractive proposition.

Initial clinical assessment

Attention has been drawn already to the importance of the history, and to the difficulties faced in establishing its accuracy. Here errors in clinical assessment which may be important in litigation will be considered, without rehearsing all the details of good clinical practice in the assessment of the patient who has sustained a head injury.

There are four primary areas of initial assessment:

(1) Level of consciousness
(2) Pupils
(3) Cranium and face
(4) Spine

(1) Level of consciousness

An accurate assessment of the level of consciousness, and its accurate recording, are essential to the subsequent management, especially if changes occur later. Therefore any failure in this first essential step may rightly be considered to be evidence of an inadequate standard of care which has contributed significantly to a patient's death or long-term neurological disability. Usually the first entry on the neurological observation chart (see Fig. 5.2) is made by the nursing staff *after* the initial assessment of the patient by a doctor. That entry is valuable in the light of subsequent sequential nursing observations and entries; but it is not a substitute for the first medical note. Nor is it sufficient for the first medical note to be simply a numerical expression of the first entries on the chart; this practice has led to confusion and a failure to recognise deterioration of the level of consciousness very soon after admission.

Therefore the initial *medical notes* should contain a clear verbal description of the level of consciousness without necessarily any reference to numerical values. Furthermore, within each individual category on the observation chart there can be small differences in the patient's level of consciousness, which may become important if there is deterioration, and which may be examined later in the course of litigation. A delay in diagnosis of an acute extradural haematoma which causes early deterioration in the level of consciousness is one such example.

Some examples of expressions which are useful in amplifying and increasing the accuracy of neurological observation charts, and which can indicate slight changes in level of consciousness, are:

- Fully alert, orientated, logical conversation, no gap in memory.
- Irritable, unco-operative, uncommunicative, resents examination.
- Obeys by inappropriate actions.
- Purposeful movements to remove localised stimuli.
- Eyes follow visual stimuli. Blinks to approaching object.
- Extends limbs locally to local stimulation.
- General extension of limbs to local stimuli.
- Spontaneous extension of limbs.

(2) *Pupils*

There are few doctors who will not know of the importance of the pupils in the management of a patient who has sustained a head injury. Unfortunately there are many who do not appreciate the essential abnormality which may indicate potentially remediable intracranial pathology. Too often one sees the medical entry 'PERLA'; this abbreviation for 'pupils equal reacting to light and accommodation' omits the *size* of the pupil; in fact it is the small pupil which shows most clearly that the third cranial nerve is functioning satisfactorily. Conversely, a dilated pupil shows that the third cranial nerve is compressed, unless the dilation of the pupil is due to direct injury in the region of the orbit.

Failure to observe and record the size of the pupils in head injuries is common. This is very difficult to defend, especially when all doctors should know that dilatation of one or both pupils may well be associated with major intracranial pathology. Thus, in head injury management the size of the pupil is generally more informative than its reaction to light. Indeed, when a pupil is very small, its reactions may be difficult to assess.

(3) Cranium and face

It might seem obvious to the layman that a careful examination of the head and face is an essential part of the assessment; but at times this seems to escape the attention of medical practitioners. Errors that have become apparent during the course of litigation include:

- Failure to suspect a penetrating skull injury, or failure to observe cerebrospinal fluid (CSF) rhinorrhoea or otorrhoea, all of which may lead to meningitis and/or intracranial abscess.
- Failure to observe orbital or ocular injury which may be associated with an intraocular foreign body.
- Failure to detect a fracture of the mandible, which may cause airway obstruction.
- Failure to observe the signs of displaced fracture of the upper third of the face with subsequent meningitis or a cosmetic deformity.

(4) The spine

The subject of spinal injury is covered in Chapters 6, 7 and 8. In the context of head injury, the failure to suspect clinically a cervical or thoracic injury may result in severe disability in a patient who would otherwise have recovered completely from the head injury. Although an impaired level of consciousness makes the clinical diagnosis very difficult soon after injury, the error is much less acceptable when the consciousness level has improved sufficiently for the relevant neurological defects to be detected and for appropriate radiographs to be obtained. The tendency to omit assessment of upper or lower limb function once the critical period of the head injury has passed, and to mobilise patients, increases the risk of error, which in litigation can lead to very substantial damages.

Indications for admission and skull radiographs

The traditional indication for admission following a head injury has been loss of consciousness, for however brief a period. The implication was that this feature alone was sufficient to admit the patient. In such cases the purpose of admission was observation. Thereby any complication, should it occur, would do so when the patient was in hospital, the changes would be observed immediately, action such as the evacuation of an extradural haematoma would be taken without delay, and subsequent damage would be prevented. For reasons already discussed (see above), to this indication could be added: alcohol; a lack of any reliable witness, especially if there were problems with communication; crime; and accidents occurring at speed, even if the patient denies loss of consciousness.

The traditional indication was generally accepted irrespective of skull radiographs; therefore skull radiographs were not an obligatory part of the assessment in deciding the need for admission. In a move to reduce the number of patients admitted on this basis, alternative guidelines have been formulated, so that it would be reasonable not to admit some patients even if there had been a brief period of loss of consciousness. In those circumstances, the additional requirements for non-admission would be: the patient did not have any headache; the neurological examination, including orientation and all other aspects of the level of consciousness, was entirely normal; skull radiographs were normal.

The reason for including a skull radiograph is that the presence of a skull fracture has been shown to be associated with a significantly increased risk of the patient developing an intracranial haematoma. The risk of developing an intracranial haematoma when there has been a brief period of loss of consciousness without a skull fracture is very much less. However, it should be added that the detection of a fracture on a skull radiograph does depend upon the quality of the radiography and also the experience of the doctor viewing the radiographs. From this there arose the approach that when a skull radiograph did not show, or there could not be seen, a fracture, the otherwise remote risk of an intracranial haematoma developing later could be disregarded. It is ironic that, at about the time these views were being formulated, radiologists were pleading for a reduction in the number of unnecessary skull radiographs.

In a number of medical negligence actions, the central issue has been the failure to admit, or the premature discharge of, a patient who later developed a compressing intracranial haematoma, and the resultant unnecessary delay in the removal of the haematoma, with grave consequences.

Irrespective of the causation arguments, the traditional or more recent approaches may cause difficulties. The introduction of the skull radiograph raises questions concerning the quality of the radiographs, which depends upon the skill of the radiographer and the co-operation of the patient; and also on the competence of the doctor viewing, and reporting on, the radiographs, which would include the quality of the films for the purpose of recognising a fracture. All this requires considerable expertise. Therefore, it is not surprising that failure to recognise the skull fracture has often been a major medical and legal issue.

Furthermore, a radiologist's formal report of a skull vault fracture, or a fracture involving the skull base and/or the paranasal sinuses, or the presence of intracranial air, may not reach the clinical notes for two or more days, especially if a weekend intervenes. Likewise, a verbal radiologist's report may not be given any earlier, and in those circumstances the management in relation to the presence or absence of a skull fracture is dependent upon a relatively inexpert view of the radiographs. In other cases, the formal typed radiologist's report may not have been seen by the clinicians, before or after being filed in the notes. Just such an error, which is hardly acceptable or unavoidable, has contributed to delays in the diagnosis of meningitis and cerebral abscess following head injury.

There are implications for medical practice if avoidable errors are to be prevented. They include: the competence, seniority and supervision of casualty officers; the ready availability of more senior medical opinions, for example registrars or senior registrars; and the availability of a radiologist to give an immediate opinion on skull radiographs, particularly those which are deemed to be negative, and upon which depends the decision *not* to admit the patient. These requirements are not 'defensive medicine'; they are simply another example of medico-legal considerations leading to higher standards of medical practice.

CT scanning

The advent of CT scanning has brought great benefits in the management of patients following a head injury, especially in the early non-invasive demonstration of compressing intracranial haematomas. In the UK this is now available in most district general hospitals. Before CT scanning, and before its availability in district general hospitals, the possible courses of management available to general and orthopaedic surgeons were either to seek neurosurgical advice and then neurosurgical admission, or to observe the patient in the district general hospital; and occasionally to perform burr holes and then a craniectomy for removal of an acute extradural haematoma. In that situation the surgical action was dictated by the plain skull radiographs, and the patient's clinical condition; there were clear traditional protocols for such actions. It should not be forgotten that many patients were saved from impending death or severe disability by expeditious and competent action in general departments, even though transfer to a neurosurgical department would have been preferable *had time permitted*.

The use of CT scanning in district general hospitals has, in general, allowed prompt referral to neurosurgical departments. It has largely removed the need for cranial surgery outside neurosurgical departments, surgery which could be ill-judged and poorly executed. It has much reduced unnecessary and sometimes harmful transfer of patients over considerable distances to neurosurgical departments, which can interrupt essential continuing intensive care.

However, as negligence actions have shown, there are errors which can occur because CT scanning is available outside neurosurgical centres to doctors who are not entirely conversant with intracranial pathology. For example, a negative CT scan on admission soon after injury may reassure doctors falsely that the risk of a complication has passed, and therefore clinical observations are relaxed. A scan which does not show a compressing haematoma may provide evidence of raised intracranial pressure and brain swelling which may be overlooked by the less experienced doctor. Therefore the patient is not transferred to a neurosurgical department for non-operative management, a transfer that should have occurred on the basis of the clinical signs alone.

More disturbing still is the time lost in obtaining a CT scan at a district general hospital, instead of urgently transferring a patient, when the clinical signs and a skull fracture are consistent with an acute extradural haematoma at a time when there is rapid deterioration in the level of consciousness and dilatation of one or even both pupils. In neurosurgical departments, time has been lost by CT scanning when immediate surgical action should have been taken on the basis of the clinical signs.

These are examples of misuses of CT scanning which have contributed to morbidity which might have been avoided. They may be a reflection of inexperience by more junior members of a district general hospital, or of a neurosurgical team, who have never had to deal with patients without CT scanning. Such inexperience may be open to criticism in medical negligence actions.

Organisation of transfer to a neurosurgical department

The clinical indications for seeking advice from, and transfer to, a neurosurgical department have been referred to in previous sections, including Chapter 2. Accurate sequential observations, and their careful recording by medical and nursing staff, are essential; neither of these steps is complex, and deficiencies in these respects are hard to defend in negligence actions. The methods of communication in neurosurgical departments and the organisation of transfer are equally important, and these also may be deficient - deficiencies which are also difficult to defend.

Problems arise from the level of experience and seniority of the member of the district general hospital team who communicates by telephone with the neurosurgical team. This is equally applicable to the members of the neurosurgical team who receive the call, offer advice and accept or decline the patient for admission. The district general hospital doctor may fail to give accurate and full information; the neurosurgeon may fail to elicit, by questioning, the essential information. Either may lead to unnecessary transfer, or to a delay in transfer. The former has been associated with death *en route*, due to pulmonary complications; the latter with avoidable mortality or morbidity due to intracranial haematoma. Therefore the onus is on the district general hospital team, and the neurosurgical team, to ensure that those responsible for communication are of appropriate seniority, and have sufficient experience.

Even when decisions have been taken to transfer the patient urgently, unacceptable delays of several hours have contributed to a grave outcome. The factors here include:

- Unclear instructions by medical staff and nursing staff to summon an ambulance.
- Confusion in the medical team regarding this responsibility.
- Unavailability of a doctor, and particularly an anaesthetist, to accompany the patient.
- Time spent on unnecessary general medical investigations and radiography before transfer.

In general, the ambulance services respond rapidly to calls for urgent transfer of patients, and when avoidable delays occur, the ambulance patient report form and the ambulance station log-books may provide incontrovertible evidence that the fault lay in the hospital organisation, be it medical or nursing. There may be other reasons for delays in transferring patients, but whatever the reasons, the timings and the accuracy of the ambulance services' recordings are essential. Thus, in one case, an ambulance station recorded a call at 13.45 for an urgent transfer from a district general hospital to a neurosurgical service. The arrival of the ambulance at the district general hospital was at 14.17. But the ambulance did not leave the district general hospital until 15.00 or possibly later, arriving at the neurosurgical department at about 15.45. The anaesthetic chart for craniotomy did not start until 17.15. The ambulance records of timings proved very important for the arguments in court on causation, as well as for those on liability.

Pathology in medical negligence actions

In this section, attention is drawn to some particular clinical disorders or situations which have been the subject of negligence actions. No doubt there are many others which the author has not so far encountered.

Acute extradural haematoma (EDH)

This is the most remediable of all the traumatic intracranial lesions. With prompt diagnosis and correct management, there is every prospect of a full recovery without any residual disability, because usually at the moment of impact there is not any primary brain injury. For anatomical reasons, EDH occurs most commonly in children and young adults. Therefore when a satisfactory result is not achieved, there is likely to be earnest enquiry into the management of the case and, not surprisingly, this may lead to an action for medical negligence.

Such actions have implicated all stages of management, either singly or jointly. The *GP* is likely to be involved during the interval between the initial injury and the subsequent deterioration in level of consciousness, particularly with children. The difficult task is to identify those children who are at risk, and to refer them at this very early stage to a hospital for observation. With these difficulties, the practitioner's decision is more often a case of intuition than judgement based upon experience. This includes instructing parents or relatives to act as observers in the home. GPs have been defendants in cases where acute deterioration occurred before admission to hospital for observation; and unlike the hospital doctor, who is supported by nursing staff and radiography, the GP usually has only one opportunity to assess the patient and to make the appropriate decision. This unenviable predicament may not engender the sympathy of a court, when clinical issues may include:

- The severity of impact, such as a child falling from a playground swing onto concrete, or a fall from a bicycle.
- Bruising or swelling of the scalp in the temporal region.
- Vomiting, a common unspecific symptom in childhood.
- Sleepiness, which is thought to be no more than a child's usual habit.
- Irritability, which is so hard to define as abnormal when there has been a seemingly minor domestic drama.

Instructions to parents or relatives, and assessment of their reliability, can be very difficult, but at least that is an acceptable way of sharing responsibility.

The predicament for the GP may be even more difficult when a patient has been seen in an accident and emergency department, assessed, not admitted and given instructions to call a GP if he or she or the relatives are worried. It is reasonable for a GP to expect the assessment of a patient in the accident and emergency department of a reputable district general hospital to be thorough. The casualty officer should be of at least senior house officer standing (pre-registration house officers are not permitted to act as casualty officers), and the casualty officer has access to more senior staff such as specialist registrars in medicine, surgery or orthopaedics. The casualty officer, or his or her seniors, has immediate access to radiology. The time for which the patient is in the accident and emergency department under observation is important; the longer it is, the more the GP is reassured.

For these reasons, most GPs feel, quite rightly, reassured by knowing that the

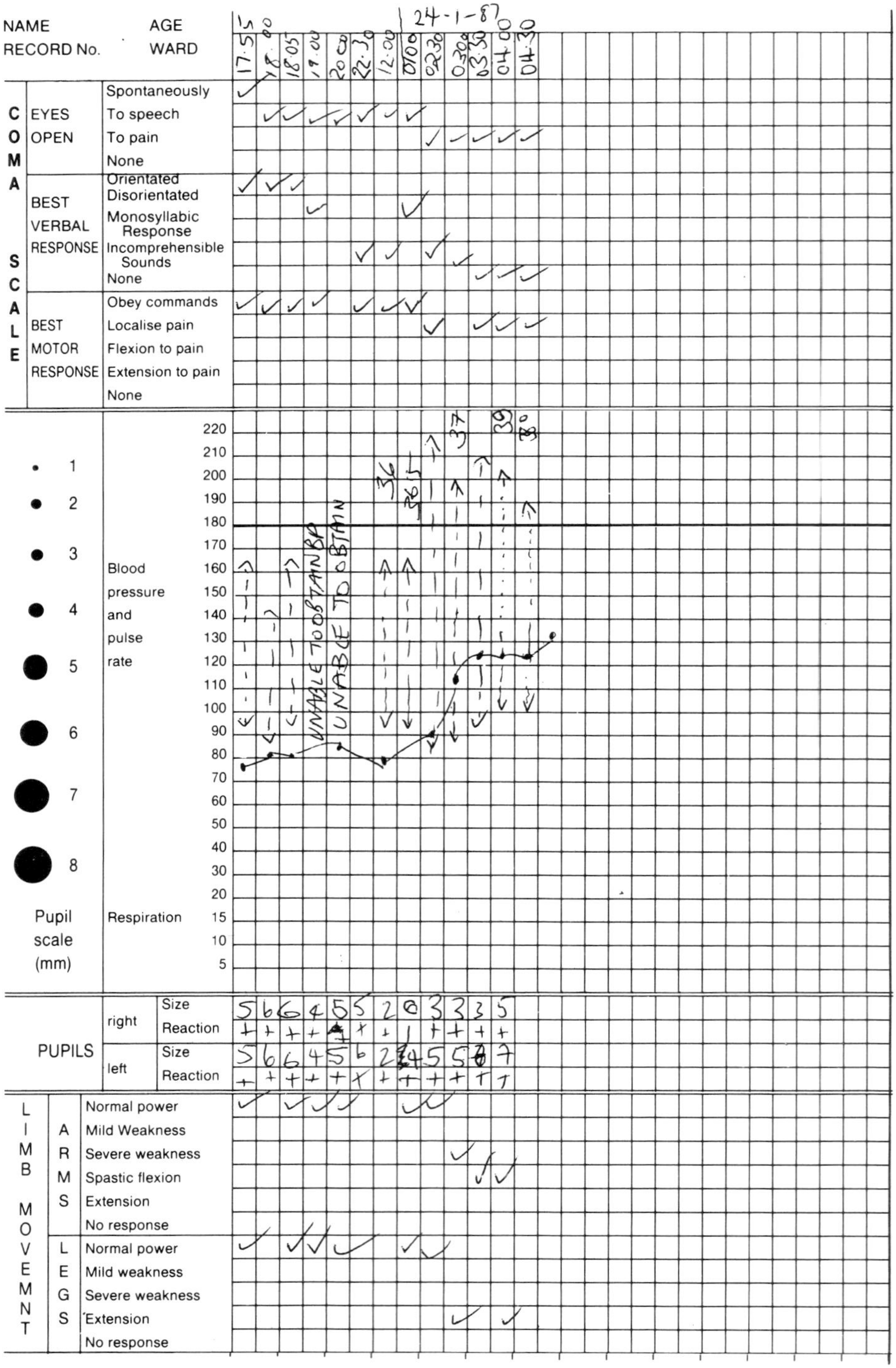
NAME
AGE
RECORD No.
WARD
24-1-87
17.55
18.00
18.05
19.00
20.00
22.30
12.00
01.00
02.30
03.00
03.30
04.00
04.30
COMA SCALE
EYES OPEN
Spontaneously
To speech
To pain
None
BEST VERBAL RESPONSE
Orientated
Disorientated
Monosyllabic Response
Incomprehensible Sounds
None
BEST MOTOR RESPONSE
Obey commands
Localise pain
Flexion to pain
Extension to pain
None
Blood pressure and pulse rate
220
210
200
190
180
170
160
150
140
130
120
110
100
90
80
70
60
50
40
30
20
Respiration
15
10
5
Pupil scale (mm)
1
2
3
4
5
6
7
8
UNABLE TO OBTAIN BP
UNABLE TO OBTAIN
PUPILS
right
left
Size
Reaction
LIMB MOVEMENT
ARMS
Normal power
Mild Weakness
Severe weakness
Spastic flexion
Extension
No response
LEGS
Normal power
Mild weakness
Severe weakness
Extension
No response

patient has been assessed at the district general hospital and considered fit to be at home. In those circumstances, the GP cannot be expected to maintain the same degree of alertness and instant attendance on the patient should there be a further call. He or she also has a right to expect the patient, and the relatives, to have been given a card of head injury instructions in the accident and emergency department. The GP cannot be expected to visit the patient *routinely* unless there has been a specific and direct request from the hospital for him or her to do so. Points such as these have occasioned considerable argument on issues of liability, causation, and particularly apportionment of damages.

In *the accident and emergency department*, the problem can be similar to that facing the GP; by then the very early or indeed the later signs of cerebral compression may be evident. Errors at this stage have been covered previously in this chapter. Once the process of admission has been initiated, a further error which has had grave consequences is failure of communication between casualty nursing staff, casualty officers and ward doctors; as a result, each has assumed that the other had completed the assessment of a child, and that formal decisions about management had been made.

Errors in the *district general hospital* have already been covered; all are applicable to EDH. To these can be added the very rare cases in which EDH causes deterioration after an interval of several days. The mechanism and precise pathology is uncertain, negligence actions occasion much divided expert opinion, and the issues of management hinge upon the patient's condition if his or her discharge is subsequently proved to be premature.

In *neurosurgical departments*, the error which has been open to criticism is delaying surgery while a CT scan is obtained. At night, if the radiographer is not resident, this delay can be considerable. Thus if a patient presents to the neurosurgical department with rapid deterioration in the level of consciousness, dilatation of one pupil and a fracture visible in the right temporal region on the skull radiographs, it would be very difficult to justify a delay of, say, up to an hour or more awaiting the result of a CT scan. In these particular circumstances, there will be much less criticism of the neurosurgeons making a burr hole in the region of the fracture and, if an EDH is present, evacuating it immediately by craniotomy or craniectomy. If an EDH was not found, it would

---

Fig. 5.2 Illustration of delay in transfer to a neurosurgical department, despite a well-kept neurological observation chart at a district general hospital.

At 18.00 there is the first indication of a deterioration in level of consciousness. From 22.00, there is further decline marked for best verbal response and thereafter for eye opening. The accompanying signs of raised intracranial pressure are the rise in blood pressure, and the rising pulse which could indicate severe brain stem compression. Although the pupils appear to react throughout, their size, especially the enlarged left pupil, was significant. Despite this eloquent chart which showed clear indications for urgent referral to a neurosurgical department from 19.00 onwards, the patient remained at the district general hospital until 04.30.

then be reasonable to proceed to CT scanning, without the patient suffering the delay which could well determine the outcome. Other areas of neurosurgical responsibility and criticism include surgical technique and postoperative intensive care (see below).

Acute subdural haematoma

Acute subdural haematoma is rarely an isolated feature of intracranial pathology following a head injury. It is usually associated with significant primary brain injury, which can include cerebral contusion, diffuse or localised intracerebral haemorrhage and brain swelling, which may occur soon after injury.

The medico-legal implications are that full recovery following appropriate management is far less likely than with acute extradural haematoma. Therefore in negligence actions, there may be a strong defence on causation, even if the defence on liability is weak.

With acute subdural haematoma, management rarely involves GPs, and few casualty officers are troubled by decisions about admission, the needs for which are usually obvious. If there is any GP involvement it may have been from a police surgeon, when the deterioration in level of consciousness was less acute, and occurred while the patient was in police custody. Causation arguments are usually concentrated on the postulated pathology during that period, and at what stage the haematoma was present and having a clinical effect.

The main liability issues in cases of subdural haematoma include:

- Standard of intensive care
- Adequacy of respiration, and its control
- The use of osmotic diuretics (e.g. Mannitol)
- Fluid balance
- Anaemia
- The management of other injuries, particularly thoracic and abdominal
- The indications for, and the timing of, repeated CT scanning.

From these liability issues flow causation arguments, mainly about aggravation of brain swelling and of infarction, arguments which may be very difficult to resolve.

Neurosurgical causation arguments may depend upon the surgeon's assessment of the relative effects of the subdural haematoma (its thickness and extent) and the associated brain swelling and intracerebral haemorrhages. Hence the importance of full descriptive operation notes. The extent of surgery, including removal of a swollen, contused portion of the frontal or temporal lobe, has led to disputes over the cause of long-term neurological and psychiatric disability.

Cerebrospinal fluid leak, meningitis and cerebral abscess

Meningitis following head injury usually means that at the time of the injury a communication was established between the scalp and the subarachnoid space, or between a paranasal sinus and the subarachnoid space. Over the skull vault, the evidence for such communication is the presence of a compound depressed fracture. If fragments of bone or foreign bodies are driven inward and perforate the dura mater, the arachnoid and the pia, and enter the surface of the brain, and there is an overlying scalp laceration, a route of entry for infection is created. If the fracture is recognised promptly and dealt with surgically, meningitis or cerebral abscess are very rare. Failure to diagnose such a fracture, or failure to elevate the fragments and repair the dura, with subsequent development of cerebral abscess, has been the cause of litigation.

More commonly post-traumatic meningitis arises from fractures of the base of the skull, or fractures involving the paranasal sinuses, with or without evidence of CSF rhinorrhoea. The liability issues in negligence actions have included:

- Failure to test clinically for CSF rhinorrhoea before a patient was discharged from hospital.
- Failure to recognise the presence of intracranial air visible on a skull radiograph, and failure to read a radiologist's report.
- Failure to use prophylactic antibiotics, which is still a matter of controversy.
- Failure to recognise the early symptoms of cerebral abscess.

Some of these errors, which occur in orthopaedic and general surgical departments, arose because relatively junior staff were unsupervised, and there was no regular review of admissions by senior staff. The defence on causation was usually weak.

Postoperative intensive care

Following technically successful surgery for an intracranial haematoma, deficiencies in further care may affect adversely the outcome. The most obvious of these is failure to ensure that postoperative respiration is satisfactory. To have to re-intubate and reventilate a child after apparently successful evacuation of an acute extradural haematoma, when preoperatively respiration was already inadequate, does not indicate an adequate standard of care. If thereafter the child does not make a good recovery, the causation arguments may well turn some measure of liability on to the hospital care and away from the GP or casualty officer who was responsible for the initial delay in diagnosis. These arguments are less persuasive when the primary intracranial pathology is less remediable (e.g. acute subdural haematoma).

Neurosurgical technique

Neurosurgeons, even quite senior neurosurgeons, are not above committing surgical errors in dealing with intracranial haematomas. One example is to 'plunge' the perforating drill point into the brain when making a burr hole in the thin squamous temporal bone at the start of a craniectomy or a craniotomy for an extradural haematoma. This has caused cerebral laceration and an intracerebral haematoma which has resulted in a severe neurological deficit. Surgeons may also fail to evacuate a haematoma adequately, or to take the usual steps to prevent re-accumulation of an extradural haematoma, errors which have been difficult to defend.

Conclusions

Head injuries are common. The organisation and administration of a head injury service calls for attention to detail, but the management of the individual patient does not usually require great intellectual effort. Presence 'in the shop' of medical staff of appropriate seniority is the most important factor in preventing avoidable errors, errors which may rightly lead to litigation. The rush to the CT scanner, and a blind faith in its results, has tended to diminish the attention to basic clinical observation and management in dealing with intracranial, and especially associated extracranial, injuries.

Indefensible errors in the management of patients with head injury can arise from what appear to be failures of organisation, and from defects in nursing care. These are generally failures at a simple basic level, which are not due to lack of great expertise, and therefore a court will find such errors unacceptable. It will also be apparent that medical staff have a clear responsibility for the organisation of a department in which they have agreed to work.

LEGAL COMMENTARY

M.A.M.S. Leigh

Closed head injuries are probably the largest single category of neurosurgical disaster to come the lawyers' way. Comparatively few of them come to trial because liability is so often clear. John Garfield is drawing on 25 years' experience as the Medical Defence Union's principal adviser on all of these cases and thus describes far more claims than have ever been considered by the courts.

As he says, ambulance service records are usually reliable and should always be available to casualty officers. However, in a significant proportion of cases clinicians have missed vital information as a result of not reading the ambulance records. Because the information should have been available, cases have had to be settled principally on these grounds. The one thing that the ambulance service often does acquire is a history from the person who was looking after the patient at home or at the site of the road traffic accident. If that person fails to accompany the patient to hospital the history, which is frequently more important than the findings on examination, may be lost.

John Garfield describes the problems posed by alcohol which again makes many cases indefensible. Severe alcohol intoxication frequently mimics closed head injury. It is hard not to sympathise with a junior casualty officer who is dealing with a patient who appears to be semi-stuporous as a result of consuming a quantity of alcohol which appears to be routine. In such cases it seems as if the patient has to be admitted for observation for no better reason than having been brought to hospital. It seems very unfair that the junior should be indefensible for having permitted the patient to return home to the bed in which he or she normally sleeps when in this condition. These cases demonstrate that the junior hospital doctor in these circumstances has to admit those in whom he or she cannot exclude a potentially life-threatening injury. The doctor is not permitted to discharge those in whom the presence of the injury cannot be demonstrated.

In many cases involving an extradural or subdural haematoma or other closed head injury, the patient's condition deteriorates over a period of anything up to 24 hours. As the lesion progresses it becomes increasingly clear that the patient's condition presents a more extreme emergency. A clinical response which appears in retrospect to have been unduly lethargic or complacent to begin with, may in fact have been a conventional and appropriate response to the clinical picture at the time. Initially the patient presents with signs of head trauma and a history of loss of consciousness. This merits an X-ray, which reveals no fracture and the patient is appropriately admitted for observation. Four hours later, equivocal focal neurological signs or symptoms are apparent. Appropriately a neurologist is called. Two hours later, signs of intracranial bleeding or pressure are apparent and a CT scan is organised to take place, in the knowledge that, as it is the middle of the night, there will be an hour's delay. Suddenly the patient shows signs of acute raised intracranial pressure and an operation has to be done as an emergency. All of these responses may in fact have been appropriate at the time; but if they are going to be justified in court, we have to be able to rebut the impression which inevitably arises that the team should have been aware of the likely future evolution of this clinical picture. It can only be done if there are meticulous notes available which reveal precisely what the clinical picture was and why the doctors acted as they did at each stage in the procedure. If there is an absence of neurological observation which leads the court to be able to infer that the picture evolved faster than the doctors responded, then the defence will be unsustainable.

When the patient does have to be transferred to a neurosurgical centre, this often seems to cause far greater delays than one might expect. On page 94 John Garfield describes a case in which a 45-minute ambulance journey resulted in a delay of three and a half hours between the decision to transfer and anaesthesia for craniotomy. By the time the patient reached the neurosurgeon there was very little need for anaesthesia, and very little that the lawyer could do to defend the delay. In such cases, it may be difficult to identify precisely the delay on which the defence will founder in court, but it is evident that the total period of time which elapsed cannot be defended.

Other cases have to be settled because the patient deteriorated in the ambulance. It may be that there was a failure to secure a portal of venous access or a failure to intubate before departure. The fact of the matter is that such a saga implies that the clinicians failed to appreciate the severity of the condition with which they were confronted.

Closed head injuries, like so much else in medicine, are now associated with much higher expectations on the part of patients and public. Whereas it used to be accepted that a patient with a closed head injury was likely to die or necessarily be the victim of disabling surgery, today a failure to produce an optimal result has to be justified. If the patient was conscious or had an absence of sinister neurological signs on arrival at hospital, people are reluctant to accept that a subsequent demise was something that could not have been prevented with reasonable care. The doctors are victims of a higher expectation which they have themselves fostered.

Further reading

Bartlett, J., Kett-White, R., Mendelow, A.D., Miller, J.D., Pickard, J. and Teasdale, G. (1998) Guidelines for the initial management of head injuries. Recommendations from the Society of British Neurological Surgeons. *British Journal of Neurosurgery* **12**(4), 349–52.

Douglas Miller, J. (1984) Aggressive medical care of severe head injury – is it justified ethically and economically? In *Dilemmas in the Management of the Neurological Patient* (C. Warlow and J. Garfield, eds), pp. 223–33. Churchill Livingstone, Edinburgh.

Group of Neurosurgeons (1984) Guidelines for initial management after head injuries. *British Medical Journal* **288**, 983–5.

Miller, J.D. (1987) Head injury. In *Northfield's Surgery of the Central Nervous System*, 2nd edition (J.D. Miller, ed.), pp. 795–870. Blackwell Science, Oxford.

Miller, J.D. (1992) Evaluation and treatment of head injury in adults. *Neurosurgery Quarterly* **2**(1), 28–43.

Reilley, P. and Bullock, R. (eds) (1997) *Head Injury: Pathophysiology and Management of Severe Closed Injury*. Chapman and Hall, London.

Teasdale, G. and Jennett, B. (1974) Assessment of coma and impaired consciousness: a practical scale. *Lancet* **2**, 81–4.

Teasdale, G.M., Murray, G., Anderson, E., Mendelow, A.D., MacMillan, R., Jeanette, B. and Brooks, M. (1990) Risks of acute traumatic intracranial haematoma in children and adults; implications for managing head injuries. *British Medical Journal* **300**, 363–7.

Appendix
Head injury: medical negligence actions

Cases reviewed, 1977 to 1998, total 90

Acute extradural haematoma: 30

Errors of diagnosis, delay or failure to admit, delay in transfer, GPs, accident and emergency departments, district general hospitals.

Skull fracture: 9

Errors or failure of diagnosis of simple or depressed fractures. Failure to elevate fracture.

Acute or subacute subdural haematoma: 16

Failure or delay in diagnosis.

CSF leak and infection: 8

Alcohol: 5

CT scan: misinterpretation or delay: 2

Intracerebral haematoma: 3

Miscellaneous: 17

Chapter 6

The Cervical Spine: Trauma and Degenerative Disease

R.A. Johnston

Cervical trauma

The cervical region is the most mobile section of the spine and the least well protected. The incidence of cervical spine injury in the UK is approximately 20 cases per million per year, of which about one-third are associated with primary neurological damage. The usual causes are road traffic accidents and falls, although sports-related trauma often receives a higher profile. Equestrianism, rugby football, rock climbing and diving into shallow water are those leisure activities usually associated with cervical spine injury in the UK. Failure to diagnose a cervical spine injury is probably the most common source of medical negligence action associated with this condition.

Diagnosis in cervical trauma

The patient with cervical spine trauma will often complain of neck tenderness and pain and will, in many cases, hold his or her neck relatively immobile, resenting attempts at movement during examination. The presence of external evidence of trauma around the face, head, chest and limbs may indicate the direction and degree of force which was involved. These signs and symptoms are not necessarily present in lesser degrees of cervical trauma which have nevertheless caused vertebral fracture or subluxation. Some patients will provide a history of transient neurological symptoms including tingling, paraesthesia or numbness in all four limbs or in the trunk, together with an inability to move any limb. This may last for only a few seconds, but is an experience clearly recalled and deeply appreciated. It also indicates that the cervical spinal cord has been primarily damaged, albeit to a limited extent, and that the cervical spinal canal has been compromised by abnormal movement of cervical vertebrae or discs. These symptoms are a relatively common experience for patients who present with cervical injury following sports/leisure-related spine trauma such as that associated with rugby, shallow water diving or horse-riding. The importance of eliciting these transient neurological symptoms and recognising their implications cannot be overestimated.

Those patients who are quadriparetic or even quadriplegic at the time of first assessment would appear to present no special diagnostic difficulty. However, in five selected cases in recent years the diagnosis of traumatic quadriplegia was not recognised by hospital medical staff for up to 12 hours. In two cases, the patient was discharged and actually carried out of the hospital. It is perhaps the relative rarity and lack of familiarity with cervical spine trauma that causes the symptoms of myelopathy to be misdiagnosed as local limb trauma, alcohol-related weakness and, in particular, hysterical paralysis. The following case illustrates that a patient's circumstances, prejudice, and a medical mind which has already been 'set', can result in an obvious neurological diagnosis being ignored.

Patient A, an alcoholic itinerant, was assaulted by a third party with a wooden stake and in the course of this was struck violently across the face and head, although he was not rendered unconscious. He was taken to an accident and emergency department in a large city, where he complained of being unable to move his arms and legs. Following a cursory clinical examination, a diagnosis of hysterical paralysis was written in the admission sheet. The patient continued to make protestations about his neurological deficit. In reaction to this diagnostic challenge the registrar, despite contrary advice from a more junior colleague, arranged that the patient be stood up on his feet with the help of non-medical staff, whereupon he promptly fell to the floor when the support was withdrawn. Labelled with the diagnosis of hysteria, the patient was eventually carried out of the hospital and returned to a site close to where he was originally found. Later he was rediscovered and returned to the same department, where the correct diagnosis of a C6 fracture with quadriplegia was confirmed.

The management given by one junior doctor in this case was clearly indefensible. The clinical notes indicated an examination conducted in a way designed to conform with a diagnosis of hysteria, made in advance, and which was adhered to despite strong signals to the contrary. In fact, the patient was probably quadriplegic when he was first discovered, and it was argued subsequently that, despite the poor quality of management he received, the spinal cord injury was not made worse, although such small chance of recovery as might have existed was probably eliminated.

The term 'hysterical paralysis' is one which should be studiously avoided by all who do not have immediate access to high-quality spinal (and cranial) imaging, neurophysiological testing and cerebrospinal fluid (CSF) analysis and who cannot rely on years of neurological or neurosurgical diagnostic experience. Even then this author prefers not to use the term, let alone write it in the case records. It is better, and safer for all concerned, to maintain an open mind and if necessary record the clinical neurological findings, but indicate that no organic pathological cause has yet been identified. Undoubtedly patients do present with paralysis of limbs for reasons of a psychological or psychiatric nature, but an accident and emergency department is an unsafe place to make this diagnosis, and few junior medical staff have the neurological experience to eliminate other possible causes. Traumatic spinal cord lesion is probably significantly more common than hysterical quadriplegia, and the consequences of a misdiagnosis are profound. Alcohol consumption by the patient will cloud the issue and other factors may bring diagnostic prejudice to the surface. The scenario is not uncommon and exposed medical staff must be aware of this recurrent diagnostic pitfall.

Following a carefully elicited history and, arguably less importantly, a clinical neurological examination, a plain X-ray of the cervical spine is the most important initial diagnostic investigation. In all cases where there is reasonable suspicion that a cervical spine injury has occurred, a good-quality lateral X-ray of the cervical spine must be carried out. The type and force of the injury will raise or lower the probability of cervical spine injury, though penetrating injuries, including gun shot wound, are a rare cause of cervical spine trauma in the UK.

The plain X-ray of the cervical spine should be carried out under controlled circumstances, particularly if there is a strong suspicion of injury, but the immediate requirements of a patient undergoing urgent resuscitation will dictate the order of action. In such cases, the cervical spine can easily and rapidly be stabilised using Gardner–Wells (or similar) traction. This can be applied in a few seconds to provide excellent control of cervical movement. Otherwise an external cervical orthosis such as a Philadelphia-style collar and lateral sandbags should be used until such time as cervical trauma can be definitively confirmed or excluded.

The X-ray must include all seven cervical vertebrae, but the patient with cervical trauma may have secondary protective muscle spasm around the shoulders and neck, thus preventing adequate views of the lower cervical vertebral bodies. This in itself provides an indicator that cervical spine trauma has occurred. Reasonable efforts should be made to obtain a view of the C7 vertebra by varying the radiological technique or by pulling the shoulders downwards. If this fails then the patient should be imaged by computerised tomography (CT) and the investigation completed (Fig. 6.1).

After a fall, Patient B was taken to an accident and emergency department, where she provided a history of neurological symptoms in all four limbs. This history was not recognised by the junior medical staff and an X-ray of the cervical spine down to C5 was considered sufficient. The patient was returned home by ambulance and carried into her house. She was readmitted later on the

(a)

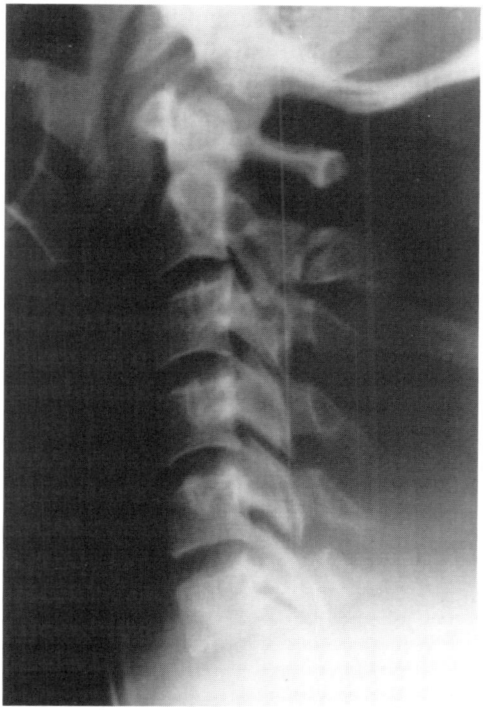

(b)

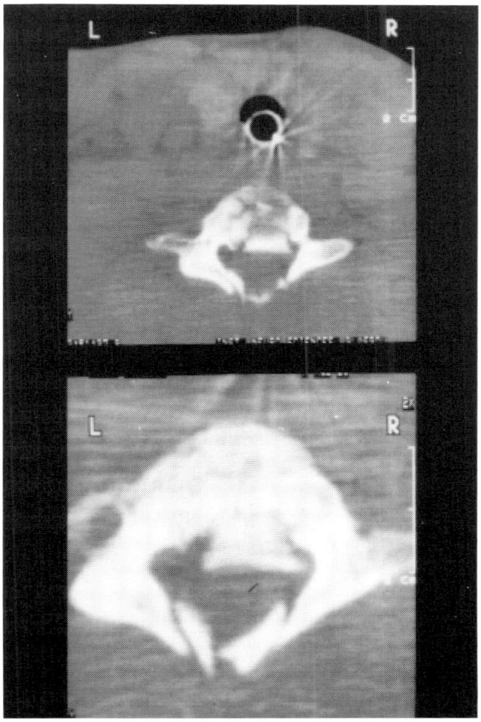

Fig. 6.1 (a) Lateral X-ray of cervical spine in which only C1–C6 can be seen. (b) CT scan through the fractured C7.

same day and was found to have a bilateral facet dislocation of C5/6. The liability issue was indefensible on two counts. First, the failure of the medical staff to recognise the importance of the patient's neurological symptoms, and second, on the glaring inadequacy of the lateral cervical spine X-ray (Fig. 6.2).

The essential minimum requirement is to obtain radiological imaging of all seven cervical vertebrae, by whatever means necessary, in a patient in whom there is a reasonable clinical suspicion of cervical spine trauma. Dynamic cervical spine X-rays, carried out in flexion and extension, add information concerning the stability of the cervical spine and will occasionally reveal a hitherto unrecognised facet joint injury. These should be carried out by reasonably experienced medical staff, and provided the amount of flexion and extension is adequate and properly controlled, the technique is valuable and completely safe. Uncontrolled and violent movements of the cervical spine are dangerous and may lead to secondary cervical spinal cord damage. Spinal stability is a factor to be taken into account by those involved in the definitive management of the cervical spine injury. Stability is not an 'all or nothing' phenomenon, but is present (or absent) in varying degrees. Generally speaking, the more ligamentous and bony damage present, the greater the degree of instability and the less the force required to produce secondary spinal cord damage. Cervical spines which are clearly and significantly unstable on static views do not require dynamic views to be taken.

Failure to recognise cervical spine trauma from an X-ray is a very reasonable fear of many junior and some senior clinical staff who are called upon to make comments on these X-rays. There is a diverse radiological range of cervical spine trauma, but a few general rules can be applied to the plain X-ray. First of all, ensure that all seven cervical vertebrae are present and look for swelling of the pre-vertebral tissues which could indicate haemorrhage (Fig. 6.3). Check the alignment of the anterior and posterior cortical margins of the vertebral bodies which should form a gentle lordotic curve with no sudden breaks. Look for the oblique angle of the facet joints, usually easily seen between C3 and C7. If a facet joint is subluxed, dislocated or fractured the clear, dark oblique line of the joint will be missing. It may not be possible to determine exactly what has happened to the joint, but it will be clear that something is amiss. Some fractures and subluxations are easily identified, while others remain covert until dynamic views or more sophisticated spinal imaging is carried out. It can be easy to miss an undisplaced Anderson type II fracture of the odontoid process or a relatively undisplaced, but nevertheless potentially highly unstable, flexion tear drop fracture of the mid-cervical region. Confidence in the interpretation of cervical spine X-rays following trauma can only come with years of experience in looking at normal and abnormal X-rays. For this reason the only sensible advice that can be offered to junior staff, particularly those in the accident and emergency department, is to ask for a senior opinion on any spinal X-ray which causes concern or which they do not feel confident in recognising as normal.

(a)

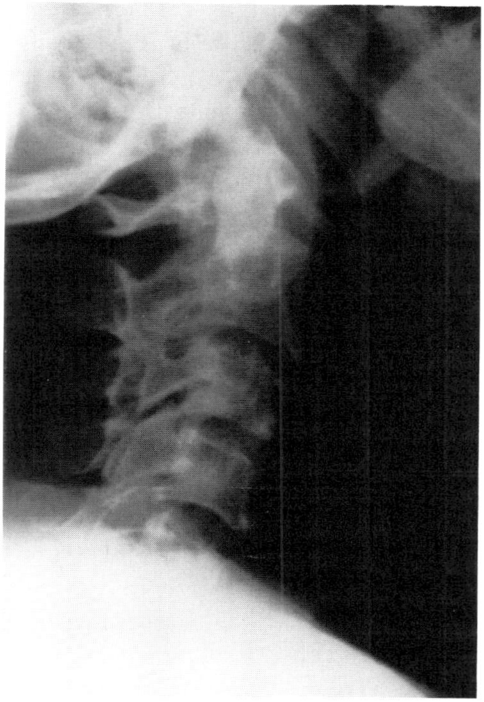

(b)

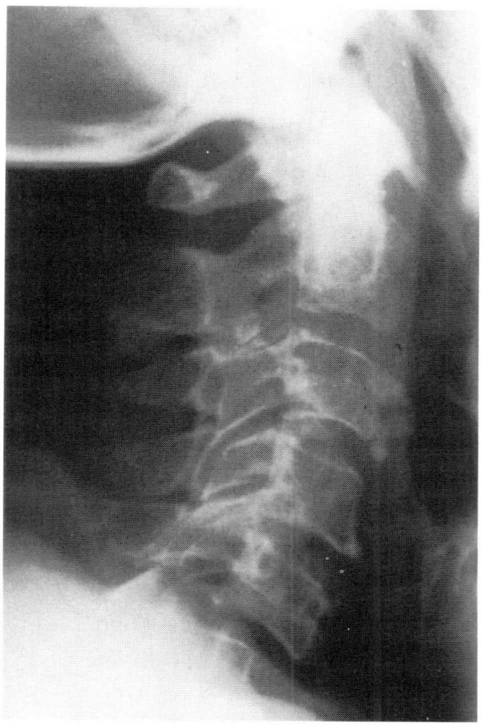

Fig. 6.2 (a) Initial X-rays of cervical spine showing only the vertebrae C1–C4. The patient was discharged following this X-ray. (b) Same patient showing the malalignment at C5/6. X-rays taken at the second assessment some hours later. C7 vertebra still not seen.

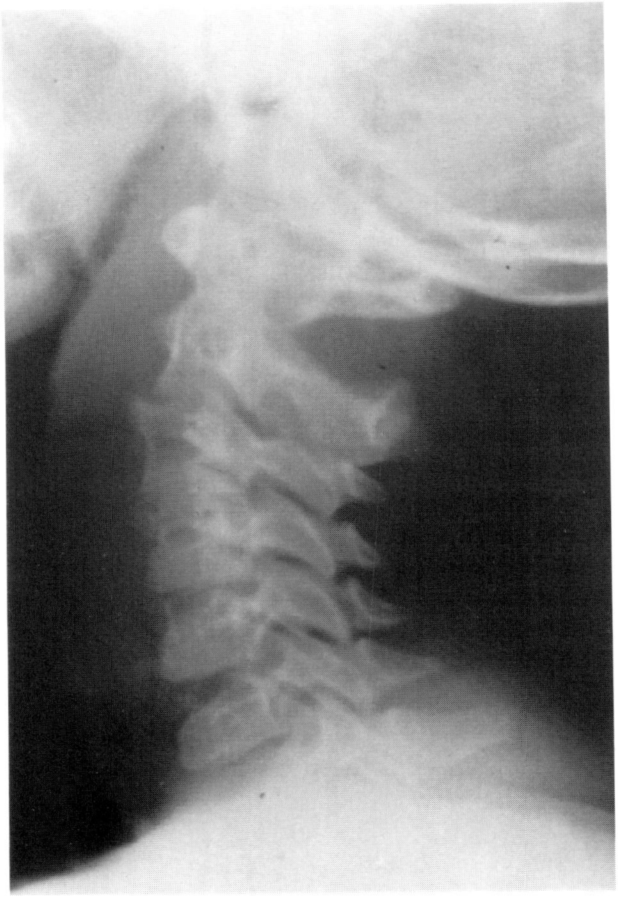

Fig. 6.3 Pre-vertebral swelling but no vertebral damage following an extension injury in a child.

In addition to the trauma, other incidental pathological conditions may obscure the diagnosis, resulting in inappropriate management. Patient C fell downstairs and developed a fracture subluxation at C6/7 which caused partial primary spinal cord damage. The fracture was recognised on the plain X-ray, but the junior medical staff failed to recognise the coexisting ankylosing spondylitis and to employ the necessary but difficult and complex procedure necessary to immobilise the cervical spine in that individual's normal alignment. Standard traction was applied and this caused the subluxation to become worse, leading to severe secondary cord injury.

It is increasingly clear that patients with cervical spine trauma should be managed at an early stage in specialised units. Previously, for the most part, patients with cervical trauma were referred to orthopaedic units or occasionally to neurosurgical units, where the diagnosis was made and surgical management carried out. It was not unusual for a surgeon to manage only one or two cases of cervical spine trauma in a year. With the increasing tendency to surgical specialisation, especially in spinal surgery in recent years, this is becoming less acceptable and less reasonable. The experience gained by treating a very small number of cases per year is to be matched against those centres where 50 or 60 cases of cervical spine trauma are admitted each year (and a similar number of thoracolumbar injuries). Initial referral is still often to non-specialised units, where it is reasonable to expect a correct clinical diagnosis to be made, initial X-rays to be carried out and appropriate measures taken to immobilise the spine. Optimally at this point the patient should be referred to a spine specialist (either orthopaedic or neurosurgical) or directly to a spinal injury centre. Following consultation, the patient is transferred with the cervical spine appropriately stabilised. An accurate neurological assessment is carried out and definitive radiological investigation is arranged in the specialist unit. High-definition CT does not require the use of contrast to delineate fractures or fracture dislocations, and this information provides considerable help in planning surgical or non-surgical management. It should be remembered that in 10–15% of patients with a cervical spine fracture, there is a second non-contiguous fracture which can easily be overlooked when attention is focused on a more prominent lesion. High-field magnetic resonance (MR) scanning is very useful in recognising damage to the longitudinal ligaments, discs and the spinal cord itself. However, for assessment of bony vertebral damage the CT scan is superior (Fig. 6.4).

Management

Once the extent of the vertebral, disc and soft tissue lesion is clearly identified, together with the extent of any neurological deficit, the initial plan of management can be established. It may be necessary to reduce a fracture dislocation and this can be safely carried out using conventional cervical traction. The safest and most easily applied cervical tongs are the Gardner–Wells variety, the pins of which are located 4 cm vertically above each external auditory meatus. This places the traction in direct line with the vertebral bodies and appropriate extension or flexion to the cervical spine can be applied where necessary. The use of older traction devices such as Crutchfield or Blackburn tongs is much less acceptable with the availability of inexpensive, efficient and more easily applied systems. Care must be taken not to place the traction pins inside the cranial cavity, although there is inevitably a small risk of this occurring. Should this occur, it may be obvious to the person applying the tongs that cranial penetration has occurred, but if there is only a suspicion, a tangential X-ray, or if possible a CT scan, should be carried out to confirm whether or not the tip of the traction pin has penetrated the inner table of the

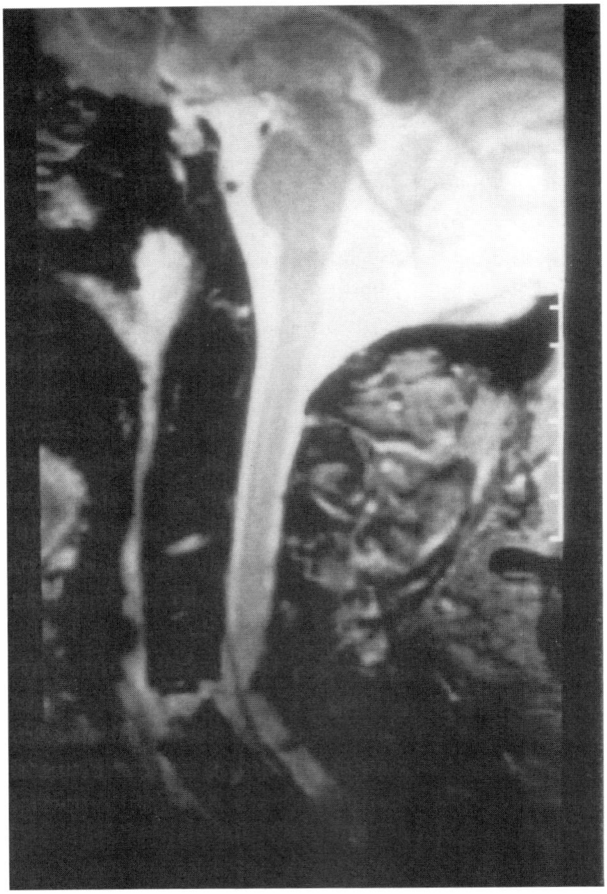

Fig. 6.4 T_2-weighted MR scan showing a mid-cervical fracture in a patient with ankylosing spondylitis. There is complete loss of stability and a haematoma retained by the posterior longitudinal ligament.

skull. If this has occurred the pin should be removed, the area locally cleaned and the traction applied elsewhere. The use of prophylactic antibiotics is an individual decision, and there is evidence in the literature which supports both the case for and against their use. The most likely infecting organism will be *Staphylococcus*. Should the traction pin penetrate the dura the risk of cerebral abscess is raised. There is a good case for holding a 'watching brief' and scanning the patient's head at regular intervals to detect early development of cerebritis or cerebral abscess. However, it would also be reasonable to treat this penetration by surgical exploration to clean and repair the damaged tissues by craniectomy or craniotomy.

Patient D was admitted with fracture dislocation at C4/5. This was reduced by traction and stabilised using an anterior cervical plate system. The procedure was technically unsatisfactory, the plate became loose and the patient was replaced in traction some days later to await a revision internal stabilisation procedure. During reapplication of the tongs the inner table and dura were penetrated. This was recognised and the tongs were relocated more securely. The second cervical procedure was carried out satisfactorily and the patient made an excellent recovery. Four weeks later he presented with diminished level of consciousness, profound hemiparesis and a large cerebral abscess. The cranial penetration had not been managed with appropriate antibiotics, surgical exploration or repeated CT scans.

Stabilisation of the cervical spine can be carried out using an external orthosis or a diverse range of internal fixation techniques. These include anterior cervical plate and screw systems, posterior lateral mass plate or rod fixators, laminar clamps, cable wire systems and transarticular screw placement for complex C1/C2 fractures. While most of these systems are relatively straightforward to use they are also easy to place incorrectly. For instance, the laminar clamp and screw system is an excellent device for posterior fixation and stabilisation across a single motion segment, i.e. the lamina above to the lamina below. When they are placed across two motion segments (i.e. three laminae) their efficiency is degraded considerably. Any method of internal fixation may need to be supplemented by an external orthosis, and this decision will be made by the surgeon after the stabilisation procedure is completed (Fig. 6.5).

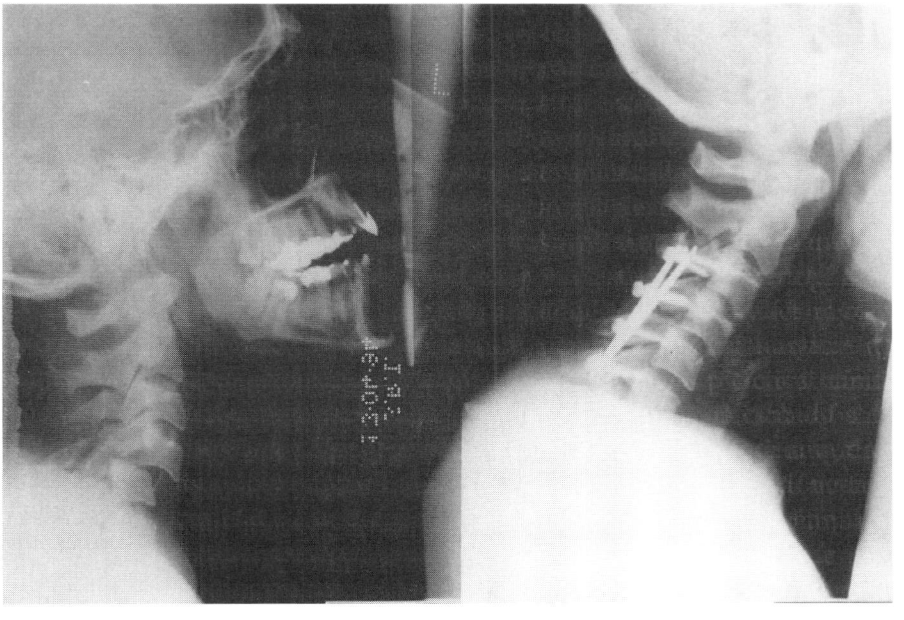

Fig. 6.5 C4/5 fracture subluxation. Stabilisation using four level to three motion segment fixation by lateral mass plates. This will require external support using a Halo or Minerva brace. Short-segment fixation when possible is preferable.

While these cervical internal fixation techniques are very effective and safe, the 'lower-tech' methods such as external orthotic bracing and Halo fixation retain a major role. It is important that selection of the method of stabilisation is made on the basis of the optimal technique for each individual fracture/dislocation/subluxation, and that newer internal fixation techniques are not chosen simply because they are currently fashionable. For many years before the development of modern sophisticated methods of internal fixation, many cervical fractures and dislocations could be successfully treated conservatively. The advantages and disadvantages of internal fixation versus conservative management should be discussed between the surgeon and spinal injury physician and, when appropriate, the options presented to the patient. Although no specific figures are available, the risk of major neurological damage associated with these methods of fixation is probably extremely small. The advantages of internal fixation are earlier mobilisation, reduction in the need for and duration of external orthotic support, enhanced bone fusion and improved long-term spine alignment.

There are few, if any, situations where surgical treatment has been clearly recognised to improve neurological outcome following primary cord injury. The object of management is to minimise the effects of the primary vertebral and neurological damage, remove the risk of secondary spinal cord damage and produce a stable, mobile, pain-free cervical spine. Where bone is fractured it is reasonable to hold the cervical spine in satisfactory position and allow bony union to occur. A Halo fixator is the most secure means of reducing cervical spine movement, although it is less effective at the lower cervical motion segments. Studies have shown that a soft cervical collar reduces flexion and extension movement by only 25%. Philadelphia-style collars, Somi braces and four-poster braces are better, but each will still permit about 30% of the normal range of flexion and extension and 50% of lateral movement.

When there is little or no bone fracture, but subluxation and/or dislocation of facet joints has occurred, the healing process will involve fibrous or ligamentous tissue rather than bone union, and consequently there is a risk of late subluxation, although this is difficult to quantify. The greater the ligamentous damage, the greater the risk. Some surgeons may prefer to acknowledge this risk and use a posterior fixation technique to ensure that bone union occurs and the risk of late subluxation is eliminated. It is possible, however, to treat such injuries conservatively, but the injury type must be recognised, immobilised properly for the appropriate length of time and the risk of late subluxation should be recognised.

Patient E was injured during a gymnastic class at school. She fell heavily after vaulting over a horse and injured her neck on landing. She had no neurological deficit at any time. At her local hospital she was placed in a cervical collar for six weeks following X-ray examination of the cervical spine. After that time the collar was removed and she was asked to return in a further four weeks for review. At this review appointment a cervical spine X-ray showed considerably worse forward subluxation at the C5/6 level, and she was referred for specialist management. By this time it was impossible to reduce the cervical spine back to normal alignment and a combined posterior and anterior fixation and fusion procedure *in situ* was carried out. Two years later repeat X-ray showed remodelling of the cervical spine resulting in improved cervical spine alignment. Fortunately she remained without neurological deficit. This case serves to illustrate a failure to recognise the degree of damage to the facet joints and the failure of inadequate conservative treatment.

Some conditions of the cervical spine make the patient more vulnerable to spinal trauma. These include os odontoideum and congenital laxity of spinal ligaments, in particular the transverse atlantal ligament and the condition of chronic atlanto-axial subluxation, which in about 60% of cases is associated with atlanto-occipital assimilation and C2/3 segmentation failure (Hensinger, 1989). It is not unusual for these conditions to be discovered incidentally. Some years ago it was thought that the ligamentous laxity associated with Down's syndrome put these patients at increased risk of neurological deficit by atlanto-axial subluxation. However, with the advantage of further studies it seems that the risk of neurological damage is considerably less than originally thought and prophylactic surgery based on X-ray appearances is probably not indicated.

Chronic atlanto-axial subluxation often occurs with total or partial assimilation of the atlas into the foramen magnum and with segmentation failure of the C2 and C3 vertebral bodies. This places considerable extra strain on the C1/2 joint, which is the most mobile segment of the cervical spine in any case. It is probable that over the years this extra strain causes attenuation of the transverse atlantal ligament, permitting excessive forward motion of the head and C1 relative to the odontoid process. This brings into question the risk of neurological damage either as a chronic progressive condition or as the result of acute trauma. There are no facts or figures to indicate this risk, although it is probably small. It is reasonable to make the patient aware of this small risk, to advise him or her to avoid high-risk situations and thereafter to observe the C1/2 joint at appropriate intervals. Alternatively it is reasonable to argue that, if the odontoid process has encroached sufficiently into the spinal canal to indicate that the transverse atlantal ligament is incompetent, and knowing that the apical and alar ligaments alone are insufficient to provide stability, surgical stabilisation should be considered as a preventative measure. Both these lines of management were found to be reasonable and acceptable in a recent court judgment.

With the condition of os odontoideum more data are available, particularly from the studies of Spierlings and Braakman (1982). In this condition, which is acquired rather than congenital, the atlas vertebra together with the os can move either anteriorly or posteriorly with respect to the axis. Spierlings and Braakman observed that only those patients in whom the antero-posterior diameter of the spinal canal had been reduced to 13 mm or less had neurological symptoms. While this study provides a useful indicator for management, it is not universally accepted and argument continues as to whether and which patients with incidentally diagnosed os odontoideum should have a prophylactic C1/C2 fixation and fusion procedure.

In each of these examples of C1/C2 abnormality, the risk of any prophylactic spinal procedure must be measured against the risk of severe neurological damage following even modest cervical spine trauma, and the long-term effects of progressive instability at this level. As yet these risks are not clearly quantified, but are probably small.

Cervical degenerative disease including cervical spondylosis and prolapsed cervical intervertebral disc

Degenerative intervertebral disease is by far the commonest pathological condition in the cervical spine causing radiculopathy and/or myelopathy. It is considerably more common than cervical trauma and patients do not generally present with acute symptoms to accident and emergency departments, but are usually diagnosed under more elective circumstances. Cervical cord trauma and coexisting cervical spondylosis is usually associated with a sudden uncontrolled extension force applied to the cervical spine leading to a central cord injury. The typical clinical features of this condition are a flaccid, lower motor neurone paralysis of the hands with spastic weakness of the lower limbs. The extension movement, it is thought, causes the spinal cord to become pinched between a pre-existing osteophyte anteriorly and a thickened, infolded ligamentum flavum posteriorly. As a result there is damage to anterior horn cells and to the cortico-spinal tract, although the detailed pathogenesis of the central cord lesion has not been fully explained. The patient will most likely have fallen forward, be of an age when cervical spondylosis is likely to be present and may have facial or forehead lacerations or abrasions to indicate the manner in which the fall occurred. The injury does not significantly compromise cervical stability, although small bone flakes avulsed from the anterior-inferior vertebral edge indicate stretch damage to the anterior longitudinal ligament. Management involves general restriction of activities for a short period with the cervical spine supported using a collar or side-supports. The condition does not require the use of cervical traction.

Secondary cord damage can theoretically be caused by reduced spinal cord blood flow secondary to low systemic blood pressure, perhaps by premature and vigorous attempts at mobilisation. The concept of spinal cord 'oedema' is often put forward as an argument against early mobilisation. Use of the term 'oedema' is really a catch-all term but what is more clear, however, is the complex interaction of microchemical changes that occur at and around the site of cord injury, including release of excitotoxic peptides (Pringle, 1992; Greene *et al.*, 1996). The influence of movements and altered blood flow on these pathopharmacological mechanisms remains to be clarified. Early MR scanning will determine whether or not spinal cord swelling is present, or the pressure of intramedullary signal change which often heralds a poor prognosis.

There is considerable contemporary research focused on laboratory and clinical methods of limiting the effect of primary spinal cord injury by pharmacological means. Once the primary injury has occurred and the cell damage takes place within the spinal cord, a variety of different mechanisms are likely to be involved in producing further spinal cord damage or extending the lesion. These include intramedullary haemorrhage, ischaemia, the release of excitatory amino acids, free-radical release, etc. Several different agents have been tried in laboratory and clinical situations including gangliosides, opiate antagonists, free-radical scavengers such as vitamin E and methylprednisolone and the amino steroid antioxidant Trilazad. The calcium channel blocker Nimodipine has been shown to be effective in the brain following subarachnoid haemorrhage and this effect is being explored following spinal cord trauma. In the laboratory situation, pretreatment with some agents serves to limit the extent of the primary spinal cord injury, and while this is interesting in that it shows us that targeted pharmacological agents can be helpful, it is hardly a practical clinical solution.

Perhaps most recent attention has been directed toward the use of high doses of methylprednisolone within the first eight hours following spinal cord injury. Three trials have been reported by the North American Spinal Cord Injury Study (NASCIS) Group on the timing, dosage and duration of methylprednisolone therapy. The use of this agent is widespread within North America, but this is a complex function of public demand and the pressure of potential litigation rather than clinical evidence. If it is to be used, methylprednisolone needs to be given within eight hours of the primary cord injury. Used after this time it may have a detrimental effect on clinical progress. In the trials, those patients who received methylprednisolone within the specified time may well have had a numerical improvement in their ultimate motor power strength compared with those patients who did not receive the drug. However, as with many major trials the results were less than absolutely convincing. For example, the two placebo groups used for control purposes in the study showed significant differences in their ultimate recovery, throwing some doubt on the results of the treated groups of patients. Despite this, however, there is some evidence that very high doses of glucocorticoids given within the first eight hours probably do make a slight difference to ultimate motor recovery. Their use in patients following spinal cord injury, for the time being at any rate, should remain an individual decision made by the consultant in charge. Prescribing initiative must not be relinquished to pressure exerted by the media or by any other non-medical body not in possession of comprehensive knowledge of the scientific and clinical evidence.

Once neurological recovery has begun to occur, as it does in over 50% of patients with central cord injury, gradual mobilisation can be accelerated. When central cord injury is considered as a potential diagnosis it can usually be verified with little difficulty. Patient F had a fall which caused a central cervical cord injury from which he eventually made a reasonable functional recovery. (Recovery in the lower limbs is generally much better than that in the hands, which frequently remain flaccid and useless.) However, the clinical diagnosis in this case was not made until some months after the injury because the patient also had congenital bilateral cerebral palsy, which confused the early clinical presentation. As a result he was mobilised more rapidly than would otherwise have been the case, and it was subsequently argued some years later that his recovery was jeopardised by this failure of diagnosis and inappropriate early mobilisation. While this may or may not have been the case, the health board's case was severely weakened yet again by the appearance of the word 'supra-tentorial' in the early initial clinical notes, a common hostage to fortune. The junior medial staff involved had done their best, but the difficulty of diagnosis in this case obviously required assessment by an experienced clinician. This will often clarify a neurological diagnosis, or at least direct the patient to an appropriate unit for appropriate management.

Patient G presented with a six-week history of cervical-thoracic spinal pain and was initially seen in an accident and emergency department. There was dispute as to whether the patient actually had neurological signs or even symptoms at this time, but he was discharged from hospital only to return the following morning with definite neurological signs. The diagnosis of 'hysterical paralysis' was made by a very junior doctor. Fortunately this was corrected by a medical registrar, who very reasonably organised an early myelogram to investigate the possibility of a surgically treatable lesion. The myelogram was in fact incorrectly reported as normal and because of this, investigations were directed at possible medical causes for his myelopathy. Eventually he was seen a small number of days later by a consultant who disregarded the apparently normal myelogram and made a neurosurgical referral. Within a few hours the correct diagnosis of a massive prolapsed C7/T1 intervertebral disc was made. The delay in diagnosis was primarily caused by the incorrectly reported myelogram and probably compromised the patient's subsequent recovery.

As with cervical trauma, the diagnosis and clinical presentation of acute disc-related myelopathy may be confused if the patient has consumed alcohol. Patient H developed a myelopathy secondary to an acute prolapsed cervical intervertebral disc. Initially his general condition was attributed, not unreasonably under the circumstances, to a high consumption of alcohol. An examination under less than optimal circumstances in police custody had failed to identify a myelopathy, and this failure was cited by the plaintiff as the cause of his subsequent poor neurological recovery. However, following his referral to a major neuroscience department, the clinical and radiological diagnosis was not actually confirmed until 72 hours later, under what can only be described as optimal circumstances. In this case, the small number of hours in which the initial diagnosis and referral was delayed by the patient's intoxicated state played no significant role in his degree of recovery.

The optimal method of investigation of cervical myelopathy due to spondylosis or disc protrusion is by MR scan or CT myelography. Myelography alone remains an acceptable and useful form of investigation, but what is less clear is the role of *cervical discography*. This technique is more closely identified with lumbar intervertebral disc disease than with cervical disc degeneration and is considered by some to help identify which motion segments or discs are the source of spinal pain.

Patient I was investigated by multiple-level cervical discography as a prelude to anterior cervical decompression surgery. Following the investigation, he developed severe and persistent cervical pain which required treatment using escalating doses of analgesia. His clinical notes recorded progressive neurological symptoms and signs, remarkable because of the failure of the junior medical staff who diligently documented them to recognise their importance. The patient was treated symptomatically and eventually the otherwise exemplary clinical notes indicated a time at which the clinical features were such that failure to investigate and make a definitive diagnosis constituted indefensible clinical practice. Post-discography pain is well recognised, but should settle rapidly, and its persistence together with the slow development of neurological signs indicates a major complication, usually infection. In this case the problem was a ventral cervical extradural abscess secondary to the discography procedure. Failure to recognise these symptoms was responsible for the patient's poor neurological condition and poor recovery.

Discography was also used in the case of Patient J, a young professional person whose leisure and professional activity was limited by cervical pain. This was reasonably diagnosed on clinical grounds to be generated from one or more sets of cervical facet joints. Plain X-rays of the cervical spine showed no abnormalities and a non-interventional regime of treatment was instigated. However, at a parallel and contemporaneous consultation it was judged that the patient had degenerative disc disease despite the appearances on plain X-ray. Cervical discography was recommended and subsequently carried out at all levels between C2/3 and C7/T1. Following this procedure, the patient complained immediately of severe cervical pain which persisted and required escalating analgesic medication. He developed systemic signs of infection and was eventually treated with antibiotics. An X-ray taken at this time showed multiple-level discitis despite which a posterior surgical fusion and fixation procedure was carried out.

The value of cervical discography has to be seriously questioned, particularly when MR scanning is available to identify normal and abnormal signs from intervertebral discs. Few UK radiologists, to the best of the author's knowledge, are skilled at direct puncture of cervical intervertebral discs, and it is likely that even fewer junior staff are aware of the complications of this increasingly redundant form of investigation.

For degenerative disc disease, there are two basic *routes of surgical access* to the cervical spine – anterior and posterior. The true lateral approach as described by Verbiest (1970) is not often used for cervical disc disease in the UK. The scope of this chapter does not include a discussion on the merits of, and indications for, the various approaches in different clinical situations. The anterior operation can be described as an anterior cervical decompression procedure which may simply remove the osteophytes and/or the disc and not include a fusion or fixation. This is entirely reasonable, as is the use of a fusion procedure, either using a cylindrical bone dowel as described by Cloward (1958) or the quadrangular graft as described by Smith and Robinson (1958). Recently, the addition of anterior cervical plate fixation to encourage bone union for multi-level surgery has increased in popularity. Using a posterior approach, the surgeon can carry out either a cervical laminectomy, a laminoplasty or confine the decompression to a nerve root by a microforaminotomy. Small lateral discs causing radiculopathy can also be removed by this latter operation.

Prior to surgery the *risks* should be discussed with the patient. The most feared complication is spinal cord damage detected immediately following the surgery. This can be due to poor positioning or handling with uncontrolled movement of the cervical spine while the patient is under anaesthetic. During an anterior procedure, if excessive and aggressive drilling is carried out the spinal cord may be damaged by direct drill impact (Fig. 6.6). It should also be remembered that the fluted drill, which is designed for the standard Cloward operation, is excellent for drilling bone and moving it backwards, but is a poor method of drilling cartilaginous disc tissue which tends to be pushed forward, i.e. in the direction of the spinal cord. Instrument impact on the ventral surface of the spinal cord is always a risk, particularly when the posterior cortical plate and osteophytes are being removed either with microcurettes, micropunches or a high-speed drill. It has been argued that a myelopathy which follows on from an anterior cervical disc procedure can be due to a combination of Surgicel and blood clot. It should be noted that the manufacturer's instructions on a packet of Surgicel indicate clearly that this material should not be left within the spinal canal and should be removed. Myelopathy can also occur if the bone graft is driven too deeply and encroaches on the spinal canal.

The risk of neurological complications, including myelopathy, caused by anterior cervical decompression surgery is approximately 0.64%. For posterior cervical surgery the risk of neurological complications is 2.18%, again an

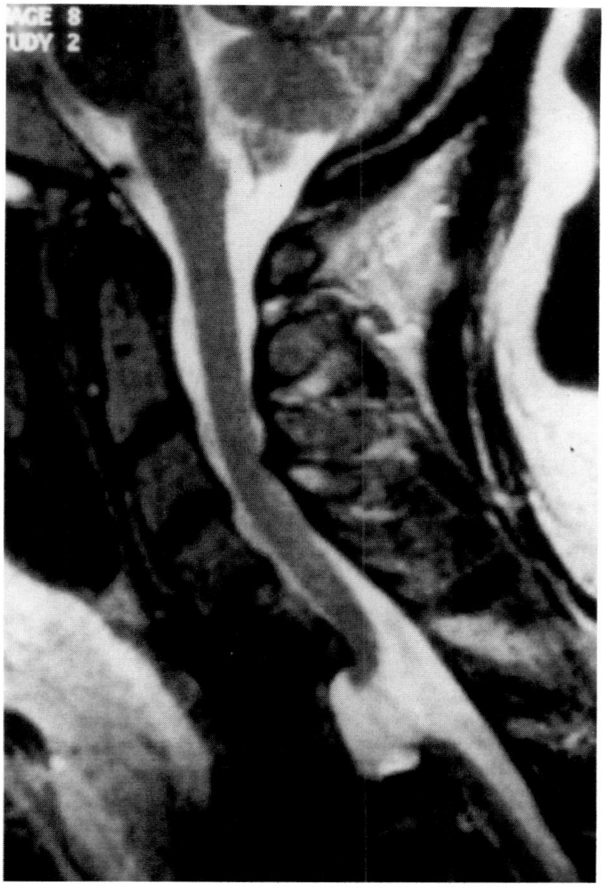

Fig. 6.6 MRI of a cervical cord directly damaged by instrument impact many years earlier.

average figure (Graham, 1989). Of course, not all of these neurological complications represent myelopathy, but it is good and standard practice to mention risks of this order, i.e. 0.5% or 2%, to patients undergoing either anterior or posterior cervical decompressive surgery (Zeidman *et al.*, 1997).

The operation of anterior cervical decompression and fusion was first described in the early 1950s and has been subsequently modified in a variety of useful ways. There are several different methods of carrying out this operation and variations in technique include the use of power drills, different methods of estimating the depth of drilling, different methods of removing the osteophytes and variations in graft material and insertion. In the 1990s, it is very difficult to justify anterior cervical surgery without the use of an operating microscope, or at least the use of loupes and appropriate illumination.

When the surgery is complete it is good practice to carry out a lateral plain X-ray of the cervical spine within 24 hours. If instrumentation is used, this should be done early and preferably while the patient is still under anaesthetic or in the recovery room following surgery. If a myelopathy has developed, it is important that this is recognised and brought to the attention of the surgeon directly. It should be investigated immediately by MR imaging (MRI) or by CT myelography. Persisting compression of the cervical cord will necessitate immediate re-exploration. In 1974 (the pre-microscope era), a study identified 70 cases of myelopathy developing after anterior cervical disc surgery and fusion. Of these, 53 occurred immediately and 17 were delayed. Surgical re-exploration produced recovery in 21% of patients while 18% improved without surgery (Flynn, 1982). The need for surgical re-exploration should be judged in each case following urgent investigation.

Following a cervical laminectomy there is a risk of myelopathy. Patient K presented with a progressive cervical myelopathy due to multiple-level degenerative disease and following investigation had a C3–C7 inclusive cervical laminectomy. He was neurologically well until the third postoperative day, when he developed progressively worsening myelopathy. This was immediately investigated by myelography but no compressive cause was found. In another case in which litigation was not involved, the circumstances were similar, except that the myelopathy became obvious within a few hours of the laminectomy. It was progressive and the patient subsequently died. An autopsy was carried out and revealed no evidence of injury to the outside surface of the cervical cord, but showed a haematomyelia running the full length of the grey matter between C1 and C7. Autopsy information on this condition is uncommon, but this case does illustrate the mechanism of post-cervical laminectomy deterioration in some cases (Fig. 6.7).

Two of the author's own patients developed a cruciate paresis (arms but not legs) immediately after an uneventful cervical laminectomy. No cause, other than the 'decompression effect', was identified and both patients made substantial but incomplete neurological and functional recoveries.

As with all operations performed on the spine, identification of the correct vertebral level is a fundamental requirement. There are a variety of ways of ensuring that this is done, mostly involving X-rays taken before, during and sometimes after the operation while still under anaesthetic. It is likely that most surgeons who carry out a large number of spinal operations have at sometime operated at an incorrect spinal level, despite taking adequate precautions to avoid this. Patient L had a thoracotomy to remove a prolapsed thoracic intervertebral disc causing myelopathy. Peroperative X-rays were taken and were marked by a consultant neuroradiologist in the operating theatre. The operation was carried out but postoperative X-rays showed that the disc removed was one level above that intended. The patient was told that the mistake had occurred despite standard and reasonable precautions. The following day the operation was carried out through the same thoracotomy wound at the correct level. The patient made a good neurological recovery and nothing further was

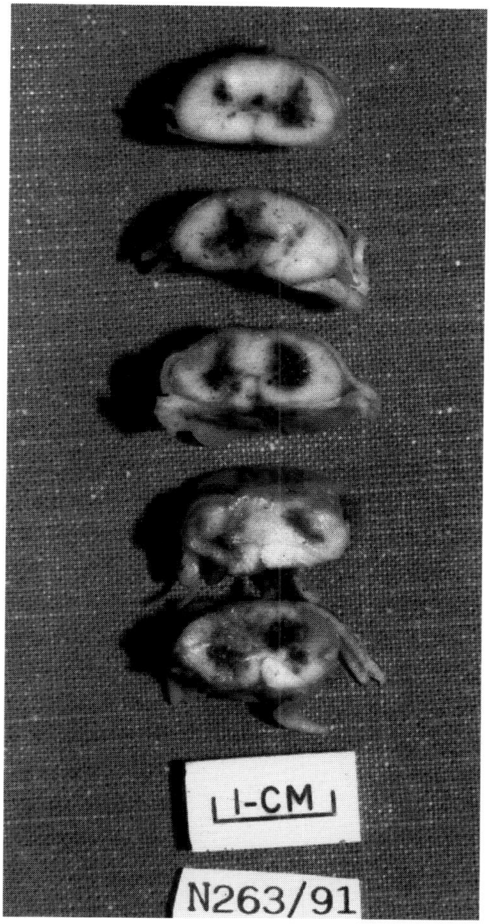

Fig. 6.7 Autopsy specimen. Posterior decompression of the spinal canal resulted in haemorrhage throughout the grey matter of the cervical cord.

heard on the matter. The frequency with which litigation arises as a result of spinal surgery at an incorrect level is high and the surgeon must not simply rely on the radiological reports, but must examine the X-rays and correlate these directly with clinical information. The number of cervical vertebrae occasionally does vary due to segmentation failure. Postoperative X-rays following spinal surgery are carried out for a number of reasons, one of which is to confirm the correct level has been the subject of the operation. It is not a risk which needs to be imparted to the patient before surgery because of its rarity and also because doing so could easily detract from the surgeon's credibility. In operation notes it is useful to record how the correct level was identified.

Sometimes during disc surgery the disc removed is not as degenerate or as prolapsed as expected from the imaging. If doubt exists whether or not the correct level has been operated at, then an instrument marker can be placed in the disc space and another X-ray taken while the opportunity exists to rectify any mistake in level under the same anaesthetic.

Cervical instrumentation

Over the past ten years there has been a boom in spinal surgery which has, to a large extent, drawn together the practices of orthopaedic surgery and neurosurgery. This was due in no small part to the availability of vastly improved spinal imaging and the development of old and new routes of access to the spine at all levels between the clivus and the sacrum. In recent years there has been a substantial increase in the variety of methods available for internal fixation of the cervical spine, and more patients have internal fixation with cervical surgery than was the case ten years ago. This applies to traumatic, degenerative, neoplastic, inflammatory and even infective lesions.

For anterior cervical fixation, plate and screw techniques include the various anterior cervical plates, which use cancellous screws, and the Caspar-type plate, which uses cortical screws that penetrate both the anterior and posterior cortex of the vertebral body. These are relatively straightforward techniques for internal fixation, and it is probable that they improve the rate of bone fusion by inducing a degree of rigidity and some compression of the bone graft. The Caspar technique requires that the posterior cortex of the vertebra is penetrated by the first millimetre of the screw in order that adequate purchase is achieved, whereas this is not required using the anterior cervical locking plate screws. These latter screws are 14 mm in length and do not reach the posterior cortex. Both techniques are safe and extremely useful in the appropriate circumstances (Maiman *et al.*, 1994; Menezes and Ryken, 1994).

The posterior cervical spine has generated a wider variety of methods of fixation, which include sublaminar wiring at multiple levels using various loops and rectangles, including the Ransford loop for occipito-cervical fixation. Sublaminar wiring is possibly the method of fixation associated with the highest risk of neurological complications in the cervical region. There is no reliable figure for the frequency of myelopathy developing following cervical sublaminar wiring, but it is common practice among surgeons who use the technique frequently to indicate a risk of about 1% prior to operation.

The technique of passing wires below the lamina in the cervical spine is different from that in the lumbar spine. In both cases, the spinous processes are removed to give easier access to the interlaminar space. The interlaminar space is opened up using a small-size, flat-base bone punch, or a high-speed drill, in order to expose the ligamentum flavum and the midline gap between the right and left halves of this ligament. Some of this ligament is removed in the midline using sharp 2 or 3 mm bone punches in order to expose the arch of the lamina in the midline. Often small amounts of bone are removed in the same fashion from the upper and lower edges of the lamina at each level to facilitate wire passage. This will present the surgeon with a midline groove through which the wire can be passed. The technique as described in the Surgicraft manufacturer's manual is for stiff wire passage in the lumbar spine and indicates that the wire should be configured into a square-shaped arrangement. This is not applicable in the cervical spine where the laminar curve is more rounded and the Cable wire leader has to be configured into a more curved arrangement in order to effect safe passage. Only flexible Cable wire with a stiff 'leader' should be used in the cervical spine. If passage of the wire leader proves difficult, it must not be pushed or forced since this is essentially a blind technique and the surgeon cannot tell what is happening to the posterior surface of the dura and spinal cord. If necessary, more bone is removed to make the passage easier and when they have been passed, the wires are carefully moved to each lateral extremity and secured in position to prevent them accidentally impinging on the spinal cord. The technique of multiple-level sublaminar wiring in the cervical spine is difficult and in inexperienced or unsupervised hands it can be dangerous. The main periods of risk to the cord are when the wires are being passed and later when they are mobilised in order to secure them to the fixator.

When cervical canal stenosis is present, the depth of the subarachnoid space, particular posteriorly, should be gauged for passage of wires. When this is only 1 or 2 mm in size, serious consideration should be given to omitting that particular level.

Other more recent techniques include the use of Halifax clamps, cervical lateral mass plates, rod and screw systems, plastic ties and the use of screws for transarticular fixation at the C1/2 joint. These techniques are all extremely useful in the appropriate circumstances and have greatly improved the options for posterior cervical fixation.

When internal fixation is used in the cervical spine, it is good practice to carry out an antero-posterior and lateral X-ray of the spine in the operating theatre or within a few hours of the operation, preferably in the recovery ward. This will check the alignment of the spine and confirm that the appropriate levels have been fixed. If a neurological complication arises at this time, or shortly afterwards, reference can be made to this X-ray without delay. In the event of a myelopathy developing, it is necessary to determine whether or not there is ongoing compression of the spinal cord, such as by a badly placed sublaminar wire or by a misplaced screw, which compromises the spinal canal. Most cervical fixation devices are manufactured in titanium which produces little artefact after CT or MR imaging. If compression is revealed, removal of the fixation device is usually mandatory. When a myelopathy occurs following sublaminar fixation and the investigation has not demonstrated any ongoing obstruction, it might be assumed that at some point in the application of the fixation system the wire has impinged on the spinal cord and further exploration is likely to be unnecessary. Over-reduction of a malalignment is a possible cause of postoperative neurological deficit after this type of surgery.

The use of new and sophisticated methods of internal fixation of the cervical spine must be kept in perspective, and their application should be confined to those patients in whom it is advantageous to use them. Internal fixation techniques should not be employed because they are fashionable, and it is important that the method selected is appropriate for the individual needs of a patient, that the surgeon is well instructed in the proper application of the technique, knows the risks and can recognise complications when they occur during and after surgery.

References

Cloward, R.B. (1958) The anterior approach for removal of ruptured cervical discs. *Journal of Neurosurgery* **15**, 602.

Flynn, T.B. (1982) Neurological complications of anterior interbody fusion. *Spine* **7**, 536–9.

Graham, J.J. (1989) Complications of cervical spine surgery. In *The Cervical Spine*, 2nd edn (H.H. Sherk, ed.), pp. 831–7. J.B. Lippincott, London.

Greene, K.A., Marciano, F.F. and Sonntag, V.K.H. (1996) Pharmacological management of spinal cord injury: current status of drugs designed to augment functional recovery of the injured human spinal cord. *Journal of Spine Disease* **9**, 355–66.

Hensinger, R.N. (1989) Congenital anomalies of the atlanto-axial joint. In *The Cervical Spine*, 2nd edn (H.H. Sherk, ed.), pp. 236–57. J.B. Lippincott, London.

Maiman, D.J., Yoganandan, W. and Pintar, F. (1994) Biomechanics of spinal instrumentation. In *Spinal Instrumentation* (E.C. Benzel, ed.), pp. 11–30. American Association of Neurological Surgeons.

Menezes, A. and Ryken, T.C. (1994) Instrumentation of the craniocervical region. In *Spinal Instrumentation* (E.C. Benzel, ed.), pp. 47–110. American Association of Neurological Surgeons.

Pringle, R.G. (1992) Effect of injury on the spinal cord. In *Surgery of the Spine* (S. Findlay and R. Owen, eds), pp. 999–1008. Blackwell Science, Oxford.

Smith, G.W. and Robinson, R.A. (1958) The treatment of certain cervical spine disorders by anterior removal of the intervertebral disc and interbody fusion. *Journal of Bone and Joint Surgery* **40A**, 607.

Spierlings, E.L.H. and Braakman, R. (1982) Os odontoideum: analysis of 37 cases. *Journal of Bone Joint Surgery* **64B**, 422–8.

Verbiest, H. (1970) La chirurgie anterieure et laterale du rachis cervical. *Neurochirurgie* **6** (Suppl.).

Zeidman, S.M., Ducker, T.B. and Raycroft, J. (1997) Trends and complications in cervical spine surgery 1989–1993. *Journal of Spine Disease* **10**, 523–6.

Chapter 7

The Lumbar Spine

David Markham and John Garfield

I PROLAPSED LUMBAR INTERVERTEBRAL DISC

David Markham

The intervertebral disc is but a part of a complex mechanical system, which includes adjacent facet joints and ligaments, enabling movement and shock absorption at levels throughout the spinal column. The normal disc is mechanically very strong, being capable of resisting massive forces. Despite this, the lumbar intervertebral disc has for many generations provided patients and the medical profession with a convenient diagnosis, actual or imaginary, of 'slipped disc', or prolapsed intervertebral disc. Indeed, the terminology has assumed the dimensions of folklore, being used to explain all forms of acute low back pain, with or without sciatica, whatever the underlying pathology and attendant disability.

The advent of imaging techniques such as computerised tomography (CT) and magnetic resonance imaging (MRI) scans has increased our understanding of the part played by the intervertebral disc in clinical syndromes, at the same time providing us with a far more accurate diagnostic aid than previous contrast studies. MRI scans in particular have led to the widespread understanding that the intervertebral disc must be degenerate, or more accurately dehydrated, in order to be vulnerable and susceptible to damage.

Whilst our understanding and investigation of lumbar disc damage is now more accurate, the long-standing problems of clinical assessment, choice of treatment, surgical pitfalls, complications and long-term associated disabilities still test the medical profession in its various guises.

Low back pain, with or without associated neurological symptoms, is one of the most common reasons for patient referral to consultant orthopaedic and neurological surgeons. Sadly, the prolapsed intervertebral disc is still regarded by many as being a simple problem carrying a surgical solution, that surgery being so straightforward as to qualify for delegation to relatively inexperienced members of a surgical team. This perception is erroneous, and is a common cause for error leading to mistakes which generate allegations of negligent management. The converse is, of course, the case. Backache, with or without radiation into the legs, is a complex symptom which can be the presenting feature of a myriad of different pathologies. Its investigation requires careful examination, detailed planning and experienced evaluation in order that errors of both omission and commission do not lead to actions for medical negligence. It is unfortunately the case that such actions are commonplace and cover many aspects of the overall management of backache.

General practitioners (GPs), who must regard low back pain as being one of the most frequent symptoms about which they are consulted, may be the first defendant in any medical negligence action where a delay in treatment is alleged. This is particularly the case in cauda equina compression, where a delay in effecting decompression of the cauda equina may lead to devastating long-term disabilities. It is true that there are associated problems relating specifically to causation which impinge upon hospital and surgical management, but the initial liability may rest with the GP. The same could also be said of physiotherapists who fail to heed symptoms that may indicate a degree of cauda equina irritation and fail to take appropriate steps to ensure urgent referral.

In essence, actions for medical negligence concerning the overall management of the prolapsed lumbar intervertebral disc can, and often do, encompass a wide range of medical and paramedical practitioners, the action of whom may be critical to the overall defensibility of any particular claim.

Errors leading to medical negligence actions

There are generally four areas of management in which errors can occur that may give rise to medical negligence actions:

(1) Clinical management
(2) Physical treatment
(3) Radiology
(4) Surgical management.

These are discussed below.

Clinical management

The initial clinical assessment of a patient complaining of backache is essential for an accurate diagnosis. The history should be detailed with recorded facts in relation to the severity of pain, its onset, duration and relationship to trauma. Previous history is important but should not be allowed to mislead the clinician into a false diagnosis of a recurrent episode of previous problems. Nowhere is this more true than in the case of the cauda equina syndrome, where a simple assumption that a further attack of backache is merely a recurrence of previous problems leads to complacency, with an associated failure to enquire about specific symptoms such as bowel and bladder dysfunction. Effectively, a previous history is essential but it must be accompanied by detailed enquiries about whether or not there are any additional symptoms or, indeed, whether current symptoms mirror those of previous occasions.

Examination is essential, as also is regular review should there be any doubt about the underlying cause for the symptoms. GPs will say that this form of clinical assessment is a counsel of perfection and that backache is such a common complaint that detailed clinical assessment, in all but a very small minority of patients, does not assist in the management. It is that small minority of patients who successfully issue writs against their doctors for failing to make a diagnosis which would have been apparent under such circumstances. The most frequent allegations made against GP defendants is a failure to carry out an accurate clinical assessment, particularly in terms of neurology, in patients who subsequently develop irreversible cauda equina syndrome or permanent neurological deficit in a limb as a result of delayed referral because the physical signs were not appreciated at an early stage.

It is recognised that there are constraints upon a GP's ability to ask for specialist advice. However, there can be few hospital practitioners who would refuse to see, as a matter of urgency, a patient who is known to have bladder or bowel dysfunction associated with acute low back pain.

Physical treatment

Physical treatment of the low back pain syndrome has in the past led to successful actions for negligence, particularly where clinical assessment has been questionable. Vigorous manipulation of the lumbar spine in the management of acute low back pain has been followed by the development of severe and irreversible neurological deficit. Our developing knowledge in relation to the vulnerability of degenerate discs may, superficially at least, seem to be an adequate defence for a medical practitioner who is alleged to have precipitated an acute disc sequestration by a manipulative procedure. However, the pragmatic view is that even if it were to be accepted that a single episode of trauma does not produce intervertebral disc prolapse, the temporal relationship between such a manipulation and the development of acute neurological deficit will lead pragmatists to an inevitable conclusion.

Radiology

Radiological investigation is central to the diagnosis and management of the prolapsed intervertebral disc. It demands close co-operation between the clinician and the radiologist. It also necessarily requires that the radiologist be adept at the interpretation of plain films and images of the lumbar spine and that he or she be party to the clinical evaluation of the patient by the clinician.

Plain radiographs enable the provisional suspicion of a prolapsed intervertebral disc by excluding a number of radiologically obvious alternative causes; these can include metastatic disease, advanced degenerative spondylosis and other esoteric abnormalities, e.g. increased interpedicular distance, sacroiliac abnormalities and mechanical derangement such as congenital spondylolisthesis. They are also effective in highlighting lumbosacral anomalies, subsequently enabling the surgeon to accurately identify lumbar disc levels when planning a surgical approach.

CT scans without intrathecal contrast, are a generally inaccurate method of investigating the prolapsed intervertebral disc. However, they are useful in excluding other pathologies such as lumbar spondylosis. They are more accurate in the presence of injected contrast medium. They should not be dismissed as a useful method of investigating the lumbar spine.

MRI scans do, of course, provide a wealth of information about the lumbar spine and, in particular, intervertebral disc disease and damage. They also enable soft tissue tumours, such as neurofibromata, to be excluded from the differential diagnosis. Careful differentiation should be established between the bulging degenerate disc, causing minimal or no irritation of the nerve root or theca, and the significant prolapse of disc material into the vertebral or neural canal, causing associated compression of their contents. This is particularly apposite in multiple-level disc disease. The clinician and radiologist must have a mutual respect for each other in relation to the interpretation of MRI scans, otherwise culpable mistakes will occur, leading to inevitable allegations of negligence. In particular, clinicians should be prepared to accept that in the interpretation of such complex images as MRI scans, a radiologist is more experienced and, therefore, more likely to advance an opinion which is both accurate and unaffected by emotional factors.

Discography is enjoying a resurgence amongst certain surgeons. It is used as a simple diagnostic imaging technique wherein leakage of contrast from a particular disc can be said to infer damage sufficient to account for the patient's symptoms. This cannot be refuted if, of course, the level is appropriate to the neurological deficit. Discography is also employed as a simple clinical test, where fluid is injected into the appropriate disc, that disc being 'diagnosed' as being responsible for the patient's symptoms if those symptoms are reproduced by the injection. It is sometimes a source of medical negligence actions. Discography is often carried out on an out-patient basis or with the patient detained in hospital for a minimal period of time. It can be painful; it can also lead to acute bacterial infective discitis, leading to pyrexia, acute pain and associated acute muscle spasm. Those symptoms are, unfortunately, often disregarded, enabling the disease to become well-established before the diagnosis is made. This leads to permanent disability which generates actions for negligence. Whilst the introduction of infection is rarely seen as a negligent act, particularly if the investigation is carried out under full aseptic conditions, the failure to diagnose such infection expeditiously has been found to be negligent.

Surgical management

The majority of successful negligence actions surrounding the lumbar intervertebral disc relate to its surgical management. Without adequate operation records and notes, indicating the pre- and postoperative clinical state, it may prove impossible to mount a successful defence. A patient with severe low back pain radiating into the leg or legs, with apparent neurological deficit, is a compelling reason for a compassionate surgeon to embark upon a surgical procedure, particularly if a relative applies pressure for 'something to be done'. This can lead to misinterpretation of MRI scans by the surgeon, in contradiction of his or her radiological colleague. The patient and relatives will not hesitate to issue proceedings when such inappropriate surgery fails to relieve the problem. It is, therefore, essential to exclude wherever possible extraneous pressures and to evaluate the patient's preoperative state, in consultation with colleagues, before deciding whether or not surgery is appropriate and likely to be successful. Even in those circumstances informed consent is essential in that despite there being a sound clinical and radiological reason for surgery, an operation may not necessarily relieve the symptoms, and may lead to a complication which further disables the patient.

Excision of the prolapsed lumbar intervertebral disc has long been regarded as a simple procedure that can be delegated to a junior member of the surgical team without specific supervision. That perception is unacceptable. Surgery is fraught with potential hazards. Furthermore, experienced spinal surgeons never fail to be surprised at the lack of correlation between preoperative indications and the appearances at surgery. Unfortunately, surgery of this nature is still delegated to inexperienced surgeons. This leads to mistakes, not only in surgical technique but in appreciation of operative findings, which lead to subsequent negligence actions.

Delay in effecting surgical excision of a prolapsed intervertebral disc is often alleged and can often be refuted. This is not the case in relation to cauda equina compression or where there are significant peripheral neurological deficits in lower limbs. The historical management of intervertebral disc prolapse is, of course, conservative. Its overall success enables negligence actions to be successfully resisted, save in those cases where preoperative neurological deficit persists.

Surgical management covers a spectrum of procedures ranging from chemonucleolysis to laminectomy. Pressures are nowadays placed upon the surgeon to detain patients in hospital for the shortest possible period of time.

This may have admirable political and administrative benefits, but it places the surgeon in potential hazard in terms of inability to accurately assess the development of any postoperative complications.

Chemonucleolysis was at one time popular, fell into disuse, and has recently enjoyed a resurgence of popularity. It generates actions for medical negligence. The procedure is usually associated with only an overnight stay in hospital. It is painful and can be complicated by the development of neurological symptoms which did not exist before the injection, and can also be followed by infection in much the same way as discography. Postoperative evaluation should be undertaken on a frequent and regular basis in order to expeditiously diagnose and treat such untoward complications.

A common error in the surgical approach is to wrongly identify the disc level. Obesity of the patient is a common underlying cause, as is lumbosacral anomaly. Errors of identification can be minimised or eradicated by the use of preoperative X-ray markers in order to accurately establish the correct surgical level. Once that level has been identified, the surgical approach must be appropriate. It is not uncommon for surgeons to explore the wrong side at the correct level. Finding no evidence of a disc prolapse, with a free nerve root, the operation is concluded without reference to documentation or radiographs. It is important, therefore, to accurately mark the patient prior to surgery and to have radiographs and images readily available in the operating theatre during surgery.

Even if all these precautions are observed, an inadequate surgical exposure can result in a failure to identify the disc lesion. Furthermore, such inadequate exposure, particularly when associated with a degree of haemorrhage, can lead to over-vigorous retraction of nerve roots with the result that not only is the disc prolapse not identified, but the postoperative deficit may be more profound than that which existed before surgery. There has in recent years been a move towards microdiscectomy. However, whatever the advantages of the minimal surgical approach, it is still essential that the exposure of the pathological area should be adequate for the prevailing conditions and the experience of the surgeon.

Surgical findings are variously described in operation notes, unfortunately with a level of detail inadequate to resist subsequent allegations that surgery was inexpertly performed. On many occasions, operation notes are written by the surgical assistant. This is a practice which should be discontinued, since it is the surgeon alone who is fully able to appreciate pathological abnormalities and the manner in which they are addressed. Even then, the interpretation of that pathology can be inaccurate to the point where inappropriate procedures are undertaken. Surgeons will find bulging of a disc where an MRI scan has shown a substantial disc sequestration; a tight nerve root in the absence of any appreciable disc problem; and various other 'abnormalities' which do not equate with the preoperative assessment. This may be due to inadequate exposure or to inaccurate assessment of the disc level. It may also accompany inappropriate surgical treatment in the presence of normal MRI scans, in other words confirming an inappropriate decision to surgically explore the spine in the first place. Failure to find that which one expects to find should lead to a reappraisal of the patient in the operating theatre, both in terms of the level and side of the lesion as well as an extension of the incision to allow adequate exposure of the disc and nerve roots, coupled with appropriate haemostasis. All of these factors must be accurately reported in the operation notes.

Damage to the dura does occur at the hands of the most experienced spinal surgeon. It does not imply negligence. However, widespread dural damage, particularly if associated with nerve root damage, identified by postoperative MRI scanning or subsequent surgery, would be seen as an indication at least of a deficient surgical technique. Again, such intraoperative damage can be minimised by adequate exposure and an experienced operator. It should always be recorded in the operation notes.

Damage to the major vessels in the posterior abdominal wall has been a source of successful litigation against surgeons. It is understandably seen to result from a deficient surgical technique and is rarely defensible.

Operative removal of a prolapsed lumbar intervertebral disc does attract a number of postoperative complications which are not necessarily the result of negligence. However, a failure to appreciate those complications, and to adequately investigate and treat them, can lead to indefensible culpability.

Neurological deficit is commonplace after lumbar disc surgery. If minor, it resolves over a relatively short time-scale and need not necessarily be a cause for concern. However, should it persist or increase in severity and extent, a failure to expeditiously investigate any underlying cause could be indefensible. Such symptoms should attract urgent MRI scanning in order to exclude compressing haematoma formation or, indeed, retention of a sizeable disc fragment adjacent to the nerve root. There is substantial debate in surgical circles about whether or not to insert suction drains after disc excision. Protagonists correctly advance the view that the insertion of a drain reduces the chance of compressing haematoma formation, whilst antagonists prosecute the view that such a drain is a conduit for infection and for cerebrospinal fluid leakage as a consequence of minor, undiagnosed dural tears. Those surgeons who do not use drainage should be alert to the possibility of compressing haematoma formation as a cause of postoperative neurapraxia. Failure to expeditiously and adequately investigate postoperative neurapraxia, coupled with a failure to re-explore the surgical site where appropriate, may present an insurmountable hurdle to the defence of any allegation of negligence.

Deep venous thrombosis plagues any surgical procedure. In some respects, presenting symptoms can mimic postoperative root symptoms following lumbar disc surgery, particularly if the affected limb is that which was symptomatic before operation. An awareness of this overlap of symptoms will minimise the potential for subsequent allegations of inappropriate post-operative care.

Postoperative discitis, usually non-infective but occasionally due to bacterial infection, is a well-recognised complication of lumbar disc surgery. It is not an indication of negligence in the performance of the operation. However, it does attract severe and protracted postoperative back pain, with associated muscle spasm and, on occasions, sciatica. It will resolve, often without specific treatment although antibiotics may be advisable if investigations yield equivocal results. Once this condition has been diagnosed - a diagnosis which is nowadays relatively easy, given the availability of MR scans - it is wise, as with all complications, to fully discuss the problem with the patient in order to abort any suspicion of underlying substandard treatment. Effectively, not only is it important nowadays to counsel patients preoperatively in relation to potential complications of surgery, but also to fully inform them of such complications when they occur. In this way suspicion leading to allegations of negligence will be minimised.

Conclusion

Contrary to popular belief, the prolapsed lumbar intervertebral disc presents complex diagnostic problems requiring detailed clinical assessment followed by multi-disciplinary investigation. Surgical management should only be undertaken when clinical and radiological abnormalities are complementary. It should not be undertaken by inexperienced surgical practitioners. Furthermore, there are specific basic requirements of the surgeon in terms of operative technique and postoperative assessment if successful actions for medical negligence in this condition are to be reduced.

LEGAL COMMENTARY

M.A.M.S. Leigh

Few areas of medicine provoke such strong feelings amongst practitioners as the management of lower back pain. As David Markham makes clear, it is a common symptom which most of us have experienced from time to time. On 99% of occasions it will be appropriate for the GP or casualty officer to whom we present ourselves to advise us in reassuring terms. Even here it is interesting to note that fashions change, and where we used to be told to go away and rest, now we are told to get off our beds and walk, if not to seek out that traditional bugbear of the medical profession, the osteopath.

However, on 1% of occasions we will have a condition which will benefit from specialist investigation and treatment, and there is an esoteric cohort, perhaps a quarter of that 1%, where our condition constitutes an acute surgical emergency. The vigour with which we protest about our symptoms may be a function of our own stoicism rather than anything else, and it is only by carefully eliciting the history and the precise nature of our complaints that the GP will be able to distinguish those cases where there is an interference with bowel or bladder function or some other localising sign, that indicates that the cauda equina or lumbar cord is critically compressed.

Nobody complains about the 99% of cases which do not need surgical referral; in practice, few complain if referral is delayed where it is indicated if there is not an acute emergency. The GP or the casualty officer will only face litigation in respect of that proportion of the 0.25% of cases where an emergency referral was indicated and it did not happen. It is futile in the vast majority of cases for the doctor to attempt to refute such claims on the basis of memory. That the patient did not present with a localising sign or symptom is a negative fact which is not in itself intrinsically memorable, and doctors are rarely able to persuade judges that they remember such intrinsically banal features of unremarkable cases without a note. It is the negative feature of a case which demands a clinical note because it is less likely to be remembered. This is, of course, the opposite of the practice of doctors which by and large is to be more assiduous in recording positive features of cases; rarely does a GP record that he or she has tested for perineal sensation except in the rare case where it is in fact absent.

If the GP or other primary care attendant is most often accused of a sin of omission in relation to cases involving a prolapsed disc, the same is not true of surgical colleagues. Occasionally it is true; we see cases where the specialist is accused of delay in responding, but far more often the specialist is concerned with sins of commission and David Markham gives a good indication of the range of these. This is major surgery by any standards, and as a result a proportion of the patients will be victims of those complications which beset any other surgery.

To begin with there are the problems of assessment and diagnosis. There are numerous claims arising from the complications of investigations. If myelography is now less commonly used, it is also treated with far more suspicion than before. Discography and other investigations require patients to be counselled about the implications. Even MRI, the last invasive investigation, gives rise to complaints if it is not handled sensitively. Today the diagnosis can be made more clearly preoperatively than ever before. The images of nerve root compression and the nature of the causative factor can be seen on MRI with a clarity which was often not available even to the surgeon 20 years ago. Because these images will be available to the doctors' critics in the event of complication or other adverse outcome, the importance of accurate preoperative interpretation cannot be overstated. It is essential that the interpretation is documented and that any discussion (for example, with a neuroradiologist) which has led to a multi-disciplinary diagnosis is clearly documented. Rarely is this the case.

The aspirations of the surgeon for the patient even with this clear imaging should be modest. It is remarkable how commonly surgical removal of a lesion which is not followed by amelioration of symptoms is followed by litigation. It is vital that the communication between doctor and patient which forms the therapeutic alliance should be clearly recorded. If the doctor is only operating to avoid a deterioration in an already dysfunctional anatomy then that fact should be recorded. If there are risks, particularly of grave matters such as paraplegia or incontinence, then the discussion of these should be recorded. Where surgery is planned electively at an out-patient consultation, it is sensible to record the implications of the operation. A copy of any letter to the patient should go to the GP. I know of no legal obligation of this nature at the time of writing, but public expectations of communication, as of other aspects of surgery, are constantly rising. Inevitably when we are in pain, many patients will volunteer for any sort of surgery. It is this lack of stoicism, which makes us such enthusiastic volunteers in the presence of pain, which will make us similarly intolerant afterwards. Most surgeons approach spinal surgery recognising that the operation is a major event for them to perform and a potentially life-changing event for the patient to undergo. It is trite to say that the preoperative documentation should be appropriate to this sort of event.

Similarly, the quality of clinical notes made by surgeons is inadequate in the vast majority of cases in the courts. This is partly because the standard of clinical documentation which is required increases. Very rarely do surgeons describe with sufficient clarity and detail the precise nature of the surgical approach; all too often they wish to record that which interests them, which is usually the pathology for which they think they are operating. That which they are least enthusiastic about recording, which is the perioperative complication such as the torn dura, is recorded in least detail. Whereas a court will readily understand the emotional response which leads a surgeon to adopt this attitude, this does not mean to say that such a court will find for the doctor against the patient.

When complications are encountered it is all the more important to document events clearly and to enlist the appropriate specialist assistance. This may be medical, neurosurgical or microbiological. The surgeon who encounters complications in the management of major surgery of this nature has to ensure that the patient receives the appropriate specialist skill that he or she needs.

Surgeons must realise that spinal surgery is probably second only to obstetrics in its ability to generate ill-founded allegations. Come what may, there will be numerous children born tragically handicapped with cerebral palsy, and their parents will naturally seek to investigate whether there may have been an obstetric component to their causation. Similarly, many patients will come to spinal surgeons in extremes of discomfort and disability which are not remediable by surgical means. The quality of oral evidence on both sides is likely to be unimpressive to the court. The patient will have been in too much pain postoperatively to be able to describe the more subtle features of his or her condition, which are so important, with any degree of clarity. The doctor will usually be unable to give relevant evidence on his or her own behalf because the important features are negative and memory is fallible. If doctors are going to defend themselves successfully against ill-founded complaints, it must be on the basis of accurate clinical notes which are consistent with the objective results of the investigations which were carried out at the time.

II COMPRESSION OF THE CAUDA EQUINA BY LUMBAR PROLAPSED INTERVERTEBRAL DISC

John Garfield

Lumbar prolapsed intervertebral disc (LPID) is a very common condition which affects thousands, but which rarely causes neurological damage. Medical negligence actions usually arise over failure of duty of care (liability), and specifically the failure to diagnose neurological deficit at a potentially remediable stage. The more complex arguments (causation) which ensue are largely over the time at which neurological deficit could, or should, have been prevented by surgical intervention, had the diagnosis been made earlier.

The subject is important because the disability due to cauda equina damage is particularly distressing, as it may interfere with bladder, bowel and sexual function; it frequently occurs in relatively young adults; it is usually life-long; and quantum is high. A critical evaluation of the relevant anatomy and pathology, and of the neurosurgical literature on causation, is essential in assessing the merits of allegations in this field. The following aspects will be covered briefly.

(1) Anatomy and function of the cauda equina.
(2) The effects of compression of the cauda equina.
(3) Management of the compression and probable outcome.
(4) Evidence on outcome in the literature.

Anatomy and function of the cauda equina

The cauda equina – so named from its appearance which is reminiscent of a horse's tail – is formed by the descending lumbar and sacral nerve roots. The roots emerge above from the lower segments of the spinal cord, which ends at the level of the intervertebral disc between the first and second lumbar vertebrae.

The roots descend in the subarachnoid space which is contained within the dura and leave the theca and then the bony canal by passing out through foramina at the different levels of the lumbar spine and sacrum. There are five lumbar motor and sensory roots and five sacral roots on each side.

At the level of any intervertebral disc, all the roots still remaining within the theca will be those which will leave the spinal canal below that level. Thus, at the level of the L4/L5 disc, the roots L5 and S1–S5 will still be within the theca.

In order to reach their appropriate exit foramina, the roots must lie progressively more laterally (away from the midline) as they descend towards the level at which they will leave the spinal canal and theca. Throughout the length of the cauda equina, the roots which emerge at the lowermost levels (e.g. S2–S5) will have a more central position (i.e. nearer the midline) in the theca. Therefore any mass which compresses the cauda equina and which is placed in the midline, or extends across the whole width of the spinal canal (termed central or bilateral), will usually affect the lower roots of the cauda equina.

Disc prolapse is most common between L5 and the top of the body of the sacrum (lumbosacral disc or L5/S1), between L4 and L5, and less commonly between L3 and L4, and even less commonly between L2 and L3 and L1 and L2.

The main motor functions of the cauda equina are conveyed in the motor lumbar and first sacral nerve roots which supply the musculature of the lower limbs. The sensation of the lower limbs is largely subserved by the lumbar and first sacral sensory roots.

The complex functions of the bladder, bowel and external genitalia are largely subserved by the sacral roots below S1. The main functions of these roots are:

(1) Sensation of bladder and bowel, especially the rectum and anus; this includes the sensation of filling of the bladder.
(2) The control of the motor activity of bladder and bowel which includes initiation of evacuation of the bladder and bowel, as well as prevention of those evacuations when they are undesirable.
(3) Sexual functions which are required for potency and reproduction; this includes erections.
(4) Sensation of the skin in the perineum, perianal region and the medial areas of the buttocks.

Effects of compression of the cauda equina

A disc may protrude or extrude directly backwards (termed a central protrusion) into the spinal canal, acutely or subacutely. This is commonly with, but may be without, a preceding history of backache and/or unilateral lower limb pain. Because of the propensity for disc prolapse to occur at L5/S1 or L4/L5 levels, a central protrusion (extrusion) will affect particularly the lowermost lumbar roots, and especially the sacral roots. Therefore the 'classical' and specific symptoms and signs of such a central prolapse (extrusion) at those levels causing compression of the cauda equina are:

- Pain in the back radiating to *both* lower limbs.
- A sense of numbness in the buttocks, perineum and sometimes down the back of both thighs.
- Difficulty, leading to inability, to pass urine; initially there may be preservation of the sensation of the bladder filling and becoming distended. The sensation is then lost, and the bladder overflows (so-called overflow incontinence) due to the distention, and the failure of the mechanism which usually prevents the escape of urine (paralysis of the sphincter).
- Voluntary expression of urine by the bladder (action of the detrusor muscle) is also lost.
- Inability to achieve or to maintain an erection.

The *physical signs* include:

- Distention of the bladder.
- Reduced, or loss of, sensation in the areas described above, especially in the perineum.
- Absence of the ankle tendon reflexes (ankle jerks) which are subserved by L5 and S1.

It is not necessary for all of these signs to be present, and their degree may vary from case to case. As in all neurological disorders, the history is often more eloquent and important than the physical signs in arriving at a diagnosis. There may, or may not, be weakness in the lower limbs, particularly of plantar flexion and less so of dorsiflexion and eversion of the feet, depending upon the level and severity of the lesion.

Management of cauda equina compression and probable outcome

The objective is to relieve the compression of the cauda equina before irreversible damage and loss of function has occurred. The usual manoeuvre is laminectomy, which allows access to the spinal canal and removal of the protruded and extruded disc. The general principle is that decompression should be done as soon as there is any evidence of cauda equina compression. Confirmation of the pathology is radiological, by myelography with or without CT scan or by MRI. As with all neural structures, the longer and more severe the compression and the greater the neurological deficit, the less the prospect of any recovery of function following decompression. On this general principle, time is of the essence. Few surgeons would *not* advise urgent decompression in the hope of improving the outcome, and would not wish to deny any patient the chance of improvement, however small that chance might be.

The debate, which has led to prolonged arguments on causation, flows from the *uncertainties of probable outcome* in the individual patient. There are many good reasons for this debate, and for the expression of conflicting views. Some are factual; others rely upon the literature and upon a surgeon's own experience. The points leading to difficulties of assessment include:

(1) Uncertainty of the time of onset of the mechanical derangement (disc protrusion/extrusion).
(2) The speed at which the anatomical derangement progresses; for example, the size of the disc protrusion/extrusion, and the movement of any extruded disc material within the spinal canal, as well as the time actually required for the process of extrusion of disc material.
(3) The pre-existing shape and size of the spinal canal into which the disc protrudes/extrudes. The canal may be reduced in size by changes associated with other forms of degenerate disease (for example, degenerative lumbar spondylosis, and enlargement of interlaminar joints by a process similar to osteoarthritis). Also, the sagittal diameter of the canal may be constitutionally or congenitally reduced. Clearly the smaller the canal, the greater the risk of compression of the cauda equina.
(4) The time of onset of compression of the cauda equina sufficient to cause interference with the function of the nerve roots; this depends upon the interpretation, by the patient and by the doctors, of the symptoms and signs described above.
(5) The severity of that disturbance.
(6) The anatomical completeness of the decompression when it is finally achieved.
(7) The degree of continuing neurological deficit which is compatible with a 'normal/reasonable/socially acceptable' life. This is particularly relevant to bladder, bowel and sexual function. For example, patterns of micturition, especially frequency, normally vary from person to person, especially in women, without causing any more comment than having a 'weak bladder'. Even though more sophisticated urological investigations (e.g. urodynamics) may reveal a neurological disturbance of bladder function, a patient may still have 'socially acceptable' control of micturition.

Evidence on probable outcome contained in the literature

(1) All studies conclude that the correct attitude is to operate as soon as possible after the onset of the cauda equina syndrome, especially if there is loss of bladder function. A very reasonable point is that earlier operation will probably prevent a 'partial' lesion from becoming complete.

(2) So far the literature does not contain any evidence concerning operation within 6 or 12 hours of the onset of retention. Thus Shapiro (1993), reviewing 161 patients in five major reports, found only 24 patients operated on within 48 hours; 60% had surgery two to four weeks after the onset of retention.

Some studies (e.g. Kostuick, *et al.* 1986) 'did not establish a correlation between the severity or duration of either the symptoms or clinical findings and the extent of recovery of neurological and bladder function'; and further, '... no correlation between length of time between onset of symptoms and surgery and the extent of recovery'.

(3) Gleave and MacFarlane (1990) drew attention to the lack of evidence concerning very early surgery (i.e. 6 or 12 hours). That was the burden of their message concerning other papers, and their own material. Nevertheless, in their 20 group I patients (onset followed by retention within 48 hours), despite a mean delay of 3.3 days to surgery, results for urinary recovery were excellent (full control within six weeks) or good (recovery ultimately full but delayed) in 14 patients. For the 13 group II patients (relentlessly progressive history of sciatica ultimately culminating in bladder paralysis), excellent or good urinary recovery was achieved in 12 patients. Therefore, although Gleave and MacFarlane state that the timing of surgery appears to be relatively unimportant, that can only refer to the hypothetical 6, 12 or even 24 hour delay. Their own material does not support the statement, 'We believe that the die is cast at the time the prolapse occurs', although the prospect for recovery after an acute onset of cauda equina symptoms is worse than in the more chronic development of the syndrome. These conclusions can only be used in referring to patients with a mean delay to surgery following retention of 3.3 and 4.1 days. The numbers of patients who had 'fair' or 'poor' recovery are too small to allow any conclusions about delayed surgery (e.g. three fair, 2.9 days; two poor, 5.0 days). Gleave and MacFarlane continue to support the standard advice that urgent surgery for an incomplete cauda equina compression is essential as it may prevent complete paralysis (their reference to Jennett, 1956).

(4) Shapiro's (1993) material is small but valuable within that limitation. The key time in this paper is 48 hours: of the 14 patients, 13 had incontinence of urine or stool. Eleven developed all the symptoms of cauda equina syn-

drome within 24 hours; in 3 it developed over a 'number of weeks'. Overall all the seven patients who had surgery within 48 hours of the onset of incontinence (which was probably overflow incontinence due to retention with a paralysed bladder and probably with loss of bladder sensation) regained control of micturition. Of the six patients who had surgery more than 48 hours after the onset of retention, only two regained control.

(5) Nielsen *et al.* (1980) also reached similar conclusions about 'two days delay'.

(6) The literature also contains reference to better outcome for motor function in the lower limbs with surgery before, compared to after, 48 hours. Also, the persistence of impaired perineal sensation cannot be correlated with persistence of bladder symptoms.

Conclusions

The literature does *not* conflict with the traditional neurosurgical advice that, in the presence of a cauda equina syndrome due to compression of the cauda equina by a lumbar prolapsed disc (massive/central/extruded), urgent decompression is indicated. The only 'hard' evidence of the better results of urgent surgery relates to a delay of less than 48 hours compared to longer than 48 hours.

From the facts available, it is impossible to draw definitive (proven) conclusions about the efficacy of decompression after a delay of 6, 12 or even 24 hours. Nevertheless, on the basis of the '48-hour' figures, and the general principles of nerve damage and duration, it is reasonable to surmise that the earlier the decompression, the better the outcome.

References

Gleave, J.R.W. and MacFarlane, R. (1990) Prognosis for recovery of bladder function following lumbar central disc prolapse. *British Journal of Neurosurgery* **4**, 205–10.

Jennett, W.B. (1956) A study of 25 cases of compression of the cauda equina by prolapsed intervertebral disc. *Journal of Neurology, Neurosurgery and Psychiatry* **19**, 109–16.

Kostuik, J.P., Harrington, I., Alexander, D., Rand, W. and Evans, D. (1986) Cauda equina syndrome and lumbar disc herniation. *Journal of Bone and Joint Surgery* **68a**, 386–91.

Nielsen, B., de Nully, M., Schmidt, K. and Iversen, H.R. (1980) A urodynamic study of cauda equina syndrome to lumbar disc herniation. *Urology International* **35**, 167–70.

Shapiro, S. (1993) Cauda equina syndrome secondary to lumbar disc herniation. *Neurosurgery* **32**, 743–7.

Further reading

Hellstrom, P., Kortelainen, P. and Konnturi, M. (1986) Late urodynamic findings after surgery for cauda equina syndrome caused by a prolapsed lumbar intervertebral disc. *Journal of Urology* **135**, 308–21.
Young, M.A. (1994) Letter. *Neurosurgery* **34**, 199.

III DEGENERATIVE LUMBAR SPONDYLOSIS

John Garfield

Definitions, anatomical considerations and sources of confusion

Strictly speaking, spondylosis implies disease of joints or articulations between the skeletal structures of the spinal column. Inevitably the addition of 'degenerative' focuses attention upon the intervertebral discs, which are the most easily recognisable site of degenerative changes, changes which can be more correctly described as the normal process of ageing. Herein lies the origin of some of the confusion between the primary effects of lumbar intervertebral disc disease, especially 'prolapse', and those of the 'spondylosis' changes which may be quite distinct and separate from those associated with disc disease. As is discussed below, this confusion is one of the major causes of error in management, including surgical, which may result in litigation.

The anatomical or pathological changes of the 'spondylosis' element are well-known and can be summarised. The interlaminar or posterior synovial joints undergo osteoarthritic changes, which result in loss of the synovial membrane, overgrowth or hypertrophy of the joint surfaces and the processes which bear them, leading to enlargement of all aspects of these joints. As they lie postero-laterally, the anterior aspects of the joints form the postero-lateral boundaries of the intervertebral foramina, which in reality are at the lateral limits of the so-called lateral recesses of the spinal canal. Thus, enlargement of these joints will in itself narrow the intervertebral foramina and lateral recesses, and may compress their contents, namely the nerve roots lying within the dural sleeves and the accompanying radicular vessels. More medially, the compression can affect the whole width of the theca. If in addition to this compression from behind and laterally there is also narrowing of the intervertebral foramina from in front by osteophytes on the margins of the vertebral bodies, and by an element of disc protrusion, the effect of the spondylotic changes will be increased. Therefore it is essential that the relative parts played by the distinct but associated changes be clearly defined when planning management, especially surgical approach and objectives. The most serious error which can lead to cauda equina damage at surgery is to mistake spondylotic compression for compression by disc protrusion, and a relatively limited surgical access may preclude safe exposure of the disc and nerve roots, and will not achieve a therapeutic decompression. Other elements in compression, such as thickened ligamenta flava and the pre-existing sagittal diameter of the spinal canal, may also lead to surgical errors.

Degenerative lumbar *spondylolisthesis* is best regarded as an advanced stage of *spondylosis*, as distinct from congenital or pars interarticularis defects. The occurrence of changes in the interlaminar joints are usually severe, and although the malalignment of the posterior aspects of the adjacent vertebral bodies (usually L4/L5 or L5/S1) may be obvious, it is the interlaminar joint changes which are most commonly responsible for neural or vascular compression. Therefore, the surgical management does not differ significantly from spondylosis without spondylolisthesis, and the place of fusion is a matter of dispute, and of secondary importance to achieving a decompression of neural and vascular structures.

Symptomatology

In order of frequency of occurrence, the symptoms of degenerative lumbar spondylosis (DLS) can be listed as follows:

- Pain low in the back (lumbar and lumbosacral).
- Pain of a radicular distribution in the lower limbs, with or without other sensory symptoms and/or sensory loss.
- Weakness and wasting in the lower limbs and/or buttocks.
- Problems of micturition.
- Pain of a radicular distribution but of ischaemic origin (neurogenic claudication or intermittent ischaemia of the cauda equina).

The purpose of careful assessment of symptoms is first, to establish their severity and the degree of disability which those symptoms are causing; and second, to determine the elements of DLS which are responsible for the symptoms, and therefore whether those elements are likely to be remediable. Although radiology is essential before reaching final conclusions about pathology and remediability, major errors with ill-advised and inappropriate surgery may be the result of a failure to assess symptoms correctly *before* turning to radiology and imaging.

From the perspective of medical negligence actions, there are certain specific failures of assessment which merit particular attention. *Pain in the back*, the most common of all symptoms, may have different origins that may be present singly or in combinations. Thus, pain may arise in the posterior or interlaminar joints, from the intervertebral ligaments, the posterior divisions of the spinal nerves, and be associated with spasm of the erector spinae muscles. It is very doubtful whether any form of decompressive surgery will bring relief in these circumstances, despite the radiological appearances of severe and compressing DLS; but it may be difficult to deny a patient surgery once the radiological appearances have been made known to the surgeon and particularly to the patient. If decompressive surgery on this basis involves removal of the medial facets of interlaminar joints at several levels, it may lessen pain in the back, but at the expense of potential instability.

'*Neurogenic claudication*' (intermittent ischaemia of the conus medullaris and cauda equina) can usually be differentiated from 'intermittent claudication' (lower limb muscle ischaemia pain) by a careful analysis of the distribution of the pain. If this distribution conforms to a radicular pattern, this is consistent with neurogenic claudication, and if there is radiological demonstration of severe compression of intervertebral foramina bilaterally at several levels, surgery to decompress the radicular arteries as they pass through the foramina may be effective. But there are pitfalls: neurogenic claudication and intermittent claudication may exist together; absence of popliteal or foot pulses does not exclude neurogenic claudication as the main cause of a patient's disability; atheromatous narrowing of radicular arteries, and particularly the ostia of the lumbar arteries in the walls of the calcified aorta or common iliac arteries, may be far more significant than narrowing of the intervertebral foramina by enlarged interlaminar joints. For these and other reasons, the results of decompressive surgery may be unpredictable. Therefore, consent for operation must be fully informed before major surgery is embarked upon, especially as this is often in the elderly patients.

Radiology

Misinterpretation, correlation with anatomy and symptomatology

Since negligence actions can arise and come to trial many years after the events, the older and now often superseded radiological procedures may still be central in disputes on liability. MRI, when available, has rightly replaced myelography and CT scanning, but can bring its own problems in the management of patients, especially in decisions about surgery and the extent of surgery.

With the advent of CT there was rightly a move away from myelography, irrespective of the earlier change from Myodil to the safer, water-soluble contrast media. But it should not be forgotten that good-quality myelography, which demanded radiological and radiographic expertise, could demonstrate very accurately the configuration of the theca and nerve roots within the spinal canal and out to the intervertebral foramina bilaterally. Furthermore, with antero-posterior, lateral and oblique projections, the images corresponded to the views obtained at surgery, throughout the whole length of the lumbar canal down to the level of S1 or S2. It was therefore possible to compare accurately the degrees of distortion of nerve roots on each side at different levels. Finally, myelography would reveal unexpected tumours such as Schwannomas or ependymomas; cerebrospinal fluid (CSF) examination might also contribute to diagnosis.

CT scanning *without* intrathecal contrast, lacked many of these features, but did avoid the invasive aspects of myelography, including the adverse effects of lumbar puncture. The degree of disc protrusion was not always clear, an essential point in determining the type of surgery in DLS. Intrathecal tumours could be overlooked completely, the changes of DLS being so common that symptoms could be readily ascribed to that pathology to be followed by inappropriate surgery. Such errors have been the basis of negligence actions.

CT scanning *with* intrathecal contrast overcame many of the limitations of 'plain' CT scanning, but because the accent was upon the CT images, the full benefits of myelography were not sought, nor was sufficient weight accorded to information clearly available from the initial examination, which was often sufficient to proceed to surgery without further delay. The radiologist's choice of levels for the tomographic cuts might not always be appropriate. These are aspects of management which have had to be examined in allegations of unnecessary, inappropriate or delayed surgery.

MRI has none of the defects or complications of myelography or CT scanning, and provides a remarkable range of anatomical and pathological information unequalled by any previous method of investigation. With its increasing availability to patients before they reach a neurologist or neurosurgeon, and with the patients' awareness of the widespread changes of DLS which have been shown, the neurosurgeon may be persuaded to operate without careful enough assessment of the severity of symptoms, the degree of disability and the vertebral levels truly responsible for the disabling symptoms. Whereas in the past careful assessment was obligatory before embarking upon invasive procedures, the entirely non-invasive procedure has lessened that obligation. Indeed the day may have passed already when the surgeon can assess the patient clinically *before* being made fully aware of extensive pathology which may or may not be relevant to the patient's symptoms.

Surgery

The above description of potential errors in preoperative assessment and management have underlined the main source of errors which can jeopardise the success of surgery and increase its risks. Here attention is drawn to some surgical mishaps which have played a part in medical negligence actions:

- Damage to the cauda equina
- Tearing of the dura and arachnoid
- Multiple operations

Damage to the cauda equina

This has been associated with inadequate exposure as a consequence of the mistaken preoperative belief that the main pathology at one or two intervertebral levels was a disc protrusion; in reality, the essential pathology was DLS with compression by diseased interlaminar joints and a narrow spinal canal. In attempting an interlaminar approach to a supposed disc protrusion, with removal of only the ligamentum flavum, visualisation of the theca and nerve root can be very difficult. Excessive and 'blind' retraction, and bleeding from extradural veins which cannot be identified and safely coagulated, have resulted in extensive damage, not only to one or two nerve roots on the side of the exploration, but to the contents of the theca. So-called bilateral foraminotomy with lateral recess decompression may jeopardise nerve roots when done by inexperienced surgeons, especially if appropriate instruments are not used.

Tearing of the dura and arachnoid

This does not necessarily imply lack of care. Much depends upon technique when using bone nibblers and the attempted level of entry to the extradural space; if this is at the level of the enlarged interlaminar joints, there is a greater risk of tearing the dura, a risk increased by enlargement of the joints posteriorly towards the midline. Should a *postoperative pseudomeningocele* develop, with a valvular propulsion of CSF into a large cavity between the muscles and fascia, there may be considerable morbidity following an operation for which the original indication may be questioned. In these circumstances, details of operative technique can be scrutinised by a court, as well as the surgeon's awareness of the difficulties which can be encountered in such operations. The level of experience and expertise to be expected of a surgeon, and the appropriateness of delegation, may become the subject of further and prolonged legal argument.

Multiple operations

Surgery for DLS, even when clearly indicated and correctly performed, may not relieve the patient's symptoms. In many cases the cause of persisting symptoms may be very difficult to define, even after further investigation including CT, myelography or MRI. If there is radiological evidence of extradural fibrosis, further surgery is often not successful, or only temporarily successful. Second, and even more, subsequent operations are often very difficult, the normal anatomical structures and planes are disorganised, and therefore the risk of damage to the dura and cauda equina is greater. There is thus a greater onus on the surgeon to inform the patient of any risks beyond those normally associated with the first operation. Because of the difficulties, subsequent operations should only be done by, or delegated to, surgeons of considerable experience. Finally, surgeons should beware of being led into performing many operations on the same patient, simply because symptoms have not been relieved and the surgeon is reluctant to admit defeat. All these points have arisen in medical negligence actions.

Conclusion

Safe surgical technique should be a reflection of an awareness of the potential dangers and difficulties occasioned by the specific deformities of the spinal canal, lateral recesses, and intervertebral foramina. Every surgeon should develop his or her own techniques with these factors in mind. Equally important is the accurate assessment of radiological anatomy, and especially the differentiation between the elements of joint hypertrophy and disc protrusion. Failure to appreciate the potential difficulties in managing patients with DLS, which may also lead to inappropriate delegation of surgery, has been the main cause of medical negligence actions in this condition.

Further reading

Blau, J.N. and Logue, V. (1978) The natural history of intermittent claudication of the cauda equina. *Brain* **101**(1), 211–22.

Garfield, J. (1984) Uncertainties in degenerative lumbar spondylosis. In *Dilemmas in the Management of the Neurological Patient* (C. Warlow and J. Garfield, eds), pp. 188–95. Churchill Livingstone, Edinburgh.

Manucher, J.J. and Eldad, J.H. (1998) Long-term follow-up review of patients who underwent laminectomy for lumbar stenosis: a prospective study. *Journal of Neurosurgery* **89**, 1–7.

Roberts, G.M. (1978) Lumbar stenosis. The significance of the narrowed lumbar spinal canal and its diagnosis in spondylotic cauda equina syndrome. MD Thesis, University of London.

IV FRACTURES OF THE LUMBAR SPINE

David Markham

Fractures of the lumbar spine have always been relatively common, being associated with injuries at work, leisure activities and accidents in the home. The increase in high-velocity injuries associated with road traffic accidents, coupled with the increasing popularity of physically dangerous sporting activities, has further increased their incidence. Additionally, improvements in the resuscitation and emergency transfer of the seriously injured patient have led to a notable improvement in the survival of such patients. Lumbar fractures are not uncommonly a feature of such multiple injuries, increasing the demands upon medical staff for their expeditious, accurate diagnosis and subsequent treatment.

Whilst the management of these fractures does not attract a great deal of litigation, when there are complaints of negligent management they range from a failure to diagnose a minor fracture to inadequate investigation leading to the persistence of neurological deficit associated with inadequate or inappropriate surgical management.

Spondylolisthesis, although not often traumatic in origin, is included in this group since, despite rarely provoking accusations of negligence, the principles of its investigation and management mirror those of acute fractures.

Understandably, fractures of the spine cannot be categorised by the layman into those of minimal significance and fractures of a more serious nature. Indeed, the English language has for centuries contained allegorical reference to the perceived severity of such an injury such as 'back breaking work' and 'breaking the back' of a problem. It is for this reason that plaintiffs find it difficult to accept that the negligent failure to diagnose a minor fracture in the lumbar spine is of no long-term consequence.

Radiological diagnosis

Simple, stable fractures of the lumbar spine, either affecting the vertebral body or its appendages, defy recognition by casualty officers with disappointing regularity. However, even when they are missed, the patient is usually treated in appropriate fashion by the prescription of analgesia coupled with advice to rest. Effectively, this is the form of treatment which would have been used in the event of accurate diagnosis, since such patients are rarely admitted to hospital unless there are compelling social rather than medical reasons. It would appear, therefore, that failure to make such a diagnosis should not engender any long-term disability, leaving the plaintiff patient with little or nothing of a case to prosecute for negligence. However, patients who have been subjected to a delay in diagnosis of a minor fracture and who subsequently learn of their injury will attribute continuing back symptoms to the delay in diagnosis or believe, at least, that their symptoms have been protracted by the failure to appreciate the fracture. In other words, any backache persisting as a result of a minor fracture within the lumbar spine is, under the circumstances of delayed diagnosis, ascribed to the delay rather than the trauma. Whilst this would appear to be unfair, it is difficult to admit failure in such circumstances while at the same time denying any responsibility for causation of associated symptoms. Casualty officers and junior surgical staff should have a high index of suspicion where there has been a significant back injury, potentially sufficient to cause a fracture, particularly where there are physical signs which could explain such a lesion. There should be a good recall system in a situation where casualty X-rays are subsequently reported upon by a radiologist.

Before the advent of sophisticated imaging techniques, plain X-rays in various projections were used to provide a simple classification of lumbar spinal fractures into those which were stable, unstable or potentially unstable. This was a very inaccurate method of assessment but, as now, relied entirely upon the radiological techniques available at the time. More sophisticated imaging has revealed how inaccurate and potentially hazardous were our previous conceptions of such injuries. Whilst plain X-rays are still the vanguard of investigation, they should be followed by CT scans where there is clinical evidence of severe local injury or of neurological deficit, however minor. Such scans should also be undertaken if plain X-rays show any suspicion of facet injury, abnormality of the pedicles or disruption of the posterior wall of a fractured vertebral body. Additionally, angular kyphosis at a single level, particularly where it is associated with an apparent increase in the interspinous distance, should dictate more sophisticated investigation.

The widespread use of CT scans has markedly changed attitudes to the management of such fractures, particularly in the presence of neurological deficit. It was at one time believed that neurological deficit was largely a feature of the traumatic event, particularly where there was little in the way of gross vertebral disruption or dislocation. This led to the acceptance of such deficit and its conservative, expectant management. CT scans regularly reveal a degree of post-traumatic devastation impossible to conceive by the study of plain X-rays. Large fragments of bone, cancellous and therefore difficult to see on plain X-ray, disc material and haematoma are regularly seen within the vertebral canal, impinging upon neural elements. Such changes dictate emergency surgical management in the form of removal of the fragments, with decompression of the neural elements, followed by surgical stabilisation. It is clearly insufficient to assess a fracture by plain X-ray, to classify it as potentially unstable or to classify it as unstable and proceed to surgical stabilisation without a CT scan, since such restricted surgery will not include removal of fragments, will not decompress the neural elements and will result in permanent neurological deficit. Significant fractures of the lumbar spine should always be investigated by CT scan. Failure so to do would make subsequent allegations of inadequate investigation and treatment difficult to refute, particularly if later CT scans reveal stenosis at the level of the injury sufficient to account for any continuing neurological abnormalities.

Pathological fractures within the lumbar spine are commonplace, particularly in the more elderly patient. However, they should not necessarily be accepted as a consequence of osteoporosis, common as that condition may be. This is particularly true in men or in younger patients where osteoporosis would not feature as an epidemiologically appropriate condition. It is, therefore, insufficient to diagnose a pathological fracture, where the trauma is minimal, without considering further investigation such as a biochemical survey coupled, perhaps, with a bone scan or MRI scan. Successful allegations have been generated by inadequate investigation in such circumstances when later investigation has revealed more widespread disease such as myeloma or metastases. Whilst later discovery of serious pathology may not be considered by the defendant surgeon to have affected the plaintiff patient's life expectation, it is again difficult to persuade a court that earlier diagnosis and appropriate treatment would not have prolonged life expectation or, at least, improved the quality of life.

Haematobiochemical survey is neither time-consuming nor expensive. When used as an adjunct to the diagnosis of a pathological fracture, it may indicate whether or not further investigation is appropriate, while enabling the surgeon to indicate an awareness of potential associated pathology and a willingness to investigate its cause. This will markedly strengthen the defence against any potential allegations of inadequate assessment of the patient.

Spondylolisthesis can be associated with trauma but is more commonly found in relation to congenital defects in the pars interarticularis. It causes backache, can cause sciatica, but is frequently symptomless. Although it does not often engender complaints in medical negligence, it can be the source of allegations in relation to complications in its surgical management or in its implication relating to symptoms which are subsequently found not to arise therefrom. Backache should not, therefore, be necessarily ascribed to the finding of a spondylolisthesis on plain X-ray, even if such an X-ray is accompanied by oblique views revealing congenital abnormalities. If there is any doubt about the anatomical distribution of the patient's symptoms, especially if they are neurological, or if there are inconsistent neurological signs, an MRI scan is necessary. Such an investigation is, in any event, essential prior to any surgical stabilisation of this condition.

A notable case, successfully prosecuted by the patient, involved successful stabilisation of a lumbosacral spondylolisthesis with continuation of the symptoms leading to progressive deterioration. Various opinions were obtained before an eventual MRI scan revealed a tumour at the level of the conus medullaris. Causation arguments were unsuccessful in rebutting a substantial claim. Despite the widely held belief that dual pathology is rare, spondylolisthesis is a relatively common condition, may be symptomless and may occur in the presence of other pathology which would cause backache and neurological abnormalities.

Clinical diagnosis

It is difficult to excuse or successfully defend the failure of a medical practitioner to undertake and record in detail a clinical examination. This is particularly true of neurological examination in the presence of a fracture within the lumbar spine, however minor such a fracture may appear to be on plain X-ray. It is often such a neurological examination which dictates the further investigation and management of the patient. Nowhere is that more true than in the case of the severely injured patient, particularly where there has been a degree of head injury.

Differentiation between physical signs attributable to other injuries and those which may be associated with lumbar spinal injury can be difficult. However, careful local examination of the lumbar area, even in the unconscious patient, can lead to a suspicion of severe spinal injury, since such fractures are almost invariably associated with a degree of clinically appreciable bruising. If there is any suspicion on clinical grounds that lumbar spinal injury has occurred, plain X-rays are mandatory since, clearly, failure to appreciate an unstable fracture of the lumbar spine can lead to further neurological damage if, in the management of the patient's other injuries, inappropriate movement is utilised or allowed. The patient who suffers multiple injuries is subjected to variable tangential forces which cannot be analysed and which may easily have resulted in spinal injury. Even in accidents where the ergonomics of the accident are more easily identified, it is sadly the case that the lumbar spine escapes suspicion of injury. An example is in a fall from a height where there are severe painful fractures of the os calcis sufficient to clinically mask pain arising from a fractured lumbar spine.

Surgical management

This should be preceded by imaging of the spine in order to exclude remediable abnormalities within the vertebral canal. Thereafter, management takes the form of surgical stabilisation, with or without primary decompression, depending upon the scan findings. Allegations of negligence fall into two categories, failure to decompress the spine and failure of surgical technique.

Whilst matters concerning decompression of the spine have already been detailed, it should be said that decompression of the acutely fractured lumbar spine is a daunting procedure which should not be delegated to the inexperienced surgeon. It is an operation which is complicated by extensive soft tissue damage and by considerable haematoma and intraoperative bleeding. These factors demand experience on the part of the surgeon and meticulous attention to the search for disc and bone fragments which are, or may be, responsible for neurological compression.

There are numerous devices available and utilised for the stabilisation of the lumbar spine. These range from posterior fixation devices to techniques involving anterior and posterior stabilisation of the lumbar spine, coupled with bone grafting. Where anterior instrumentation or stabilisation is undertaken, particularly in male patients, adequate preoperative counselling should be given in relation to potential impotence complicating such surgery. The incidence of this complication is sufficiently high to make it a necessary component of preoperative counselling. It generates complaints in relation to lack of informed consent.

Posterior stabilisation of the lumbar spine can involve the insertion of interpedicular screws or the utilisation of laminar wires. Both have led to successful actions for negligence; pedicular screws when they breach the cortex of the pedicle and impinge upon the adjacent nerve root, a complication which can be avoided by the marriage of meticulous surgical technique with intraoperative radiological monitoring. Where there is postoperative neurological deficit in the presence of an X-ray showing a malpositioned interpedicular screw, allegations of negligence are difficult to refute. The same can be said of sub-laminar wires which breach the theca, leading to traumatic meningoceles or more serious neurological entrapment.

Pseudoarthrosis, particularly occurring in the stabilisation of spondylolisthesis, is an acknowledged complication of the procedure. It does not imply negligence and can be refuted, provided that the instrumentation can be shown to be adequate and properly inserted, and provided that preoperative warnings in relation to this complication have been given.

Conclusion

Fractures of the lumbar spine are commonplace, are not always as simple as they would appear to be on plain X-ray and require detailed investigation. They may deflect the clinician from diagnosis of a more serious and sinister pathology which, in itself, requires specific evaluation. Surgical stabilisation cannot be guaranteed and should be preceded by detailed counselling in relation to potential permanent disabling symptoms. Simple fractures carry psychological connotations which should be eliminated by prompt diagnosis and reassurance, in order that future concerns can be avoided in advance of mild, chronic low back symptoms, which would otherwise be ascribed to any delay in their diagnosis.

Chapter 8

The Thoracic Spine

David Markham and John Garfield

I SCOLIOSIS

David Markham

The management of scoliosis – curvature of the spine – has taxed the ingenuity and inventiveness of orthopaedic surgeons since the very inception of orthopaedic surgery, the specialty deriving its name from the recognition of the need to treat this condition. Whilst great progress has been made in treatment, this has been at the expense of increasing litigation against those surgeons who supervise and operate upon scoliotic patients. So time-consuming and exacting is such work that a relatively small number of surgeons dedicate their professional life to this aspect of surgery. This, in turn, leads to a somewhat introspective view of acceptable complications in this sphere of medicine, raising the philosophical argument as to whether or not general principles should be used in assessing culpability, or whether practitioners of their art should be judged by their peers and, by definition, their broader-based view of acceptable postoperative complications.

These issues directly affect considerations of alleged medical negligence, particularly in relation to the complexity of this type of surgery which necessarily dictates a detailed and comprehensive discussion of potential complications between the surgeon and patient. Given that in the majority of cases the patient is a minor, such discussions need to be undertaken in a 'family forum' in order to ensure that adequate informed consent is received prior to surgery.

Whilst this is not the place for discussion of the aetiology of scoliosis, it is, perhaps, worthwhile outlining the fact that this covers a significant spectrum of disease, from tuberculosis through poliomyelitis and other neuropathies to congenital anomalies of vertebral bodies, to the so-called idiopathic scoliosis – a condition which has, as yet, defied accurate understanding. Since poliomyelitis and Pott's disease are now far less common, the majority of corrective procedures are carried out for spinal anomalies and idiopathic scoliosis.

There is a predominance of girls among those suffering from this condition. It tends to affect young people and to become a distressing disfigurement in adolescence.

Clinical management

Often appearing in early childhood, scoliotic deformity may not necessarily be progressive, although the more aggressive forms of the disease do increase in severity with growth. Early management is often difficult, in that it is designed to conservatively resist progressive deformity until such time as any perceived surgical procedure can be safely undertaken without stabilisation, in itself producing specific iatrogenic complications. It is generally accepted that surgical stabilisation is inappropriate until adolescence. Conservative clinical management in the early stages of the disease ranges from repeated clinical monitoring, with frequent radiological review, to external splintage in its various forms.

Actions in medical negligence are rarely, if ever, associated with this phase of management.

Radiological assessment

The very nature of scoliosis, producing three-dimensional deformity of the spinal axis, often over a significant segment of the spine, is a challenge to radiographers and radiologists. The radiographer must be skilled at producing accurate radiographs which, wherever possible, should be identical with previous X-rays. Therefore, the projections should be reproductions so that accurate measurements can be undertaken in order to assess any progression in the curvature over any given time-scale. This is a daunting task, requiring considerable experience and expertise.

Imaging techniques have been of some assistance in the assessment of progressive scoliotic deformity. However, the disease again is such as to markedly complicate the production of diagnostic images as well as to challenge the radiologist in his or her interpretation. Myelography has to a certain extent been superseded by computerised tomography (CT) and magnetic resonance imaging (MRI) scans. However, the interpretation of the images is exceedingly difficult, particularly in relation to whether or not the deformity is causing, or may cause, compromise of the spinal cord at the level of maximum curvature. Again, radiologists involved in this sphere require considerable expertise in the interpretation of X-rays and images obtained in this condition. Close collaboration between the radiologist and clinician is, perhaps, more essential in this condition than many others.

Indications for surgery

As in most conditions where surgery is a treatment option, there has always been debate about the indications for operative correction and stabilisation of the scoliotic spine. This is entirely appropriate given the complexity of the condition and the potential for improvement, with or without complication, in this distressing condition.

The majority of scoliotics are young girls. Cosmetic considerations are, therefore, often paramount in discussions as to whether or not surgical correction of the deformity is appropriate. However, where serious complications do follow surgery, the preoperative mobility of the patient provides a poignant reminder of the need to give careful consideration to such major surgery as a cosmetic exercise.

Decisions in relation to surgery are better defined where there is neurological deficit or where it can be shown that there is a potential for such problems in the absence of corrective procedures. Again, the difficulties experienced in producing images which can be accurately interpreted leads to dispute in medical negligence actions, where radiologists advising the adversaries may apply widely differing interpretations of particular images. Such situations do not develop where there are clinical signs of progressive neurological deficit.

Cardiopulmonary compromise has historically been an indication for correction of the scoliotic spine. However, this remains a controversial issue, some clinicians believing that there is a long-term improvement in pulmonary function following correction, while others maintain that such improvement is so small as to be negligible when compared to the extensive nature of corrective surgery.

It is not difficult to appreciate that the relatives of a scoliotic child are understandably anxious to obtain as much cosmetic improvement as possible. This makes it dangerously easy for a surgeon to advocate surgery. Indeed, it is often easier to accept a need for surgery than to resist pressures for surgical correction in inappropriate situations.

Preoperative counselling

It is difficult to envisage any other area of surgery wherein detailed and repeated preoperative counselling is an essential adjunct to operative treatment. The indication for surgical correction, the manner by which the correction is to be achieved and, more importantly, details of postsurgical complications must be discussed at length in a forum containing all interested parties. The indications for surgery are often accepted without demur by relatives who are anxious to see an improvement in the patient's cosmetic disfigurement. However, their understandable desire to accept, and in some cases demand, surgery should not distract the surgeon from giving a detailed account of the reasons for operation, at the same time recording those indications in the notes.

It is in the distressing area of serious postoperative complications that surgeons have been known to be disingenuous to a degree sufficient to enable the patient to successfully plead lack of informed consent on the basis that the severity of the complication was not spelt out to him or her in terms before he or she agreed to surgery. It is insufficient for a surgeon to use bland terms such as 'weakness of the legs' to describe frank paralysis. There is understandable reluctance on the part of some surgeons to spell out in accurate detail to a teenage girl and her parents that a possible complication of operative correction of scoliosis is paraplegia. However, oblique terms used to describe that condition enable a plaintiff to successfully plead that the terms used were so misleading as to deliberately misrepresent the severity of that potential complication. Well-intentioned, experienced, compassionate and caring surgeons have in the past been unsuccessful in defending postoperative paraplegia through failure to accurately express the risk of postoperative paralysis. It is remarkably easy for a paraplegic person to persuade a judge that, had paralysis been expressed in terms as a complication of surgery, he or she would never have agreed to the operation!

In essence, therefore, preoperative counselling should be detailed, undertaken in simple terms, be recorded and accompanied by a follow-up session, wherein patients and relatives can avail themselves of additional advice before assuring the surgeon that they fully understand the complexity of the procedure and its potential complications. Only in this way can a surgeon minimise the risk of being found culpable because of a lack of preoperative informed consent, by leaving the plaintiff patient with the weak allegation of '*res ipsa loquitur*'.

Surgical treatment

Whilst there are many different forms of instrumentation available to correct and stabilise scoliotic deformity, the complications which they engender are common to most of them. Surgical approaches to the scoliotic spine are essentially thoracoabdominal or posterior.

The transthoracic or thoracoabdominal approaches do attract the hazard of potential non-negligent damage to the often anomalous blood supply to the spinal cord in the dorsal region.

Posterior instrumentation, as in transthoracic approaches, can be complicated by paraplegia. Indeed, this complication is by far the greatest cause of medical negligence actions associated with scoliosis. There are a number of potential causes, including damage to the anomalous thoracic blood supply, postoperative haematoma formation, dislodgement of bone graft material into the vertebral canal and excessive distraction caused by over-correction of the deformity. These factors are not necessarily associated with negligent technique, provided that it can subsequently be demonstrated that appropriate care, monitoring and, where necessary, investigation coupled with re-exploration are undertaken. In other words, the complication does not often infer negligence, but failure to recognise at an early stage that such a situation is developing, coupled with failure to expeditiously address the problem, can be difficult to defend.

The electrophysiological monitoring of the spinal cord is routinely utilised by many scoliosis surgeons. It represents one method of highlighting at an early stage the development of abnormal spinal cord function. Utilised during surgery, it forms an invaluable adjunct to other clinical assessments which may herald potential complications at a time when they can be reversed or, at least, addressed. Failure to employ this form of intraoperative assessment can represent a significant weakness to the overall defensibility of a surgeon faced with a negligence action because of postoperative paraplegia.

The 'wake-up test', where the level of anaesthesia is altered during surgery in order to enable the patient to undertake lower limb movements on command, remains an area of controversy in scoliosis surgery. Its supporters consider the test to be appropriate, whilst its detractors feel that it is an unscientific and flawed method of assessing spinal cord function during surgery. Failure to utilise the wake-up test is an allegation frequently made by plaintiffs. Taken in isolation, it is probably insufficient to prove negligence.

It is difficult to defend a surgeon who procrastinates in the investigation of postoperative paraplegia. Patients having undergone major corrective surgery for scoliosis are necessarily nursed in intensive care situations. They are, as should be the case, regularly monitored, not only in terms of their cardiovascular and pulmonary function but also in relation to their neurological state. Failure to appreciate any developing neurological deficit and to expeditiously address potential problems makes a defence difficult.

Investigation of paraplegia should include early plain X-rays coupled, wherever possible, with appropriate CT scans. MRI scans cannot, of course, be employed because of the metallic internal fixation devices. If these investigations reveal a surgically remedial problem such as haematoma or displaced bone fragments, urgent surgical removal of those compressive agents allows the patient a chance of recovery, even though they may not necessarily prove to be the underlying cause of the paraplegia. Similarly, in the presence of apparently normal X-rays, the surgeon is faced with a decision as to whether or not the patient should be returned to the operating theatre for release of the distraction, with or without removal of the instrumentation. Such decisions are exceedingly difficult in the emergency situation. However, failure to address potential problems and re-explore the operative area at an early stage can leave the surgeon open to justifiable criticism, even though the exact cause of the paralysis may not be known. Essentially, indolence in the presence of post-operative paraplegia can be perceived to have denied the paraplegic patient a chance of improvement.

Conclusion

Surgery for scoliotic deformity of the spine is a highly skilled, high-risk branch of surgery which, of necessity, attracts a greater level of postoperative complications than other forms of spinal surgery, ranging from irritating discomfort to total paraplegia. In many cases these complications occur in young people who consequently require a high level of personal care for the remainder of their lives. This markedly inflates the monetary considerations in cases which are considered to be indefensible or which are successfully prosecuted at trial. Detailed preoperative counselling, using simple and direct terminology, coupled with meticulous attention to intraoperative detail and postoperative investigation are mandatory if litigation in this field is to be satisfactorily controlled.

II THORACIC INTERVERTEBRAL DISC PROTRUSION

John Garfield

It is fortunate that thoracic prolapsed intervertebral disc (TPID) is relatively rare because the management of patients with this condition is difficult, and surgery may be dangerous, especially if the approach to the lesion is inappropriate. In the neurosurgical literature, these dangers are recorded very carefully, as are the subsequent evolution of surgical approaches to lessen the risks.

The clinical presentation of TPID may lead to errors in diagnosis, especially when the clinical picture mimics that caused by a thoracic spinal tumour. Confusion may be compounded by misinterpretation of the radiology; this was especially the case in the past when the surgeon had to rely on myelography. The advent of CT scanning, and even more so MRI, has made diagnostic errors largely unacceptable.

The anatomical background to the sinister reputation of earlier surgical methods can be summarised as follows:

(1) The thoracic spinal canal is narrow and there is little 'free space' surrounding the spinal cord. This is in contrast to the lumbar spinal canal

where there is a copious subdural and subarachnoid space in which lies the cauda equina and, at L1–L2, the lower end of the spinal cord (conus medullaris).

(2) The compressing lesion lies *in front of* the spinal cord. Therefore any approach to what may be a very hard, often calcified mass will jeopardise the spinal cord unless the approach is, at least to a large extent, by an anterior or antero-lateral route. A posterior approach is also unlikely to relieve the compression of the spinal cord.

(3) Compression of the thoracic spinal cord, especially from in front, will easily compromise the blood supply of the spinal cord. This depends upon the important anterior spinal artery, which is fed in a variable and often inadequate fashion by arteries at different levels, some being more substantial than others. A spinal cord which is already suffering from a degree of ischaemia will be particularly vulnerable to ill-advised manoeuvres in attempting to remove a TPID.

The main issues in medical negligence actions related to TPID have been:

(1) Surgical approach and surgical expertise.
(2) Consent for operation.
(3) Preoperative uncertainties of diagnosis and delay in diagnosis.

Of these issues, it is the surgical approach which has caused the greatest difficulty.

Surgical approach

The traditional approach to lesions compressing the thoracic spinal cord was posteriorly by laminectomy. With TPID this was known to carry a considerable risk of increasing the neurological deficit to the extent of causing paraplegia. Therefore, alternative approaches have been developed, the main objective being to approach the disc protrusion and the disc space from in front, or at least from the side. This avoids any retraction or displacement of the spinal cord, which was almost inevitable in trying to expose and then remove the disc protrusion by any posterior approach.

The 'safer' surgical approaches which have been described include:

- Costotransversectomy and modified costotransversectomy.
- Transpedicular and transfacet approaches, which are essentially postero-lateral.
- Lateral extracavitary approach.

- Transthoracic approaches which may be extrapleural or transpleural (thoracotomy).

(For surgical details of these different approaches see Russell, 1992.)

It is recognised that there are risks of deterioration in spinal cord function with all these approaches. Nevertheless, there is strong evidence that overall these alternative approaches carry significantly lower risks than the older posterior approach by laminectomy. Therefore, in a number of medical negligence actions in which the surgeon was aware of the diagnosis, it has been very difficult to defend the older or more traditional approach.

More equivocal have been the medical negligence actions in which the surgeon was uncertain of the diagnosis, and there was a distinct possibility that an intradural spinal tumour was present. If the latter proved to be the case, laminectomy with longitudinal opening of the dura provides the simplest and safest access to the lesion. The alternative approaches, in these circumstances, would put the surgeon at a grave disadvantage. Such difficulties have arisen when, for whatever reason, the more sophisticated investigations such as CT scanning and especially MRI were not available. But that radiological deficiency may in itself prove to be unacceptable, especially in a regional neurosurgical service.

An additional issue in medical negligence actions has been the expertise and experience of the surgeon. As TPID is a rare condition, it is impossible for every neurosurgeon to have sufficient experience of approaches other than laminectomy. This situation will become more common with increasing specialisation within neurosurgery, and the development of spinal neurosurgery as a recognised specialty. In a medical negligence action concerning a patient who might have benefited from urgent surgery, a neurosurgeon with expertise in one of the alternative approaches was not available. The causation issue then included the degree to which the neurological deficit might have been avoided had an approach other than laminectomy been used.

Consent for operation

In general, TPID is not a surgical emergency; the most common type of spinal cord disturbance is of gradual onset and slow progression. If radiological investigations, for example by MRI, have been adequate, there is rarely any doubt over the preoperative diagnosis. In a medical negligence action it has been alleged that adequate warning of the risks of surgery was not given, and that had it been given the patient would have declined surgery. Such an issue should not arise if the surgeon is conversant with the surgery that is appropriate, and its risks. If liability is accepted, then the causation argument will centre upon the natural history of the condition, and the likely deterioration once a cord disturbance (myelopathy) is established.

Errors of diagnosis

These have occurred when the cord lesion has been acute in contrast to the more common gradual presentation. The diagnosis and surgical decision was made on the basis of the myelography. The difficulty has been to justify the failure to obtain at least CT, or ideally MRI, which would have indicated the correct diagnosis; the appropriate operation would have followed.

Conclusion

TPID is a rare condition. Medical negligence actions have largely arisen in connection with the surgical approaches. Improved radiology, e.g. MRI, and specialisation within neurosurgery will make it increasingly difficult to refute allegations of ill-advised surgical approaches, and errors of preoperative diagnosis. The corollary of specialisation is that neurosurgical departments accepting acute admissions must ensure that appropriate surgical expertise is always available in this field.

References

Hulme, A. (1960) The surgical approach to thoracic intervertebral disc protrusions. *Journal of Neurology, Neurosurgery and Psychiatry* **23**, 133–7.

Logue, V. (1952) Thoracic intervertebral disc prolapse with spinal cord compression. *Journal of Neurology, Neurosurgery and Psychiatry* **15**, 227–41.

Russell, T. (1992) Thoracic intervertebral disc protrusion. In *Surgery of the Spine* (G. Findlay and R. Owen, eds), pp. 813–20. Blackwell Science, Oxford.

Stillerman, C.B., Chen, P.C., Couldwell, W.T., Zhang, W. and Weiss, M.H. (1998) Experience in the surgical management of 82 symptomatic herniated thoracic discs and review of the literature. *Journal of Neurosurgery* **88**, 623–33.

Chapter 9

Spinal Tumours and Infection

C.J. Earl and John Garfield

I MEDICAL ASPECTS

C.J. Earl

Spinal cord function may be affected by tumours in the spinal canal which compress the cord (extrinsic tumours), or as the result of the growth of tumours within the substance of the spinal cord itself (intrinsic tumours). Extrinsic tumours are much more common, and timely diagnosis and prompt surgical treatment will often result in a complete cure. Late diagnosis may cause irreparable damage to the cord and serious persisting disability, which may lead to allegations of negligence if the delay is regarded as unjustifiable. Positive features suggesting spinal compression are pain and tenderness in the spine, that is in the neck or the back, and the presence of associated root pain. The characteristic clinical picture of spinal cord dysfunction in patients with spinal tumour of either sort is a progressive loss of motor and sensory function in the upper and lower limbs, the exact clinical picture depending on the level of the tumour. Disturbances of sphincter function will be present sooner or later.

The usual reason for a delayed diagnosis is that the signs of spinal cord disease are attributed to some other intrinsic disease of the cord. In the past, multiple sclerosis has been the commonest diagnosis made in error in cases of spinal tumour. Less often, some form of 'degenerative' spinal cord disease, such as motor neurone disease, may be thought to be responsible for the clinical picture.

Multiple sclerosis

The diagnosis of multiple sclerosis is often relatively easy. Most cases present the classical features, often summarised as a clinical picture which can be interpreted only by the occurrence of neurological lesions that are 'disseminated' in space and time. Unfortunately, there are patients with proven multiple sclerosis who present with a progressive, unremitting and localised neurological disorder. Once the diagnosis of this progressive form of multiple sclerosis has been made, it is very easy for this diagnosis to remain fixed in the mind of the physician. Fortunately this diagnostic error is much less common since the introduction of magnetic resonance imaging (MRI) which in a patient with multiple sclerosis will almost always reveal evidence of lesions in the brain which may have caused no detectable clinical abnormalities.

Thus, in patients with increasing signs of progressive spinal cord disease, the presence of a tumour or other compressing lesion must be excluded absolutely before the diagnosis of multiple sclerosis is accepted. An erroneous diagnosis of progressive multiple sclerosis affecting the spinal cord could not be defended successfully where appropriate steps had not been taken, by either scanning techniques or myelography, to rule out spinal cord compression. In the past, the fear of possible harmful effects of myelography in patients with multiple sclerosis increased the difficulties of management. Now that non-invasive MRI is available that may reveal positive evidence of multiple sclerosis or of spinal cord compression, the decision about investigations is no longer a difficult one. There should be no hesitation in requesting this investigation when there is a history of progressive impairment of spinal cord function.

There are other conditions whose remitting clinical course resembling that seen in multiple sclerosis may sometimes lead to an erroneous diagnosis. Spinal vascular malformations, for example, may give rise to recurrent episodes of impairment of spinal cord function. Meningiomas in the spinal canal (or in the cranial cavity) may increase in size in pregnancy and cause symptoms which may clear up spontaneously after delivery. A mistaken belief that pregnancy causes a relapse in multiple sclerosis may easily lead to an erroneous diagnosis of this disease. Spinal meningiomas may also cause a clinical picture with 'remissions and relapses' from haemorrhage which may recur spontaneously in vascular tumours and produce transient symptoms which might well give rise to an action for medical negligence, if the true diagnosis is seriously delayed. The use of modern non-invasive imaging techniques should make errors of this sort very uncommon.

Combinations of physical signs simulating multiple sclerosis

The presence of a compressive lesion, usually a meningioma, at the level of the foramen magnum, with involvement of the uppermost segments of the spinal cord and of structures in the posterior fossa, may produce the clinical picture with a combination of a spinal cord disorder and ataxia, or other signs referrable to disturbance of function of structures in the posterior fossa. This combination may be misinterpreted as indicating the existence of more than one lesion in the nervous system, when in fact a single large tumour spreading above and below the foramen magnum has caused this pattern of abnormal physical signs. Pallor of one or both optic discs may be interpreted as clinical evidence of previous and optic neuritis, and when spinal cord signs are present such disc pallor may easily but wrongly be accepted as confirmatory evidence that multiple sclerosis is the cause of the spinal cord disease. There are many other causes of disc pallor and, if there is any doubt at all, further advice should be sought and investigations carried out. From the neurological point of view, a pale optic disc that is the result of optic neuritis will almost always be associated with an increase in the latency of the visual evoked cortical potential.

The neurologist's ability to establish a firm diagnosis in cases of this type has been made much easier in recent years by the development of scanning techniques. Magnetic resonance (MR) scanning has proved particularly useful: not only will it demonstrate and localise abnormalities in the spinal cord clearly, but it will often give an indication of pathology. As already stated, in patients with multiple sclerosis it will almost always show multiple abnormal areas in the white matter of the nervous system that are virtually diagnostic. It should be stressed that the interpretation of images produced by any recently introduced techniques is not always straightforward; where such techniques are used, reliance should be placed only on opinions provided by radiologists with appropriate training and experience.

II SURGICAL ASPECTS

John Garfield

The general issues concerning spinal cord and cauda equina compression are described in Chapter 2. Meningitis, the most common remediable infection of the nervous system, is covered in Chapter 10. This section deals with the surgical problems which have arisen in medical negligence actions, where the pathology has been:

- Intraspinal neoplasm
- Tuberculosis
- Spinal extradural abscess.

The main issues in medical negligence actions in these conditions have been:

- Delay in diagnosis
- Inadequate or misdirected radiology
- Neurosurgical technique and instrumentation

- Consent for operation
- The natural history and operability of intramedullary tumours
- General medical assessment
- Neurological deficit related to delay in diagnosis.

Spinal tumours

The most common spinal tumour in neurosurgical practice is the extradural spinal metastasis. It has rarely been the source of a medical negligence action. This is probably because the overall prognosis and life expectancy is usually poor, and any neurological damage following a breach of duty of care is relatively brief. Only with the more indolent and treatable neoplasms, such as prostatic carcinoma or lymphoma, has delay in diagnosis and treatment been the cause of a medical negligence action.

Benign extramedullary tumours, despite their rarity, have been the basis of medical negligence actions. Schwannomas and meningiomas, because of their slow growth, may produce a progressive neurological deficit so gradually, and even intermittently, that the diagnosis may be overlooked and delayed for many years. The erroneous diagnosis of multiple sclerosis in these circumstances has proved difficult to defend. A delay in diagnosis has also occurred when the clinician's and radiologist's attention has been focused upon obvious and severe degenerative changes in the lumbar region, while the evidence of a spinal tumour at the upper limit of myelography was completely overlooked.

Example

> An elderly woman, with a year's history of pain in the thigh and sacroiliac region and numbness over the shin and the forefoot following a fall, had absent ankle jerks, and radiographs showed mild degenerative changes at the L4–L5 and L5–S1 levels. Within about eight months there were definite motor and sensory abnormalities, ascribed to the degenerative changes. Lumbar myelography taken up to the level of T9 showed multiple-level narrowing of the spinal canal. Lumbar laminectomy and discectomy improved the symptoms and also the neurological deficit. Within three months the patient developed a progressive, almost complete paraplegia with a sensory level at T10; myelography then showed a complete block at T3 and at operation a meningioma was removed, resulting in a partial recovery. The liability issues involved the clinical diagnosis, the extent of myelography and the severity of the lumbar abnormalities shown prior to the first operation. The causation issue was the probable outcome had the thoracic meningioma been shown earlier by more extensive myelography.

During the time that a tumour has been allowed to continue to enlarge, it may become adherent to the spinal cord which becomes increasingly compressed, so that the risks of surgery are increased. These are points which arise in legal arguments on causation, in addition to those on liability.

Before advances in surgical technique for the removal or partial removal of *intramedullary spinal tumours*, it could be argued that earlier diagnosis would not have resulted in a more favourable outcome, because whenever the diagnosis had been made the tumour would have been considered inoperable; and attempted removal would probably have resulted in a severe neurological deficit. In those circumstances, even if liability for delay in diagnosis was admitted, there could be a strong defence on causation.

Example

The spinal radiographs of a 30-year-old man with a three-year history of lumbar back pain radiating to the buttocks and lower limbs showed a mild L5–S1 spondylolithesis (grade 1) to which his symptoms were ascribed. When further neurological symptoms developed with loss of one ankle jerk, traction was prescribed. A computerised tomography (CT) scan did not show a lesion, a myelogram was considered to be technically unsuccessful, and the diagnosis remained one of instability and a facet joint disorder; discography was recommended and a spinal fusion planned. Eventually only partial removal of an ependymoma involving the conus medullaris and the cauda equina was possible.

This illustrates the dangers of accepting a radiological diagnosis in the face of progressive clinical changes; the fallibility of CT scanning for spinal tumours; and the dangers of not repeating technically unsatisfactory investigations. Causation arguments centred upon the time at which the tumour would still have been operable, and the likely outcome.

Improved surgical techniques, such as the use of the operating microscope, the ultrasonic aspirator and possibly the laser have made removal of intramedullary tumours, especially when small, more feasible and relatively safer, thereby weakening defensive arguments on causation. These advances in this specialised surgical field place increasing responsibility upon the general practitioner (GP), general physician and neurologist to heed relevant symptoms and signs and to initiate appropriate referral and investigation. The realities of litigation are such that without any sustainable defence on causation, it may be more difficult to sustain a defence on liability, even though it may be argued that such lesions are very rarely seen by practitioners. Conversely, if a defence on liability fails, a defence on causation becomes that much more difficult to sustain.

These and other advances in surgical technique have been the subject of arguments regarding surgical liability in cases where removal of tumours has been followed by severe neurological deficit, including paraplegia and quadriplegia. If the surgeon did not use, or there was not available, the operating microscope and the ultrasonic aspirator or laser, some experts would consider that he or she had not provided an acceptable standard of care.

Example

A 34-year-old man with a two-year history of a progressive neurological deficit was shown radiologically to have a diffuse expansion of the cervical spinal cord. The extent to which there was explanation by a senior specialist of the proposed operation and of its risks remained uncertain. The signed consent form was for cervical laminectomy. At operation, an intramedullary tumour, which was a partially cystic astrocytoma, was found and some part of it removed. Postoperatively the neurological deficit was greater. The liability and causation issues were complex, and were closely interrelated. They included: informed consent for operation and explanation of the risks of surgery; surgical aspects of the length of the surgical exposure, the use of the operating microscope and other instrumentation; the natural history of the tumour; and the prognosis had the surgical technique been different.

Litigation may follow very many years after the events occurred. At the time the treatment was undertaken, either the current technology was not available, or only a minority of surgeons were using it; and the benefits had been neither established nor published. Therefore, the courts should take notice of the age of experts and their surgical experience and practice at the time that the events occurred. There has been a tendency in some medical negligence actions for reliability to be placed upon experts who do not have any personal experience of the conditions and technology available at the time that a particular operation was performed. The curriculum vitae and the age of such experts may have to be examined critically in court.

Issues of *informed consent for operation* have been of considerable importance in cases of severe neurological deficit following removal of spinal tumours, and particularly intramedullary tumours. The preoperative assessment of risks of increased or profound deficit may be difficult, and figures vary from one surgeon to another, and from one publication to another. In the English jurisdiction, recent judgments have indicated that a surgeon is not compelled to warn a patient of any specified list of complications which may follow an operation, but that the courts will inquire into the complications of which the patient was or was not informed.

Despite the seemingly tolerant attitude of the courts, it has been very difficult to deny negligence in cases in which the surgeon failed to inform the patient, in whatever terms, of the risk of severe neurological deficit associated with removal, or attempted removal, of intramedullary or even extramedullary spinal tumours. The view that to inform a patient of that risk would deter the patient from agreeing to an operation that was necessary has been weak. By contrast, it has been possible to establish that, although it was admitted that a patient was not informed of the risk of quadriplegia, he or she would nevertheless have agreed to the operation had he or she been informed of that risk. In such a case, although liability for failure to inform was admitted, causation was successfully denied. However, this type of defence is not one upon which any surgeon should rely!

Mistaken preoperative, clinical and radiological diagnosis of a tumour which was thought to be extramedullary but which proved to be intramedullary have been insufficient grounds for defence of the failure to warn of the risk of postoperative quadriparesis.

On occasions courts have enquired into *details of surgical technique*, which do not depend upon any advanced technology. In operations for removal, or attempted removal, of cervical tumours, such details have included degrees of retraction of the spinal cord, division of dentate ligaments, extent of laminectomy, extent and position of myelotomy, and the method and depth of exploratory needling of the cord.

Tuberculosis

Although relatively rare in European practice, spinal tuberculosis continues to be a significant cause of medical negligence actions. In the majority of these, it is the failure to consider tuberculosis as a possible, or even probable, diagnosis which had led to a delay in management, and thereby the patient was denied a chance of full neurological recovery and cure. The most common erroneous diagnoses which have been made are: dorsal spinal extradural metastasis; cervical spondylosis; and an ill-defined polyarthritis. These errors have been attributable to:

- Failure to take into account the ethnic origin of the patient, since tuberculosis in the UK is more frequent among members of the Asian community.
- Failure to inquire into a past history or family history of pulmonary tuberculosis.
- Failure to obtain or examine carefully plain radiographs of the thoracic spine in patients complaining of chronic thoracic, as opposed to lumbar, back pain.
- Failure to recognise the radiological distinction between malignancy and infection.
- Failure to observe paraspinal or pre-vertebral swelling on plain radiographs.
- Failure to take note of a raised erythrocyte sedimentation rate.
- Failure to examine the patient carefully for localised spinal tenderness or deformity.

Such errors can be very difficult to defend; so also is the denial that earlier effective treatment, often by chemotherapy alone, would have prevented neurological deficit, and also disease in other organs, and that it would have achieved a complete and lasting cure.

Example

> A 28-year-old man of Asian origin presented with a three-month history of neck pain, and more recently numbness and paraesthesiae in the upper limbs, and then paraesthesiae over the trunk and thighs. There was no definite neurological deficit, and the initial differential diagnoses included ankylosing spondylitis and an inflammatory arthropathy. Radiographs of the cervical spine were considered to show mild degenerative changes. One month later the finding of a motor and sensory deficit in the upper limbs prompted a diagnosis of a cervical disc protrusion, consistent with further plain radiographs. Immediately following myelography there was profound neurological deterioration, and operation revealed extensive tuberculous osteomyelitis and a chronic extradural abscess.
>
> The liability issues included: the primary clinical diagnosis and the extent of the clinical neurological examination; the significance of the patient's ethnic origin; the interpretation of the earlier radiographs; the need for more generalised investigations. The causation issues centred on the likely results of early investigation, and on the course which would have followed if myelography had been done before there was evidence of any neurological deficit.

The surgical approach to cord compression by tuberculous pus or granulation tissue has been central to some medical negligence actions, particularly when the preoperative diagnosis was metastatic malignancy. Laminectomy in those circumstances may not provide a decompression, it may not allow evacuation of pus, and the anterior compression of the dura and cord can be aggravated, causing a significant and potentially irreversible increase in the neurological deficit, to the extent of paraplegia. It is then very difficult to deny that an antero-lateral approach (e.g. costotransversectomy) would have prevented those complications. Such surgical errors are less likely when a thoracic kyphosis or kyphus is present, the correct preoperative diagnosis is more obvious, and anterior approaches – lumbar or transthoracic – are more clearly indicated.

Spinal extradural abscess (non-tuberculous)

Despite its rarity, this condition has led to medical negligence actions, mainly owing to the failure of early diagnosis, referral and treatment which would have prevented the onset of a severe spinal cord lesion, which can develop very rapidly and may not be improved by decompression. The clinical presentation often includes severe lumbar or thoracolumbar pain associated with spasm of the erector spinae muscles at a stage when the neurological examination may be normal apart from a limitation of straight-leg-raising. The patients are often young adults, who are apyrexial, and there is usually nothing in the recent or past history to raise the suspicion of infection.

The onus in such cases usually falls on a casualty officer, who is drawn towards a diagnosis of prolapsed lumbar intervertebral disc, or, as has happened, considers the patient to be hysterical. The rarity of the condition does not provide a defence on liability when neither the preceding history nor the severity of the symptoms are consistent with the diagnosis of prolapsed lumbar intervertebral disc, common as that condition is.

Example

A 19-year-old woman with recurrent boils in her axilla and on the back of her neck presented with very severe low back pain radiating to both lower limbs, without any neurological deficit. Forty-eight hours later she was admitted with evidence of a severe thoracic cord lesion which had come on within the previous 12 hours. Clinical differential diagnoses were Guillain–Barre syndrome or transverse myelitis. It was not until 36 hours after admission that she reached a neurosurgical department, where a large staphylococcal spinal extradural abscess was evacuated.

The liability issue was not the failure to make a diagnosis of spinal extradural abscess, a very rare condition. It was, in the first place, the failure to admit a young woman with very severe back pain; and, secondly, the failure to consider spinal cord compression as the one condition calling for very urgent referral as soon as the patient was admitted.

The issue of causation may sometimes be a live one, in that although prompt surgical drainage of extradural pus is mandatory, when the volume of pus found at operation is small it can be argued that the cord lesion was due to vasculitis and ischaemia rather than compression, and that earlier surgery would probably not have prevented the cord lesion. In addition to diagnostic errors in the accident and emergency department, there are cases in which there has been a delay in referral of the patient to a neurosurgical department after admission to a general medical ward, even after the onset of lower limb weakness; this has also been followed by some further delay after the patient had reached neurosurgical hands. In these circumstances, it may be extremely difficult to apportion the degree of damage attributable to the different stages of management. Apportionment arguments between the different parties can be very important financially, whether liability is admitted or denied. Unfortunately, hard neurological data upon which cogent arguments can be based are often lacking.

Further reading

Cooper, F. and Epstein, F. (1992) Intramedullary tumours. In *Surgery of the Spine* (G. Findlay and R. Owen, eds), pp. 587–600. Blackwell Science, Oxford.

Ho, E.K.W. and Leong, J.C.Y (1992) Tuberculour spondylitis. In *Surgery of the Spine* (G. Findlay and R. Owen, eds), pp. 608–18. Blackwell Science, Oxford.

Johnston, R.A. (1992) Intramedullary infection. In *Surgery of the Spine* (G. Findlay and R. Owen, eds), pp. 621–8. Blackwell Science, Oxford.

Chapter 10

Infections of the Central Nervous System

C.J. Earl

Acute bacterial meningitis

The special diagnostic problems related to acute meningitis in infants are discussed in Chapter 12. In adults and in older children, the diagnosis of meningitis is usually more straightforward, with its characteristic features of headache, usually fever, and a clouded mental state. Physical examination reveals neck stiffness and limited straight-leg-raising. In meningococcal meningitis, the characteristic skin rash may be prominent. If diagnosis and treatment are delayed bacterial meningitis may be fatal, or leave the patient with persistent neurological disability.

Failure to diagnose established meningitis would be difficult to defend, but there are cases which have given rise to actions for negligence, where the symptoms at the time of the doctor's visit were simply those of an acute generalised systemic infection without any of the specific signs of meningitis. Where virulent bacteria are the cause of generalised systemic infection, meningitis due to spread of highly virulent organisms by the blood stream to the meninges may develop very rapidly and the patient's life may be at risk within a very short time; even within a few hours. In cases of this sort, when the diagnosis of meningitis is eventually made, treatment may be of no avail. The doctor who saw the patient first may be blamed for failing to diagnose meningitis in its early stages, when in fact all that was present at first was evidence of a systemic infection. Defending the management of cases such as this may be difficult, because with the benefit of hindsight it is only too easily but wrongly assumed that a diagnosis of developing meningitis should have been made.

A case in which this type of fulminating infection occurred involved a 55-year-old woman who developed pain in both ears. At about 11.00 AM she visited a hospital accident and emergency department, where it was thought that she was suffering from otitis externa. Later that day she developed, in addition, symptoms of generalised infection with headache and fever. She was seen that evening by her family doctor who found signs of otitis media and prescribed antibiotics. Later that night when she became confused and drowsy she was admitted to hospital. She was found then to have signs of meningitis, which was eventually proved to be due to *Streptococcus pneumoniae*. Intravenous antibiotics in high doses were ineffective and she died in the early hours of the following morning.

Chronic meningitis

Tuberculous meningitis, meningitis due to fungal invasion of the subarachnoid space, and malignant meningitis due to spread of malignant disease in the meninges are all examples of meningitis of a chronic type. The diagnosis of malignant meningitis is rarely likely to lead to effective therapeutic endeavour, but both tuberculous meningitis and mycotic meningitis are readily treatable once the diagnosis is made. The onset of either of these conditions is usually insidious, with gradually worsening headache over a period of days or weeks, low fever, and the general symptoms of infection. Signs of local neurological disease may be present – usually as a result of focal ischaemic lesions due to inflammatory changes in arterial walls leading to occlusion.

Treatment of meningitis must depend on accurate diagnosis, which in turn depends on competent and expert examination of the cerebrospinal fluid, demonstration of the responsible organism and a study of its sensitivity to antibiotics. Before the sensitivity of the cultured organisms can be established in acute meningitis, treatment may need to be started, normally with a combination of broad-spectrum antibiotics.

In the past, a very real and serious dilemma sometimes existed affecting decisions about lumbar puncture. Fortunately, this is no longer the case. The problem arose because it is important to avoid lumbar puncture in a patient complaining of headache unless one is fully satisfied that there is nothing to suggest the presence either of an intracranial mass or of obstructive hydrocephalus with ventricular enlargement. Where either of these situations exists lumbar puncture may have disastrous consequences, because removal of cerebrospinal fluid may precipitate herniation of the brain, at the level either of the tentorial hiatus or of the foramen magnum with brain stem compression and serious, often fatal, consequences. Decisions on clinical grounds alone are made even more difficult by the fact that neck stiffness of the type seen in meningitis is a prominent feature of impending herniation. This risk can now largely be eliminated by CT brain scanning, which will readily reveal evidence of any contraindication to the removal of cerebrospinal fluid. It must be said, however, that brain herniation may occur when there is no evidence either of a mass or of hydrocephalus as the result of generalised brain swelling which may not be obvious on a scan.

Late complications of meningitis may be related to the interval which elapses between the onset of meningitis and the beginning of treatment, although with some highly virulent organisms even early treatment seems to be of no avail. However, patients who suffer from late and persistent sequelae of meningitis may well have a claim on a doctor if it can be shown the treatment was unreasonably delayed. Hydrocephalus with ventricular enlargement may be unavoidable as a complication in chronic meningitis, but occasionally may occur also in acute meningitis, and where it occurs the question of the promptness of treatment may be raised.

Sensorineural deafness is a well-known sequela of bacterial meningitis and occurs, for example, in up to 31% of patients with meningitis due to *Streptococcus pneumoniae*, but does not appear to be related to the number of days before the patient was admitted to hospital for treatment (Dodge *et al.*, 1984).

Cerebral abscess

The diagnosis and subsequent management of cerebral abscess have been greatly simplified by the use of brain scanning techniques. In the early stages of cerebral abscess, symptoms and signs of local cerebral disease may be entirely absent and clinical differentiation from simple meningitis may be very difficult. Scanning in the early stages of abscess formation, when suppuration has not yet taken place, will show evidence of local brain swelling from inflammatory oedema. In a patient with headache where there are other clinical features, which might suggest the possibility of a cerebral abscess, failure to arrange for early scanning could be difficult to defend when a delay in diagnosis gives rise to some persistent disability, which might have been avoided by prompt treatment. The situations in which the possibility of cerebral abscess might be suspected are local sepsis in the skull (frontal sinusitis or otitis media), chronic chest infection (e.g. bronchiectasis) or cyanotic congenital heart disease.

There have been recent changes in the surgical techniques used in treating cerebral abscess, with the introduction of methods using stereotaxic apparatus combined with scanning to direct the aspirating needle with an accuracy which would be impossible without such assistance. This technique is now available in most neurosurgical centres in the UK and, except in cases of extreme urgency, is clearly the method of choice, the most likely to be effective, and the least liable to cause complications.

Reference

Dodge, P.R., Davis, H., Feigin, R.D., Holmes, S.J., Kaplan, S.L., Jubelirer, D.P., Stechenberg, B.W. and Hirsh, S.K. (1984) Prospective evaluation of hearing impairment as a sequela of acute bacterial meningitis. *New England Journal of Medicine* **311**, 869–74.

Chapter 11

Iatropathic Lesions of Peripheral Nerves

George Bonney

Introduction

Doctors damage peripheral nerves during their work because of:

(1) Insufficient familiarity with topographical anatomy.
(2) Lack of appreciation of the vulnerability of nervous tissue.
(3) Ignorance concerning the functioning of peripheral nerves.
(4) Unfamiliarity with the clinical signs of nerve damage, and in particular with those of continuing damage.
(5) Ignorance of techniques for nerve repair.
(6) Failure to observe conditions rendering peripheral nerves abnormally susceptible to damage.
(7) Adverse local factors such as distortion of anatomy by scarring and involvement of nerves in malignant processes.

The elements of the peripheral nervous system are so widely distributed in the body that the opportunities for damage are many.

Most of the damage is, no doubt, done during operative surgery under local, regional and general anaesthesia, but there is a steady toll of disability from failure to recognise nerve injury in the accident department, from failure to recognise impending ischaemia in a limb, from the use of drugs toxic to nerves and from injection injury. Birch *et al.* (1998a) classify iatropathic or iatrogenous injury to nerves thus:

- Administration of drugs liable to cause neuropathy.
- Administration of anticoagulant drugs liable to cause bleeding into or around a nerve.
- Injection of a tissue-damaging agent into or near a nerve.

- Pressure from bleeding caused by accidental or deliberate arterial puncture.
- Closed pressure or traction during general anaesthesia.
- Traction during manipulation under anaesthesia or during delivery.
- Production of or failure to recognise ischaemia of a limb.
- Damage in the field of operation.
- Ionising radiation.

Little can be done about doctors' general unfamiliarity with topographical anatomy: the subject is no longer accorded the precedence that it once received and was thought to deserve, and the graduate clinician must learn from his or her errors with regard to patients. Patients may not see the matter quite in this light. It may, however, be possible to persuade doctors and those in high places who determine the form of medical training that some knowledge of the structure and function of the peripheral nerves is desirable in the interests of patients and of those indemnifying them for the effects of iatrogenous injury.

The peripheral neurone

The peripheral neurone consists of the cell body, its dendrites and its prolongation, the axon. In the case of the efferent or motor neurone, the cell body is usually situated in the anterior horn of the grey matter of the spinal cord; the axon is single, and extents peripherally in the anterior root to its termination in skeletal muscle or other organ. In the case of the afferent or sensory neurone, the cell body is situated in the posterior root ganglion; the axon is bifurcated, one limb proceeding centrally by the posterior, or less often by the anterior, root to the posterior horn of the grey matter of the spinal cord, the other proceeding distally in the peripheral nerve to its junction with a sensory receptor. In the peripheral nerve, formed at the intervertebral foramen, motor and sensory roots come together and efferent and afferent axons are mingled.

The neurone is and functions as a single cell, receiving impulses through its dendrites or terminals and conveying them by the axon to end organs such as skeletal musculature or to the cell bodies of other axons. The nutrition of the neurone and the supply of transmitters at its terminals are mediated by orthograde and retrograde axonal transport.

The nerve fibre is made up of the axon, the sheath composed of Schwann cells and, in the case of the larger axons, the myelin sheath. The large fibres are contained singly in Schwann cell/myelin sheath tubes; the smaller, unmyelinated axons are contained in bundles in Schwann cell sheaths. The function of the myelin sheath is to effect rapid conduction. Different fibres have different functions: the largest myelinated fibres convey position and vibration sense; rather smaller myelinated fibres conduct impulses to skeletal muscle; small myelinated fibres convey pain sensibility; the smallest, unmyelinated fibres conduct impulses to the blood vessels and sweat glands and also convey 'slow' pain sensibility.

In the peripheral nerve, the fibres are arranged in bundles (fascicles) surrounded by a perineurium; the bundles are contained in an epineurium, which is a prolongation of the dural sleeve of the nerve roots. Peripheral nerves have a good blood supply, derived from longitudinal and segmental vessels, communicating freely with an intraneural plexus.

Reactions to physical injury

Although a nerve can be damaged by any one of a number of physical agents or by a combination of two or more of these, its reactions conform to simple patterns. With transient ischaemia, the product of short-lived local pressure or traction, there is a simple failure of conduction without lasting structural change. When pressure is more severe or more prolonged, myelin is squeezed away from the site of pressure and the axon ceases to conduct. Recovery is mediated over the course of days or weeks by the remyelination of the demyelinated segment. These are examples of non-degenerative injury, in which the axon is largely unaffected. Neurapraxia is a good term for this type of lesion (Seddon, 1943).

When the insult is more severe or lasts longer, the axon itself is damaged, and the whole of the effector cell of the unit suffers. Distal to the site of injury, the axon degenerates and the myelin sheath fragments; proximally, the axon shrinks, the dendrites retract and changes occur in the cytoplasm of the cell body. In the case of damage to sensory axons, changes take place in the cells of the posterior horn of the grey matter, with effects on pain and skin sensitivity (Iadarola and Caudle, 1997; Mantyh *et al.*, 1997). If continuity of the axon is not re-established, the cell body eventually disappears. Such lesions are termed 'degenerative'; they are produced by such physical agents as traction, burning, crushing and cutting. Most lesions of peripheral nerves short of section represent mixtures of the various types of lesion.

In one type of iatrogenous lesion – the birth injury of the brachial plexus – the nerve lesion can be entirely different: the roots are ruptured intradurally or avulsed from the spinal cord. The axons in the anterior root degenerate, but those of the sensory system in the posterior root distal to their cell bodies survive and function despite the interruption of their central processes. Birch *et al.* (1998b) suggest the term *neuradetosis* for this type of lesion.

Recovery after a degenerative lesion must be mediated by centrifugal regeneration of the axon. If the force used on the nerve is insufficient to interrupt the basal membrane of the Schwann cell tube, the axon may regenerate spontaneously along its original path, so that good recovery is achieved; if the basal membrane has been interrupted, as for instance by cutting, orderly peripheral regeneration can only be achieved by accurate bridging of the gap between the nerve ends, so that the axon can regenerate along its former paths. It is plain that nerve growth factors, released at the time of injury, have a major role in the regenerative process and in the guidance of regenerating axons to their peripheral targets. Axonal regrowth proceeds at a rate of about a millimetre a day - the speed of slow orthograde axonal transport.

Clinical features of nerve injury

It is plain from the above that the sooner continuing damage is arrested or continuity of the axon is restored, the better the prospects for recovery will be. Therefore, it is vitally important that the clinician should:

(1) Recognise the fact of nerve injury.
(2) Identify the nerve or nerves involved and the level or levels of injury.
(3) Determine whether the lesion is partial or complete.
(4) Appreciate the depth of the lesion.
(5) Determine whether there is continuing injury.

The symptoms of nerve injury are:

- Weakness or paralysis
- Impairment or loss of function
- Numbness
- Pain
- Other paraesthesiae.

The signs are muscular weakness or paralysis, and alteration or loss of sensibility. Pressure alone rarely produces a lesion of the small fibres of a nerve, so in neurapraxia, vasomotor and sudomotor function are not impaired. However, if the nerve has been cut or if there has been bleeding within it, vasomotor and sudomotor function are lost, and the extremity is dry and warm. Pain in acute injury is a common indicator of continuing damage; it is a constant feature in ischaemia. Progressive deepening of the lesion is an indication of continuing injury, as by ischaemia or pressure or distortion.

Enhanced susceptibility to injury

Clinicians should not forget that the susceptibility of peripheral nerves to injury can be enhanced in systemic conditions such as diabetes mellitus, alcoholism, hypothyroidism and rheumatoid arthritis. Vulnerability varies according to age: the proportion of myelinated fibres increases up to the age of three years, and declines progressively after the third decade of life. Sometimes the susceptibility of a peripheral nerve is affected by the presence of a lesion more proximal in the nerve trunk.

Possibilities for treatment

The critical decision is whether to act as a matter of urgency to repair or to relieve the affected nerve or nerves of a continuing noxious process, or to wait and see. The decision is based primarily on clinical findings, but may be aided by electrophysiological examination and other investigations, magnetic resonance imaging (MRI) in particular. Here are two good rules:

(1) If a patient comes with a cut over the line of a main nerve, however inflicted, and with motor, sensory, vasomotor and sudomotor affection in the territory of that nerve, the last must be assumed to have been cut unless it is proved otherwise by exploration.

(2) If there has been an intervention in the region of a trunk nerve or nerves and the patient complains of motor and sensory symptoms and pain in the territory of those nerves, it must be assumed that there is a continuing lesion and that action must be taken to halt it.

The courses open to the clinician are:

- Relief of ischaemia by fasciotomy with or without restoration of flow along the axial vessel.
- Neurolysis by removal of a compressing or distorting agent including haematoma.
- Nerve repair by direct suture or by graft.

Iatrogenous lesions in practice

Injection injuries

Substances can be injected into nerves during intramuscular administration of drugs or during infiltration with local anaesthetic agents or steroid. The damage is done by the neurotoxic effect of the particular drug, by the mechanical effect of the fluid and probably by bleeding into the nerve. It is more likely to be severe in intrafascicular than in interfascicular injection. The agents principally responsible for damage are non-steroidal anti-inflammatory drugs, steroids, local and general anaesthetic agents and benzodiazepines. It is very likely that injection of one of the more neurotoxic drugs, such as diazepam, near a main nerve is sufficient to damage it. Injection into a nerve of a conscious patient is marked by instant pain and paraesthesiae and by progressive motor and sensory paralysis in the area of distribution. When the injection is near the nerve the onset of symptoms is delayed. All components of the nerve are damaged, so that the lesion is commonly degenerative.

Often enough, these accidents occur in places where facilities for urgent investigation and treatment are lacking. The lesion has to be left to follow its course, with regenerative recovery along a fibrosed nerve. The occurrence of such an accident in a hospital where there are facilities for exploration should be the signal for action within 12 hours: the nerve should be exposed at the site of injection and the epineurium should be opened to allow the escape of blood and the injected substance. The nerve and the field should be irrigated with saline. Because the opportunity for and the will to such decisive action are so generally absent, the best to which most practitioners will be able to aspire is the late mitigation of pain by exposure and epineurotomy of the damaged nerve. All practitioners, however, can avoid the introduction of noxious substances into nerves by eschewing the buttock and upper arm as sites for injection, and by knowing that the median nerve runs, as its name suggests, down the middle in the front part of the elbow, forearm and wrist. The safest sites for intramuscular injection are the uppermost part of the deltoid muscle, the upper lateral quadrant of the buttock and the lateral side of the thigh.

Injuries with the needle point

Special hazards attach to 'interscalene block' (Winnie, 1970), in which regional anaesthesia is produced by infiltration around the most proximal part of the brachial plexus. Birch *et al.* (1998c) describe the cases of three patients who suffered serious neurological damage from this procedure. In one case, the damage was almost certainly produced by occlusion of one vertebral artery, brought on by penetration with the needle point. The responsible lesion may have been a simple spasm, since vertebral angiography 48 hours later showed no arterial lesion.

Similarly, damage can be done with a needle point during insertion of a pacemaker into the subclavian vein, venepuncture at elbow level or arterial catheterisation. In the first case, the lateral cord of the brachial plexus is damaged; in the last, there is bleeding into the brachial (Colville and Colin, 1998) or femoral sheath; and in the second, the ulnar artery is penetrated with consequent bleeding into the deep compartment of the forearm and compression of the ulnar nerve. These are accidents which happen in hospitals; there is no excuse for a delay in diagnosis and action, but frequently both occur.

External pressure

Occluding cuffs

The occluding cuff is still quite often used to produce a bloodless field for operations on the limbs. It is, or should be, well-known that when a cuff round the arm is inflated to above systolic pressure, there is a progressive paralysis of the limb below the cuff, first affecting the largest nerve fibres and finally affecting even the smallest. These phenomena were, of course, investigated by Lewis *et al.* (1931), whose experiments formed the basis of much subsequent work on the relationship between fibre size and function. The paralysis is caused by transient ischaemia of the sections of the nerves underlying the cuff. Evidently, such paralysis occurs whenever a 'tourniquet' is used in operative surgery; the effect almost always wears off over a few minutes when the pressure is released. Rarely (but once is enough) the paralysis is deep and degenerative, and does not recover over a few minutes. The causes are usually:

- Undue susceptibility of nerves
- A more proximal lesion of nerve or nerves
- Lack of protective covering for the nerves through wasting of the limb
- Application of the cuff at an incorrect level
- Use of too narrow a cuff
- Too high a pressure in the cuff
- Occluding cuff applied for too long a period
- A combination of two or more of these factors.

An occluding cuff should never be applied over a prosthetic arterial replacement.

Here again, prevention is better than cure, not least because there is no cure. The operating surgeon must himself or herself see that the cuff is applied to the correct part of the correct limb; pressures in aneroid gauges should be checked against those in mercury manometers; pressures suited to limbs should be used, and they should be recorded; times of inflation and deflation should be recorded in the operating theatre and in the notes; maximum periods of application should be laid down and observed; occluding cuffs should not be used in patients with known neuropathies.

Pressure from the operating table

The ulnar nerve at elbow level and the common peroneal nerve just below the knee are specially vulnerable to outside pressure, because of their situation superficial to bone and just deep to skin. Both can be damaged in the unconscious patient by pressure on the operating table and in bed after the operation. Injury to the ulnar nerve is signalled by paraesthesiae and alteration of sensibility in the ulnar two digits, and by weakness noticed most in the small muscles of the hand. The patient may not be allowed time to draw these symptoms to the attention of a nurse or doctor before he or she is discharged from hospital; even when they are disclosed, the symptoms may be dismissed as a natural consequence of the operation, likely to recover spontaneously. Yet the situation of the ulnar nerve at this level – passing medial to the elbow joint and under the arcade of origin of the flexor carpi ulnaris muscle – makes it possible or even probable that the pressure paralysis will develop into a continuing entrapment syndrome. If there is no early evidence of recovery, the advisability of decompression should seriously be canvassed.

With pressure on the common peroneal nerve at the level of the fibular head, the consequent paralysis of the evertors of the foot and the extensors of the foot and ankle is more often than not recoverable; but the paralysis is sometimes deep, and sometimes permanent. Doubtless, factors similar to those operating on the ulnar nerve at the elbow come into operation. When such a paralysis follows arthroplasty of the hip, it is necessary to distinguish it from that produced by injury to the sciatic nerve at the level of the hip. Electrophysiological investigation is helpful and may be decisive here. If there is no early sign of recovery, the question of decompression should be raised.

Internal pressure and distortion

The brachial plexus is particularly liable to damage from internal pressure and distortion, because of its situation connecting fixed axial structures to the mobile shoulder girdle, and because of the potential hazards that it encounters on its way from the neck to the upper limb. Thus, in cardiac operations, when the sternum is split and the halves of the hemithorax are separated, the lower trunk is liable to distortion over the edge of the first thoracic rib. In operations through the axilla, when the limb is abducted on the trunk, the upper part of the plexus can be stretched over the front of the shoulder joint or trapped by the rising clavicle against the axial skeleton. A particular hazard is created when, during operation on the prone patient, the upper limbs are held elevated above shoulder level. Usually the whole plexus is initially involved, though the affection of the upper part is usually deeper than that of the lower.

Cooper *et al.* (1988) made a thoughtful contribution to the study of this complication, indicating an incidence of 0.02% in 15,000 operations of all types under general anaesthesia over 12 months. They noted predisposing factors, showed various mechanisms of damage and indicated precautions.

Although the outlook for recovery is generally good, no patient appreciates having an upper limb partly out of action for a year or more.

Traction

Birth injury of the brachial plexus

Despite a rising rate of delivery by Caesarean section and improvement in techniques of antenatal monitoring, the rise in the average birth weight in the UK has, it seems, been responsible for maintaining a steady toll of injury to the brachial plexus during parturition. Macrosomia and malposition combine during delivery to cause the mobile shoulder girdle to be wrenched away from the axial skeleton. The nerves and nerve roots of the brachial plexus connecting the two are stretched or ruptured, or pulled away from the spinal cord. Intradural rupture of roots or avulsion from the cord may damage the blood supply to the ipsilateral cord and affect the long tracts. Commonly, the upper part of the plexus is involved; less commonly, the lower part; rarely, the whole plexus is involved.

The view has persisted over many years that nearly all such lesions are spontaneously recoverable, and that no more need be done than to observe progress and to maintain flexibility of the joints whose movers have been paralysed. It has, however, long been known that some lesions go on to cause permanent disability and to produce deformity of the shoulder from subluxation and even dislocation.

The work of Narakas (1981), Gilbert and Tassin (1984) and Morelli *et al.* (1984) did much to dispel the rosy illusions about prognosis in birth lesions of the brachial plexus, and to define those cases in which operative repair was necessary if disability were to be avoided. It is no longer acceptable for the clinician asked to see a newborn child with a lesion of the brachial plexus to give general reassurance and to indicate the need to maintain joint mobility. The child should be seen by a clinician with special experience of such lesions; the extent and depth of the lesion should be determined; investigations should be done; and if there are indications for repair by operation the options should be discussed with the parents.

Traction lesions in the adult

Traction is used in a number of procedures done under general anaesthesia: arthroscopy of the hip; manipulation of the shoulder; limb lengthening; and in certain cases, arthroplasty of the hip. Lundborg and Rydevik (1973) showed that venous flow in the nerve was blocked by stretching by 8% of its resting length, and that stretching by 15% produced ischaemia. Rupture by surgical procedure is rare, but nerves so treated may suffer degenerative lesions with consequent long-lasting disability.

Ischaemia

Unrecognised peripheral ischaemia

The continued omission of instruction and practice in the surgery of the blood vessels from the training of surgeons dealing with accident cases leads to a steady toll of cases in which ischaemia from damage to main vessels associated with limb fractures goes unrecognised. Less common now, perhaps, is the failure to recognise ischaemia resulting from increasing pressure within fascial compartments associated with fractures of long bones. Muscle does not tolerate complete ischaemia for longer than six hours; nerves are rather more tolerant, but certainly suffer permanent damage if subjected to ischaemia for longer than 12 hours. Usually all the evidence is there: fracture through the lower humerus, the junction of the middle and lowest thirds of the femur or the upper tibia; persistent pain; numbness of digits; loss, first, of vibration sensibility and, later, of other modalities; pallor, coldness and loss of peripheral pulses. Too often the fatal mantra 'spasm' is pronounced, and remedial action comes too late, when the clinician's first thought should be that there is arterial obstruction requiring intervention. The result may be a ruined limb; in the worst cases, it may be no limb at all.

It is not easy during operative surgery to devascularise a nerve: the blood supply is too rich and stems from too many sources. It is possible with the ulnar nerve: transposition for chronic neuropathy involves the mobilisation of a considerable length of the nerve, and if the accompanying vessels are not mobilised with it, there may be irreversible ischaemia with serious pain and loss of function. It is principally for this reason that prudent surgeons prefer the simple decompression of the ulnar nerve as the first operation for chronic neuropathy. Transposition becomes inevitable in cases of severe deformity or osteophytosis of the elbow, of recurrent subluxation of the nerve, and of recurrence of symptoms after simple decompression.

Damage during operation

Operations for conditions affecting nerves

Clearly, any intervention on or near a nerve whose function is already compromised carries a risk of further damage to that nerve. This is particularly the case in operations on benign tumours of nerves, and especially in solitary neurofibroma of a trunk nerve. Schwannomas of main nerves can usually be enucleated without causing damage to function, but, as Kehoe *et al.* (1995) revealed, the correct diagnosis is not often made before operation. Frequently, the diagnosis of 'ganglion' or 'enlarged lymph node' is made, and an operator imperfectly acquainted with structure, function and pathology is let loose on an enterprise classed as a 'minor operation'. If the tumour is central in the nerve, the operator may think that he or she has found a 'malignant tumour' and may proceed to remove a length of a main nerve or even of the upper trunk of the brachial plexus. If the tumour is laterally placed, the operator may think the diagnosis of 'ganglion' justified and may proceed to removal, taking with the 'ganglion' part of a main nerve. The error may be compounded by a failure after the operation to heed the patient's complaint of numbness and paralysis, or by an attribution of those symptoms to 'neurapraxia' or 'bruising of the nerve'. Some, lost to all shame, may pronounce the mantra 'neuropraxia'.

Usually, this is no matter of deep knowledge being required; it is simply a matter of remembering that there are important structures including the brachial plexus at the root of the neck and under the skin in limbs; of being suspicious about a 'ganglion' which is tender to pressure; of heeding what patients say; of not taking anything for granted. In one case, indeed, things were more difficult: a schwannoma of the facial nerve was mistaken for a mixed parotid tumour, and irretrievable damage was done to the nerve during removal.

Invasive and malignant tumours

Malignant nerve sheath tumours are usually associated with defects of conduction; adequate removal usually involves further interference with neural function. Here, in particular, it is necessary to inform and warn the patient and to expose to him or her the options for treatment and the balance of risk and advantage. Evidently, it is for the patient to make the decision, but the clinician should not shrink from indicating the course that seems to him or her the best. Treatment of the singular condition of musculo-aponeurotic fibromatosis may involve some hard choices: the condition is invasive but non-metastasising; it may surround nerves so closely as to make it impossible to extract them. One or more main nerves may have to be sacrificed if removal is to be complete; plans for treatment must include this possibility.

Operations for entrapment syndromes

The advent of 'endoscopic release' for carpal tunnel syndrome has opened up new possibilities for damage to the median and even the ulnar nerve. The warning by Thomas *et al.* (1993) should be compulsory reading for all aspirants in this field:

> 'Endoscopic surgical technique requires rigorous training in order to avoid dangerous pitfalls: it must be performed by experienced hand surgeons.'

De Smet and Fabry (1995) go further:

> 'We should be wary about yielding to pressure to use endoscopic carpal tunnel release from instrument makers, medical supply houses, insurance companies and patients.'

The British surgeon should perhaps add 'managers' to that list.

Even open decompression of the median nerve exacts a toll of damage to the main nerve or to its motor and palmar branches; devascularisation of the ulnar nerve during anterior transposition has been mentioned; surgeons have mistaken an anomalous head of the triceps slipping to and fro over the medial epicondyle for a subluxing ulnar nerve and have unnecessarily transposed the last.

Operations for decompression of the lower trunk at the thoracic outlet are hazardous for the patient when the operating surgeon is unfamiliar with the anatomy of the region. The price paid may be high: a deep and possibly irrecoverable lesion of the lower part of the plexus or a chronic neuropathy. In some cases of distortion of the lower trunk over the first rib or over a seventh cervical rib, the neural tissue may be so much attenuated that the surgeon may in error divide it. In attempting to remove a first thoracic or seventh cervical rib, the surgeon can exert such force on the lower trunk that it ceases forever to function. The signs of impending acute ischaemia from thrombosis of the subclavian artery may be missed; critical ischaemia may supervene and extensive grafting may be needed. There may be bleeding after the operation so severe as to compress the lower trunk and cause a deep lesion. The transaxillary approach of Roos (1981) is an admirable route for removal of the first rib or for a second operation on the outlet, but it is not one for the casual surgeon. It presents dangers to the plexus and, in particular, to the subclavian vein.

Operation for entrapment syndrome gives good results when it is correctly indicated and properly performed; the results of an operation incorrectly done or done for the wrong indications are uniformly bad and generally irreversible.

Operations in general

The cutaneous nerves

The importance of damage to the cutaneous nerves has, perhaps, been underestimated. Damage to the terminal part of the superficial radial nerve, to the palmar branch of the median, to the infrapatellar branch of the saphenous and to the sural nerve can produce a painful state with cutaneous hyperaesthesia which is resistant to all methods of treatment. So too, of course, can damage to other cutaneous sensory nerves: the first four seem to be those most often injured. Surgeons who operate on the neck and limbs should familiarise themselves with the position of these nerves and should preserve them. If a nerve is accidentally divided or if the situation necessitates division, and if there are early signs of a developing painful state, steps should at once be taken to repair the damaged nerve. It may be necessary to bridge a gap; in this situation freeze-thawed muscle grafts are useful (Thomas *et al.*, 1994).

Malignant disease

If radical removal of a malignant growth requires removal of functioning tissue, that hard decision has to be taken and, if necessary, the damage has to be repaired later. Thus, the spinal accessory nerve may have to be sacrificed in radical clearance of the neck. On the other hand, it is usually possible to preserve the nerve to the serratus anterior muscle in radical removal of the breast. Surgeons operating in the area are, or should be, especially careful of it during clearance of the axilla (Dudley, 1982).

The neck

Maran *et al.* (1993) deal well and wisely with the subject of damage to the facial nerve during operations on the parotid gland. They point out that although 90% of tumours of the gland turn out to be pleomorphic adenomas (mixed tumours), it is not always easy before operation to be certain about the distinction between malignant and benign growths. Hence, advice and warning before operation should always include mention of the risk of facial paralysis. Maran *et al.* (1993) go so far as to suggest that should a tumour be found at operation to be so extensive and invasive as to require sacrifice of the facial nerve, and should preoperative warning and consent have been inadequate, the patient should be woken, acquainted with the facts and asked for specific consent to that proceeding.

The important aspects of operation for removal of a probably benign tumour of the parotid gland are: methodical approach to the growth, with early identification of the facial nerve; use of the stimulator during the operation to identify the nerve's branches; and stimulation of the main nerve at the end of the procedure to confirm structural integrity. In cases in which the nerve has been sacrificed deliberately or cut accidentally, there is a strong case for early exploration and for repair by graft. The results of repair should be good, because the facial nerve is largely composed of efferent fibres. As Karnes (1993) notes, there is still uncertainty about the presence or otherwise of proprioceptive fibres in the nerve; certainly, there are few if any spindles in the facial muscles. It may well be that the afferent fibres from these pass to the brain in the branches of the fifth (trigeminal) nerve. In practice, Samii (1980) records good results after repair by grafting of lesions of the facial nerve.

The spinal accessory nerve runs through the sternocleidomastoid muscle to cross the upper part of the posterior triangle on its way to innervate the trapezius muscle. In this site it is close to the skin, and close, too, to the lymph nodes of the neck. Lymph node biopsy exacts a regular tribute of damage to the spinal accessory nerve by cutting, clamping and burning. The results are serious: function of the shoulder girdle is gravely impaired by the loss of the trapezius; pain arises from damage to afferent fibres in the nerve, from traction on other tissues from the dropping of the shoulder and from distortion of the suprascapular nerve at the suprascapular notch. Avoidance is best: lymph node biopsy in the neck should not be left to apprentices; paralysis of the trapezius after such an operation should be the signal for instant exploration and repair. The results of early repair are good; the results of late repair and of no repair are uniformly bad.

The upper part of the plexus is not immune to the attentions of the biopsist, although generally damage to the upper trunk is the result of the mistaken identification of a benign tumour as an enlarged lymph node. Damage to the recurrent laryngeal nerve is not the prerogative of the thyroidectomist; in extensive operations on the cervical spine and on tumours of the brachial plexus, dissection may proceed to the region where the nerve leaves the aorta or brachiocephalic artery to retrace its steps to the tracheo-oesophagus. Similarly, the superior laryngeal nerve and even the hypoglossal nerve can be damaged during the approach to the uppermost cervical vertebrae by the anterior route.

Cervicothoracic sympathectomy by the supraclavicular route has now largely been replaced by the endoscopic operation by the transthoracic route, but there may still be cases in which it is required, as when the pleural cavity is obliterated. The upper trunk of the brachial plexus has been mistaken for the tendon of the scalenus anterior and divided; the lower trunk or the first thoracic nerve has been mistaken for the ganglionated chain and removed. The latter error is in theory possible with the transthoracic approach; it has been seen with the removal of a benign tumour above the apex of the lung through a thoracotomy.

The upper limb

The most common error in operations on the shoulder is damage to the musculocutaneous nerve or the lateral cord of the brachial plexus during capsulorrhaphy for recurrent dislocation of the shoulder. One one occasion, the axillary artery was involved also. Many operations for recurrent dislocation involve detachment of the coracoid process, with later reattachment in its original site or to the front of the glenoid neck. Most procedures involve division of the tendon of the subscapularis muscle and opening the glenohumeral joint, with later plication of capsule and subscapularis muscle. The lateral part of the brachial plexus is very near the scene of these procedures; the musculocutaneous nerve arises from the lateral cord and runs laterally to pierce the short head of the biceps muscle arising from the coracoid process. It can be damaged during the division of the coracoid process and the mobilisation of the short head of the biceps muscle; the lateral cord and even the axillary artery can be included in one or more of the sutures used for reuniting the ends of the subscapularis tendon. The consequences are, of course, serious for the patient. Inclusion in a suture is usually signalled by pain; simple division is indicated by paralysis of the biceps and brachialis muscles. The motor paralysis may at first be masked by the ability of the brachioradialis muscle to flex the elbow against gravity. Action must be instant and decisive: divided nerve must be repaired; constricting sutures must be removed.

The close relation of the radial nerve to the humerus makes it a likely victim during operations on the shaft of that bone, as does the close relation of the ulnar nerve to the back of the medial epicondyle in fractures of the lower end.

The lower limb

Two operations are principally concerned:

(1) replacement arthroplasty of the hip; and
(2) operations for varicose veins.

The deserved popularity of replacement arthroplasty of the hip, chiefly for the relief of pain from degenerative disease, has made it one of the most commonly done procedures in the UK. Pike and Hollingsworth (1995) reckoned that 40,000 such operations are done yearly. Operation involves major proceedings on a joint in close relation to three main nerves – the sciatic, femoral and obturator – and to two branch nerves – the superior and inferior gluteal. It is not surprising that there is a steady toll of damage to nerves, principally the sciatic and femoral. In Schmalzried and Amstutz's (1991) series of patients from the University of California Los Angeles (UCLA), there were 53 involved extremities in 3,126 patients – an incidence of 1.7%. The sciatic nerve was involved in 43 cases, the femoral in five, and both nerves in seven. The cause of the nerve lesion was unknown in as many as 55% of these cases. The incidence was highest (5.8%) in arthroplasty done for the late effects of congenital dislocation. All agree about the increased risk in that condition and in second and third operations. There is also an increased risk of nerve damage in cases in which degenerative change is secondary to protrusio acetabuli.

The causes of damage are:

- Transection
- Mangling by a reamer which has broken out of bone
- Inclusion in a wire suture used to reunite the detached great trochanter to the femur

- Traction
- Pressure and distortion by retractor or during dislocation
- Distortion by extruding cement (Siliski and Scott, 1985)
- Heat from polymerising cement
- Diathermy burn
- External pressure from haematoma
- Internal pressure from intraneural haemorrhage.

The lesion may be non-degenerative and quickly recoverable, or degenerative but in continuity and recoverable, at least in part, over a long period. Evidently, transection or mangling or severe burning of the nerve produces a lesion which is recoverable only if repair is done. The critical decision for the clinician here, as elsewhere, is to determine the necessity or otherwise for instant and decisive action.

When the sciatic nerve is damaged, the usual complaint is of 'foot drop', though in serious cases a more extensive paralysis is noticed. There may be pain; that symptom is especially common with thermal lesions and with irritative lesions produced by inclusion in a suture. Examination is not easy in a patient, often elderly, who has just undergone a major operation on a major joint, but the extent and depth of the lesion must be established early. A partial lesion confined to the extensors and evertors of the foot and ankle may well indicate simple pressure damage to the common peroneal nerve at the level of the knee. A deep, complete lesion with sensory and motor paralysis, involving the knee flexors and all muscles below the knee, indicates that the sciatic nerve has been damaged at the level of the hip. The association of persistent pain indicates the likelihood of thermal or other irritative damage, such as that caused by traction or encirclement. If the patient is receiving anticoagulant drugs, the possibility of haemorrhage into or around the nerve is raised. The finding of warm, dry digits almost certainly indicates transection or bleeding into the nerve, but whereas the former causes paralysis observed immediately after operation, the latter's onset is usually delayed.

Examination must be extended to determine the function of the gluteal muscles and to exclude damage to the femoral and obturator nerves. The operation site should be examined for swelling due to haematoma; radiographs taken after operation should be examined for evidence of extrusion of cement. Indications for action are:

- Deep complete paralysis immediately after operation.
- Deep paralysis associated with persistently severe pain or evidence of large-wound haematoma.
- Deep paralysis of late onset in a patient receiving anticoagulant drugs.
- Persistent paralysis unchanged after a week, associated with electrophysiological evidence of axonal degeneration.

The decision about action is often difficult, because of the generally advanced age of these patients and their not uncommon unfitness for further operation. Evidence of haemorrhage must, of course, indicate cessation of treatment with anticoagulants.

Action involves exploration of the sciatic nerve and removal of the damaging agent with, if necessary, repair of the nerve. There is no doubt about the nature of action when the nerve is encircled by a suture, burnt by cement, distorted by cement or cut: the distorting agent must be removed and the nerve repaired. When the nerve has been partly mangled by a reamer or retractor, the damaged part can be resected and repaired by graft. Things are much more difficult when a non-conducting lesion in continuity, probably caused by a combination of traction and pressure, is found. It is unlikely that the effects of traction can be reversed by replacing the implant so that the nerve is no longer under tension, although that might give relief from pain. More evidence is required in this situation.

The common peroneal nerve at the level of the knee is the occasional victim in operations for ligation of varicose veins. The damage can be limited by prompt recognition and instant repair.

Radiation neuropathy

Interest in radiation neuropathy was revived in 1994 and 1995 by the publication, on the initiative of the Royal College of Radiologists (London), of a review by Bates and Evans (1994) and of a report of a committee chaired by Maher (1995). Because of the frequency of carcinoma of the female breast and the proximity of the brachial plexus to the affected field, most reports concern neuropathy of the plexus of women. The condition is not unknown in men: Bowen *et al.* (1996) consider the cases of six men who received radiotherapy to the groin and para-aortic glands for testicular malignancies, and who later developed neuropathy affecting the lumbosacral roots. Pathological examination of the conus medullaris and cauda equina was possible in one case: there was a 'vasculopathy of the proximal spinal roots, with preservation of motor neuronal cell bodies and spinal cord architecture'. Radiotherapy for lymphoma may, of course, produce neuropathy in either sex and in the nerves of upper and lower limbs. It is not known whether the neuropathy that may be associated with the primary condition predisposes to radiation neuropathy in these cases.

Difficulties are posed by the often long periods intervening between radiation and the onset of neuropathy, the lack of evidence concerning incidence, the need to distinguish radiation neuropathy from that caused by local recurrence, and uncertainty about the place of operation in treatment of the established condition. The lesion is dual: there is sclerosis of nerve trunks with axonal affection; and there is an element of external compression from sclerosis of structures related to the plexus. Symptoms are initially sensory; later, there is progressive motor paralysis, and pain may be serious and persistent. Rather rarely, the condition spontaneously comes to a halt and even regresses.

Recognition may be difficult: the early symptoms are those of 'carpal tunnel syndrome' or 'ulnar neuritis'. Even when the nature of the condition is recognised, it may be hard to exclude the possibility of local recurrence. MRI is sometimes helpful; electrophysiological testing is more likely to show myokymia (DeLisa *et al.*, 1994) in radiation than in 'metastatic' neuropathy. The last resort in diagnosis is exploration: the opportunity offered by this may be used to decompress the plexus or – more ambitiously – to attempt revascularisation by pedicled omental or musculocutaneous flap. It should, at least, be possible to offer relief from pain and a halt to the progress of the paralysis. There is good hope that increasing awareness of the condition and changes in the plan of radiotherapy will reduce the incidence of this distressing complication.

Risk management

The following 12 maxims are offered to aspirants in and practitioners of operative surgery:

(1) Peripheral nerves are widely distributed and vulnerable to damage by physical agents.
(2) The nerves of many patients are rendered abnormally susceptible to damage by existing conditions.
(3) Damage to peripheral nerves often causes serious disability.
(4) Cut nerves rarely recover spontaneously.
(5) The earlier a cut nerve is repaired or a compressed nerve freed from compression, the better will be the result.
(6) No patient's complaint of pain and dysfunction should be disregarded.
(7) Suspicion of nerve injury should lead to examination to determine the nerve involved, the level of the lesion and the extent and depth of injury.
(8) Evidence of a deep, complete lesion of a nerve after operation is usually an indication for exploration.
(9) If a surgeon has been around a main nerve with a knife in his or her hand, and if after operation there is deep paralysis in the distribution of that nerve, it has been cut.
(10) It is better to explore and find no remediable lesion than to wait and see and allow a remediable lesion to become irremediable.
(11) The use of a simple nerve stimulator during operations near nerves facilitates identification of conducting tissue.
(12) The prevalence of medical negligence actions following iatrogenous

lesions of peripheral nerves makes the topic of great importance for all who practise operative surgery, whether or not that is related primarily to any part of the nervous system. Practitioners should study to improve.

LEGAL COMMENTARY

M.A.M.S. Leigh

The defence of claims involving iatropathic lesions of peripheral nerves is bedevilled by the absence of evidence. A typical case on its facts was that of *Delaney* v. *Southmead Health Authority* which was considered by the Court of Appeal in 1992. Three to four days after an uneventful cholecystectomy, the patient complained of pins and needles in her left hand and clawing of the third and fourth fingers. Six days after this she was seen by a neurologist who diagnosed a brachial plexus lesion. The plaintiff pleaded *res ipsa loquitur*, that the damage would not have happened unless the arm had been hyper-abducted during the operation. Amongst those who gave evidence for the defence was Christopher Earl and the judge accepted his opinion that it was not necessary for the arm to be abducted beyond 45° during the course of the operation in order to cause the lesion.

The case is important as an illustration of how a defendant can refute the proposition of *res ipsa loquitur* partly by coming up with an alternative theory, but more importantly by calling the doctors involved who are able to impress the judge that they were cautious professionals who very probably did their best. Frequently, ulnar nerve palsies are not diagnosed until later than Mrs. Delaney's and there is often no real evidence available to the court as to whether they were caused in the operating theatre or sustained as a result of casual handling on the way back to the ward, in the recovery room or post-operatively.

Damage to the sciatic nerve is regularly reported following total hip replacement. Explanations put forward include stretching or traction injuries, direct or indirect pressure on the nerve and ischaemic lesions of the nerve due either to occlusion of the artery or thrombosis. A typical case was *Bentley* v. *Bristol and Western Health Authority* (1991). The precise explanation that the court is likely to accept as to the causation of the injury depends upon the approach to the operation. In the *Bentley* case, again the plaintiff pleaded *res ipsa loquitur* and Christopher Earl again gave evidence for the defence and suggested a vascular cause of the injury to the nerve. The judge rejected this. He accepted that the sciatic nerve is vulnerable to some extent in a hip replacement and that damage could occur in the absence of negligence, but the surgeon failed to persuade him that he had not been negligent. He pointed out that comments on the surgeon's 'own present credibility in relation to the operation is of limited assistance bearing in mind that 10 years have now elapsed since the relevant operation. He appeared to be a reasonably straightforward witness but he has no present recollection of the details of the operation according to him, and he could only describe his normal procedure. Various orthopaedic witnesses described his operation as good or adequate but this must be on the footing that nothing untoward that (he) regarded as worthy of comment occurred. I doubt whether that was the position at the time of the operation.'

This is a telling illustration of the way in which judges attack evidence. A contemporaneous written note will be regarded as cogent in a way in which a wealth of oral evidence from the witness box may simply fail to persuade. This is just as important in cases involving peripheral nerve lesions as it is in relation to any other cases.

In order to defend the hospital where an allegedly iatropathic lesion has been sustained, it is vital to demonstrate that appropriate procedures were followed. Some of these lesions are sustained in operating theatres, as with the ulnar and sciatic palsies. If the court has to decide whether the patient was subjected to untoward pressure on an ulnar nerve or stretching of a sciatic nerve, then it is essential to produce evidence that proper procedures were followed. It can be a help if there is documentary evidence in the form of protocols existing before the operation which indicate what procedures should have been followed. Increasingly these protocols are recognised as being a part of the way in which a properly organised operating theatre is supposed to work, and lawyers seek them out and will soon begin to comment on the absence of a protocol as being evidence in itself of a less than meticulous attitude to the problem in issue.

George Bonney describes numerous hazards which must be skirted either by act or omission which it is not the present practice to record. American operating notes are characteristically more detailed than those made in the UK. If the present generation of British surgeons finds such operating notes irritating, they will no doubt be displeased to learn that to the lawyer they look very much like the pattern for the future.

When confronted with a disastrous adverse outcome, the judge will certainly give the first precedence to contemporaneous records. However, this does not mean to say that there is not an important role for oral evidence. One example' of a case which was won by the defence largely on the basis of oral evidence is that of *Michelle Howard* v. *Wessex Regional Health Authority* (1994). Here the neuropathy involved was of central rather than peripheral nervous tissue, but nevertheless it illustrates the principle. A young woman was found to be tetraplegic as a result of a cervical cord infarction after an oral surgical procedure. The only way in which the defendant could explain the catastrophe was to suggest that the plaintiff might have had an ischaemic lesion caused by a fibrocartilaginous embolus. This explanation relied more on theory than observation. What may have led the court to accept that the patient's catastrophe was due to this rather than some sort of untoward jerking manoeuvre in the course of the procedure was the fact that the written records were supplemented by impressive oral evidence from virtually everyone in the operating theatre.

If the defence wishes to persuade the judge that nothing untoward happened it is a good tactic not to send the surgeon into court alone, but to call everybody who might have observed the untoward event that may be alleged. Some surgical disasters take place in deep body cavities out of sight of everyone except the surgeon and possibly the assistant and scrub nurse. Other disasters such as those occurring in the course of minimal access surgery, take place on television screens visible to everyone and are frequently recorded on videotape as well. Injuries to the peripheral nerve are somewhere in between: they usually result from inappropriate pressure or stretching manoeuvres. They may be caused by the surgeon or the anaesthetist or, in some cases, those who manoeuvre the patient between the operating theatre table and the ward. An effective tactic for the defence can be deployed by calling as many of these people as possible.

From the medical point of view, George Bonney stresses the importance of early repair. It now seems to be clear that remarkable results can be achieved by early repair of the divided peripheral nerve.

From the lawyers' point of view, this means that a successful defence requires us to prove that the lesion was recognised promptly, referred swiftly and repaired at an early stage. In order to achieve this, we have to demonstrate that the lesion did not exist at an earlier stage when it should have been recognised. Once again the lawyer needs records of the absence of signs and symptoms.

The severity of the lesion is something which doctors (and lawyers unless prompted) tend to overlook, but which is a factor of the first importance. Patients are less likely to sue in respect of transient lesions, being apt to suppose that they should be accepted as misfortune where the complete and permanent loss of a peripheral nerve could indicate carelessness. Furthermore, they tend to suppose that a complete palsy should be evident to the most indifferent examiner.

Finally it is important to note the role of Audit and Clinical Governance. The National Health Service (NHS) and private insurers are increasingly reluctant to accept surgical misfortune without enquiry. It is part of the proper processes of a hospital to note when things go wrong and to hold internal inquiries to find out why. The written fruits of those processes are not immune from discovery and plaintiff's solicitors may demand discovery of any documentation whenever created that may assist or inhibit the attempt to prove their case. Where a patient has suffered a peripheral nerve lesion the court may expect to see a written record of an inquiry of some sort, and this will have particular cogency because it may be expected to have come into existence shortly after the event, at a time when all those involved still had a clear memory of what had happened.

Commentary references

1. *Delaney* v. *Southmead Health Authority* [1995] 6 Med LR 355.
2. *Bentley* v. *Bristol and Western Health Authority* [1991] 3 Med LR 1.
3. *Michelle Howard* v. *Wessex Regional Health Authority* [1994] Med LR 57.

References

Bates, T. and Evans, R.G.B. (1994) *Brachial Neuropathy Following Radiotherapy for Breast Cancer*. Report of the review commissioned by the Royal College of Radiologists, London.

Birch, R., Bonney, G. and Wynn Parry, C.B. (1998a) Classification of iatropathic injury of nerves. In *Surgical Disorders of the Peripheral Nerves*, p. 295. Churchill Livingstone, Edinburgh.

Birch, R., Bonney, G. and Wynn Parry, C.B. (1998b) Reactions to injury. In *Surgical Disorders of the Peripheral Nerves*, pp. 44–6. Churchill Livingstone, Edinburgh.

Birch, R., Bonney, G. and Wynn Parry, C.B. (1998c) Interscalene block. In *Surgical Disorders of the Peripheral Nerves*, p. 298. Churchill Livingstone, Edinburgh.

Bowen, J., Gregory, R., Squier, M. and Donaghy, M. (1996) The postirradiation lower motor neurone syndrome. Neuronopathy or radiculopathy? *Brain* **119**, 1429–39.

Colville, R.J.I. and Colin, J.F. (1998) Median nerve palsy after high brachial angiography. *Journal of the Royal Society of Medicine* **91**, 387.

Cooper, D.E., Jenkins, R.S., Bready, L. and Rockwod, C.A. (1988) The prevention of injuries of the brachial plexus secondary to malposition of the patient during surgery. *Clinical Orthopaedics and Related Research* **228**, 33–41.

DeLisa, J.A., Lee, H.J., Baran, E.M., Lai, K., Spielholz, N. and Mackenzie, K. (1994) Myokymic discharge. In *Manual of Nerve Conduction Velocity and Clinical Neurophysiology*, 3rd edn, pp. 417, 458. Raven Press, New York.

De Smet, L. and Fabry, G. (1995) Transection of the motor branch of the ulnar nerve as a complication of two-portal endoscopic carpal tunnel release. *Journal of Hand Surgery* **20A**, 18–19.

Dudley, H. (1982) Modified-radical and radical mastectomy. In *Rob and Smith's Operative Surgery*, 4th edn (H. Dudley and W.J. Pories, eds), pp. 262–76. Butterworth Scientific, London.

Gilbert, A. and Tassin, J.L. (1984) Réparation chirurgicale du plexus brachial dans la paralysie obstétricale. *Chirurgie (Paris)* **110**, 70–75.

Iadarola, M.J. and Caudle, R.M. (1997) Good pain, bad pain. *Science* **278**, 239–40.

Karnes, W.E. (1993) Diseases of the seventh cranial nerve. In *Peripheral Neuropathy*, 3rd edn (P.J. Dyck, and P.K. Thomas, eds), pp. 818–36. W.B. Saunders, Philadelphia.

Kehoe, S., Reid, R.P. and Semple, J.C. (1995) Solitary benign peripheral nerve tumour. *Journal of Bone and Joint Surgery* **77B**, 497–500.

Lewis, T., Pickering, G.W. and Rothschild, P. (1931) Centripetal paralysis arising out of arrested blood flow to the limb. *Heart* **16**, 1–32.

Lundborg, G. and Rydevik, B. (1973) Effects of stretching the tibial nerve of the rabbit: preliminary study of the intraneural circulation and the barrier function of the perineurium. *Journal of Bone and Joint Surgery* **55B**, 390–401.

Maher, J. (1995) *Management of Adverse Effects Following Radiotherapy*. Report of the Maher Committee. Royal College of Radiologists, London.

Mantyh, P.W., Rogers, S.D., Honore, P., Allen, B.J., Gilhardy, J.R., Li, J., Daughters, R.S., Lappie, D.A., Wylie, R.G. and Simone, D.A. (1997) Inhibition of hyperalgesia by ablation of lamina I spinal neurones expressing the substance P receptor. *Science* **278**, 275–9.

Maran, A.G.D., Gaze, M. and Wilson, J.A. (1993) Tumours of major salivary glands. In *Still and Maran's Head and Neck Surgery*, pp. 264–95. Butterworth Heinemann, Oxford.

Morelli, E., Raimondi, P.L. and Saporiti, E. (1984) Il loro trattamento precoce. In *Le Paralisi Ostetriche* (F. Pipino, ed.), pp. 57–76. Aulo Gaggi, Bologna.

Narakas, A.O. (1981) Brachial plexus surgery. *Orthopaedic Clinics of North America* **12**, 303–22.

Pike, J. and Hollingsworth, R. (1995) Audit of postoperative autotransfusion of shed blood in arthroplasty. *Journal of the Royal Society of Medicine* **88**, 522P–523P.

Roos, D.B. (1981) Essentials and safeguards of surgery for thoracic outlet syndrome. *Angiology* **32**, 187–92.

Samii, M. (1980) Repair of the facial nerve. In *Management of Peripheral Nerve Problems* (G.E. Omer and M. Spinner, eds), pp. 527–33. W.B. Saunders, Philadelphia.

Schmalzried, T.P. and Amstutz, H.C. (1991) Nerve injury and total hip arthroplasty. In *Operative Nerve Repair and Reconstruction* (R.H. Gelberman, ed.), pp. 1245–54. J.B. Lippincott, Philadelphia.

Seddon, H.J. (1943) Three types of nerve injury. *Brain* **66**, 237–88.

Siliski, J.M. and Scott, R.D. (1985) Obturator-nerve palsy resulting from intrapelvic extrusion of cement during total hip replacement. *Journal of Bone and Joint Surgery* **67A**, 1225–8.

Thomas, C., Merle, M. and Gilbert, A. (1993) Endoscopic treatment of carpal tunnel syndrome. In *The Hand*, vol. IV (R. Tubiana, ed.), pp. 487–98. W.B. Saunders, Philadelphia.

Thomas, M., Stirrat, A., Birch, R. and Glasby, M. (1994) Freeze-thawed muscle grafting for painful cutaneous neuromas. *Journal of Bone and Joint Surgery*, **76B**, 474–6.

Winnie, A.P. (1970) Interscalene brachial plexus block. *Anesthesia and Analgesia, Current Researches* **49**, 455–66.

Chapter 12

Paediatric Neurology

Edward M. Brett

Introduction: some general considerations

The special status of the child in society, together with his or her differences neurologically and developmentally from the adult, result in specific problems in the medico-legal aspects of childhood neurological disorders. On the one hand the child, especially at younger ages, is vulnerable, helpless and dependent, and on the other he or she usually represents a precious vessel loaded with a cargo of the many hopes of his or her family for a happy and golden future.

The child also, far from being a miniature adult (an earlier distorted view), is an individual constantly changing and developing from fetal life to adolescence and adulthood, programmed to advance and to gain new skills to enable him or her to function independently and competitively in a demanding social milieu. At every age the normal child is different from all other ages. Each child's development must be viewed against the background of the norm for his or her age, so that the basic questions as to whether that development is normal and, if it is abnormal, whether it has always been abnormal or has diverged from a normal path, may be answered. It is on these answers that the important decision as to whether the child may be suffering from a static or a progressive disorder is based. Until the child has reached an age at which he or she should have achieved various developmental milestones, such as independent sitting, crawling, walking, speaking in words or sentences, and self-care skills, it is not possible to recognise that he or she shows delay. Hence the recognition of mental retardation and motor deficits, such as cerebral palsy, is inevitably often delayed, even though there may have been suspicion, because of risk factors, a family history or abnormal neurological findings in the newborn period, that these might develop. The same applies to the recognition of visual and hearing problems. The recognition of seizures in childhood may be delayed because parents, and sometimes doctors, fail to realise that the episodes are indeed fits.

Another difficulty, not unique to childhood, is the non-specific presentation of many acute neurological diseases, such as meningitis, including tuberculous meningitis, herpes simplex virus encephalitis and other encephalitis, with features of upper respiratory or gastrointestinal tract infection. The presentation of more chronic neurological illnesses may be insidious, with initially intermittent symptoms. Thus intracranial tumours, hydrocephalus, subdural haematomas and effusions, and other causes of raised intracranial pressure may take time to declare themselves clearly enough to be suspected and detected. The expandable skull of the young child allows readily for unduly rapid growth so that the effects of raised pressure may be delayed; an abnormal rate of growth of head circumference is therefore a vital clue, and regular measurement, recording and charting of this figure is a basic part of a paediatric examination – sadly often neglected. Within the spinal canal, pressure on the spinal cord, whether from within or without the cord, is a serious danger to cord function likely to declare itself earlier rather than later.

The importance of a detailed family history is probably greater in children than in adult practice. This may involve examination of parents or siblings, as well as taking an ordinary history. In diseases with autosomal dominant inheritance, an affected parent may show only mild features, so that a diagnosis may not have been made. Examples are tuberous sclerosis, neurofibromatosis, facioscapulohumeral and myotonic dystrophy, and hereditary motor and sensory neuropathy. Particular difficulties attend the recognition of childhood-onset Huntington's disease and of an affected parent.

Certain common diagnoses should always be kept under review so that the label does not induce a false sense of security, overlooking the possibility of an underlying progressive disorder. The label 'cerebral palsy', for example, implies a non-progressive pathology, but an occasional patient so labelled will prove to have a genetic disorder of progressive type or a spinal cord tumour. Similarly, the diagnosis of migraine to explain recurrent headaches should not stifle consideration of an alternative, more sinister cause.

Common pitfalls in paediatric neurology

The history

Listen to the mother

Although the history has been defined as 'an account of the patient's experience *in his own words*', in the paediatric field it is largely, but not wholly, obtained from the 'carer' – usually the mother, sometimes the father or other relative – and occasionally from an outsider such as a teacher, whose observations can be helpful.

In talking to parents, it is important to ensure that they understand the question, and answer *that*, and not some other question. This may need great patience; to keep some witnesses to the point at issue (as most lawyers will know) can be hard work. In dealing with symptoms which are outside the experience of most people, one often encounters an unwillingness, at times a refusal, to try to describe an event. This is especially common with episodes which may, or may not, be epileptic. Stephenson (1990) has written instructively of the problems of getting an accurate history in his monograph *Fits and Faints*. Often the reply is, 'Oh, you know, he had a fit.' Gently and tactfully one must explain that you *don't* know; he or she knows and one depends on his or her record. It is helpful to suggest that in future episodes a written account be made at the time in a diary, including all the details which are needed, mode and speed of onset and ending, previous event or precipitants (stress, fever, posture, etc.), associated features, duration and condition immediately afterwards (confusion, headache, speech disorder or weakness, general or hemiplegic). More errors are made in child neurology from inadequate history-taking than from other transgressions. It is unfair to label a parent as 'a bad historian'; the doctor is the historian, and it is his or her task to ferret out the truth, however difficult this may be.

That 'mothers are usually right' is a sound axiom, and many mistakes result from ignoring or discounting a mother's concerns about her child. Mothers usually know, perhaps intuitively, when there is a problem, and all paediatricians are familiar with the long-delayed diagnosis of certain disorders, both static and progressive. The reasons for this are not hard to find, and are referred to in the introduction above.

Talk to the child

Despite the major importance of the mother's contribution to the history, that of the child himself or herself must also be stressed. Only the child knows just what he or she experienced, yet his or her evidence is often neglected.

The older, more articulate child can describe the bizarre distortions of perception in some complex partial seizures; the focal onset in the face and tongue of fits in benign Rolandic epilepsy; the premonitory feelings of malaise in a syncopal attack; or the occurrence of early morning myoclonic jerks in juvenile myoclonic epilepsy. Failure to search for such clues often results in failure to recognise that a *generalised* convulsion, witnessed and described by a parent, had its onset focally, or that other seizure types are present, which place the case in a specific category of epilepsy syndrome, often with vital prognostic and therapeutic implications. For example, many children with juvenile myoclonic epilepsy are treated as if subject only to generalised convulsions through a failure to ask about myoclonic jerks; as a result they are often treated with carbamazepine, which may have a disastrous effect on their myoclonus. 'Leading questions' are often denigrated in medicine, as in law, but they are needed in the field of childhood epilepsy. Sometimes verbal accounts are inadequate and the doctor must demonstrate a range of seizure patterns (clonic convulsions, myoclonic jerks, infantile spasms, etc.) and offer them to the parent. Legally, this might be called 'leading the witness', but in the medical context it is sometimes a necessary tactic.

Leave a little room for doubt

Doctors are brought up to believe patients, and such trust is desirable. Nonetheless, it would be a naive doctor who believed that no parent had ever tried to mislead him or her. The recognition of the phenomena of non-accidental injury in childhood, and of child sexual abuse, was long delayed, because doctors could not believe such things could happen. The fields of non-accidental injury and child sexual abuse are minefields, for doctors and lawyers alike, and errors arise in both directions, i.e. over-diagnosis and under-diagnosis. Both errors can be catastrophic for the child and his or her family. The reader is referred to Hobbs *et al.* (1993) for a good review of child abuse and neglect.

The examination

'Hasten slowly'

The neurological examination of a child, particularly a very young child, is often more difficult than that of an adult. The normal toddler or young child may well regard the routine approach of the adult neurological examination as an assault on his or her person, and react with appropriate vigour. Hence a great deal of information must be obtained, and *can* be painlessly obtained, by simple observation of the child in the 'free range' situation. As the history is taken from the mother or another informant, the doctor can observe how the child reacts to the mother and to the strange person talking to her. Most gross degrees of developmental retardation and most gross motor deficits, as well as many features suggestive of a syndrome, will already become evident at this early and informal stage. The mobile child may well be ranging around the room exploring the furniture and equipment. Interest or lack of interest in his or her surroundings, ability to focus on a target, visual and auditory function, and gait, whether hemiplegic, diplegic, foot-drop, waddling, ataxic, etc., can quickly be assessed. Manipulative abilities, the presence of tremor, ataxia or dystonic movements can also be assessed by observation alone, with the more formal aspects of examination coming later, when the child's confidence has been won. The examination should ideally not become a battle, but even when the child fights off the doctor's closer attentions, the latter can at least gain useful information from his or her aggressive activity.

Certain specific aspects of the examination are of great importance, and their neglect has often led to litigation over a delayed diagnosis and treatment. Some of these do require closer handling of the child, and parental assistance can sometimes overcome any resistance.

Head circumference

The importance of regular and early measurement of head circumference has already been mentioned, but cannot be over-emphasised. It is the most neglected vital statistic of all. Cajolery and play-acting may be needed: 'Let's measure Mummy and Daddy for a funny hat, and now *you!*' Sometimes the child will allow the mother to measure him or her. It should seldom be necessary forcibly to hold the child down to take the measurement, but this is sometimes the lesser of two evils.

Examination of the spine

This must be examined throughout its length from neck to coccyx to exclude midline defects, such as hairy patches, sinuses, naevi or lipomata suggestive of spina bifida occulta. (The word occult is used as a contrast to aperta or cystica and is actually inappropriate, since the clues are usually there to be seen, if looked for.) If one such lesion is found, one must look for others, since they are often multiple and at different levels. The risks of undiagnosed spina bifida occulta are well-known. The neurological risk to limb and sphincter function often operates in later childhood, with the growth spurt, but meningitis is a greater and an earlier hazard when there is open communication between skin and theca, and it is particularly important in any child with bacterial meningitis, above all with recurrent episodes, to examine the spine carefully.

Scoliosis must never be neglected or overlooked. It has many causes, but from a forensic point of view, its main importance may well be as a possible pointer to a spinal cord tumour. A painful scoliosis must be taken seriously, and the same is true of an acquired torticollis, which may indicate a cervical cord or cerebellar tumour. Spinal deformity, whatever its cause and whether symptomatic or idiopathic, is itself a potential hazard capable of impairing spinal cord function, as well as respiratory efficiency.

Skin stigmata

The neurocutaneous syndromes loom large in child neurology, from the readily recognised Sturge–Weber syndrome, through the common tuberous sclerosis and neurofibromatosis with their myriad presentations, to the rare syndromes, such as incontinentia pigmenti and hypomelanosis of Ito. These are usually easily recognised if a thorough search is made. Their implications in terms of prognosis, genetics and general management are so weighty that a failure to diagnose them can have medico-legal consequences.

Tuberous sclerosis often presents with infantile spasms at three to nine months of age. If the child has received a vaccination such as diphtheria–pertussis–tetanus (DPT) shortly before the onset of the spasms, the possibility of brain damage due to pertussis vaccination is often raised. It is probable that compensation for this has been granted in the past in cases in which tuberous sclerosis was present, but had not been recognised (see below). The fact that the precise onset of infantile spasms is often difficult to date, since they may not have been recognised as seizures, makes the problem more complex. Tuberous sclerosis is inherited classically as an autosomal dominant condition, although most cases arise as a new mutation. Failure to make the diagnosis or, having made it, to examine both parents and any siblings for stigmata of tuberous sclerosis (which may be minimal, confined perhaps to a lumbar shagreen patch) will mean that appropriate genetic advice is not given, and will put those involved at risk of litigation.

In neurofibromatosis type I, the common, early-onset form, inheritance is also autosomal dominant. The classical *café au lait* patches may not be evident until some years have passed. The axillae should be examined carefully for the 'freckling' often found in that area. Lisch nodules should be looked for in the eyes. For the neurologist, neurofibromatosis conjures up glioma of the optic pathways and neurofibroma, so that the skin of children presenting with visual problems and acquired nystagmus, especially if unilateral, or with features suggestive of spinal cord compression, must be examined for the tell-tale stigmata. The genetic implications are similar to those of tuberous sclerosis.

Raised intracranial pressure

Recognition of this, and hence of the serious causal lesions, may be delayed for the reasons mentioned above. Headache is common in children and has many causes, mostly benign, but headaches which are frequent and prolonged, associated with vomiting, and are worse on waking or wake the child from sleep must be taken seriously. With posterior fossa tumours, a head tilt and a painful stiff neck are often present.

Examination of the optic fundi may be difficult in young children. Mydriatic eye drops are often used to facilitate examination, but they should be avoided, since they rob the observer of the valuable data to be gained from the pupil reactions. When the child is referred to the neurological or neurosurgical centre it may be difficult to know if his or her large inactive pupils are due to the effect of a mydriatic or dysfunction of the third nerve, which have very different outcomes.

Meningitis (think of meningitis)

The classical features of meningism – fever, headache and vomiting, irritability, lethargy, neck stiffness and Kernig's sign – are often absent in infants and young children. Bacterial meningitis often presents in the context of an apparently banal upper respiratory infection or otitis media, which is often treated (sometimes inappropriately) with an antibiotic. This may have the effect of suppressing the clinical features of meningitis for a time and delaying the diagnosis. Partially treated bacterial meningitis is a common and difficult problem; sometimes no organism can be cultured and hence no sensitivities established.

The diagnosis is especially difficult in the newborn and in young infants in whom the signs are often subtle and non-specific. Fever is present in only 50% of neonates with meningitis. Commoner features are lethargy, lack of interest in feeding, vomiting or diarrhoea, jaundice and changes in respiration. Irritability, a valuable clue in older patients, is seen in only a third of neonates with meningitis. Seizures and a bulging anterior fontanelle occur late: the latter may be absent if the child is dehydrated. Most cases of meningitis follow an initial phase of bacteraemia, and features suggesting infection should always raise the suspicion of meningitis, even when a clear site of infection has been found. This applies above all in the newborn period, when lumbar puncture is an important part of the screen for infection, together with blood culture. The outcome of untreated or late-treated meningitis in the neonate is dismal, but is much improved with early diagnosis and appropriate treatment, the mortality being 15–20%, a figure little changed in the past two decades.

Meningitis may sometimes present, as may other bacterial infections, with a 'febrile convulsion'. There has been debate about the need for lumbar puncture in febrile fits. The special difficulty in diagnosing meningitis in those under six months of age (Rossi *et al.*, 1986) means that it is essential for the first febrile convulsion in this age group, and most authorities recommend lumbar puncture in all children under 18 months of age. Lumbar puncture should also be performed with complex seizures with fever, and when there seems to be serious underlying disease not otherwise explained. A sound rule is to do a lumbar puncture when there is any doubt. One very rare problem the author has encountered, having a disastrous outcome with brain damage and subsequent litigation, is the occurrence of hyperglycaemia in bacterial meningitis, which led to the incorrect diagnosis of diabetes mellitus.

Meningitis is a particular concern in the child with immune deficiency, whether congenital or acquired, with communication between skin and spinal theca, as in spina bifida occulta, with cerebrospinal fluid shunts and with recent neurosurgical procedures.

The skin must also be carefully examined for cutaneous features which give a valuable early clue in some forms of meningitis. The well-known, rapidly spreading purpuric rash of meningococcal septicaemia (sometimes seen also in pneumococcal and *H. influenzae* sepsis) is one of the most dramatic and vital clinical signs, which must lead to prompt investigation and antibiotic therapy. A UK campaign to educate the public (and doctors) on the significance of this rash which does not fade on pressure has saved lives and limbs, although there are some concerns that an impression may be given that an absence of the rash excludes the diagnosis of *any* form of meningitis.

The choice of antibiotic in children with bacterial meningitis is much debated. A vast array of agents is available. Changing patterns of antibiotic sensitivity keep the doctor on his or her metaphorical toes. Treatment must be started *before* the sensitivities of the organism are reported by the laboratory: in some cases no organism is isolated. These problems are well discussed by Levin and Walters (1997) in a wide-ranging review.

Supportive care and treatment of the complications of meningitis, which may be life-saving, require management in hospitals with full intensive care facilities, to which the child should ideally be moved by staff experienced in resuscitation and transport of critically ill children. The specific problems of raised intracranial pressure with cerebral oedema, acute hydrocephalus and subdural effusions, respiratory support, control of seizures (which occur in 20–30% of patients), hypotension, multi-organ failure and critical care neuropathy often present a major therapeutic challenge to the medical and nursing team involved.

Many children with meningitis have neurological deficits at the time of discharge from hospital, but considerable improvement may occur over time, giving grounds for guarded optimism.

Significant hearing loss is a common complication of bacterial meningitis, occurring in 2.4–29% of cases. At follow-up all children should have their hearing tested.

Tuberculous meningitis

Involvement of the central nervous system is the most serious complication of tuberculosis. Tuberculous meningitis is a common cause of mortality and lasting morbidity in children in areas where tuberculosis is prevalent, especially the Indian subcontinent and regions in the West with high immigration from Asia.

Since the onset of tuberculous meningitis is usually insidious over a matter of weeks and the early symptoms are vague and non-specific, a high index of suspicion must be maintained. Within days or a few weeks, evidence of severe brain damage usually appears, with declining consciousness, seizures, focal or generalised, cranial nerve palsies, signs of raised intracranial pressure and pyramidal tract signs. Meningism is often present. Fundoscopy may show papilloedema and choroidal tubercles. Delayed diagnosis and treatment reduce the chances of a full recovery.

Diagnostic delay is often caused by a failure to consider the diagnosis, preferring a commoner disorder, such as a viral or partially treated bacterial meningitis or a space-occupying lesion. A family history may show family members with known tuberculosis, and 'case-finding' is an important public health measure.

Misinterpretation of the laboratory findings in the cerebrospinal fluid is another common cause of delay. The protein level may be slow to rise. Although lymphocytosis is usual, a preponderance of polymorphs may be found in the cerebrospinal fluid. The cerebrospinal fluid glucose level is often normal in the early stages, and moderately reduced levels may not be followed up persistently enough to exclude tuberculosis. Hence the search for the bacteria may not be sufficiently diligent: this important examination is demanding and time-consuming. The clinician must be prepared to insist on a prolonged search, if necessary on a further cerebrosinal fluid specimen. Fluorescent microscopy may be helpful.

Although the Mantoux test is positive in most patients with tuberculous meningitis, a negative result does not exclude it. Nor does a normal chest X-ray, since this is only abnormal in about half the cases.

Computerised tomography (CT) or magnetic resonance (MR) imaging is often helpful in showing enhancement in the basal meninges, cortical thrombophlebitis, infarction, tuberculomas and hydrocephalus, and is useful in the management of the latter. Levin and Walters (1997) have reviewed the investigation and management of tuberculous meningitis.

General examination

To neglect general examination in favour of only one system is clearly unwise, and a holistic approach is needed here as in all aspects of medicine. Many factors, such as asphyxia and ischaemia, can affect other targets besides the central nervous system. Multisystem diseases can present neurologically. The neurological complications of leukaemia and related diseases, and of their treatment, are increasingly recognised. Cardiac lesions may underlie cerebrovascular events in childhood, as at other ages, and cardiomyopathy occurs in various diseases. Friedreich's ataxia, Duchenne muscular dystrophy and their ilk must be remembered. The blood pressure should never be neglected, since hypertension may be a symptom or a cause of neurological disease; lower motor neurone facial palsy in childhood may be a symptom of hypertension, an association not as well-recognised as it should be. Suspicion of trauma, however acquired, must prompt a search for other evidence, in bony lesions, perhaps of various ages, in the retina with retinal haemorrhages, in the skin and elsewhere.

Collecting the evidence

The expert who is asked to prepare a report on condition and prognosis, causation and life expectancy can only be expected to do this if he or she has all the available evidence. In paediatric cases, this usually means the obstetric and neonatal notes, and the records of the child's biography before and after the event which is the subject of litigation, whether this be in pregnancy, in labour or at a later stage.

The process of obtaining copies of the records is often arduous and lengthy, but it is an essential preliminary to a critical review of the data. In some cases, earlier records are unobtainable, having been destroyed or lost after the lapse of years, or for other reasons. A degree of *obsessionality* is a requisite in both medicine and law, and equally or more so in medico-legal work. A poorly copied 'neurological observation chart' or a nurse's cardex record has sometimes provided vital evidence, not documented elsewhere, as to when a child's pupil reactions became abnormal, giving an earlier date for the onset of severe neurological dysfunction than was otherwise evident. The expert should insist on the provision and review of as much documentation as possible, and should make it clear when a report is based on incomplete documentation. Indeed, in some cases it is wise to refuse to express an opinion when the records are totally inadequate.

Cerebral palsy

It is in the field of cerebral palsy that litigation most often arises in relation to childhood neurological handicap, and it is necessary to consider the definition of these disorders, and also the historical development of the concepts of their causation from the nineteenth century onwards. Only in this way can the previously dominant mind-set and received wisdom, and the more recent 'wind of change' which has blown away many misconceptions, be understood.

Definition

Several definitions have been suggested, but a good one is 'a persistent but not unchanging disorder of movement and posture caused by non-progressive pathological processes of the immature brain'. An alternative definition, 'the name given to the motor manifestations of the non-progressive brain damage sustained during infancy and childhood', is less desirable. This implies that damage to the brain is the only possible cause, and ignores the possibility that the abnormal brain function may result from prenatal factors such as maldevelopment of the brain, an aetiology which is increasingly recognised since the advent of CT and MR imaging. Such a definition can only support the widespread mistaken and simplistic equation of disordered brain *function* with brain *damage* as its invariable cause. This confusion is present in many lay people's and some doctors' minds, as if *trauma* were the only ill to which the young brain is heir.

As in all paediatric problems, a chronological approach is necessary. One must consider not only the process of delivery itself, and the difficulty which the fetus may experience in coping with its potentially harmful effects, and in adjusting to independent existence, but also the earlier period of fetal brain development during which an almost miraculous evolution occurs, culminating in the structural and functional complexity of the normal human brain. Historically, the emphasis in seeking the roots of cerebral palsy has been on the process of delivery and the perinatal period, but increasing attention is now focused on intrauterine life, with its potential for adverse effects.

It is important to stress that in cerebral palsy motor function is not merely *delayed* but is also *deviant*, following a course never seen in a normal child.

The situation is made more complex, in comparison with the neurology of older patients, by the fact that the paediatrician and child neurologist are dealing with a small person who is programmed to develop in a remarkable way, acquiring new skills in motor, language and cognitive function as he or she grows older. Each child must be considered in the context of his or her age and the level of development considered normal for that age. The 'test of time' is one of the commonest, and least expensive, investigations applied, particularly in paediatric neurology, in order to decide whether, in what way and to what extent, the child's development is delayed and deviant. This feature is at the same time one of the difficulties and one of the attractions of the specialty. It can be a potent source of dissatisfaction, or even anger, to parents that the doctor only diagnosed the child as 'spastic' after a year or more, 'when I've been telling him all along there was something wrong'.

The very concept of cerebral palsy is in some ways an artificial one, since the term covers a very wide range of disparate neurological disorders, with the clinical picture influenced also by other symptoms caused by the underlying brain disorder, whether this be known or not. Thus the two other common chronic neurological handicaps of childhood, mental retardation and epilepsy, are often associated with cerebral palsy, all these problems stemming from a common root and interacting. In addition, a wide range of sensory deficits, visual, auditory and even tactile, may coexist, and superimposed skeletal problems with contractures and deformities of limbs and spine may sometimes, despite vigorous therapy aimed at prevention, compound the child's problems. The degree of cognitive impairment and the child's own motivation to improve, related to this, are other important prognostic factors. If seizures are frequent and intractable, management is rendered more difficult and prognosis less favourable.

Classification

It is clearly naive, though common, to generalise about such a heterogeneous group of disorders (just as it is to speak of childhood epilepsy as if it were one condition). The different categories of cerebral palsy are associated with different aetiological, prognostic, therapeutic and educational features (for a historical review of the classification of cerebral palsy the reader is referred to the classic monograph of Ingram (1964) and to Ingram (1984)). Unfortunately, the terminology of the subject is, in places, tortuous, so that different words may be used for the same concept, particularly in the field of involuntary movements caused by impaired function of the extrapyramidal system. Here one encounters the terms athetoid, athetotic, choreic, choreiform, choreoathetoid and dystonic, used to describe certain types of abnormal movement with some features in common. The word dyskinesia is sometimes used to cover the range of abnormal movements.

It is understandable that judges and lawyers may sometimes have difficulty in understanding and even pronouncing the various terms. At times resorting to *imitating* the abnormal movements, or showing a video record of them, is a better way to convey to others what is going on than by the spoken or written word. (Videos and photographs are also very useful in child neurology in showing how a child functioned at an earlier age, when there is uncertainty about the onset of a problem.)

The *distribution* of the motor deficit is an essential element in classification. The widely used categories are hemiplegia (self-explanatory); diplegia, meaning bilateral deficit more marked in the legs than the arms; and tetraplegia (the pure Greek derivation is preferable to the mongrel (Latin and Greek) quadriplegia), for four-limb deficit with the upper limb deficit as severe as, or severer than, the lower. The term bilateral or double hemiplegia is sometimes used instead of tetraplegia, but can be criticised since tetraplegia constitutes a more severe deficit than the summation of two hemiplegias, with mental retardation, epilepsy and bulbar problems often being present. The words monoplegia and triplegia are applied to one-limb and three-limb involvement, but these are rare situations in clinical practice.

Movement and posture in cerebral palsy are disordered by alterations of tone, by weakness, by unwanted movements and by ataxia, in various combinations. Hypertonia in cerebral palsy, as in diseases of later onset, may be of a primarily spastic or rigid type, although features of both may be present. Extrapyramidal rigidity is often associated with involuntary movements of dyskinetic, choreoathetoid or dystonic type. Hypotonia is usually a transient phase in the evolution of tone towards the hypertonic state, although short-term variations in tone occur in any children with cerebral palsy, in relation to physiological and other factors.

Ataxia is another element of disordered movement. Pure ataxic cerebral palsy is relatively uncommon and more often the picture is a mixed one of 'spastic–ataxic diplegia', with varying degrees of the two elements in different patients.

Associations

Certain associations are well-recognised between types of cerebral palsy and their commoner aetiologies. For example, in the days before effective treatment and prevention were available for severe neonatal jaundice, due to rhesus (Rh) or ABO blood group incompatability or other causes, kernicteric brain damage affecting particularly the basal ganglia and auditory nerve (but also sometimes other cerebral structures) led to postkernicteric choreoathetoid or dyskinetic cerebral palsy, with sensorineural deafness, often associated with a defect of voluntary upward gaze and with greenish staining of the first teeth. With appropriate management in the developed nations, this has become a rarity. Since the introduction in 1969 of the administration of anti-D immunoglobulin to mothers after delivery, the incidence of haemolytic disease of the newborn has plummeted. Nonetheless, a warning note was sounded by Letsky and de Silva (1994), who pointed out that in Britain the rate of RhD sensitisation is still unacceptably high, at around 1.5%, so that more than 1,000 Rh-negative women each year develop anti-D antibodies in association with the delivery of a Rh-positive infant.

In premature infants, kernicterus may still lead to athetoid cerebral palsy, often with a contribution from hypoxia. A rather similar picture of dyskinetic cerebral palsy occurs in term infants who have suffered perinatal hypoxia, but signs suggestive of 'pyramidal' dysfunction are often also found, and deafness, abnormal upgaze and dental staining are not seen.

Spastic diplegia, with upper limb function better than lower, and often with relatively preserved intellect, has long been known to develop, and still does so, in a significant proportion of infants born prematurely with appropriately low birth weight. This is often correlated with the presence of periventricular leucomalacia demonstrable on imaging and pathologically.

In some cases, intraventricular haemorrhage (shown by ultrasound or other imaging) and hydrocephalus can result, causing additional brain damage and dysfunction.

With spastic hemiplegia and tetraplegia, the aetiological correlations are less consistent, and evidence is increasing that these problems often originate prenatally, sometimes in cerebral maldevelopment (often of unknown cause), and sometimes from damage to the brain *in utero*, in relation to a variety of insults, such as maternal infections and other illnesses. Congenital spastic hemiplegia is seldom if ever genetically determined, but some syndromes of bilateral spasticity may be inherited. With ataxic and spastic–ataxic pictures, the possibility must always be considered of an underlying genetic disorder, progressive or non-progressive, of undetected hydrocephalus which may be successfully treated, or even of a posterior fossa tumour.

Historical perceptions, epidemiology and changing views

The seminal paper of Little (1862) led to a widespread acceptance of such factors as abnormal parturition, difficult labour, premature birth and asphyxia neonatorum as being commonly responsible for what later came to be known as cerebral palsy. This perception dominated medical thinking for over a century after his paper. Even so, Freud (1897), during his phase as a child neurologist, questioned Little's view and pointed out that the abnormalities noted in the perinatal period might sometimes be the *result* of disordered brain function rather than the cause of the subsequent impairment. Berendes (1969), in discussing fetal distress and its significance in neurological and mental impairment in childhood, was later to suggest that many factors might be involved, and that perinatal difficulties may be 'an insult on prepared soil'.

Illingworth (1985) was the author of one of the first of a series of more critical reviews of the aetiology of cerebral palsy. Impressed by the readiness with which doctors accept the diagnosis of brain damage at birth, he asked, 'Why is it called birth injury?' He stressed that in most cases severe difficulties in delivery and severe birth hypoxia are not followed by evidence of 'brain damage,' and that the maternal history showed a significantly greater incidence of relative infertility, and of pregnancies associated with low birth weight or intrauterine growth retardation, postmaturity, antepartum haemorrhage, pre-eclampsia or infections. Genetic factors, congenital anomalies and pathological evidence of underlying abnormality were often present. He concluded that there was an interaction of numerous factors, pre-, peri- and postnatal, and that it was simplistic to ascribe 'brain damage' to single factors, such as breech delivery or hypoxia at birth, without considering the antecedent causes of these factors.

More recent epidemiological studies of cerebral palsy from many parts of the world have examined this question critically. Two studies of large defined populations have looked retrospectively from the known neurological outcome and attempted to estimate the proportion of children in each population likely to have cerebral palsy as a sequel to intrapartum events.

A large North American cohort study, the Collaborative Perinatal Project (NCPP) of the National Institute of Neurological and Communicative Disorders and Stroke, dealt with births between 1959 and 1966 (Nelson and Ellenberg, 1986) and considered hundreds of variables. The follow-up of 41,018 children showed that at seven years of age, cerebral palsy not acquired through known illness or injury after the first month of life was present in 189 of these children. The estimate of the proportion of cerebral palsy associated with intrapartum asphyxia in births in the NCPP was in the range of 3–13% (and did not exceed 21%).

The Western Australian case-control study using a total population-based cerebral palsy register, which included children diagnosed up to 1985 (Blair and Stanley, 1988) showed results in close agreement with the NCPP. Of 183 cases of cerebral palsy, only 4.9% were considered very likely to have experienced intrapartum damage, and this was considered possible in a further 3.3%, while in 91.8% intrapartum injury was considered highly unlikely to account for the disability.

There is a very significant association of cerebral palsy with low birth weight. Analysis of cerebral palsy data from the Mersey region of the UK between 1967 and 1984 (Pharoah *et al.*, 1990) showed that during this period there was no change in the prevalence of cerebral palsy among infants of normal birth weight, but the prevalence of all types of cerebral palsy among low-birth-weight infants (<2500 g) at least doubled. The increase was most marked for those of the lowest birthweight (<1500 g). Stanley and Blair (1991), reviewing the Western Australian data and many other studies with sound methodology, asked the (rhetorical) question, 'Why have we failed to reduce the frequency of cerebral palsy?' They concluded that cerebral palsy proportions in low-birth-weight infants are rising in most developed countries, coincident with increases in the neonatal survival of low-birth-weight babies, that few cases of cerebral palsy seem to be caused by birth asphyxia and that those which are may not have been preventable by obstetric care. The Swedish survey (Hagberg and Hagberg, 1989) of 'the changing panorama of infantile hydrocephalus and cerebral palsy over 40 years' shows similar findings and illustrates this point well. The authors compared the two periods 1979–82 and 1967–70 to assess the hypothetical 'gains' and 'hazards' of the decreasing perinatal mortality in terms of non-cerebral palsy and cerebral palsy in survivors. The decrease in perinatal mortality from 17.5 to 7.4 per 100,000 births/year entailed a 'gain' of nearly 4000 'healthy' infants (at least free from cerebral palsy) compared with the earlier period. This was at a 'cost', however, of nearly 300 cases of cerebral palsy. These included a new category of extremely preterm infants (who previously would have died), with combinations of severe neurological impairments, cerebral palsy, mental retardation, hydrocephalus, epilepsy and retinopathy, which are cause for alarm. Hagberg and Hagberg believed that as long as the survival of preterm infants continues to increase and extends to ever lower gestational ages, there will be yet more such damaged children, a conclusion with which it is hard to disagree.

The contribution of neuropathology to the understanding of the aetiology of cerebral palsy is limited. Mortality in general is low, and is highest in the most severely affected patients. When death occurs it tends to be long delayed; the largest pathological study of cerebral palsy, that of Christensen and Melchior (1967), found that the results were unrepresentative for this reason.

Nelson (1991) reviewed the prenatal origins of hemiparetic cerebral palsy and the mechanisms by which it may arise. She pointed out that the birth-weight distribution of this form of cerebral palsy is less skewed towards low weight than in other types, although in recent years the prevalence of hemiplegia has increased in low-birth-weight infants.

Neuroimaging, especially the newer, non-invasive techniques, offers more help in seeking an aetiology. Ultrasonography is particularly helpful, since it can be used relatively close to the time of presumed pathogenetic events (Leviton and Paneth, 1990). The report of Scher *et al.* (1991) of six term neonates with intracranial lesions dated by ultrasonography to pathological processes occurring before the onset of labour is an example of the value of neuroimaging techniques in the timing of cerebral lesions. Two Swedish studies of early-onset hemiplegia gave evidence for the prenatal onset of disability in most of the children born at term. In preterm infants, hemiplegia may often be related to early postnatal events or to an interaction between prenatal and perinatal factors (Powell *et al.*, 1988; Wiklund and Uvebrant, 1991). Population-based studies now in progress of imaging in preterm babies and sample studies of term infants will allow a correlation between their later neurological status and prenatal brain lesions detected by ultrasound. A recent Japanese MRI study of 70 patients with cerebral palsy (Sugimoto *et al.*, 1995) concluded that most were of prenatal origin and only 12.8% were caused by birth asphyxia.

Nelson (1991) considered the well-known association of prenatal brain damage with *twinning*; the prevalence of cerebral palsy was six times higher in twins than in singletons in a recent population-based North American study. Ten percent of the cerebral palsy children were twins. Factors involved in this higher morbidity in twins include a tendency to low birth weight, and an excess of congenital anomalies and obstetric complications including cord entanglement. Twin-to-twin shunting of blood through anastomotic channels may produce the transfusion syndrome. When one of a pair of twins dies, disruption of the survivor may occur due to release of thromboplastic substances or to embolisation, haemodynamic shifts or other factors. If this occurs early in gestation, before 16 weeks, microgyria and neuronal heterotopia may occur in the surviving twin (Barth, 1987). Twinning ascertained by ultrasound early in pregnancy is more frequent than at the time of delivery – 'the vanishing twin' phenomenon – (Landy *et al.*, 1986) – so that the potential contribution of twinning to cerebral palsy may be greater than is realised. As Nelson (1991) stressed, although there are *many known* mechanisms by which fetal brain damage can occur, there may be many more still to be discovered.

Reviewing the evidence in the individual case

Clearly the doctor reviewing a patient with cerebral palsy in an attempt to determine the cause, whether in a medico-legal context or in ordinary practice, must hunt for every possible clue and scan the records very closely – a situation which is akin to detective work. Uncritical acceptance of undocumented statements is unwise. Sadly, the documentation in many cases referred for review is incomplete. Obstetric and neonatal notes may not contain essential data, such as Apgar scores, head circumference measurements and biochemical results. It is as unwise to offer an opinion in a medico-legal case when data available are not produced, as it would be in a purely medical context. It is sometimes necessary to insist that a search be made, when the gap may occasionally be filled. Bedrick (1989) wrote that we must be prudent and exact in our medical documentation of infants with a complicated adaptation to extrauterine life.

Terminology is important; terms such as perinatal or birth asphyxia, and hypoxic–ischaemic or postasphyxial encephalopathy are often loosely applied, and ideally should not be used until or unless some evidence specific to an asphyxial origin for neurological illness in the neonate is available. Bax and Nelson (1993), in a statement on birth asphyxia, recommended that the above terms should be replaced by 'neonatal encephalopathy of early onset'. Whether or not their advice is followed, such a formula might well decrease the common tendency to beg the question of asphyxia.

In a valuable article, Freeman and Nelson (1988) reviewed the relationship between intrapartum asphyxia and cerebral palsy. They concluded that virtually no single sign or symptom has sufficient correlation to enable prediction of later cerebral palsy with a reasonable degree of medical certainty. For cerebral palsy to be attributed to prior asphyxia with reasonable certainty, they suggested that four conditions be fulfilled:

(1) Marked and prolonged intrapartum asphyxia did occur.
(2) The infant, as a newborn, showed signs of moderate or severe hypoxic-ischaemic encephalopathy, with evidence also of asphyxial injury to other organ systems, such as renal or cardiac (this aspect was reviewed by Perlman *et al.* (1989)); when evidence of transient renal impairment is documented, it is a valuable clue, but milder degrees may well be overlooked in dealing with a sick infant's more pressing problems).
(3) The child's neurological condition is one that intrapartum asphyxia could explain.
(4) Other conditions have been ruled out.

With regard to the first condition, Freeman and Nelson discussed assessment during labour with special reference to the role of fetal heart monitoring. Continuous electronic monitoring is now widely used, but its value is undergoing reassessment. It appears that its use in *low-risk* pregnancies results in a higher rate of Caesarean sections and forceps deliveries, but with little evidence of improved outcome. Nonetheless, abnormalities of the cardiotocograph (CTG) are often adduced as evidence in litigation, and an expert opinion from an obstetrician or neonatologist familiar with the subject should be obtained in such cases (the author does not believe that the average general or paediatric neurologist can provide a good opinion on this specialised issue). Interestingly, although the incidence of neonatal seizures (regarded as one measure of fetal outcome) may be reduced by electronic monitoring, a study in Dublin found no difference in deaths secondary to asphyxia, or in outcome of survivors between those labours monitored electronically and those monitored by auscultation (MacDonald *et al.*, 1985).

Meconium staining of the amniotic fluid is an indication that fetal distress has occurred, and staining of the skin or cord suggests that the insult occurred at least four to six hours prior to membrane rupture (Fiyikura and Klionsky, 1975). However, meconium staining does not of itself predict later outcome.

Acidosis, measured by scalp or cord blood pH, might be thought to provide the best measure of severity and duration of intrauterine asphyxia and to correlate with outcome, but studies have shown little correlation of severe acidosis with Apgar score, neonatal neurological status or outcome, although the reported series did not contain many infants with a low pH (<7.0), a group in which better correlation with outcome might be expected. A normal pH, on the other hand (>7.2 and perhaps even lower), can be taken as evidence that substantial asphyxia has *not* occurred in the recent past.

Regarding Freeman and Nelson's (1988) criterion that other possible causes have been ruled out, it is debatable how far investigation should be carried in a purely medico-legal context, in contrast to a medical one. If the brain has not been imaged previously, should CT or MR imaging be arranged? The results are not predictable, and might support or demolish a case for causation, either showing appropriate imaging findings, no abnormality, or features of a prenatal disorder, such as a neuronal migration defect. The parents must understand this clearly. When a child would need sedation or anaesthetic to achieve a scan, ethical concerns arise. Pressure should not be put on parents to agree to an investigation that they do not want.

The review by Freeman and Nelson (1988) is a reminder of the sequence of events required for *near certainty* that intrapartum asphyxia was responsible for cerebral palsy in a particular patient. It provides useful guidelines for the doctor in his or her search for a causal link, whether in a clinical or medico-legal context. When the sequence is well documented, the expert can feel fairly confident of this link. When, despite detailed documentation, one or more of the four criteria are not fulfilled, there must be doubt. When, as sadly often happens, the necessary data are missing, as a result of substandard note-taking (illegibility, incomprehensibility, for example idiosyncratic abbreviations or acronyms) or of unavailability of records, perhaps destroyed after the passage of many years, the expert cannot give a clear statement, and should be prepared to say so.

Despite the basic soundness of these guidelines (which it would be beneficial for members of the legal profession to understand), the experienced paediatrician or child neurologist will encounter cases in which they may seem too strict. An important example of this occurs in the field of dyskinetic (extrapyramidal) cerebral palsy. Rosenbloom (1994), in a review of the relationship between this type of cerebral palsy and intrapartum asphyxia, pointed out that the reviews on which these guidelines were based did not distinguish between the dyskinetic and the spastic and mixed forms of cerebral palsy. Of a group of 17 term infants with dyskinetic cerebral palsy in the Mersey region, 10 were likely to have sustained intrapartum asphyxial brain damage as the cause. In this situation, a characteristic pattern was usually seen of severe fetal distress occurring late in labour, severe but short-lived birth asphyxia and only mild or moderate hypoxic–ischaemic encephalopathy. This clinical picture should be distinguished from the pattern of birth asphyxia which precedes the development of spastic tetraplegic cerebral palsy. Rosenbloom stresses that the whole sequence of events is necessary for a causal link with dyskinetic cerebral palsy to be established, as opposed to mild or moderate hypoxic–ischaemic encephalopathy.

Stillbirths and neonatal deaths

In a recent monograph on cranial haemorrhage in the term newborn infant, medico-legal aspects are helpfully discussed by Wigglesworth (1993) from the perspective of the neuropathologist giving advice in litigation. He stresses the importance of a skilled post-mortem examination with photographic and radiological records as well as full examination of the brain if an infant or child dies in circumstances which could lead to litigation. If parents are blaming the hospital for the death, it may be necessary to involve the coroner; the autopsy is ideally performed by a regional perinatal pathologist on the coroner's behalf. Careful gross and microscopic examination of the brain is important, but, as Wigglesworth points out, is often inadequate. He stresses the need for widespread sampling of the brain from at least six areas, including frontal lobe, temporal lobe with hippocampus, thalamus, midbrain, pons, cerebellum and medulla, as well as several levels of the spinal cord and from gross lesions, in order to assess whether there is underlying ischaemic damage apart from any traumatic lesion.

Risk management strategies

Wigglesworth (1993) also stresses the need to develop 'risk management strategies' in response to the rising tide of medical litigation, not in the sense of 'defensive medicine', but rather specific targeting for improvements in investigation and record-keeping in those areas where litigation is most likely to arise. The reason for any specific procedures, obstetric or neonatal, especially if not standard, should always be stated in the notes; in this regard neonatal records are normally better than obstetric notes. Paediatricians should be careful not to label their neurologically disabled patients as having suffered severe birth asphyxia or trauma if they have not personally studied the obstetric records, since unfounded references to 'severe fetal anoxia' may encourage groundless actions. Any infant who develops signs of encephalopathy, which could be due to either trauma or asphyxia, should have imaging studies by real-time ultrasound or CT scan performed as soon as possible to provide an initial baseline and show whether prenatal damage is present. Copies of all ultrasound scans should be kept with the notes or X-rays. These are sound rules, reflecting good practice, yet honoured more often in the breach than in the observance; it is the wise doctor who learns from the mistakes of others rather than from his or her own.

That ideal standards of management are not always met is shown by a recent (March 1995, HMSO, 1995) confidential enquiry into stillbirths and deaths in infancy in the UK which has analysed the contributory factors. Failure to react to abnormal CTGs was the commonest reported problem; others were lack of experienced senior supervision during inductions, inadequate monitoring, and overdosage with prostaglandins or oxytocin. Nearly two-thirds of the intrapartum and early neonatal deaths were attributed to asphyxia. Almost 40% of stillbirths or infant deaths were associated with serious obstetric complications such as antepartum haemorrhage, ruptured uterus or shoulder dystocia. The commonest criticism of obstetricians was failure to act appropriately; of midwives and general practitioners (GPs) it was failure to recognise problems. Communication between professionals was often poor, especially between senior and junior staff, and in foreseeing the need for a paediatric presence at delivery.

Such criticisms are often made by experts in cases in which it is alleged that cerebral palsy has resulted from intrapartum asphyxia. In many cases, the infant's condition at birth was such that he or she was thought unlikely to survive.

A forthright consensus statement was recently issued by the Australian and New Zealand Perinatal Societies (1995) in response to those problems and litigation. Current Australian data indicate that the public are largely unaware that more than 15% of pregnancies will miscarry, 6–8% of babies will be born preterm, 1% will die around the time of birth, 5% will have a notifiable birth defect and 0.2–0.25% (2–2.5 per 1000 liveborn) will have cerebral palsy. The authors state that there is a great need to teach health professionals and the public that the causes of cerebral palsy are often hidden, and are almost always prenatal, only to become apparent after birth. Ideally this would need to be part of a widespread public educational programme in normal physiology, health and disease.

These two reports may appear contradictory. This is symptomatic of the rapid advances in knowledge in recent years flowing from the many detailed epidemiological studies of cerebral palsy, and from improved methods of investigation, particularly the new imaging techniques. Recent large series of cerebral palsy patients investigated by MRI, for example, have confirmed the prenatal origin in many cases, yet it is probable that most children with cerebral palsy are not investigated in this way, whether or not they are the subject of litigation. From the perspective of the epidemiologist, and that of the medical expert in litigation, the relative contributions of prenatal and perinatal factors may appear very different, and for the public these issues are confusing.

Life expectancy

A prediction of the length of survival of a handicapped child with cerebral palsy and/or other neurological disorders is often sought by lawyers in order to assess the sum (quantum) required to provide for the child's needs. They often seek precise figures and many physicians find this difficult.

Data are emerging from epidemiological studies which provide some guidance (Table 12.1). A survey of the survival of children with cerebral palsy in the South-East Thames region of the UK born between 1970 and 1979 (Evans *et al.*, 1990) showed that 90% were still alive at follow-up. Survival varied considerably among the different diagnostic groups: those suffering from spastic 'quadriplegia', dyskinetic and 'mixed' cerebral palsy were the most severely affected, with respective mortalities of 26, 9 and 25%. Immobility and mental subnormality, which were frequently associated, were independent and the strongest predictors of mortality, but the majority of even the most severely affected patients survived to adulthood.

Table 12.1 Mortality in 35 patients classified by mobility and mental status (from Evans *et al.*, 1990).

	Number (%) alive or lost to follow-up	Number (%) dead	Total
Immobile and severely subnormal	65 (69)	29 (31)	94
Immobile but not severely subnormal	27 (93)	2 (7)	29
Severely subnormal but not immobile	59 (97)	2 (3)	61
Neither immobile nor severely subnormal	258 (99)	2 (1)	260
Total	409 (92)	35 (8)	444

Although preliminary analysis showed an association between epilepsy and poorer survival, this was really owing to the strong association between epilepsy and mental subnormality. However, there is an impression that intractable epilepsy, particularly with episodes of status epilepticus, adversely affects survival; neurological and cognitive deterioration may correlate with status epilepticus which can rarely be fatal. Severe feeding difficulties, particularly related to gastro-oesophageal reflux with a tendency to aspiration and chest infection, are another important adverse factor, as is severe spinal deformity, which reduces the efficiency of the lungs and predisposes to pneumonia and cor pulmonale. Bladder problems, urinary tract, and other infections, and bedsores are further adverse factors.

In a more recent survey of all children with cerebral palsy born during 1966–84 in the Mersey region of the UK, the main outcome measures were the effect of functional ability (ambulation, manual dexterity and mental ability), sex, birth weight and gestational age on survival (Hutton *et al.*, 1994). Life expectancy in this group of children was greater than that found in some previous studies. The best statistical model used gestational age and the number of severe functional disabilities as predictors. Twenty-year survival for the whole cohort was 89.3% for females and 86.9% for males. For those without severe functional disabilities, the 20-year survival was 99%, while those severely disabled in all three functional groups had a 20-year survival of 50%. Epilepsy is not discussed in this survey.

In considering the life expectancy of children with cerebral palsy living in the UK, who enjoy the benefits of a relatively uniform standard of medical care under the National Health Service (NHS; now 50 years old), it seems most appropriate to refer to the two UK surveys mentioned above, rather than the surveys conducted on populations elsewhere, such as the Californian studies of Eyman *et al.* (1996), in which the patients may have been receiving more varied levels of care. It is interesting, however, that a recent survey from California (Strauss and Shavelle, 1998), analysing data on individuals aged 15 years and over between 1980 and 1995, found that the key predictors were lack of basic functional skills, mobility and feeding: those lacking these skills had much reduced life expectancies, as short as 11 years for the worst functioning groups (which would imply survival to age 26 and over). The life expectancies of adults of a given age could differ by 40 years or more, according to their functional level.

It must be admitted that the estimation of life expectancy in children with cerebral palsy is one of the most difficult questions which medical experts are asked by lawyers. There can never be any certainty on these matters, and the expert can only give an opinion based on his or her own clinical experience and a review of the literature. It is reasonable to feel more optimistic about a child born in the 1990s, who can benefit from advances in the management of gastro-oesophageal reflux, spinal curvature and other orthopaedic problems, infections and epilepsy, than might have been justified in assessing a comparable child some decades ago. There is today a more positive attitude to the management of the handicapped than prevailed earlier. This is seen, for example, in more interventionist or 'aggressive' management of scoliosis in boys with

Duchenne dystrophy and girls with Rett's syndrome, in the greater attention paid to the associated problems of people with Down's syndrome, and in the encouraging developments in methods of non-verbal communication. The motto 'small profits, slow returns' is an appropriate one in chronic neurological handicap. An apparently small improvement in mobility, independence, feeding or communication may represent a great step forward for a child and his or her family with improvement in quality of life.

Mental retardation without cerebral palsy as a result of perinatal brain damage

Mental retardation is often associated with cerebral palsy, and sometimes also with epilepsy. These three common neurological problems often occur together because they have a common root cause, whether dating from the prenatal, perinatal or postnatal period.

The question sometimes arises as to whether mental retardation *without* clinical features of cerebral palsy can be the result of adverse factors in the perinatal period. Parents are often keen to pursue this line of enquiry, not only in their understandable need to know the cause of their child's problems, but also sometimes with a view to litigation against a hospital, and an expert opinion is then sought on causation. Sometimes there has been documented evidence of difficulties in delivery or of problems in the newborn period, which may have been adduced as causing or contributing to the developmental delay.

The causes of mental retardation are numerous, but in some cases no clear cause can be recognised. A detailed perinatal and family history is needed. The contribution of chromosomal anomalies, especially X-linked mental retardation, is well-known, and such easily diagnosed disorders should be excluded, as should as far as possible the many genetic disorders associated with mental retardation. The presence of dysmorphic features increases the chances of a malformation syndrome. When microcephaly is present, it is important to know whether this was already present at birth, or whether it was 'acquired', as a result of deceleration in head growth, as may occur after perinatal hypoxia and ischaemia, as well as in certain syndromes such as those of Rett and Angelman. Microcephaly present at birth is unlikely to be the result of brain damage at that time.

The consensus of 'received wisdom' is that mental retardation on its own is seldom caused by adverse perinatal factors. As with most 'rules' in medicine, there are occasional exceptions. Brain imaging, preferably MRI, in this situation occasionally shows an unusual abnormal appearance known as ulegyria, which is known to result from perinatal asphyxia in the more mature brain from term, i.e. 36 weeks gestation onwards, and associated with developmental retardation and acquired microcephaly. Such findings on MRI may strongly support a perinatal origin for a child's delayed development. The appearance of ulegyria, with 'waisting' of the bases of the gyri, the greatest damage tending to lie in the watershed zones of the brain in the frontal and parietal regions, is quite unlike the gyral anomalies seen in the various malformations of prenatal onset.

EPILEPSY

Classification

Epilepsy is a common disorder in childhood, affecting some 6–8 per 1000 children of school age. Like cerebral palsy it is very variable in its manifestations, and generalisations are even more misleading. The subject is well reviewed by O'Donohoe (1994) among others. The classification of epileptic seizures into those which are *primarily generalised* contrasting with *partial* seizures starting locally which may or may not show *secondary* generalisation is important. The further subdivisions of partial seizures into simple and complex, the latter with some impairment of consciousness, is also extremely helpful to the clinician. The recognition of numerous *syndromes* of epilepsy, which may be relatively benign or malignant in terms of prognosis, and also age-related, is very helpful in considering aetiology, prognosis, treatment and genetic aspects. Thus, syndromes of primary generalised epilepsy such as childhood absence epilepsy (true *petit mal*) and juvenile myoclonic epilepsy are seldom, if ever, caused by demonstrable organic brain disease such as cerebral tumour. Benign Rolandic epilepsy (benign focal or centrotemporal epilepsy of childhood) is seldom the result of detectable brain pathology, by contrast with many other cases of simple or complex partial seizures, with or without secondary generalisation, in which history and brain imaging often indicate a 'lesional' aetiology. There is no area of neurology in which a clear, detailed and accurate history from an observer, and when possible from the older child patient, is so important.

Epilepsy, being one of the chronic neurological handicaps of childhood, is commonly associated with cerebral palsy, mental retardation and the occurrence of troublesome and intractable seizures, especially status epilepticus, and therefore is an important factor in prognosis, including life expectation in the severely neurologically handicapped child.

Risks for the child with epilepsy

The child with epilepsy is at risk of injury during fits; occasionally, litigation may centre on the warning that parents and other carers were given by medical advisors of these risks. In general, restrictions on a child's activities should be as few as seems compatible with common sense. Some parents, understandably, wish to restrict their child's activities to an unnecessary degree, and gross 'overprotection' can adversely affect the chances of normal development, marking the child out even more as abnormal. Swimming, cycling and horse-riding are areas needing discussion with parents. O'Donohoe (1994) provides valuable guidance on 'what the child with epilepsy should be allowed to do'. Clearly young children should not go swimming or cycling unaccompanied. Careful supervision of swimmers in the water is essential; a pairing system, by which all children are expected to swim in pairs, is a simple and prudent strategy.

Drowning in the family bath-tub is actually a greater hazard to the patient with epilepsy than swimming, yet this risk is often not appreciated and is not discussed with parents and children. Patients should not lock themselves in the bathroom nor should they bathe in a full bath; a water depth of only 5–7.5 cm is advisable. Unfortunately even showering has its risks, since the patient in a fit may fall through glass or plastic or against hot water taps. It seems appropriate that the paediatrician or neurologist advising the child's parents should discuss these risks as part of the general advice on management and lifestyle. It should be mentioned also that there are dangers in the child locking the lavatory door, since it may be impossible to rescue him or her if he or she has fallen in a fit. It must be admitted that the co-operation of the child, especially the teenager, may not be easy to obtain in these areas.

The problem of 'vaccine damage'

The neurological complications of immunisation against various infectious diseases have different causes and mechanisms. Aicardi (1992) lists 'immunoallergic complications associated with protection against influenza, rabies, rubella, measles, and diphtheria–pertussis–tetanus (DPT).'

The more controversial topic of brain damage associated with DPT immunisation has attracted much attention and has produced fierce debate since the publication of reports questioning the safety of pertussis vaccine led to a serious loss of confidence in the immunisation programme and a steep decrease in acceptance rates (Kulenkampff *et al.*, 1974). In the UK, a system of 'vaccine damage' compensation was set up, with financial awards in cases in which it was considered more likely than not that severe neurological handicap (80% or more) had been caused by immunisation. Such decisions were difficult, since seizures and other features of acute encephalopathy often occur at the ages when DPT vaccination was usually performed. The lack of any specific test or pathology for 'vaccine damage', the fact that the children involved might have been neurologically and developmentally abnormal *before* the vaccination without this having been recognised, and the wide variation in the attitudes of experts towards the concept of vaccine damage (ranging from easy acceptance to total scepticism) contributed to this difficulty.

In the UK, the National Childhood Encephalopathy Study (NCES) was set up in 1976 with the aim of examining the causes and outcome of severe acute neurological illnesses in young children, with particular reference to the possible role of pertussis vaccine as an aetiological agent (Alderslade *et al.*, 1981; Miller *et al.*, 1981). The results indicated that there was a relatively higher risk of children suffering from an acute neurological illness in the seven days following DPT immunisation than in control cases. The attributable risk of serious neurological reaction was 1 per 100,000 immunisations. This apparent small increase in the risk of neurological damage induced by pertussis vaccination needs to be weighed against the mortality and neurological damage induced by pertussis itself in unvaccinated children (Miller *et al.*, 1986).

In a later report, the results of a follow-up study by the NCES of over 80% of cases and controls were reviewed by Miller *et al.* (1993). The conclusions of the study were that DPT vaccine may on rare occasions be associated with the development of severe acute neurological illnesses that can have serious sequelae in some children, that the illness may occur by chance, or may have other causes. The role of pertussis vaccine as a prime or concomitant factor cannot be determined in any individual child. The balance of possible risk against known benefits from pertussis immunisation supports continued use of the vaccine. Japanese experience of the catastrophic effects of withdrawing the vaccine following two deaths of recently immunised children in 1976 certainly favours this view (Kanai, 1980).

For the doctor faced with the decision whether to vaccinate a child or not, the above statistics may be comforting yet not entirely reassuring. A personal or close family history of seizures, with or without fever, has in the past often been taken as a contraindication to vaccination against pertussis for fear that a febrile reaction to the vaccine might trigger a fit. In children liable to febrile seizures, the use of diazepam given by the rectal route (Stesolids©) has been a valuable therapeutic strategy, and appropriate advice should be given on the use of paracetamol and other antipyretic measures.

It is clearly important to be aware of any neurological disorder in a child candidate for vaccination. Neurocutaneous syndromes in which external stigmata point to the diagnosis may go unrecognised unless the skin is carefully examined. Tuberous sclerosis is an example of a disease which may not be diagnosed until some years have passed, although the skin will show the characteristic amelanotic macules long before facial adenoma sabaceum becomes evident. A common presentation of tuberous sclerosis is with seizures, particularly infantile spasms (West's syndrome). These are an age-specific type of generalised seizure with onset usually between three and nine months of age, and with a poor neurodevelopmental prognosis. Often they are not recognised as seizures until some weeks or even months have passed, and may be mistaken for episodes of colic. It is therefore difficult to determine their precise date of onset and to relate this to the timing of a vaccination. Clearly if a child shows evidence of tuberous sclerosis or of other identifiable pre-existing neurological disease, vaccination cannot be claimed as the primary cause of his or her problems.

An important practical point is the need to avoid vaccination in a child with a current or very recent infection.

The officially accepted contraindications to immunisation noted in the UK by the Joint Committee on Safety of Vaccination and Immunisation change periodically and are published regularly in the *British National Formulary*. In 1987, the recommendations were that pertussis vaccination should not be done in children with a history of any severe local or general reaction, including a neurological reaction, to a preceding dose, or with a history of cerebral irritation or damage in the neonatal period, or who have suffered from fits or convulsions.

Special consideration, falling short of absolute contraindications, is recommended in certain other groups: children whose parents or siblings have a history of 'idiopathic' epilepsy; those with developmental delay thought to be due to neurological defect; and children with neurological disease. The risk of vaccination may possibly be higher in these groups than in normal children, but in them the effects of pertussis itself may be more severe, so that the benefits of vaccination may be greater. The risk versus benefit balance in each case must be carefully assessed.

The wishes and fears of parents should be considered in this area, and vaccination should *not* be performed against their expressed wishes. In the author's experience, when this has been done and problems have arisen soon afterwards, parental feelings have run high and they have been convinced of a causal relationship and are sometimes determined to seek legal redress. This is particularly - and understandably - common when there has been an apparent adverse reaction to a previous vaccination which has been ignored or discounted by professionals. Stories are told of the child being snatched from the unwilling mother and vaccinated despite her protests. Whether true or not, this has been the mother's perception, and such actions cannot be condoned.

The importance of measuring the head circumference

Paediatricians and all doctors should understand the importance of measuring, and recording, the maximum occipito-frontal head circumference from birth onwards, and charting its growth on a standard chart, in the same way as weight and height are recorded. Special charts should be used for premature babies, and correction made for the degree of prematurity.

In some cases, unduly rapid growth of the head circumference may be the only clue to hydrocephalus or to subdural collections. The significance of a single measurement on its own is difficult to interpret, since it must be related to earlier figures to decide whether head growth is following the same centile line, or is crossing centiles. Similarly, microcephaly (small head), should be viewed against the background of earlier figures. Ideally the head circumference at birth is recorded, and it can be seen whether later measurements at, say, 6 or 12 months are on the same centile, or whether there has been deceleration in the rate of head growth, as occurs, for example, in Rett's syndrome, in the infantile form of Batten's disease and in some patients with perinatal brain damage. Congenital microcephaly is unlikely to be caused by problems occurring at the time of delivery and favours a prenatal aetiology. It is remarkable how often there is no record at all of the head circumference.

Genetics

The parents of a handicapped child want to know why this tragedy has happened, what it is, what can be done about it, what will happen in the future to their child, and will it occur again if they have more children? Often the answer to the last question, and the only bright spot in a gloomy scenario, is a firm negative. Sadly, however, the answer is sometimes affirmative, with a recurrence risk of one in four or one in two, and this realisation is the sorrow's crown of sorrows for the devastated parents.

Accuracy in genetic counselling is important, but it can be difficult. The basis is a firm diagnosis; the genetic risks for most recognised disorders are now well understood. The high-risk disorders must be diagnosed, and the appropriate risks calculated and given. For the low-risk disorders, a reassuring view can be taken, but for non-specific mental retardation it is wise to advise a slightly higher risk than the normal 1%.

Errors in genetic counselling stem from two main sources. One is a geneticist's lack of diagnostic expertise and the giving of advice without making a clear diagnosis. The other is a lack of genetic expertise in a paediatrician or child neurologist who undertakes genetic counselling without support from an expert. Ideally it should be a combined operation, with input from the experienced clinician who is aware of the many diagnostic possibilities including the latest advances, and from the geneticist familiar with the newest developments in molecular biology. Communication and co-operation are of paramount importance in this field, as in so many others, and patients suffer when these are lacking. So complex has the 'new genetics' become that the clinician is wise to consult an experienced geneticist whenever possible. Neither can hope to get it right always; problems will arise when an example of a 'new' syndrome is first encountered, and many experienced clinicians have seen the emergence of syndromes previously unknown in recent decades;

examples are the eponymous syndromes of Rett and Angelman, the mitochondrial and the peroxisomal disorders, and the recognition of the 'dystrophinopathies'. Probably many more syndromes are still hidden in the womb of time, to be delivered to recognition after longer gestation. Prenatal diagnosis is now possible for many disorders.

This vast field cannot be fully covered here, and the reader is referred to the review of practical genetic counselling by Harper (1994). The London Dysmorphology Database (Winter and Baraitser, 1991) provides valuable guidance to the clinician struggling to recognise a syndrome and to keep abreast of the ever-growing legion of disorders.

LEGAL COMMENTARY

M.A.M.S. Leigh

Paediatric neurology for the lawyer falls into two very different categories. The first is where the paediatric neurologist is the defendant. These cases are few and far between. There are many reasons for this. Sadly one of them is the poor prognosis for the majority of patients who consult paediatric neurologists. Even where cases do have an initially better prognosis with optimal management, such as meningitis, the majority of claims are made against general practitioners or other primary care physicians who failed to refer the patient more promptly. This may in part be because of the very high standard of care rendered by paediatric neurologists.

The ways in which paediatric neurologists nevertheless can get it wrong are well described by Edward Brett. In many cases it will be as a result of failing to listen carefully enough to what the patient or the parent is saying. Sometimes it is as a result of taking what they say too literally.

Where the very small child is concerned no history will be elicited from the patient and the extent to which this disables the doctor is illustrated by the primacy which is accorded to history taking in the assessment of the adult patient by the neurologist.

Where the examination is concerned Brett describes in detail the importance of simple observation of the child. There is a clear analogy here with the general practitioner's assessment of the overall impression that the child makes upon him. The general practitioner will be greatly reassured by the child who does not appear to be ill; Brett describes how the specialist observes numerous aspects of specific behaviour in the course of a simple observation of the child in the free range situation. The difficulty for the lawyer is that it is rare, indeed, for the doctor to document the numerous aspects of the movement of the child with the detail that Brett describes. As with the general practitioner, we have in some way to recreate the examination before the judge's eyes to demonstrate that numerous negative observations were made.

In paediatric cases notes are of particular importance because of the decades which may elapse between examination and litigation. In any given case it will be difficult for a doctor to persuade a judge that an examination was performed or an aspect of behaviour observed if there is no note to support the claim. In paediatric cases there will usually be no recollection either. As far as the judge is concerned, if it is not recorded usually it did not happen. If the neurologist protests 'but in those circumstances *I would always* observe the child's interest or lack of interest in his surroundings, his ability to focus on a target, his visual and auditory function, his gait whether hemiplegic, diplegic, foot drop, waddling, ataxic etc, his manipulative abilities, the absence of tremor ataxis or dystonic movement', the judge is likely to write down that the doctor has conceded that those are the things which *should always* be observed. Once the concession is made that it should happen the search for evidence that it did so can begin. Once again, the skills are for the patient, the notes are for the doctor.

One oddity of paediatric neurology which comes across very clearly from Edward Brett's account concerns the significance of the differential diagnosis. In most other specialties the danger is that the practitioner will miss an alternative and more serious differential diagnosis. In paediatric neurology the danger is that the general examination will be inadequate, as a result of which the practitioner will miss a less sinister but more treatable diagnosis.

The second area of paediatric neurology with which lawyers are far more familiar is where they are acting as 'picking-up-the-pieces merchants', as their colleagues in general paediatrics are inclined to put it. The paediatric neurologist has little danger of being cast in the defendant's role when helping to disentangle the causes of cerebral palsy or some other species of chronic handicap. There they are acting as professional expert witnesses. Such is the demand for this work that some of them are able to do it almost full-time. Doctors should be aware that the role of the expert witness has become much more rule-governed in recent years.

Edward Brett stresses the importance of securing the basic evidence. As he says, from a risk management point of view, other specialisms could do much more to help themselves if they would record the basic information which the neurologist would need to ascertain the causation of subsequent disability. It is far more important to secure the information than it is to worry about whether or not it will in fact incriminate the hospital. There seems no reason for a modern hospital to fail to test and record the acid base status of the cord blood whenever a child has to be delivered by emergency caesarean section or has a 1 minute Apgar score of less than 5. As Brett points out, a normal pH (which he defines as ≥ 7.20) is evidence that substantial asphyxia has not occurred in the recent past, whereas a lower pH has less diagnostic and prognostic significance.

Edward Brett points out the importance which some observers attach to the 'vanishing twin' phenomenon, it being suggested that where one of a pair of twins dies, the agonal event may have disastrous consequences for the other. It has thus been suggested that a fetus papyraceous is a marker for subsequent cerebral palsy. It may be that in years to come research which is only now being carried out will substantiate this thesis. Since in these cases the death of the first twin is a first trimester event, it seems inescapable that the damage will have been done long before the child came to term, and that any apparent evidence of fetal distress or birth asphyxia occurred after the child sustained the insult of which subsequent complaint is made. Yet few hospitals search systematically for a fetus papyraceous and in most cases even when a child is born in disastrous condition, the examination of the placenta will be a cursory affair by one of the midwives in the delivery room. At least, that is the way it appears to the lawyer because the only note describing the condition of the placenta that is usually offered is in a midwife's hand and appears at the bottom of the birth summary.

Edward Brett also raises the question of the ethical concerns which arise when an MRI scan is proposed for forensic reasons. If in the absence of the scan the child has an apparently strong case for claiming compensation, then parents will usually be reluctant to consent to the investigation. If the defendant's lawyer insists upon it, the court will have to decide whether it is in the patient's interests to undergo the investigation. The plaintiff will argue that the court should not order the investigation if it will not be in the patient's interests and the defendant will say that the court ought to stay the action unless the patient agrees to co-operate. Once it is established in this country that such scanning is in fact a necessary part of a reasonable preparation for this sort of litigation, then the objections will fall away.

The first case in which this was proposed was that brought to *Caroline Robertson* v. *Nottingham Health Authority*.[1] There the patient refused to consent to an MRI on the grounds that it was too hazardous an investigation to be reasonable. However she did consent to undergo a CT scan. The CT scan appeared to reveal a condition of hydranencephaly, absence of much of the supratentorial brain, which suggested a developmental failure in the first or second trimester, long before she came to hospital at 36 weeks gestation. Confronted with this evidence the patient's advisers decided that after all it would be reasonable to undergo an MRI scan since this was the only way of saving her action. The MRI with its greater sensitivity was able to pick up strands of glial tissue so that the diagnosis changed to multicystic leukomalacia, implying that the fetal brain had formed before being destroyed by a profound insult.

In the USA, many plaintiff's lawyers refuse to commence cases unless the patient agrees to undergo an MRI at the outset. It may be that with the arrival of conditional fee arrangements those acting for patients in this country will take a similar view. Once the use of the MRI has become commonplace in such litigation, the courts will be more likely to find that it is unreasonable of the patient to refuse to undergo it, and that it is in their interests if it is a part of the normal process which they have to undergo to establish their claim to the compensation which will transform their lives.

The vaccine damage cases which Edward Brett describes represent an area of medicine which may have been more rigorously explored by lawyers than doctors. After the basic evidence was assembled by the doctors in the research which Edward Brett describes it was then rigorously examined over many weeks in trials taking place successively in Edinburgh, Toronto and London. In each case the verdict was the same: the evidence did not support the hypothesis that the vaccine could cause permanent damage. It is true that plaintiffs have succeeded in establishing these cases in other jurisdictions where the forensic process is less rigorous, but overall it seems highly unlikely that the Legal Aid Board in England will finance any further litigation of this sort, or that lawyers who work on conditional fee arrangements will risk their own money in the hope of persuading the courts to join the doctors in mistaking subsequence for consequence. The damage that this process has caused, however, has now become apparent from research recording the differential take up of vaccination and the consequent prevalence of pertussis in countries where the litigation was fashionable (Gangarosa, 1998).[2] It would be sad if society were to take a similar path with the measles, mumps and rubella vaccine on the basis of evidence which is considerably less persuasive at first blush.

For the lawyer the most important point to stress about the work of the paediatric neurologist as an expert witness is the importance of the witness having an impeccable reputation. Some experts have been criticised by the courts for acting like a 'hired gun', but they do not have to allow matters to get that far in order to lose their utility to the court and thus to the party who instructs them. The principles which an expert should follow were identified by Creswell J in a celebrated case [*The 'Ikarian Reefer'* (1993)][3] as:

(1) Expert evidence should be, and seen to be, the independent product of the expert uninfluenced as to form or content by the exigences of litigation.
(2) An expert should provide independent assistance to the court by way of objective unbiased opinion in relation to matters within his expertise.
(3) An expert witness should never assume the role of the advocate.
(4) An expert witness should state the facts upon which his opinion is based, and he should not omit to consider material facts which could detract from his concluded opinion.
(5) An expert must make it clear when a particular question falls outside his expertise.

(6) If an expert opinion is not properly researched because he considers insufficient data available, then this must be stated with an indication that the opinion is no more than a provisional one. In cases where an expert who has prepared a report could not assert that the report contained the whole truth and nothing but the truth without qualification, that qualification should be stated in the report.
(7) If after exchange of expert reports an expert witness changes his view on a material matter, having read the other side's expert reports, or for any other reason, such change of view should be communicated through the party's representatives to the other side without delay and, where appropriate, to the court.

In another case [*Sharpe* v. *Southend Health Authority* (1997)][4] the same judge, Creswell J, said that in alleged medical negligence cases where the *Bolam* test would provide a defence to those who follow any recognised school of thought, the expert witness should make it clear in his report where he or she would have adopted a different practice, and if he or she accepts that the approach adopted by the defendant was in accordance with the approach accepted as proper by a responsible body of practitioners skilled in the relevant field.

These are rules of good housekeeping but the fundamental point which is made clear by the Woolf Reforms is that experts owe their primary duty to the court, not to the party which is paying them to give evidence. Those practitioners who cling to this rule will find lawyers beating a path to their door even if it means that in some cases they have to give disappointing advice.

Commentary references

1. *Caroline Robertson* v. *Nottingham Health Authority* [1997] 8 Med LR 1.
2. Gangarosa, E.J., Galazka, A.M., Wolfe, C.R., Phillips, L.M., Gangarosa, R.E., Miller, E. and Chen, R.T. (1998) Impact of anti-vaccine movements on pertussis control: The untold story. *Lancet* **351**, 356.
3. '*The Ikarian Reefer*' [1993] 2 Lloyd's Report 68.
4. *Sharpe* v. *Southend Health Authority* [1997] 8 Med LR 299.

References

Alderslade, R., Bellman, M.H., Rawson, N.S.B. *et al.* (1981) The National Childhood Encephalopathy Study. In *Whooping Cough*, pp. 74–169. HMSO, London.

Aicardi, J. (1992) Para-infectious and other inflammatory disorders of immunological origin. In *Diseases of the Nervous System in Childhood. Clinics in Developmental Medicine 115/118* (J. Aicardi, ed.), pp. 697–731. MacKeith Press, Oxford.

Australian and New Zealand Perinatal Societies (1995) The origins of cerebral palsy – a consensus statement. *Medical Journal of Australia* **162**, 185–90.

Barth, P.C. (1987) Disorders of neuronal migration. *Canadian Journal of Neurological Sciences* **14**, 1–6.

Bax, M. and Nelson, K.B. (1993) Birth asphyxia: a statement. *Developmental Medicine and Child Neurology* **35**, 1022–4.

Bedrick, A.D. (1989) Perinatal asphyxia and cerebral palsy. Fact, fiction or legal prediction. *American Journal of Diseases of Children* **143**, 1139–40.

Berendes, H.W. (1969) Fetal distress: its significance in neurological and mental impairment of childhood. In *Perinatal Factors Affecting Human Development*, pp. 228–33. WHO Scientific Publications No. 185.

Blair, E. and Stanley, F.J. (1988) Intrapartum asphyxia: a rare cause of cerebral palsy. *Journal of Pediatrics* **112**, 515–19.

Christensen, E. and Melchior, J. (1967) *Cerebral Palsy – a Clinical and Neuropathological Study. Clinics in Developmental Medicine No. 25*. Spastics Society Medical Education and Information Unit and William Heinemann Medical Books, London.

Evans, P.M., Evans, S.J.W. and Alberman, E. (1990) Cerebral palsy: why we must plan for survival. *Archives of Disease in Childhood* **65**, 1329–33.

Eyman, R.K., Strauss, D.J. and Grassman, H.J. (1996) Survival of children with severe developmental disability. In *Diagnosis and Management of Neurological Disabilities in Childhood* (L. Rosenbloom, ed.). Bailliere's Clinical Pediatrics: International Practice and Research. Bailliere Tindall, London.

Fiyikura, T. and Klionsky, B. (1975) The significance of meconium staining. *American Journal of Obstetrics and Gynaecology* **121**, 45–50.

Freeman, J.M. and Nelson, K.B. (1988) Intrapartum asphyxia and cerebral palsy. *Pediatrics* **82**, 240–9.

Freud, S. (1897) *Die infantile cerebrallahmung (Nathnagel's specialle pathologie und therapie)*, div. 2, pt. 2, vol. 9. Holder, Vienna.

Hagberg, B. and Hagberg, G. (1989) The changing panorama of infantile hydrocephalus and cerebral palsy over forty years – a Swedish survey. *Brain Development* **11**, 368–73.

Harper, P.S. (1994) *Practical Genetic Counselling*, 4th edn. Butterworth-Heinemann, Oxford.

HMSO (1995) Confidential Enquiry into Stillbirths and Deaths in Infancy; Part I. Her Majesty's Stationery Office, London.

Hobbs, C.T., Hanks, H.G.I. and Wynne, J.M. (1993) *Child Abuse and Neglect. A Clinician's Handbook*. Churchill Livingstone, Edinburgh.

Hutton, J.L., Cooke, T. and Pharoah, P.O.D. (1994) Life expectancy in children with cerebral palsy. *British Medical Journal* **309**, 431–5.

Illingworth, R.S. (1985) A paediatrician asks – why is it called birth injury? *British Journal of Obstetrics and Gynaecology* **92**, 122–30.

Ingram, T.T.S. (1964) *Paediatric Aspects of Cerebral Palsy*. Churchill Livingstone, Edinburgh.

Ingram, T.T.S. (1984) A historical review of the definition and classification of the cerebral palsies. In *The Epidemiology of the Cerebral Palsies. Clinics in Developmental Medicine, No. 87 SIMP* (F. Stanley and E. Alberman, eds), pp. 1–11. Blackwell Scientific, Oxford.

Kanai, K. (1980) Japan's experience in pertussis epidemiology and vaccination in the past thirty years. *Japanese Journal of Medical Science and Biology* **33**, 107–43.

Kulenkampff, M., Schwartzman, J.S. and Wilson, J. (1974) Neurological complications of pertussis inoculation. *Archives of Disease in Childhood* **49**, 46–9.

Landy, H.J., Weiner, S., Carson, S.L., Batzer, F.R. and Bolognese, R.J. (1986) The 'Vanishing twin'. Ultrasonographic assessment of fetal disappearance in the first trimester. *American Journal of Obstetrics and Gynecology* **155**, 14–18.

Leviton, A. and Paneth, N. (1990) White matter damage in preterm newborns – an epidemiologic perspective. *Early Human Development* **24**, 1–22.

Letsky, E.A. and de Silva, M. (1994) Preventing Rh immunisation – much scope for improvement. *British Medical Journal* **304**, 213–14.

Levin, M. and Walters, S. (1997) Infections of the nervous system. In *Paediatric Neurology*, 3rd edn (E.M. Brett, ed.), pp. 621–89. Churchill Livingstone, New York.

Little, W.J. (1862) On the influence of abnormal parturition, labour, premature birth and asphyxia neonatorum on the mental and physical condition of the child, especially in relation to deformities. *Transactions of the Obstetrical Society of London* **111**, 293.

MacDonald, D., Grant, A., Sheridan-Pereira, M., Boylan, P. and Chalmers, I. (1985) The Dublin randomized control trial of intrapartum fetal monitoring. *American Journal of Obstetrics and Gynaecology* **152**, 524–39.

Miller, D.L., Alderslade, R. and Ross, E.M. (1986) Whooping cough and whooping cough vaccine: the risks and benefits debate. *Epidemiology Review* **4**, 1–2.

Miller, D.L., Ross, E.M., Alderslade, R., Bellman, M.H. and Rawson, N.S.B. (1981) Pertussis immunisation and serious acute neurological illness in childhood. *British Medical Journal* **1**, 1575–99.

Miller, D., Madge, M., Diamond, J., Wadsworth, J. and Ross, E. (1993) Pertussis immunisation and serious acute neurological illnesses in children. *British Medical Journal* **307**, 1171–6.

Nelson, K.B. and Ellenberg, J.H. (1986) Antecedents of cerebral palsy. Multivariate analysis of risk. *New England Journal of Medicine* **31**, 81–6.

Nelson, K.B. (1991) Prenatal origin of hemiparetic cerebral palsy. How often and why? *Pediatrics* **88**, 1059–62.

O'Donohoe, N.V. (1994) *Epilepsies of Childhood*, 3rd edn. Butterworth, Oxford.

Paneth, N. (1986) Birth and the origins of cerebral palsy. *New England Journal of Medicine* **315**, 124–6.

Perlman, E.M., Tack, E.D. and Martin, T. (1989) Acute systemic organ imaging in term infants after asphyxia. *American Journal of Diseases in Childhood* **143**, 617–20.

Pharoah, P.O.D., Cooke, T., Cooke, P.W.T. and Rosenbloom, L. (1990) Birth-weight specific trends in cerebral palsy. *Archives of Disease in Childhood* **651**, 602–5.

Powell, T.G., Pharoah, P.O.D., Cooke, R.W.I. and Rosenbloom, L. (1988) Cerebral palsy in low-birth-weight infants. I. Spastic hemiplegia: associations with intrapartum stress. *Developmental Medicine and Child Neurology* **10**, 11–18.

Rosenbloom, L. (1994) Dyskinetic cerebral palsy and birth asphyxia. *Developmental Medicine and Child Neurology* **36**, 285–9.

Rossi, L., Brunelli, G., Duzioni, N. and Rossi, G. (1986) Lumbar puncture and febrile convulsions. *Helvetica Paediatrica Acta* **41**, 19–24.

Scher, M.D., Belfar, H., Martin, I. and Painter, M.J. (1991) Destructive brain lesions of presumed fetal onset: antepartum causes of cerebral palsy. *Pediatrics* **88**, 898–905.

Stanley, F.J. and Blair, E. (1991) Why have we failed to reduce the frequency of cerebral palsy? *Medical Journal of Australia* **154**, 623–6.

Stephenson, J.B.P. (1990) *Fits and Faints*. MacKeith Press, Oxford.

Strauss, D. and Shavelle, R. (1998) Life expectancy of a child with cerebral palsy. *Developmental Medicine and Child Neurology* **40**, 369–95.

Sugimoto, T., Woo, M., Nishida, N. *et al*. (1995) When do brain abnormalities in cerebral palsy occur? *Developmental Medicine and Child Neurology* **37**, 285–92.

Wigglesworth, J.S. (1993) Medicolegal aspects. In *Cranial Haemorrhage in the Term Newborn Infant* (P. Govaert, ed.), pp. 178–87. Clinics in Developmental Medicine, No. 129. MacKeith Press, Cambridge.

Wiklund, L.M. and Uvebrant, P. (1991) Hemiplegic cerebral palsy: correlation between CT morphology and clinical findings. *Developmental Medicine and Child Neurology* **35**, 944–82.

Winter, R.M. and Baraitser, M. (1991) *Multiple Congenital Anomalies*. Chapman & Hall, London (a companion to the London Dysmorphology Database).

Chapter 13

Congenital Anomalies of the Central Nervous System

Anthony D. Hockley

Introduction

Congenital anomalies of the central nervous system, notably hydrocephalus and spina bifida, are major causes of mortality and morbidity in children. Because of this and other reasons, medico-legal problems arise relating to their diagnosis and treatment.

There is no real 'cure' for many of these conditions, with repeated medical and surgical attention from several disciplines being necessary. Survival is possible with handicap, requiring special and expensive facilities. Problems may arise from a delay in diagnosis and referral to appropriate specialists. This includes the recognition of complications which may be part of the natural disease process or due to inadequate treatment or medical care. Such complications present not infrequently as emergencies both in the home or in hospital, and at times when unfamiliar or less experienced medical staff are initially available.

Problems related to informed consent may occur both at the pre- and post-natal periods. Where a fetal abnormality *in utero* has been recognised, inadequate or no counselling with parents not afforded the opportunity to consider an abortion may result in a 'wrongful life' decision in law. After birth, the parents need to be given a realistic and experienced view of their child's problem, including its natural history and treatment possibilities. Whilst it is the child who is at the disadvantage, it will be the parents who have the burden of care, and not surprisingly there is a high incidence of resultant marital problems. Whilst public opinion generally is helpful both for parents and doctors, some lay pressure groups may be unhelpful if ill-informed. For example, a decision to let a newborn baby with Down's syndrome and multiple congenital anomalies die led to a murder charge against the paediatrician (the 'Arthur' case (Medico-legal, 1981)), and in the USA to major governmental attempts to supervise obstetrical practice with 'Baby Doe' squads (Dunea,

1983). If the medical profession is placed in continuous danger of prosecution, decisions will become more influenced by legal considerations. Ultimately it will be the patient who will suffer from this 'defensive' medicine.

Hydrocephalus

Hydrocephalus, or the excess accumulation of cerebrospinal fluid in the ventricles of the brain, is not a single disease entity but the result of different pathological conditions. Normally, cerebrospinal fluid is produced within the ventricles by the choroid plexus and circulates out into the subarachnoid space that surrounds the brain and spinal cord. It is then absorbed by the arachnoid villi over the upper surface of the brain. Apart from the excess production of the fluid by a rare tumour of the choroid plexus, hydrocephalus results from a block or obstruction to its normal circulation and absorption. This occurs at different sites and is due to various causes (Table 13.1). During the neonatal to late infancy period (zero to two years), hydrocephalus is usually caused by a developmental abnormality, aqueduct stenosis being the most common. The hydrocephalus found in babies with spina bifida usually results from the Arnold–Chiari malformation, where there is downward herniation of the cerebellum through the foramen magnum. In the older child (two to ten years), the most common causes of hydrocephalus are posterior fossa tumours and aqueduct stenosis.

Table 13.1 Causes of hydrocephalus.

Site of block	Cause
Lateral ventricle	Perinatal haemorrhage Ventriculitis
Foramen of Monro	Ventriculitis Colloid cyst Tumour
Third ventricle	Suprasellar cyst Tumour
Aqueduct	Developmental stenosis Tumour Arterio-venous malformation
Fourth ventricle	Dandy-Walker malformation Meningitis Tumour
Subarachnoid spaces	Arnold–Chiari malformation Meningitis Subarachnoid haemorrhage

The clinical features of hydrocephalus depend on the time of onset and nature of the obstruction. Under two years of age, the abnormally large head with its increased rate of growth usually attracts attention. In older children, patients may be divided into two groups. In the first group are children with pre-existing (infantile) but unrecognised hydrocephalus which may or may not be partially compensated. Neurological development may be normal, borderline or retarded. The head may be mildly or severely enlarged, and the diagnosis of so-called 'arrested hydrocephalus' may be given. These patients may rapidly deteriorate after a head injury or viral infection. There may also be endocrine changes resulting in poor growth, obesity, precocious or delayed puberty, diabetes insipidus or menstrual irregularities. These hormonal changes are probably due to abnormal hypothalamic function from raised intracranial pressure. Spasticity in the legs and comparatively poor intellectual function are common. Occasionally these patients reach adulthood before the diagnosis is suspected. The second group of children develop hydrocephalus after closure of the cranial sutures so that the head circumference remains within normal limits. Headaches and vomiting are common, with additional clinical features of the causative lesion.

With regard to investigation of hydrocephalus, plain skull X-rays may show an abnormally thin cranial vault with separated sutures, but computerised tomography (CT) and magnetic resonance imaging (MRI) scanning now provide sufficient information in most cases to proceed directly to treatment. Ultrasound scanning in the presence of a patent anterior fontanelle is another non-invasive method of assessing ventricular size. These methods have replaced the older techniques of ventriculography.

Any baby with progressive hydrocephalus will, if untreated, reach a condition of stability where no further enlargement of the ventricle or skull will take place. The child may be of normal intelligence, but more likely will be seriously handicapped. If treatment is to be worthwhile, it must improve convincingly on the natural history of the disorder. By comparing results of operative against non-operative treatment in the literature (Laurence, 1962), and allowing for differences in case selection, two conclusions may be drawn. First, at comparable periods of follow-up, the natural mortality of hydrocephalus is reduced by half after surgical treatment. Second, the number of educable survivors is double in the operated as opposed to the non-operated group (Milhorat, 1972).

The large number of operations devised for the treatment of hydrocephalus is evidence of the unsatisfactory nature of most of them. Dandy, in 1918, wrote:

> 'no form of treatment, either medical or surgical, has yet a valid claim to the cure of a single case of hydrocephalus, except in those cases caused by tumour and relieved by tumour extirpation.'

Essentially the various methods of treatment fall into two main groups. First, so-called 'physiological' operations not requiring the use of implanted mechanical tubes and valves to bypass the obstruction in the ventricular system. The physiological procedures, which include destruction of the choroid plexus (choroid plexectomy) and surgical recannalisation of occluded pathways, although seemingly attractive are not as technically satisfactory as the simpler shunting procedures which have the more widespread acceptance. These shunting procedures include intracranial operations such as Torkildsen's (1939) ventriculocisternostomy, with cerebrospinal fluid diverted by a catheter from one lateral ventricle into the cisterna magna. The method can be used for treating hydrocephalus caused by an obstruction of the aqueduct. Once drainage has been established, the incidence of late complications is much lower than with the extracranial procedures. Both ends of the catheter are bathed in cerebrospinal fluid and its function generally is unaffected by the growth of the patient.

Extracranial diversion of cerebrospinal fluid from the ventricles into the bloodstream or body cavities remains the most frequent method of treating hydrocephalus. Initially, the most widely used example was the ventriculoatrial shunt. Early experience made it clear that artificial drainage of cerebrospinal fluid from ventricles to the venous system would succeed only if it incorporated a mechanical device that could control the flow of fluid and prevent a reverse flow of blood. The invention of such a valve is credited to Holter, an engineer, and the operative technique for its insertion to Nulsen and Spitz (1952). Although there have been many subsequent modifications of the shunt components, the operation has remained substantially the same. The Holter valve comprises a short length of silicone rubber tube connecting at each end with a ball valve that allows unidirectional flow. The intermediate portion of the tube is compressible and the valve lies subcutaneously behind the ear. At its upper end it is connected to a catheter from the lateral ventricle, and at its lower extremity to another catheter passed into the internal jugular vein with sufficient length for its lower end to lie in the right atrium.

Diversion of cerebrospinal fluid into the peritoneal cavity ('ventriculoperitoneal shunt') has increasingly been employed and now, especially in children, is the preferred first option. A longer tube can be put into the peritoneum to allow for the infant's growth, and although complications do occur, they are less serious than with atrial shunts.

Shunting cerebrospinal fluid into the pleural cavity or directly into the atrium, requiring the chest to be opened, may be used when other shunt sites are no longer available. Recently the gall bladder has been used for the same reason.

Despite a very low operative mortality, complications after ventriculoperitoneal and ventriculoatrial shunts are frequent, with an incidence of approximately 46%. The most common complications that affect all shunts are shunt malfunction and infection. Shunt malfunction is usually due to obstruction of the ventricular or distal catheter, but can also result from disconnections in the tubing or failure of the valve itself. Infection may occur on the external surface of the shunt tubing, with signs of acute inflammation and sometimes scalp or skin erosion. Alternatively, infection may occur within the shunt tubing itself, usually due to a less virulent organism, typically *Staphylococcus epidermidis*, introduced at the time of the initial operation. In patients with a ventriculoperitoneal shunt, this often presents as a lower-end block due to a localised peritonitis or pseudocyst formation. In the case of a ventriculoatrial shunt, infection can produce a serious and sometimes chronic bacteraemic illness with endocarditis and shunt nephritis. Over many years, discussion has continued about whether infections can be cured without removing the shunt. Although there have been some successes with antibiotics alone, most would agree that either removal or exteriorisation of the shunt, with temporary external drainage of the cerebrospinal fluid, is necessary before the infection can be controlled and a new shunt can be inserted.

The third most frequent complication from shunts is over-drainage, which produces 'slit ventricle' syndrome, subdural fluid accumulations and craniosynostosis. These patients may develop symptoms of raised intracranial pressure from shunt malfunction, but without enlargement of the ventricles, which can lead to difficult technical problems. Sophisticated modifications in valve manufacture, including externally programmable valves and anti-siphon devices, have been introduced to try and overcome this problem. An alternative technique, favoured by the author, is to carry out a subtemporal craniectomy with opening of the dura which does not allow the ventricles to enlarge. In the shunt-dependent patient, this not only relieves intracranial pressure but does facilitate ventricular catheter revision and also provides a palpable 'fontanelle' which allows the clinical assessment of intracranial pressure.

The specific complications of ventriculoatrial shunts may be serious. Patients following shunt nephritis have developed renal failure needing transplantation. Endocarditis has led to cardiac valve replacement. Thromboembolism may also occur leading to chronic pulmonary hypertension and heart failure. Specific complications of ventriculoperitoneal shunts include intestinal obstruction and perforation.

In predicting prognosis, the nature of the primary lesion is important. For example, a patient with hydrocephalus caused by congenital aqueduct stenosis may be expected to lead a normal adult life. In comparison, a low-birth-weight premature baby with severe perinatal hypoxia and gross intraventricular haemorrhage has a high incidence of brain damage with physical and mental handicap.

The outcome of hydrocephalus changed dramatically with the introduction of shunts. Prior to their availability, outcome was very poor; children had an estimated 20% chance of reaching adulthood and a 50% chance of remaining brain-damaged should they survive. In the last four decades, however, outcome has improved so that now over 80% of patients are expected to survive long term. With regard to quality of survival, several studies now indicate that the majority of children attend normal schools, achieve social independence and are employable. The mechanical complications of shunts have been well-recognised and, ultimately, up to 80% of shunts will develop mechanical complications at some stage, one-third of which are most likely in the first year of the shunt's life. Whilst most shunt complications tend to be in young children, late problems can occur in adulthood, even after many years of 'shunt stability'. For this reason it is important that follow-up of these patients be continued, and that facilities are available with neurosurgeons familiar with this problem.

Medico-legal issues related to hydrocephalus start right at the beginning. After a diagnosis of fetal hydrocephalus, parents may question whether the delay before definitive treatment has been responsible for brain damage. As intrauterine treatment of hydrocephalus has not proved to be an acceptable form of management, there is usually no difficulty in waiting until such an infant has an established hold on life. Treatment can then be electively planned at the optimum time. In such cases, obstetricians and paediatricians need to liaise early with their surgical colleagues who will be treating the hydrocephalus. With appropriate and informed counselling, parents can cope with the position and will be most unlikely at this stage to seek legal advice.

Problems occur if there is delayed or inadequate communication. The initial care of the newborn infant with or without hydrocephalus is supervised by the paediatrician. A surgical opinion of management of the hydrocephalus may have already been obtained before delivery with the parent(s) meeting the surgeon. In such cases, clearly, a combined policy on treatment is established early. Alternatively, the paediatrician should seek a surgical opinion once the diagnosis of hydrocephalus is suspected. Communication with parents at first is the responsibility of the paediatrician, but details of surgical treatment, expected results and potential complications can only be given by the neurosurgeon or paediatric surgeon. This is 'informed consent' and is very important. Ideally, follow-up supervision should continue with both disciplines complementing each other.

A rare and serious situation can develop where the size of the infant's head from hydrocephalus will not permit a vaginal birth. With satisfactory antenatal care and supervision, obstetricians will often decide on a Caesarean delivery. Problems may arise where the disproportion was not adequately appreciated, the hydrocephalus was not previously diagnosed, antenatal attendances were poor, and for other reasons. The worse scenario is that of a low impacted head, which carries not only a risk to the baby of brain damage, but also a potential fatal risk to the mother from a ruptured uterus. It may be too late for a Caesarean delivery, and there is then no alternative but to reduce the size of the baby's head to allow completion of the vaginal delivery. In the presence of hydrocephalus, needle aspiration of the distended ventricles by fontanelle puncture is technically the easiest method and can allow the baby's survival. If there is no hydrocephalus, the obstetrician may have to consider the use of skull-destroying instruments. Assuming a baby with hydrocephalus survives such a birth, parents later may bring a claim accusing the obstetrician of causing brain damage to their infant by the needle aspiration. In such a complex case there are several issues.

First, the individual obstetrician - probably a junior doctor on emergency duty - faced with this delivery may not have attended the mother before. Needle aspiration to relieve the hydrocephalus may well have allowed the infant to survive and prevented a serious medical problem for the mother. It would be very doubtful if this action added to the child's later evident brain damage. It would not be appropriate to regard this individual doctor as negligent. However, if the obstetrical team, including its more experienced members and consultant, were aware either in the antenatal clinic or during the very early stages of labour that there was such a potential problem, action should have been possible to avoid this dangerous position. Under such circumstances, criticism of standards of care is justified and there may be a case of negligence to answer.

Infants with suspected hydrocephalus are usually referred to neurosurgeons or, still in a few centres within the UK and Europe, to paediatric general surgeons for definitive surgical treatment. Such referrals come from general practitioners (GPs), school doctors or paediatricians. In most cases, the diagnosis and referral are made easily on the basis of too rapid a growth rate of head size, but for various reasons there is sometimes a delay. The first question that specialists, both medical and legal, need answered is whether the delay in a particular case is responsible for additional damage. A ten-year-old child with long-standing hydrocephalus, unable to stand or walk, who was normally mobile five years previously, is such an example. The more difficult question is: why did the delay occur and who was responsible? It may not have been the GP or junior hospital doctor but the consultant paediatrician or surgeon who failed to make the diagnosis earlier, and whose standard of practice must be questioned.

More florid cases relate to the treatment of hydrocephalus and management of shunt complications. The majority of these complications should not be regarded as negligent but merely reflect the failure of the treatment method and implant device. However, when there has been a delay in diagnosis or inappropriate treatment of a particular complication, additional significant damage may occur and hence the large number of medico-legal claims in this area.

The most common complication is shunt malfunction, usually due to obstruction of the ventricular or lower catheter, but other mechanical causes of complications may occur. In some patients, shunt malfunction does not produce clinical symptoms. It may be that such patients no longer require a shunt ('shunt-independent') or that somehow a small amount of fluid can occasionally flow through or around the shunt tubing to maintain a normal balance. In the majority of so-called 'shunt-dependent' patients, shunt malfunction produces raised intracranial pressure that is clinically manifest either with a short history ('acute shunt failure') or sometimes with a more insidious, intermittent illness.

Acute shunt failure with headache, vomiting, fits and drowsiness which may lead to coma, respiratory arrest and death is a surgical emergency. Once suspected it is necessary to identify and rectify the cause. There may not be time for a CT scan to assess ventricular size, or X-rays to show the integrity of the shunt tubing, before the patient is taken to the operating theatre. Occasionally the patient may present in a critical situation with deep coma or respiratory arrest, when needle aspiration of some cerebrospinal fluid from the shunt apparatus or ventricle may be life-saving before definitive treatment is embarked upon. It is recognised that the history may be so short that death occurs before access to medical help is possible.

Patients with shunt malfunction may present with more subtle symptoms that include personality change, lack of interest at school and visual problems. Some patients may develop double vision or a squint from unilateral or bilateral cranial (sixth) nerve palsy.

Of very special importance is failing visual acuity that also can result from shunt malfunction. Affecting one or both eyes, loss of visual acuity even to the point of blindness may very easily be missed, especially by paediatricians and generalists. Even ophthalmologists may not appreciate shunt malfunction as a potential cause and give an alternative diagnosis. There have been, and will continue to be, a number of cases wherein the loss of vision related to shunt failure ultimately continues to be the main disability for the patient upon which quantum depends. If recognised early enough, shunt revisions may rescue visual function, partially or even completely.

Once a patient with hydrocephalus is treated, it should become the responsibility of the specialist surgical team to continue the patient's follow-up surveillance and maintenance of shunt function. This includes important counselling of the parents and education for all doctors (junior and senior) who may see the patient with regard to shunt complications and their need for prompt attention. The most reliable of all diagnostic clues is 'what mother says' and her opinion should wisely top the list. Most patients with acute shunt malfunction are appropriately managed. However, there continues to be a small number of cases where, at one or more of the above stages, standards of care fall below an acceptable level, with significant additional handicap that does deserve compensation.

Shunt infection in patients with ventriculoperitoneal shunts usually presents as shunt blockage. In patients with ventriculoatrial shunts, clinical features may be characteristically insidious, with vague poor health and only anaemia as signs of an underlying infective illness. Diagnosis by serological tests is possible. Renal and cardiac damage may persist from the nephritis and endocarditis that occurs. Because the early symptoms may be non-specific, diagnosis in this group of patients can be delayed.

Spina bifida

Embryologically, the spinal cord develops from the outer of three cell layers with a special part (neuroectoderm) forming a 'neural' tube. This tube closes like a zip, the process being called raphism. A spectrum of anomalies occur (dysraphism or spina bifida) when there is a fault in this closure; these vary from major external lesions with associated neurological deficit and hydrocephalus, to intermediate and more minor forms ('spina bifida occulta').

In its most severe form, the neural tube defect is open with an elevated alphafetoprotein level in maternal serum and amniotic fluid allowing prenatal diagnosis, in addition to diagnostic ultrasound imaging. In cases where the obstetrical team either did not follow up appropriately or inform the parents of a positive result, there have been some claims for 'wrongful life'. Alternatively, after appropriate specialist consultation involving the parents and obstetrician, a decision is made to let such a pregnancy go to term and assess treatment options once the infant has been delivered.

With regard to decisions following delivery, major spina bifida (myelomeningocele) is a good example that illustrates the importance of informed consent. Treatment is not just a question of repairing the defective skin cover over the exposed spinal cord. There will likely be significant persisting neurological deficit below the level of the lesion which will affect the limb function and sphincter control. Orthopaedic, urological and other colleagues from several disciplines will be involved in the patient's management. The majority of infants will develop hydrocephalus with all its problems. Left alone at birth, the infant will probably not die. Although some spontaneous epithelialisation of the lesion will occur, the development in later years of a spontaneously and fatal skin cancer has been increasingly reported at the site of a previously unrepaired myelomeningocele. For these reasons it is now policy in most paediatric neurosurgical departments to operate on the majority of severe or open spina bifida babies. In a very small number, however, the lesion may be so severe that survival for more than a few days is unlikely and surgery is deferred.

Medico-legal problems may occur when paediatricians refer these babies late for a surgical opinion, often after several months when the hydrocephalus has progressed and the infants have an enormous head and large ballooned spina bifida lesion. The question asked by the paediatrician to the surgeon is, 'Can you tidy things up a bit and help the nursing of this baby?' Such a late referral is bad and out-of-date practice, but there are historical reasons.

Effective surgical treatment only became possible for children with spina bifida with the development of shunts for hydrocephalus in the late 1950s. In 1971, Lorber, a paediatrician, published the results of surgical treatment in 524 cases from Sheffield and described his 'adverse criteria', correlating morbidity and handicap with more serious spina bifida lesions. There followed a trial of no treatment in 25 infants with these criteria and all but two died within six months, the remainder by nine months. This had a profound effect on medical management in the UK, where 'selection' became the standard policy. Later the issue was reopened when several centres reported cases in whom the early decision not to operate had been reversed when the children survived. In other words, emergency surgery perhaps was not always necessary, and a policy of immediate back closure became reserved for the good-prognosis group. Initial conservative treatment was advocated for the more severe cases, and providing the hydrocephalus was effectively treated, surgery to the back could be safely delayed. With this historical background, it is easy to understand why some 'older' paediatricians may refer these babies late. Bearing in mind the reduced incidence of open spina bifida now, both real and from terminations of pregnancy, the trend today has been very much back towards active treatment.

As a result of the important initial counselling of the parents by appropriately experienced medical staff, the treatment policy is decided. Operative repair of the back lesion may be undertaken during the first 48 hours or, for a variety of reasons, be deferred. Whilst there may be some different opinions related to the techniques and timing of surgical treatment, provided an experienced team in the field is supervising the infant's management and parents, there is not usually a medico-legal problem.

In contrast, there are potential medico-legal problems with regard to the management of the other and more subtle forms of spinal dysraphism. These children fall into two groups, those with an anatomical abnormality which may tether the spinal cord, or children with a dimple on the skin that may communicate with the theca and pose a risk of serious infection.

Abnormalities which anatomically tether the spinal cord include large fatty lipomas, more correctly called lipomyelomeningoceles, that also produce an obvious cosmetic deformity. The normal fibrous structure (filum terminale) that joins the termination of the spinal cord to the outer dura membrane surrounding the cerebrospinal fluid may be abnormally short and tight. There may be a bony spur (diastematomyelia) which splits and transfixes the spinal cord. Usually asymptomatic at birth, as the child grows progressive neurological and sphincter deficits may result due to presumed stretching of the cord by the fixed tethering structure. In some of these children there may be an associated curvature (scoliosis) of the spine that needs orthopaedic correction. Clearly, diagnosis and appropriate treatment of the tethering abnormality, either in advance or synchronously with the orthopaedic correction, may need to be considered.

Because there is a risk of progressive deficit, a delay in diagnosis or referral of these patients can lead to unnecessary permanent handicap. Patients with an underlying dysraphic lesion may present with cutaneous evidence such as a hairy patch, port-wine stain, lipoma or dimple, clues that should lead to further investigation. Low back pain and neurological symptoms may be unrecognised as significant. Deformities of the feet and trophic skin changes may be operated on without any diagnosis of an underlying spinal problem. Finally, altered or loss of bladder and bowel control brings the patient to the urologist and general surgeon. The author has seen an adult with recurrent osteomyelitis of the toes from sensory loss leading to amputation. Later urinary and bowel diversion operations were needed because of double incontinence. Despite a buttock fatty swelling present since birth, no serious investigation of the spine or neurosurgical referral had been considered before. As the patient subsequently developed back and leg pain, surgery was undertaken which relieved these symptoms but sadly did not influence the established handicap. When this patient was a small infant, the contemporaneous view by many at that time was to be conservative in the management of spinal lipomas. It is now accepted in paediatric neurosurgical practice that anatomical abnormalities which tether the cord should be treated surgically to prevent deficit. It is important that these operations be undertaken by a neurosurgeon actively involved in paediatric practice.

A dimple, especially in the midline above the level of the buttocks, may be the external opening of a congenital dermal sinus. These vary from a simple epithelial tube which ends blindly in the soft tissues, to an elongated tract which extends intraspinally as a port of entry for infection. At any point along the tract, usually at its termination, the sinus may expand into a dermoid cyst. Although occasionally diagnosed in asymptomatic patients, the most frequent presentation is infection with meningitis, that may be recurrent, or spinal abscess. Meningitis may also occur after incomplete surgical excision. Less frequently, the lesion may present with symptoms referable to a spinal mass lesion or tethered cord, with back pain, scoliosis or progressive neurological and sphincter deficit. In diagnosis, ordinary X-rays are of limited value but MRI scanning has now replaced invasive contrast radiology in demonstrating the extent of these lesions. The aim of treatment is to prevent recurrent infection by totally excising the tract up to and including its termination, which may be as high as the conus medullaris.

Despite this knowledge, well-described in medical and paediatric textbooks, failure to diagnose the true nature of this lesion may result in permanent deficit. This can also be a problem when surgery has to be undertaken in the acute phase for an infected dermoid cyst, when normal anatomical appearances may be obscured. Clearly, this lesion is important and continues to have legal implications. It should be stressed that the very common skin dimple found between the buttocks immediately overlying the coccyx is innocent; its intact skin base can be demonstrated and it is not a surgical problem. The large number of children with these sent to paediatric neurosurgical clinics for reassurance indicates the increased awareness by GPs and paediatricians that fortunately now exists concerning the diagnosis of potential communicating sinuses.

Other cutaneous abnormalities occur in association with underlying intraspinal anomalies which are tell-tale signs. These include a midline haemangioma or nevus, skin appendage or hairy patch indicating an underlying intradural dermoid cyst, tethered cord or diastematomyelia. It is the responsibility of the obstetrical and neonatal paediatrician to be aware of their significance and refer babies to the paediatric neurosurgeon. Although usually asymptomatic at birth, diagnoses of these problems will lead to early investigation and appropriate surgical treatment that can prevent the progressive neurological deficit which might otherwise occur.

Other congenital anomalies

The remaining congenital anomalies of the central nervous system include encephaloceles and craniosynostosis. An encephalocele is basically a sac or hernia, containing brain or its covering membranes, with a skull defect. Usually situated over the back of the head or occipital area, their embryological basis and many clinical features are similar to spina bifida. Large lesions may be diagnosed prenatally. At birth there may be deficient or ruptured skin with loss of cerebrospinal fluid and risk of infection as indications to consider their early operative repair. If there is brain (cerebellum) present in the sac the lesion is called an encephalocele and in 50% of such cases there is associated hydrocephalus. When no brain tissue is present, the lesion is called a meningocele. This is important, as infants with occipital encephaloceles and hydrocephalus have a significantly poorer prognosis both for survival and intellect. Experience and judgement are required by the specialist in counselling parents before deciding if an 'active' policy is appropriate or not. After repairing the defect, especially a large or ruptured lesion, hydrocephalus may develop very quickly and be life-threatening. By contrast, encephaloceles in the frontal area which may produce gross cosmetic deformity are rarely associated with intellectual deficit.

Usually there is no difficulty or medico-legal problem about the diagnosis of an encephalocele. Occasionally they may occur through the base of the skull, producing a cystic tumour in the nose or roof of the mouth. As infants or even adults, patients may be referred to an ear, nose and throat (ENT) surgeon who will undertake a biopsy for a presumed 'polyp'. The correct diagnosis may be immediately obvious with escaping cerebrospinal fluid, or subsequent histology reveals brain tissue, sometimes referred to erroneously as a 'nasal glioma'. Clearly there is a risk of meningitis following such a procedure, but fortunately, in practice, our ENT colleagues usually realise the position very quickly and a neurosurgical referral follows immediately, sometimes even from the operating room.

Rarely more subtle forms not visible externally can occur. For example, a small encephalocele in the roof of the nose or inside the ear associated with a fistula can lead to recurrent meningitis. If there is a history of clear (cerebrospinal) fluid leak from the nose or ear, this should lead to a neurosurgical referral for investigation.

In craniosynostosis, there is premature fusion of one or more skull sutures. This may occur as a primary disorder or secondary due to poor brain growth. A common 'secondary' cause results from shunting operations in early infancy for hydrocephalus. Craniosynostosis produces different and recognised anatomical patterns that may have cosmetic implications. In some cases, raised intracranial pressure may later be manifest by visual failure or slow mental development. Usually the diagnosis in these infants is obvious and a neurosurgical referral is made. More complex types of craniosynostosis occur with associated abnormalities affecting the orbits and face, producing so-called 'craniofacial syndromes' of which Crouzon's and Apert's are the best-known examples. Whilst treatment for some simple cases of craniosynostosis is carried out by many neurosurgery departments, the more complex forms need a multidisciplinary team approach involving collaboration with maxillofacial and plastic surgery colleagues.

From a medico-legal point of view, problems can occur with craniosynostosis. First is the question of brain damage or deficit, as a result of undiagnosed or inappropriately treated craniosynostosis. Often in practice, such an infant's skull shape and size is due to an underlying failure of brain growth ('microcephaly') which is the cause of the mental retardation. This infant does not really have craniosynostosis at all, and plain X-rays of the skull usually show patent sutures. However, there are cases of true craniosynostosis with longstanding raised intracranial pressure, presenting with visual failure. Appropriate pressure-relieving skull release surgery may rescue the position. The question of 'brain damage' is difficult, but there is much anecdotal and some scientific evidence of the benefit from appropriate skull surgery in improving intellectual progress. In dealing with a claim for late diagnosis or inappropriate treatment for craniosynostosis, there is a major difficulty, namely the 'reasonable' state of knowledge which contemporary GPs, paediatricians and 'adult' neurosurgeons are expected to have regarding this condition. Wider education of medical colleagues is needed by the specialist centres and this is being addressed.

The second problem, more straightforward medically and legally, is the unexpected disastrous sequel to surgical treatment with death or major handicap as the result. In well-experienced surgical teams with an acceptably low operative mortality and morbidity possible even for major procedures, occasional serious complications will arise. Parents need to be informed that these major operations are not risk-free. Often there are no treatment alternatives, and statistically in general the results from specialist centres are good. There have been cases, however, where standards have not been acceptable. For example, inadequate blood replacement postoperatively following a relatively minor craniosynostosis operation may result in persisting brain damage. Because the more complex conditions needing surgery are less common, it does make sense to regionalise this work into centres so that adequate numbers for experience, training and maintaining standards can be achieved.

Congenital anomalies and negligence

Congenital anomalies of the central nervous system include many clinical conditions needing treatment which may have major legal issues. Problems can arise before birth, so that obstetricians and paediatricians need to keep in touch with their surgical colleagues about current 'state of the art' methods and results for treating these conditions. Because many of these infants survive with long-term handicap, their families and later the children themselves, if they are able, will ask questions from their medical advisors. They will want to know why it happened, whether it could have been avoided and was anyone at fault. Often parents will blame themselves. Legal conflicts about a damaged child are distressing, whatever the rights and wrongs of the issues.

So much of paediatric practice, whatever the specialty, is speaking to parents and families. This is particularly important in dealing with congenital anomalies, and it is vital that appropriately senior staff deal with this area and are sensitive to the consequences of what is said, including the legal implications. The natural history of the condition must be understood and the need for appropriate follow-up and possible further intervention must be explained. The parents or family, after reflecting on what they have been told and burdened with the care of a disabled child, may seek a remedy in law.

Negligence essentially comprises one or more of the following:

(1) Failure to diagnose
(2) Failure to explain possible consequences of the condition and its treatment
(3) Failure to treat appropriately

Medical management should only be considered negligent if the standard of practice exhibited fell below a level that could be expected of the particular practitioner. With regard to congenital anomalies, a GP or junior hospital doctor will not be expected to have the diagnostic skills or experience of a consultant surgeon. Equally, a particular consultant may manage a patient in a different way to that in which the plaintiff was managed. An expert advising in such a case must give an opinion based on an overview of current, accepted and available methods of treatment rather than his or her own preference. There may be several possible causes of a delayed diagnosis and this will require the advice of an expert in general practice or paediatrics. From a surgical point of view, there are several issues that include junior staff cover and their supervision, radiological facilities and technical surgical aspects. For example, most hydrocephalus is now managed by neurosurgeons, but in a few centres this has continued under the supervision of general paediatric surgeons. The surgical expert in such a case must be aware of different choices in technique, and of opinions that are 'reasonable' but also recognise out-of-date and inadequate methods. He or she must answer questions in an unbiased manner. At the same time, the expert must avoid being unrealistically critical, or unjustifiably defensive in supporting the profession, colleagues and the hospital. Contributions to the defence organisations and hospital insurance arrangements are intended to recompense those damaged by medical negligence as well as to defend doctors when they are wrongly accused.

In assessing damage, it is crucial to know that whereas major focal consequences of brain insult are relatively unusual in children compared to adults, there is a considerable chance of lost function in terms of learning and behaviour. Evidence will be needed not only from parents but also from psychologists and developmental paediatricians. Family, social and educational consequences are likely to be different. Parents are in a unique position to influence the child's reaction to injury and may have a strong vested interest in overstating the consequences, even to the point of concealing pre-existing handicaps or exaggerating acquired disabilities.

References

Dandy, W.E. (1918) Extirpation of the choroid plexus of the lateral ventricles in communicating hydrocephalus. *Annals of Surgery* **68**, 569–79.

Dunea, G. (1983) Squeal rules in the nursery. *British Medical Jornal* **287**, 1203–4.

Laurence, K.M. (1962) The natural history of hydrocephalus. *Archives of Disease in Childhood* **37**, 345–62.

Lorber, J. (1971) Results of treatment of myelomeningocele: an analysis of 524 unselected cases, with special reference to possible selection for treatment. *Developmental Medicine and Child Neurology* **13**, 279–303.

Medico-legal (1981) Dr Leonard Arthur: his trial and its implications (legal correspondence). *British Medical Journal* **283**, 1340–1.

Milhorat, T.H. (1972) *Hydrocephalus and the Cerebrospinal Fluid*. Williams and Wilkins, Baltimore.

Nulsen, F.E. and Spitz, E.B. (1952) Treatment of hydrocephalus by direct shunt from ventricles to jugular vein. *Surgical Forum* **2**, 399–403.

Torkildsen, A. (1939) A new palliative operation in cases of inoperable occlusion of the Sylvian aqueduct. *Acta Chirurgica Scandinavica* **82**, 117–24.

Chapter 14

Subarachnoid Haemorrhage

David Sumner and John Garfield

I FAILURES OF DIAGNOSIS

David Sumner

Spontaneous subarachnoid haemorrhage is a rare disorder and published figures of its incidence vary from 6 to 20 cases per 100,000 of the population per year. It must not be forgotten that some 10–20% of patients who suffer a subarachnoid haemorrhage may die within minutes and are never seen by a doctor or even admitted to hospital while still alive. Allowing for this and for the fact that some patients are seen alive but never correctly diagnosed, it is generally accepted that the incidence is about 12 cases per 100,000 of the adult population per year. Despite this, however, allegations of failure to diagnose the condition are by no means infrequent.

On the basis of these figures, a GP in the UK may see a case of subarachnoid haemorrhage about once every two to three years, and perhaps 12 over the course of his or her career in general practice. Figures derived from general practice, however, suggest that even this figure is too high. Indeed in one large and well-documented practice of 16,000 patients, only three cases of subarachnoid haemorrhage were recorded in 30 years, and the chance of a member of the practice gaining clinical experience in making the diagnosis of this condition is remote indeed. To the GP, therefore, it is a very rare condition. The consultant general physician and the consultant in the accident and emergency department will, of course, see many more, as will the medical neurologist. Neurosurgeons see most of all. They do not perhaps have the experience of some of the difficulties of diagnosis because, in many of their cases, the diagnosis will have been made and confirmed before the patient comes under their care. On the other hand, a house officer in general medicine or surgery may see very few or even none at all. This point of frequency with which the condition is seen by doctors in different specialties and of different seniority is stressed because it may influence a judge's decision as to whether the failure to diagnose the condition is to be regarded as negligent or not.

Clinical diagnosis

The signs and symptoms of 'classical' subarachnoid haemorrhage should not be missed. The onset is of a sudden headache, which may be unilateral, in a significant proportion of cases. It cannot be stressed too strongly how important the word 'sudden' is in this context. Patients who have bled into their subarachnoid space rarely tell you that, 'During the course of the day I developed a headache.' They are much more likely to say, 'As I sat down at my desk I got this sudden headache as if someone hit me on the head.' The headache is not only sudden in onset but most patients will tell you that in severity it far exceeds any other headache they have met before. It is described as terrible, awful, crushing and feeling as if the head was bursting. Vomiting is frequent, although not invariable as some have suggested. Consciousness is said to be lost in up to 50% of patients. Despite a classical presentation of this kind, it is remarkable that in one reported series with similar symptoms and signs, an alternative diagnosis was eventually made in 23%. On the other hand a less than typical presentation did not always exclude the diagnosis.

By the time of admission to hospital most patients will display the classical signs of a subarachnoid haemorrhage. These are the signs of meningism (particularly neck stiffness) with limited straight-leg-raising, photophobia and irritability. The patient may be drowsy or even unconscious. A trap for the unwary is that, occasionally, the blood may run into the lumbar subarachnoid space and give rise to the signs of lumbar root irritation. Rarely, the patient may be so ill that muscle tone is lost and no neck stiffness is to be found. Less commonly, but more dangerously, grossly raised intracranial pressure from other causes may present with a short history of headache and neck stiffness. In these cases the onset is rarely sudden. To complicate matters further, papilloedema may develop some days after a subarachnoid bleed. In the acute stages, subhyaloid collections of blood may be seen on examination of the optic fundi. This is a rare but important diagnostic sign and must be carefully distinguished from papilloedema. Additional support for the diagnosis may be found in the appearance of cranial nerve palsies due directly to the aneurysm itself as, for example, the finding of a third-nerve palsy.

Traditionally when a clinical diagnosis of subarachnoid haemorrhage has been made or indeed if the diagnosis is only suspected, it was confirmed or refuted by the carrying out of a lumbar puncture and examination of the cerebrospinal fluid (CSF). Of equal value today, and having the advantage of being non-invasive, the diagnosis can be made by computerised tomography (CT) or magnetic resonance imaging (MRI) scanning of the brain.

Laboratory and radiological diagnosis

Lumbar puncture

There are many disadvantages associated with this investigation. In the conscious patient, it may be distressing for him or her, and if the operator is not experienced (particularly if there is significant neck stiffness) it may be a difficult procedure. It may be dangerous if the onset has not been sudden and the intracranial pressure is raised owing to some other pathology. On the other hand, it has the very great advantage that it may support or refute the diagnosis of meningitis which can (particularly in difficult and atypical cases) be a very important differential diagnosis.

One great difficulty that may arise when the CSF is found to be blood-stained is to decide whether the blood results from spontaneous haemorrhage into the subarachnoid space or whether it results from a traumatic tap; that is, blood has been introduced into the CSF by the trauma of the investigation itself. The ease or difficulty of carrying out the lumbar puncture is of no help here. A traumatic tap is as likely after an easy, perfectly executed lumbar puncture as after difficult and prolonged manoeuvring with the needle. By and large, however, the more experienced the operator, the less likely blood is to be introduced by the lumbar puncture needle. A traditional way of solving this problem is to collect the CSF into three tubes and if there is significantly less blood in the third tube, then the blood could be regarded as having been traumatic in origin. This test is not quite as valuable as it sounds and is often difficult to interpret. Too much attention should not be paid to it. It is perfectly possible too that a traumatic tap may occur in the presence of a spontaneous subarachnoid bleed.

There are, however, changes in the CSF itself after subarachnoid bleeding which distinguish blood introduced by trauma from blood resulting from spontaneous bleeding. These changes take some little time to appear but are no less valuable for this. The first and most useful of these is the appearance of blood pigments in the CSF. The earliest appearance of pigments can be detected by spectrophotometry after two to four hours in CSF which has been centrifuged to remove the red cells; but by 24–36 hours after bleeding the characteristic yellow colour ('xanthochromia') of the blood pigments may be detected by the naked eye. The presence of xanthochromia is proof positive that spontaneous subarachnoid haemorrhage has occurred, because it does not develop when the blood in the CSF results from the trauma of the investigation.

A less commonly used method of differentiating spontaneous subarachnoid bleeding from a traumatic tap is to note the ratio of white cells to red cells in the CSF. The ratio in blood is about 1 white cell to 1000 red cells. If the blood in the CSF has resulted from a traumatic puncture, this cell ratio will be unchanged. If, on the other hand, the bleeding has been spontaneous and has occurred 24–

36 hours earlier, then the CSF cell count will be abnormal and the ratio of white cells to red cells will be greater than could be expected if the blood had entered the CSF as a result of local trauma.

One very significant advantage of lumbar puncture is that examination of the CSF allows the diagnosis of subarachnoid haemorrhage to be made within a matter of hours of the bleed. If, however, the lumbar puncture is carried out to confirm or refute a negative CT scan, the procedure should be delayed for some 24 hours after the suspected bleed to allow for the development of xanthochromia or a cellular response to develop. Since xanthochromia and an increase in the white blood cells may persist in the CSF for up to four weeks after a bleed, lumbar puncture comes into its own if the diagnosis has to be made some time after the bleed was thought to have taken place.

When considering which is the more appropriate investigation, it may be important, particularly in doubtful cases, to be aware of the time at which changes take place in the CSF after a subarachnoid haemorrhage.

(1) Red cells appear within an hour of bleeding and persist for up to four weeks thereafter.
(2) An increase in white cells appears after 24–48 hours – the first cells are polymorphs and these are slowly replaced by lymphocytes, which may persist for up to four weeks.
(3) Xanthochromia appears after 12 hours (although at this stage it is likely to be found only from laboratory examination of the fluid) and persists for at least two weeks in almost all cases, for three weeks in 70% of cases, and for up to four weeks in 40% of cases.

CT and MRI scanning

These methods of investigation have the great advantage that they are non-invasive. Examination of the restless patient by this method may be difficult but no more so than would be a lumbar puncture under similar circumstances. Unfortunately, whereas a lumbar puncture can be carried out in every hospital, CT or MRI scanning are not, as yet, available in every hospital in the UK and the balance may have to be drawn between the time and travelling involved in arranging for a scan to be carried out and the ease and speed with which a lumbar puncture may be performed. In this context Vermeulen *et al.* (1992) make the clear statement:

> 'Ideally patients with suspected subarachnoid haemorrhage should be admitted only to hospitals with computed tomography scanning facilities.'

This is a view which is likely to impress a judge. Although Vermeulen *et al.*

(1992) do not make any direct reference to litigation in this context, it would be surprising if their views were not to be picked up by potential litigants or their legal advisors. This is despite the limitations of scanning which must not be forgotten.

There is some delay between the onset of the bleeding and a scan becoming positive. The incidence of positive scans in the first 24 hours after a known bleed has been reported to be between 80 and 100%. The more sophisticated the scanning equipment used and the more experienced the radiologist, the less is the risk of a false-negative result. Nevertheless, too much reliance should not be placed on the negative scan in the first 24 hours after a bleed. At the other end of the time-scale, the ability of CT scanning to demonstrate the presence of blood in the CSF is lost remarkably quickly – much more quickly than blood itself will disappear from the CSF itself. Published figures range from 50% of scans becoming normal after three days and 100% becoming normal after ten days, to blood being detectable after three weeks. It is wise, therefore, not to rely on a negative scan less than 24 hours before or more than ten days after a suspected subarachnoid haemorrhage.

It must be realised, therefore, that while scanning is a very useful and non-invasive tool in the diagnosis of subarachnoid bleeding, it is not necessarily the complete answer. Just as examination of the CSF has the great advantage of allowing a diagnosis of meningitis to be made, scanning has the great advantage in comparison with examination of the CSF in that it may, and frequently does, give an indication of the site of the bleed and whether there is an associated intracerebral haematoma.

To summarise, the advantages and disadvantages of the two methods of investigation are as follows:

Lumbar puncture

Advantages

(1) This investigation may be positive one hour after bleeding has occurred and is reliably positive between 12 hours and three to four weeks.
(2) Examination of the CSF will exclude a diagnosis of meningitis.
(3) This investigation is widely available.

Disadvantages

(1) This can be technically difficult, particularly in a restless patient.
(2) The investigation is invasive and may be unpleasant for the patient.
(3) It affords no indication of the site of the bleeding.
(4) Doubt as to the diagnosis may be raised by the occurrence of a traumatic tap.
(5) It is very hazardous indeed in the presence of papilloedema or if there is the suspicion of raised intracranial pressure.

Scanning

Advantages

(1) This is a non-invasive investigation.
(2) Scanning may give information regarding the site of the bleeding and the presence or absence of an intra cerebral clot.

Disadvantages

(1) It is only reliably positive between 24 hours and ten days after the bleed.
(2) The accuracy of interpretation depends upon the skill and experience of the radiologist and the degree of sophistication of the equipment.

At the present time, where scanning is available and within the time limits described, it is undoubtedly the investigation of choice. If there is papilloedema – even if the history is suggestive of subarachnoid bleeding – scanning rather than lumbar puncture is mandatory. There is little doubt that with the increasing availability and increased sophistication of the equipment, it will become the standard method of investigation for subarachnoid haemorrhage. There remains a place for examination of the CSF where there has been a considerable time interval between the ictus and the investigation, or where meningitis is a real possibility.

Diagnostic problems

The clinical diagnosis of a classical subarachnoid haemorrhage should be made easily, and failure to diagnose such a case will usually have to be regarded as falling below the standard of care to be expected of any doctor.

Unfortunately, not all cases of subarachnoid haemorrhage are 'classical' and it is in these cases that litigation is likely to follow.

(1) Cases where the onset is relatively slow.
(2) Cases of 'thunder clap' or 'coital' headache which may mimic very closely the headache of subarachnoid haemorrhage.
(3) Patients with recognised migraine who have an atypical and more severe headache than usual. This applies particularly to those whose haemorrhage presents with unilateral headache.
(4) Warning bleeds.

Cases where the onset is relatively slow

From time to time, the headache is neither as sudden nor (in the stoical sense) as severe as might be expected. These cases are particularly difficult if, as often seems to be the case, there is a history of headache in the past. This is a problem especially for the general practitioner (GP) who sees very many patients with headaches and very few who suffer a subarachnoid haemorrhage. It is perhaps a counsel of perfection to say that, although rarely seen, a high index of suspicion of subarachnoid haemorrhage must always be maintained. If the patient does not normally suffer from headache, does not suffer from migraine or, when the headache developed, was carrying out hard physical work, for example, or playing squash or engaged in sexual intercourse, the diagnosis of subarachnoid haemorrhage should be seriously considered.

An unnecessary lumbar puncture or scan is preferable to a disabled or dead patient. The author has never encountered litigation because of an unnecessary diagnostic lumbar puncture or scan. However, litigation after a missed subarachnoid haemorrhage is not unusual.

On the other hand, if the headache did not appear suddenly and there is significant neck stiffness, it is important that raised intracranial pressure from some other cause must be considered. It must never be forgotten that headache and neck stiffness can result from causes other than subarachnoid haemorrhage or meningitis. If there is any doubt about this, the primary investigation should be scanning (or referral to a neurosurgical unit) rather than lumbar puncture. A lumbar puncture in this situation, which led (as it might well do) to deterioration in the patient's condition or even death, would not be looked on kindly by the courts. If, however, the scanning shows no significant intracranial lesion, then the next move is to examine the CSF.

Thunderclap headaches and other possible diagnoses

From time to time, patients who have given what appears to be the history of a classical subarachnoid haemorrhage and who may have some degree of neck stiffness, are found to have a normal CSF and a negative scan. To all intents and purposes these patients can be regarded as not having had a subarachnoid haemorrhage. They can, however, be regarded as having had a 'thunderclap headache' or 'pseudo subarachnoid haemorrhage' (a term which is better not used). The frequency with which this condition is seen is difficult to ascertain, but the author's own experience and figures emanating from Holland suggest that it may be as high as 10% of all patients presenting with a clinical picture of subarachnoid haemorrhage. The converse is vital and must never be forgotten. That is to say, 90% or more of all patients presenting clinically as a subarachnoid haemorrhage have in fact bled, and it is mandatory that all these patients are investigated by examination of the CSF or scanning. Although two cases of thunderclap headache have appeared in the literature in whom later angiography revealed unruptured aneurysms, it is generally felt that the risks of angiography, small as they may be, are such that it is probably wiser in the long run to avoid this investigation unless there is blood in the CSF. In this regard, MRI scanning may be of more use than CT scanning.

Benign coital headache

This is a special subgroup of patients who, during sexual intercourse, develop a sudden severe headache, clinically indistinguishable from the headache of subarachnoid haemorrhage. Both males and females are affected and the headache is considered to result from the transitory arterial hypertension occurring at orgasm. Unlike thunderclap headaches, coital headache is not an isolated event but may occur repeatedly under the same conditions. When the pattern is well-established it is safe to ignore the headache (or treat it symptomatically), but when it is realised that 5% or more of intracranial aneurysms rupture during intercourse it is vital that when sudden severe headache occurs for the first time in this situation, it must be regarded as resulting from a subarachnoid haemorrhage until proved otherwise. Because of the bashfulness of some patients and their partners (and also of some junior doctors), the circumstances in which the headache occurred are often not made clear and the often quoted figure of 3.8% of aneurysms rupturing during intercourse is generally regarded as being too low.

Migraine

Some patients with migraine may have sudden attacks of severe headache associated with nausea and vomiting. These episodes, if seen in isolation, may well give rise to the suspicion that a subarachnoid haemorrhage has occurred. However, if there is a clear-cut history of migraine with sudden severe headaches extending over some years, it is probably safe to pursue a wait-and-see approach. However, as with coital headache, there must be an established pattern before a subarachnoid haemorrhage can be safely excluded. Once again it is better to investigate a patient with migraine than to let a subarachnoid haemorrhage pass unrecognised.

The warning bleed

Although a subarachnoid haemorrhage is commonly regarded as a sudden isolated episode, it is perhaps not widely appreciated that, if a detailed history is taken, between 30 and 50% of patients who have bled into the CSF are found to have had minor isolated headaches in the preceding few days or weeks. It has been suggested that some of these premonitory headaches result from stretching of the aneurysm before it bleeds and that some are in fact episodes of leakage of blood from the aneurysm. These warning bleeds, which are sometimes referred to as 'sentinel headaches', can present a very difficult diagnostic problem. In most cases a doctor is never consulted when the warning headache occurred. What should the practitioner do, however, about a healthy young man or woman who reports that he or she had a headache last week which lasted for a few hours, but that now he or she is very well? To all intents and purposes these warning bleeds are only diagnosed in retrospect, because unless they are followed by a clear-cut subarachnoid haemorrhage, there is little to suggest that they were a warning of anything. These warning bleeds provide a fertile ground for litigation and, of course, the more similar the warning headache is to that of a true subarachnoid haemorrhage, the more likely litigation is to follow if no investigations are carried out. In most cases where litigation arises, the plaintiff will say, 'If something had been done about these headaches, the final and possibly disabling or lethal bleed would have not occurred.'

If the patient had not consulted a doctor about the warning bleed and the history of the warning headaches was only discovered after the subarachnoid haemorrhage, then of course there is no case to answer. But what if a doctor was consulted? In this situation every case has to be dealt with on its merits. If the patient had a long history of headaches and the warning headaches were similar, the case may fail. If, however, the patient is not liable to headache and then complains of one suggestive, or even possibly suggestive, of a subarachnoid haemorrhage, then the case may be successful. This was so in an Australian case when the patient was clear that the warning headache came on suddenly, 'just as I was posting a letter in a letter box'. It was because of this sudden onset that the plaintiff succeeded. Indeed, the nearer the clinical presentation of the 'warning bleed' approaches that of subarachnoid haemorrhage, the more the diagnosis is really that of a subarachnoid haemorrhage itself than a warning. If the warning bleed comes on during the exertion of intercourse then it has, of course, to be taken even more seriously.

From the author's own clinical experience, it is very rare for a warning bleed to be diagnosed as the precursor of a subarachnoid haemorrhage except with the useful diagnostic tool of hindsight. Indeed over the years, the author has only met this once – although it has to be said that on this occasion the warning bleed was in fact a mild subarachnoid haemorrhage. If the diagnosis of a subarachnoid haemorrhage has to be considered, it must be fully investigated.

Who is most at risk of litigation?

The GP has, without doubt, a more difficult task than his or her hospital colleagues in the diagnosis of subarachnoid haemorrhage, since apart from anything else the experience of this condition in general practice is very much less. If the presentation is classical, there is really no excuse for missing the diagnosis and failure to make the diagnosis is likely to be regarded as negligent.

If the patient is clearly very ill, everyone is agreed that something must be done and that the patient should be admitted to hospital as soon as possible. Whether the patient should be referred to a neurological unit, a neurosurgical unit or to an accident and emergency department must depend upon local circumstances. There is no place whatsoever for investigation before going to hospital.

If the case is not classical, if the patient presents with a history of migraine or if the possibility is that the headache may be a warning bleed, the situation is more difficult, but there is still no place for delay or for investigation in the home or surgery. If it is felt that the diagnosis of subarachnoid haemorrhage is a real possibility, however slight, then admission to hospital should be arranged at once and not delayed for any reason.

Thunderclap headaches are not really a problem for a GP because, until the diagnosis has been excluded by lumbar puncture or scanning or both, a thunderclap headache must be regarded as a true subarachnoid haemorrhage and the same diagnostic criteria applied. The same really applies to coital headaches. The first one must be regarded as a subarchnoid haemorrhage until proved otherwise, and a diagnosis of benign coital headache should only be made if there is a clear-cut history of similar episodes in the past. To make such a diagnosis on the basis of the first presentation would, clearly, be regarded as negligent if the diagnosis proved to be a haemorrhage.

A relatively slow progressive presentation of subarachnoid haemorrhage may well tax the GP (or any doctor for that matter) to the utmost. If there is any doubt whatsoever about the diagnosis, the patient should be referred urgently to hospital where facilities for the appropriate investigations are available. Until every district general hospital has facilities for scanning, it is probably better to get the patient quickly to where the CSF can be examined than spend time arranging admission for CT scanning elsewhere.

Junior staff in accident and emergency departments should have no difficulty in making the diagnosis of classical subarachnoid haemorrhage, and it is likely that most of the cases seen there will fall into this group. Nevertheless, there will be patients who arrive in the department directly with milder symptoms, with migraine or with a slow presentation, as well as those referred by GPs. In the accident and emergency department, however, junior staff should be able to compensate for their relative inexperience of the condition by having easy access to more experienced senior colleagues, and there can be no excuse for a patient who *might* have sustained a subarachnoid haemorrhage being discharged without investigation to exclude that diagnosis.

The consultant physician, and still more the consultant neurologist, should not miss making a diagnosis of subarachnoid haemorrhage unless it is very atypical indeed, because they have access to beds and to the appropriate investigations. At this level the risk of litigation may not lie in failing to make the clinical diagnosis, but rather in failing to act upon it appropriately.

Although the above discussion has been about the diagnosis of subarachnoid haemorrhage, it must not be forgotten that to make a diagnosis is not enough.

Action must be taken when the diagnosis has been made. The strategic management of a patient who has suffered a subarachnoid haemorrhage is the responsibility of the neurosurgeon, and by strategic management is meant the decision as to whether surgery is indicated or not, and if it is indicated, when it should be carried out. It is the responsibility of those making the diagnosis either to discuss the patient with the appropriate neurosurgical unit or transfer the patient to such a unit, depending upon local circumstances, as soon as possible. In so far as the timing of surgery may be critical, no time should be lost before contact is made with the neurosurgical unit. Failure to do this has indeed been regarded as negligent, and rightly so.

Reference

Vermeulen, M., Lindsay, K.W. and van Gijn, J. (1992) *Subarachnoid Haemorrhage*. W.B. Saunders, London.

Further reading

Maurice-Williams, R.S. (1987) *Subarachnoid Haemorrhage*. Wright, London.

A useful review of the condition seen through American eyes is:

Kopitnik, T.A. and Samson, S. (1993) Management of subarachnoid haemorrhage. *Journal of Neurology, Neurosurgery and Psychiatry* **56**, 947–59.

II CAUSATION

John Garfield

The majority of medical negligence actions in connection with subarachnoid haemorrhage centre upon failures to diagnose the first, and sometimes subsequent, haemorrhages. These are not issues of neurosurgical standards of care. As has been described in the previous section, liability for standards of care devolves upon GPs, accident and emergency officers and hospital physicians. The arguments in these cases are not usually complex, but are often over the generalist's failure to take and record an accurate history of the first haemorrhage. Since the *majority* of haemorrhages present in a 'classical' or typical fashion, failures of diagnosis are rarely defensible. The standard of care is that to be expected of the relevant generalist, and not that of the neurologist or neurosurgeon. Unfortunately, experts (i.e. neurologists and neurosurgeons) do at times stray from their own specialty, and express opinions upon the standard of care provided by generalists. Although this irregularity can usually be overcome at trial, it may add weight to the plaintiff's case on liability when experts' reports are exchanged before trial.

It is the *causation* issues which concern the neurologist, and, more particularly, the neurosurgeon. It is a field in which there is often controversy which reflects divergent and sincerely held views on the management of subarachnoid haemorrhage caused by rupture of an intracranial aneurysm. It raises important medical and legal issues concerning evidence-based medicine, and the basis of 'reasonable'/'acceptable' decisions about management of an individual patient. In the evolution of case law, the progression from *Bolam* to *Bolitho* is particularly relevant in subarachnoid haemorrhage (see Chapter 1).

The main topics in causation issues in subarachnoid haemorrhage are:

(1) The causes of subarachnoid haemorrhage
(2) The natural history of aneurysmal subarachnoid haemorrhage
(3) The objectives of treatment
(4) The overall effects of delay or failure of diagnosis
(5) Specific factors which a court would examine in deciding the causation issue.

Causes of subarachnoid haemorrhage

These have been set out in the previous section. The majority of medical negligence actions in subarachnoid haemorrhage are concerned with subarachnoid haemorrhage due to rupture of an intracranial aneurysm. Haemorrhage from an angioma (arterio-venous malformation) is rarely the subject of a medical negligence action because the risk of an early and potentially fatal or disabling second haemorrhage is very much less than that following rupture of an intracranial aneurysm.

Natural history of aneurysmal subarachnoid haemorrhage

There are many publications on this subject; there is now little dispute over the facts. Although there is some variation depending upon the site of aneurysm, overall the risks of a further haemorrhage are in the order of 10% in the first week following the first haemorrhage, 12% during the second, 7% during the third, and 8% during the fourth. During the fifth to twelfth weeks it is a further 12%. Thus overall during the first three months, following the first haemorrhage, there is a 50% chance of a further haemorrhage, which can occur at any time; *the time cannot be predicted.*

The mortality following a second haemorrhage is in the region of 60%; and 85% following a third haemorrhage.

Thus, in summary, during the first year following a haemorrhage, 60% of the patients will rebleed with a mortality between 60 and 65%. Therefore 35–45% of patients who have survived the first haemorrhage will die from a further haemorrhage within one year.

Objectives of treatment

Put simply, the purpose of treatment is to obliterate the aneurysm, and thus prevent any subsequent haemorrhage. In view of the natural history, it is impossible to determine in an individual patient when a further haemorrhage will occur. Although overall figures for the probable timing of further haemorrhages are readily available (see above), the figures give no more than the probability of the risk at the time. This is certainly taken into account in the management of a patient, especially in conjunction with other factors which may, at a particular time, militate against action required to obliterate the aneurysm. But in the absence of any other adverse factors, the figures will not provide a defence against allegations that an operation was not done at a time when it would have prevented a further haemorrhage. It is the other adverse factors and their management which usually form the basis of causation arguments (see below).

Overall effects of delay in diagnosis

On the basis of the natural history of aneurysmal subarachnoid haemorrhage, and the results of neurosurgical management (operative and non-operative), it is possible to evaluate the overall effects of delay or failure of diagnosis of the first haemorrhage. Without delay in diagnosis, two-thirds of patients will make a good recovery, and fewer than 10% will die. When diagnosis is delayed, fewer than half will make a good recovery and one-fifth will die. Of all the pre-operative factors, rebleeding shows the strongest association with an unfavourable outcome.

Factors in deciding causation issues

The neurosurgical literature on the management of ruptured intracranial aneurysms is extensive. This extent is a reflection of the many factors to be considered in deciding optimum management for an individual patient. The relevance, or weight, of different factors may be more or sometimes less well-established and accepted in neurosurgical practice. Indeed, different neurosurgeons may have different views on the weight which they accord to each factor, and therefore the extent to which their practice is influenced by each factor. It is this divergence of opinion which may occupy much time in causation arguments, and which may entail extensive and selective reference to the neurosurgical literature. Such exercises may make the court's task very difficult. Therefore it is not surprising that the court will either recommend a financial compromise, or a meeting of experts, without prejudice, to narrow or even resolve the causation issues.

Accepting that the primary objective of treatment is the prevention of further haemorrhage which can occur at any time, the main arguments in medical negligence actions have been over *timing and outcome of surgery* had the diagnosis been made at the appropriate time. More than a brief reference to some importance points is beyond the scope of this chapter.

- Since a further haemorrhage can occur at any time, obliteration of the aneurysm should be done urgently.
- The overall morbidity and mortality of surgery is related to the patient's neurological condition immediately following haemorrhage, and to some extent, immediately prior to surgery.
- When the patient's neurological condition is favourable, the overall result of surgery is significantly better than that of the natural history, at least during the first six weeks following the first haemorrhage. In most cases now, the morbidity and/or mortality of surgery is less than 10%.
- There are some conflicting reports concerning the management outcome of very early (i.e. within 48 hours of haemorrhage) surgery compared to delayed surgery.
- There are logistical factors (e.g. radiology, anaesthesia, operating time, availability of neurosurgical beds) which may be relevant in a particular case.
- The management of a patient should be viewed in the light of the generally accepted practice at the time of the event. This may be different from the accepted practice at a later date. The grounds for acceptance of that practice may be examined. Its logical basis will be questioned.
- The state of the cerebral circulation and of cerebral function is an important factor in determining the outcome following surgery; hence its importance in deciding the timing of surgery. The clinical state remains the most important indicator. Radiological features (e.g. blood shown on CT scan, cerebral vasospasm shown on angiogram) are additional, but not more important, indicators.

Conclusions

Subarachnoid haemorrhage due to ruptured intracranial aneurysm has occasioned important causation arguments in medical negligence actions. Although alternative endovascular methods of obliterating aneurysms are becoming available, overall surgery remains the most widely available and effective method of preventing a further, and potentially disastrous, haemorrhage. Since the time of a further haemorrhage cannot be predicted for the individual patient, in general, obliteration of the aneurysm as soon as the diagnosis is made is urgent. Claims that surgery would in any event have been delayed beyond the time of the second haemorrhage, or that the outcome of surgery before the second haemorrhage would have been unfavourable, will need to be supported by complex arguments. Such arguments, with extensive reference to the neurosurgical literature, may not be attractive in the face of a more commonsense approach.

LEGAL COMMENTARY

M.A.M.S. Leigh

There are not many cases on subarachnoid haemorrhage which have come to trial. This is a pity because it is a lesion fraught with potential forensic difficulty. As John Garfield says, the purpose of surgery is usually not to treat the bleed which brings the patient to hospital, but to prevent a second or subsequent bleed.

In many cases, the claims are not brought against neurosurgeons but against GPs and accident departments who fail to recognise that the patient is suffering from a neurosurgical condition. The clinical picture which is reported by the primary physician under fire is often a non-specific picture. There may be signs and symptoms of raised intracranial pressure with no more than a history of sudden onset of pain to distinguish it from meningitis or another non-surgical condition. Usually the allegation is not that the defendant should have diagnosed a subarachnoid haemorrhage, but that he or she should have recognised that the patient needed specialist care.

The difficulty is that, as John Garfield says, there are divergent and sincerely held views about the urgency with which surgery should be embarked upon. Some, like John Garfield, insist that as soon as the patient is stable and fit for surgery, any delay is unacceptable.

However, the defendants are able to call upon others who will point out that on the basis of the figures quoted above the risk of further haemorrhage in the first week is only 10%, and that if the risk of mortality from a second bleed is 65% then the patient is being subjected to a risk of mortality of only 6.5% if surgery is delayed for a week. The adherents of this school of thought may well delay surgery by up to a week in the hope that the operation itself will be safer.

Where the defendant is somebody who it is alleged was negligent in the speed with which they referred the patient for surgery, the result may well be a defence which is very similar in principle to that advanced in *Bolitho*: even if the defendant was negligent, nothing was lost because if matters had been handled correctly there would have been no effective intervention in time to prevent the disaster.

Commentary references

1. *Bolitho* v. *City and Hackney Health Authority* [1998] AC 233.

Further reading

Kassel, N.F., Torner, J.C., Jane, J.A., Hayleay, E.C. and Adam, H.B. (1990) The international co-operative study on the timing of aneurysm surgery. Part II. Surgical results. *Journal of Neurosurgery* **73**, 37–47.

Le Roux, P.D., Elliott, J.P., Downey, L., Newell, D.W., Grady, M.S., Mayberg, M.R., Eskridge, J.M. and Winn, H.R. (1995) Improved outcome after rupture of anterior circulation aneurysms: a retrospective ten-year review of 224 good-grade patients. *Journal of Neurosurgery* **83**, 394–402.

Maurice-Williams, R.S. (1987) *Subarachnoid Haemorrhage. Aneurysms and Vascular Malformations of the Central Nervous System*. Wright, Bristol.

Miyaoka, M., Sato, K. and Ishii, S. (1993) A clinical study of the relationship of timing to outcome of surgery for ruptured cerebral aneurysms. A retrospective analysis of 1622 cases. *Journal of Neurosurgery* **79**, 373–8.

Neil-Dwyer, G. and Lang, D. (1997) 'Brain attack' – aneurysmal subarachnoid haemorrhage: death due to delayed diagnosis. *Journal of the Royal College of Physicians of London* **31**(1), 49–52.

Sengupta, R.P. and McAllister, V.L. (1986) *Subarachnoid Haemorrhage*. Springer Verlag, Heidelberg.

Taylor, B., Harries, P. and Bullock, R. (1991) Factors affecting outcome after surgery for intracranial aneurysm in Glasgow. *British Journal of Neurosurgery* **5**, 575–84.

Chapter 15

Intracranial Tumours

C.J. Earl and John Garfield

I DIAGNOSTIC ASPECTS

C.J. Earl

In cases of cerebral tumour, the usual reason for allegations of negligence is a delay in diagnosis. In some cases of malignant gliomas, this may make little difference to the patient's ultimate fate, but where benign tumours are concerned the later the diagnosis is made, the larger the tumour has become and the risk of operation, in respect of both mortality and postoperative morbidity, is significantly greater. The diagnosis of such intracranial mass lesions has become much easier in the past 25 years since the development of non-invasive imaging techniques, i.e. computerised tomography (CT) scanning and magnetic resonance imaging (MRI).

In some cases the diagnosis is straightforward on clinical grounds and will give rise to few problems. Many doctors, for example, will quickly recognise the underlying pathology in a patient who presents with a progressive hemiparesis and increasing headache, but some more subtle symptoms may remain unrecognised or their significance may not be appreciated for months or years. Some of the important features of cases of this sort are considered below.

Assessment of symptoms

Headache

Headache is a well-recognised symptom of intracranial tumours, but headache generally is a very common symptom and in the vast majority of cases it is not of serious significance. One important type of headache which may be readily recognised and may have serious consequences is considered in Chapter 14. Features of headache due to intracranial tumour almost always have much less dramatic characteristics, but a delay in reaching a correct diagnosis in such cases is frequently a cause of legal action for negligence. There is no infallible way of avoiding error in coming to decisions about the cause of headache, and there are some situations where in the event of legal action the doctor's conduct can be firmly defended. There are some tell-tale features in the headache which may put the doctor on his or her guard: the classical teaching that headache in intracranial tumours is at its worst in the morning after a night's sleep in the horizontal position is often borne out in practice, and may be seen in the type of case in children described later in this chapter. Symptoms associated with the headache are especially important and failure to elicit and react to a history suggestive of focal neurological disease in a patient whose main complaint is headache may lead to legal action if the headache proves to be caused by some treatable intracranial lesion. Unfortunately, severity of headache in itself is not usually helpful. For example, the headache of migraine may be as severe as any headache related to an intracranial mass and can have the same characteristics, such as worsening with exertion, straining and stooping, an association with vomiting and relief temporarily, to a greater or lesser extent, by analgesics.

One special problem in dealing with cases that have led to litigation arises from the understandable, and often quite proper, provision of a report by a neurosurgeon for the patient's solicitors. While an estimate of the damage suffered by the patient on account of any delay in diagnosis may properly be made by a neurological surgeon, an opinion on the significance of the presenting symptom of isolated headache, which may have been present for a long time before other features appeared, is not something which falls within the experience of a neurosurgeon. In the UK (the situation may well be different where other systems prevail and patients with headache may consult neurosurgeons on their own initiative), such patients will rarely come into the neurosurgeon's care until the diagnosis of intracranial tumour has been made. Therefore, it may be properly suggested that a neurosurgeon, in expressing an opinion about the significance of headache, may be giving an opinion based on experience largely outside his or her own field.

Tumours in specific situations

Supratentorial tumours

Psychological illness is very common, and patients suffering from anxiety states, depression or some other serious mental disease may take up a great deal of a doctor's time. The detection of psychological symptoms which are organically based often depends on adequate experience and training, and psychological symptoms caused by emotional factors are so common that it may be easy to dismiss too readily the possibility of some underlying organic disease.

Apparent personality change, lack of energy, failure to keep appointments, inability to carry out the ordinary routine tasks of one's occupation or daily living may be seen in a depressive illness, but since there will also usually be a change in mood with feelings of misery and unhappiness, the diagnosis may be reasonably clear. However, similar symptoms may occur in patients with lesions affecting the frontal lobes of the brain. These psychological symptoms are particularly likely to be present in isolation if the non-dominant frontal lobe (usually the right frontal lobe) is affected, and large masses may exist in the frontal region on the non-dominant side with little or nothing in the way of detectable physical abnormality.

It is very important that the general practitioner (GP) consulted by such a patient with progressively disabling psychological symptoms should seek the opinion on diagnosis of an appropriately experienced psychiatrist. It is worth pointing out that it may be dangerous to refer patients of this sort directly for treatment to a psychotherapist, who sometimes may not be medically qualified, when the diagnosis has not been established. Once treatment along psychotherapeutic lines begins, the view that the symptoms are psychologically based tends rapidly to become established, and other possible causes of the patient's symptoms are perhaps forgotten. The author has experience of a number of cases of this sort where, for want of an exact psychiatric diagnosis, the most extraordinary conclusions have been reached. For example, in one adult patient suffering from nocturnal urinary incontinence this symptom was readily attributed by a lay psychotherapist, to whom the patient had been referred, to the patient's wish to humiliate his wife with whom he shared a bed. A large frontal meningioma was subsequently removed. There was some postoperative morbidity which could be attributed to the size the tumour had reached by the time the diagnosis was made, and the patient was successful in obtaining damages from the doctor who had referred him directly for psychotherapy. Expert opinion from an experienced psychiatrist sought in connection with the litigation was that, had the patient been referred initially to a psychiatrist for diagnosis and not to a psychotherapist for treatment, no competent general psychiatrist would have failed to come to the conclusion that the symptoms were those of organic cerebral disease.

Tumours in the non-dominant temporal lobe may not betray their presence by any sort of persistent physical abnormality. Their only manifestations may be attacks of temporal lobe epilepsy. The strange pattern of some attacks may suggest, to the inexperienced, the description 'bizarre'. In fact, to those who are familiar with such cases the attacks may give the strongest clue to the site of the trouble. If one adds to this the fact that patients with structural lesions in the temporal lobe may develop very striking psychological abnormalities (e.g. depression and personality change), it is easy to see how the diagnosis may be missed, if the doctor is too ready to ascribe any symptom of a psychological nature to some psychological cause.

Tumours affecting function in the dominant cerebral hemisphere (temporal or frontal region) are likely to be recognised earlier on account of the speech disturbance which will often be present; but even speech difficulty may be attributed to some other pathology. This occurred in the case of a patient who suffered from developmental dyslexia, a disorder of speech, particularly of reading, dating from early life. He developed a personality change which was attributed to a psychological reaction to his developmental dyslexia, and was treated with group psychotherapy which, incidentally, he found very difficult. As time went on it became clear that his problems were caused by a benign meningioma involving the dominant temporal lobe. In this case once this erroneous diagnosis of psychological symptoms owing to his dyslexia had been made, it became more and more difficult as treatment continued for the therapist to question the original diagnostic formulation. The correct diagnosis was reached only when he attended another hospital where he presented with an acute exacerbation of his long-standing headaches and transient obscurations of vision, which were the result of severe papilloedema from raised intracranial pressure.

An even more difficult diagnostic problem may arise when symptoms develop that are clearly of a functional nature in a patient previously of stable mentality, as a result of a tumour that is interfering with frontal lobe function and producing an abnormal change in personality.

Dementia often associated with behavioural disturbances occurring without focal neurological signs, particularly in a patient past middle age, may be the earliest manifestation of a frontal lobe tumour. Where the tumour is benign (the commonest variety being a meningioma), a remarkable recovery of intellectual function and return to a normal personality may follow surgical removal. As with other tumours, the complications of surgery may impair recovery and, as explained earlier in this chapter, this is dependent among other things on tumour size, so that the delay in diagnosis may be critical in respect of the eventual outcome.

Posterior fossa tumours

Tumours in the posterior fossa may affect cerebellar function and often give rise to a characteristic clinical picture with inco-ordination of the limbs on one or both sides and impairment of balance. This classical clinical picture should lead readily to conclusions about the situation of the causative lesion. Associated symptoms, such as headache and vomiting and the history of a steady decline, may raise strong suspicions of the presence of an intracranial mass. There are other cases in which the situation is less clear and which may give rise to errors in diagnosis. In some instances, the disturbance of function may affect only the patient's balance, with co-ordination of the limbs remaining normal.

When this symptom complex occurs in children the true diagnosis may remain unsuspected for some time. In children there may also be a strikingly variable pattern in the symptoms and signs which can be very deceptive. Thus, a child may complain of morning headache and sickness which will be severe enough to prevent his or her going to school. By the middle of the morning the symptoms may have disappeared. When this pattern of apparently serious symptoms and spontaneous recovery has repeated itself over a period of weeks, suspicion may be aroused that the child is unwilling to go to school, and that this is the cause of his or her illness. This may in turn lead to a referral not to a paediatrician but to a child guidance clinic, and in two cases in the author's own experience the correct diagnosis was reached only after vision became irreparably damaged by chronic swelling of the optic discs with secondary optic atrophy. Such consequences of a delay in diagnosis may well lead to legal action and the award of substantial damages.

Tumours affecting optic nerves and optic chiasma

Tumours arising in the pituitary itself or close to it will often present with visual symptoms which may consist of partial or complete loss of vision in one or both eyes. It is important in any case of progressive visual loss where there is no clear evidence of ocular disease to consider the possibility of optic nerve or chiasmal compression. As with other intracranial masses, the diagnosis has in recent years become much easier than it was in the past, because of remarkable developments in imaging techniques, but patients may still suffer as a result of failure by the medical advisors to consider the possibility of compression of the optic nerves or chiasma.

Pituitary tumours

The classical features of hypopituitarism are often associated with pituitary tumours and may lead at once to the correct diagnosis, when such patients present to an ophthalmologist with visual failure. But these signs may not be obvious to the ophthalmologist in a busy clinic. What is more, the symptoms of hypopituitarism that may accompany a pituitary tumour, i.e. lack of energy, cold intolerance, loss of libido, or potency or amenorrhoea, are symptoms which the patient may not associate with his or her visual problems and, which he or she may fail to mention altogether. What is more, patients suffering from hypopituitarism may have a degree of apathy which leads them to be rather slow to complain about any of their symptoms. The commonest errors in this respect arise from an erroneous diagnosis of chronic progressive optic neuritis, which is a condition that can be diagnosed only when optic nerve or chiasmal compression has been absolutely excluded. The second cause of delay in diagnosis is the presence in the retina of some abnormality to which the visual loss is erroneously ascribed. It is important to remember that small macular lesions, while capable of causing a small scotoma, and a severe reduction in visual acuity, will not cause extensive field loss. Extensive loss of visual field in the absence of a correspondingly large retinal lesion must be caused by a disturbance of optic nerve function.

Apart from pituitary tumours, the effects of which in most instances are readily reversible when the compression is relieved, other causes of compression are craniopharyngioma and meningioma. Until the advent of recent imaging methods the definitive diagnosis, particularly of meningioma compressing one optic nerve, was sometimes extremely difficult; with the methods now available, even small tumours may be readily detected by appropriate studies.

General considerations

Since facilities for CT scanning and MRI are now widely available in the UK, it is very difficult to justify a delay in diagnosis when there are persistent symptoms which may be due to serious intracranial disease even when the physical examination is normal. Investigations carry no serious risk, and once the equipment has been installed the real cost of examination is small. Certainly in retrospect many scans that are normal are fully justified in terms of what has been excluded. Skull radiographs, on the other hand, are of much less value. The appearances of pituitary tumours may be obvious and some meningiomas may be strongly suspected, but a normal skull X-ray excludes very little. Until the advent of CT scanning, investigations to exclude intracranial tumour (arteriography and air encephalography) were unpleasant, entailed risks of their own, and were undertaken only when it had been decided that these risks and discomforts were amply justified.

It is also important to remember that the interpretation of abnormal findings on imaging studies may at times be as difficult as it is often straightforward. Radiologists who are not seeing abnormal head scans regularly and who have not had appropriate training in a neuroradiology department should be ready to seek a more experienced opinion when they are confronted with an abnormality on a scan.

II SURGERY, CONSENT AND CAUSATION ISSUES

John Garfield

In medical negligence actions criticism of operative surgical technique is relatively uncommon, by comparison with criticism of delay in diagnosis. This may reflect a general acceptance that intracranial surgery for life-threatening conditions carries inherent risks, even in the most experienced and skilled hands.

Provided the neurosurgeon is adequately trained, and appropriate instrumentation, such as the operating microscope, the ultrasound aspirator, and perhaps the laser, is available and is used, it is rightly difficult to fault surgical technique to the extent of allegations of negligence.

In neurosurgery there is often a choice of general and detailed operative manoeuvres, few of which merit didactic teaching or rigid guidelines. If the truth be known, at many stages of the more difficult and delicate operations the surgeon may regret a particular manoeuvre, performed in good faith, which can or cannot be corrected immediately. In aneurysm surgery the choices may lie within a space of millimetres or less, and this may lead to disaster or success. Until the day arrives when every neurosurgical procedure has to be recorded on video and retained against a future threat of litigation, intracranial surgical manoeuvres are only rarely a subject for examination in court.

The main aspects which have to be considered in medical negligence actions relating to *intracranial tumours* are few. They have included:

(1) Consent and explanation of the risks of surgery.
(2) Specialisation within neurosurgery.
(3) The effect of a delay in diagnosis in benign and malignant tumours.
(4) Raised intracranial pressure, and especially hydrocephalus, leading to loss of visual acuity and reduction in visual fields.
(5) Loss of vision due to pituitary tumours and craniopharyngioma.
(6) Surgical approaches to certain tumours, for example acoustic schwannoma.
(7) Operations on the wrong side of the head.
(8) Toxicity of anticonvulsants, particularly phenytoin.

Consent

This subject has been covered in Chapters 1 and 2, and the principles are applicable to surgery for intracranial tumours, as they are to all other operations. The majority of patients suffering from intracranial tumours are well aware of the gravity of their condition and of the general risks of a major intracranial operation, without the need for any medical knowledge. But problems have arisen with tumours which, at least to the patient, are causing only minor symptoms that are not disabling, although an operation even at that stage carries major risks of severe disability. The acoustic schwannoma is notorious in this respect. This tumour, while still only producing loss of hearing, with or without tinnitus, may have reached a size which is causing distortion of the brain stem to which, over the years, the tumour has become adherent. The mortality, and even more so the morbidity, of operations in these circumstances are well known to neurosurgeons, but they are difficult to quantify because much depends upon anatomical details which cannot always be accurately foreseen preoperatively.

How forcefully the risks of surgery are spelled out is a matter for the individual surgeon; but in some actions there have been difficulties when the patient has not been aware, or claims not to have been made aware, of the risks. With a very slowly growing tumour which is causing few and only minor symptoms, it may be difficult to deny that a correct explanation of the risks of surgery would have deflected the patient from consenting to the operation, which was followed by severe disability, even though there were reasonable grounds for advising surgery.

Other examples of tumours which may cause relatively minor symptoms, but in which operation is associated with significant morbidity and mortality, are:

- Subfrontal or falx meningioma
- Posterior fossa and clivus meningioma
- Inner third sphenoid ridge meningioma
- Colloid cyst of the third ventricle.

Surgical specialisation

Under the terms of employment of the National Health Service (NHS), a consultant neurosurgeon has full and overall responsibility for patients admitted under his or her care. Certainly in the past a consultant was considered to be competent to perform the majority of neurosurgical procedures; appointment committees had a clear duty to be satisfied that the consultant's training and experience was satisfactory. As neurosurgery developed, it was recognised that the results of some of the more difficult and complex operations were related to the experience of the surgeon, to specialisation, and to the concentration of certain types of cases in particular neurosurgical departments. Fortunately, the organisation of neurosurgical departments on a regional basis related to population has largely ensured a concentration of the different neurosurgical conditions in each department, sufficient for the development of specialised surgical expertise.

Nevertheless, in medical negligence actions problems have arisen in which it has been alleged that patients who have suffered complications following surgery should have been referred to a different department whose results for such surgery were known to be better. Acoustic schwannoma is one example. This problem has also arisen in connection with other difficult skull base tumours, such as posterior fossa meningioma. The increasing trend towards specialisation is likely to lead to an increase in allegations, not overtly of incompetence, but at least that the patient was denied adequate surgical expertise that was available elsewhere, especially when the operation was not urgent. In these circumstances, lawyers will certainly examine the standards of practice in a neurosurgical department, and the experience and the surgical results in that field of the surgeon. A similar situation has arisen in spinal surgery, particularly because in recent years some neurosurgeons have come to be regarded as specialists in spinal surgery, and do little else.

Causation issues

In the majority of medical negligence actions related to intracranial tumours, liability is centred on a failure to make a clinical diagnosis and to initiate appropriate investigation. Such cases concern GPs, physicians and sometimes neurologists. The causation issues which follow are more directly neurosurgical. Some relevant pathology merits attention.

Acoustic Schwannoma

This histologically benign tumour, which arises on the eighth cranial nerve, usually causes deafness and/or tinnitus at an early stage. Medical negligence actions are usually concerned with the failure to consider this possible diagnosis and to refer the patient for investigation at an early stage. As the tumour enlarges in the cerebello-pontine angle it causes pressure upon the brain stem, to which it becomes adherent. The brain stem becomes distorted and displaced laterally, and to some extent posteriorly, and is rotated. The intracranial pressure rises owing to the compression of the fourth ventricle and the obstruction to the flow of cerebrospinal fluid (CSF), and this produces hydrocephalus. The intracranial pressure may also rise owing to the presence of the tumour irrespective of any effect upon the flow of CSF, and not necessarily related to the size of the tumour. Accurate correlation between the duration of deafness and the size of the tumour and its adherence to the brain stem is difficult, and it is accepted that tumours grow at different rates.

The larger the tumour, the greater are the risks of surgery being followed by significant neurological deficit; and the greater is the mortality. This is especially so when the tumour has become firmly adherent to the distorted and displaced brain stem, and to the basilar artery or its branches. Hence the probable rate of enlargement of a tumour can be the central point in evaluating prognosis following surgery at different stages of the tumour's evolution, and the times at which the diagnosis could or should have been made. When a series of different doctors and hospitals have been involved in the management of the patient, apportionment issues also arise.

Modern imaging techniques (CT and MRI) provide good evidence that acoustic schwannomas may enlarge only very slowly, and may not change over many years. In the absence of earlier images, the likely size of a tumour some years before the diagnosis was eventually made is often a matter of speculation.

Much depends upon the presence or absence of symptoms referrable to a disturbance of the brain stem, as opposed to symptoms referrable solely to a disturbance of the eighth cranial nerve. Even this differentiation may be difficult in the context of vertigo, with or without nystagmus.

The prospects for preservation of seventh nerve function and the avoidance of facial palsy are directly related to the size of the tumour. Hence the probable size of the tumour is important in assessing the likelihood of an unpleasant cosmetic deformity, especially for a woman, at the time when operation should have been done. At present, preservation of useful hearing is rarely a matter for causation arguments, because even with small tumours the prospects for preservation of useful hearing are generally less than 50%.

Consent for operation has on occasions been an issue in surgery for acoustic schwannoma. Because of the histologically benign nature of the tumour, surgery is usually advised. But the potential complications of surgery, even for tumours which have not so far produced any neurological disturbance beyond the eighth cranial nerve, are such that it may be very difficult for the patient in seemingly good health to accept the realities of informed consent. In these circumstances the surgeon alone, and no other member of the team, must be responsible for obtaining consent for operation. If a mishap occurs, it is the surgeon who should be in a position to recall immediately exactly what was said preoperatively, supported by his or her usual practice. An inability to recall the conversation is unimpressive.

There is a further issue which will become of greater importance in the future. Surgery for large acoustic tumours carries a significant morbidity and even mortality. It is accepted that the risks of surgery are related to the experience, skill and expertise of the surgeon, and therefore to the number of such cases referred to a particular department and to a particular surgeon. Thus, there may be strong arguments for referring patients to a surgeon and a department with particular expertise. When things go wrong the expertise, and particularly the size of a surgeon's practice, may have to be examined with the issues of liability, causation and apportionment.

Example

> A young adult presented with a nine-month history of reduced hearing and tinnitus in one ear; no diagnosis was made and there was no follow-up. Three years later he was completely deaf in that ear, there were trigeminal symptoms, headaches and ataxia. Within six weeks there were visual symptoms and he had papilloedema. CT scan showed a large (5 cm diameter) acoustic schwannoma. Surgery was associated with major neurological complications, the tumour was only partially removed, and there were further operations in the course of the ensuing years. The patient remained very severely disabled.

The main liability issue was the failure to refer the patient for intracranial investigation at the first presentation. It was causation which occasioned greater deliberations. These included:

- The probable size and anatomical relationships of the tumour three years before surgery.
- The likely rate of growth of such tumours.
- Morbidity and mortality had surgery been done three years earlier.
- The degree of specialisation of the surgeon.
- The acceptable complication rates in appropriate hands.
- The surgical approach.

Malignant glioma

In the past, the term malignant glioma was equated with a death sentence at whatever stage the diagnosis was made, and whatever treatment was offered. That view was based largely on the assumption that such tumours were probably glioblastoma multiforme, or at best anaplastic astrocytoma. Therefore, even if liability for a delay in diagnosis was admitted, there would be a strong defence on causation: nothing had been lost in terms of survival and quality of life.

During the past 30 or more years, the scene has changed for a number of reasons, a change which has an important effect on causation arguments in medical negligence actions. Non-invasive methods of investigation (e.g. CT and MRI) allow earlier diagnosis of intracranial tumours, and doctors are no longer reluctant to submit patients to these investigations, as they were with the earlier invasive procedures of ventriculography, air encephalography and cerebral angiography. In recent years, brain tumour therapy trials have led to a clearer identification of different histological types for malignant glioma, and to a statistically validated correlation between histological characteristics and prognosis, with or without specific methods of treatment. There have also been some trials which have shown a statistically valid response to treatment within certain parameter, such as age, histological grading, and preoperative status and disability. The literature is already extensive and is growing steadily, as are the available treatment options.

Example

At the age of about 20 a woman developed symptoms characteristic of idiopathic migraine, which continued over the years with variable severity. At the age of 39 the attacks began to be associated with episodes of confusion and a sense of imbalance. At the age of 41, over the course of about six months she developed visual symptoms and more persistent confusion with increasing headache and a left homonymous hemianopia. CT scan showed a large right parietal partly cystic tumour. At operation a malignant oligodendroglioma was partially removed; this was followed by radiotherapy.

The main liability issue was the continued acceptance of the diagnosis of migraine at the age of 39 and 40, and the failure to refer the patient for intracranial investigation at those times. Much depended upon the description of the symptoms and the quality of the contemporaneous records.

The causation issues were more complex. The histology at the time of operation was a malignant oligodendroglioma. It could be argued that the tumour had been present for many years as a relatively benign oligodendroglioma, and had only latterly undergone malignant change. If that was so, earlier diagnosis might have resulted in removal of the tumour at a stage surgically and pathologically more favourable. A contrary argument could be that earlier removal would not have been advisable because the symptoms were truly of migraine, and not related to the tumour; the risk of surgery in a patient without neurological deficit would not have been acceptable. It might also be argued that earlier surgery does not usually affect the long-term outlook, irrespective of the stage of evolution of the tumour. Finally, the value of radiotherapy at any particular time would occasion disagreement between experts. This case illustrates the complexity and multiplicity of causation issues, while the liability issue may be relatively more straightforward.

The implications for causation arguments can be summarised as follows:

(1) Preparatory work for trial must include a very careful review of the available neuropathological evidence. Occasionally, there may be important differences of opinion expressed by different neuropathologists. Histology is the single most important prognostic factor. Thus, surgery for pilocytic astrocytoma and well-differentiated astrocytoma may be curative. Furthermore, there is now good evidence that the prognosis following surgery and oncological treatment in anaplastic astrocytoma is significantly better than that for glioblastoma multiforme. Similar favourable results have also been obtained with oligodendroglioma.

(2) Expert neurosurgical advice must cover the treatment options available at the relevant period, and particularly those which have been validated by well-designed and completed trials. Despite the 'reasonable body of opinion' test, a general aversion to treating patients with malignant gliomas should not be relied upon as a defence on causation.

Example

A 35-year-old man presented with a five-day history of headache and vomiting. The initial diagnosis was of a gastrointestinal disorder. Four weeks later he re-presented with unequivocal symptoms and signs of raised intracranial pressure, and he underwent surgery for an extensive frontal glioblastoma multiforme.

It was alleged that, had the diagnosis been made four weeks earlier, appropriate management would have resulted in a period of relief from neurological or other disability for anything from several months to several years. The causation argument centred upon the probable outcome for a patient with a tumour of this particular histology. On the basis of statistically validated trials of surgery, radiotherapy and chemotherapy, the probability of survival at one year was between 10 and 20%; and at 20 months it was zero.

Raised intracranial pressure, hydrocephalus and failing vision

Delay in diagnosis of an intracranial tumour causing raised intracranial pressure, with or without CSF obstruction hydrocephalus, has been the basis of medical negligence actions. The most difficult causation issue has centred on the loss of visual acuity and the reduction in the visual fields due to the period of unrelieved raised intracranial pressure, rather than on visual impairment due directly to the tumour itself. The difficulties have been increased by the lack of any record of visual acuity at different times.

The ophthalmological and neurosurgical experts have had to rely upon imprecise observations by the patient and by the relatives; opinions become largely speculative. In addition, it is difficult to find specific guidance in the literature on the degree of recovery to be expected in relation to the degree of visual impairment, and the duration and severity of raised intracranial pressure. Causation issues, which may have started with the admitted breach of duty by GPs, soon pass to the neurosurgical management, including the emergency relief of raised intracranial pressure by ventricular drainage of CSF, and surgery for the tumour itself. Indeed, the causation issues may lead to considerations of neurosurgical liability and third-party proceedings.

Conclusion

Causation issues are generally more difficult to resolve than are issues of liability. Increasing specialisation within neurosurgery will inevitably mean that the individual surgeon's experience and expertise in a particular type of operation will be examined. So also will the organisation of neurosurgical departments which should ensure that patients with non-urgent conditions receive an appropriate standard of care, including surgery. In addition, the resolution of causation arguments depends upon a critical evaluation of the available literature to determine the natural history, and the expected outcome following surgery for different intracranial tumours.

Further reading

Couldwell, W.T., Fukushima, T., Giannotta, S.L. and Weiss, M.C. (1996) Petro-clival meningiomas. Surgical experience in 109 cases. *Journal of Neurosurgery* **84**, 20–28.

Foy, P.M. (1987) The meningiomas: haemangioblastoma. In *Northfield's Surgery of the Central Nervous Sysgem*, 2nd edn (J.D. Miller, ed.), pp. 255–88. Blackwell Science, Oxford.

Hildebrand, J., Sahmoud, T., Mignolet, F., Brucher, J.M., Afra, D. and the EORTC Brain Tumour Group (1994) Adjuvant therapy with dibromodulcitol and BCNU increases survival of adults with malignant gliomas. *Neurology* **44**, 1479–83.

MacFarlane, R. and King, T.T. (1995) Acoustic neurinoma (vestibular Schwannoma). In *Brain Tumours. An Encyclopaedic Approach* (A.H. Kaye and E.R. Laws, Jnr, eds), pp. 577–641. Churchill Livingstone, Edinburgh.

Thomas, D.G.T. (ed.) (1990) *Neuro-oncology. Primary Malignant Brain Tumours*. Edward Arnold, London.

Chapter 16

Neuroradiology

B.E. Kendall

Introduction

When avoidable mistakes in diagnosis or damage during treatment occur, the question of individual responsibility and apportioning of blame may arise. Neuroradiology is now an established sub-specialty but many images are interpreted by radiologists with limited neurological experience. These radiologists are responsible for the opinion they express; in situations where the diagnosis is in doubt and a mistake could result in significant neural damage or death, consideration should be given to issuing a provisional report and referral of the images for a specialist opinion.

The radiologist should provide images of diagnostic quality which demonstrate any important abnormalities described in the report, or should state the reason(s) why these have not been achieved. The report should emphasise relevant diagnoses which cannot be excluded because of poor image quality.

The orientation of the images should be clearly indicated, as well as the exact siting of pathology relative to adjacent structures and superficial landmarks when appropriate. It is of particular importance to avoid ambiguous terminology, as, for example, when transitional lumbar vertebrae are present; or when the format of image presentation is unconventional, in which confusion could lead to surgery on the inappropriate side. It is the radiologist's responsibility to ensure that there can be no misunderstanding.

Localisation as near as possible to the time of surgery is necessary when pathology may be mobile, as, for example, with foreign bodies or parasites within the subarachnoid space or foreign bodies within blood vessels. Localisation in the operating theatre, as in a surgical approach through a deep bony structure such as the body of the sphenoid or a particular vertebral body, must also ultimately be the responsibility of the radiologist.

Clinical responsibility during imaging studies is shared between the radiologist and the referring clinician. It is a joint responsibility to ensure that:

(1) An accurate clinical assessment has been made and an appropriate imaging method is used to elucidate a suspected diagnosis.
(2) The patient is in a satisfactory condition for transfer to the imaging department, and appropriate medical attention is maintained during the imaging studies.

The radiologist should decline to perform any invasive studies which cannot provide information necessary for the solution of a clinical problem.

To produce perfect images, the patient should be still. Patients may be unable to co-operate because of confusion, dementia, intoxication, fear or claustrophobia. With informed consent, rapidly reversible sedation or occasionally general anaesthesia may be appropriate in order to obtain diagnostic studies.

In the presence of acute or rapidly changing neurological status, particular attention should be given to the prevention of secondary hypoxic and/or ischaemic brain damage or elevation of intracranial pressure. Adequate ventilation is a particularly important consideration when intracranial mass lesions are suspected, because vasodilatation due to carbon dioxide retention will raise intracranial pressure.

It is a duty of the radiologist to ensure that imaging studies are performed in an appropriate order and are not dangerously prolonged.

Imaging methods

Although these should be selected as effectively as practical for the solution of each problem, they frequently provide complementary data and it may be necessary to rely on a combination of studies.

Non-invasive neuroimaging procedures

Magnetic resonance imaging

Magnetic resonance imaging (MRI) is the modality of choice for elucidation of most conditions affecting the central nervous system. The reasons for this include:

(1) Its inherent high sensitivity facilitates discrimination between both normal tissues and pathologies. MRI is in general much more sensitive than computerised tomography (CT), though in some cases it is less specific and the methods should be considered to be complementary.

(2) Freedom from bone-induced artefacts; these are particularly common when

CT is used for assessment of regions near the skull base. Bone-induced artefacts on CT may mask pathology in the inferior temporal, posterior fossa and foramen magnum regions.

(3) Multiplanar imaging – the longitudinal disposition of the central nervous system, particularly in the spine, renders essentially transverse imaging modalities such as CT inappropriate as primary studies in cases in which clinical localisation is imprecise.

(4) An absence of ionising radiation.

There are certain specific contraindications to MRI. These include the presence of:

(1) Potentially mobile ferromagnetic foreign bodies which may be present due to wounding; occupational hazards such as intraocular bodies in welders which may cause retinal detachment; or surgical implants including, in particular, ferromagnetic aneurysm clips, movement of which could cause fatal intracranial haemorrhage (Klueznik *et al.*, 1993). Most of these conditions can be anticipated from the history or shown on a preliminary plain X-ray.
(2) Radio frequency-sensitive implants such as certain cardiac pacemakers or neurostimulators.
(3) Early pregnancy – there is no evidence that MRI damages the fetus, but current advice is against its use in the first trimester.

Computerised tomography

CT has particular advantages for the demonstration of:

(1) Ossified structures – fractures, bone destruction and new bone formation and dysplasias are best appreciated on a combination of plain X-rays and CT.
(2) Calcification is a component of several pathological processes and may have diagnostic significance. Supplementary CT may be important after MRI in supporting a diagnosis of certain granulomas, tumours and hamartomas.
(3) Recent blood clot – although blood clot and breakdown products are generally best elucidated by MRI, recent clot gives very specific appearances on CT. Particularly in the context of acute neurological deterioration such as may occur following trauma, CT is a more generally available and easily applied modality than MRI. It also has advantages for the simultaneous elucidation of chest and/or abdominal pathology, for example in multiple trauma cases.

Invasive neuroimaging procedures

Contrast media

The administration of contrast medium often provides additional information which may be essential or useful in diagnosis. In such circumstances the small risk, in the region of 0.007% for iodine-based and 0.001% for gadolinium-based contrast media, of inducing a life-threatening reaction is justified provided that the correct precautions are taken and facilities for resuscitation are available. The precautions include:

(1) Consideration of steroid or other drug cover for high-risk cases.
(2) Maintenance of the endovascular connection during the study.
(3) Immediate availability of emergency drugs.
(4) Facilities for intubation tracheostomy, suction of air passages and cardiac defibrillation.

Severe reactions occurring in circumstances where contrast media have been administered without adequate reason can lead to successful negligence actions.

Angiography

Digital subtraction is now routine and is of considerable importance for limiting the time of catheterisation and contrast medium dosage. In the case of cerebral angiography, screening facilities must be adequate to allow immediate recognition of intimal damage so that appropriate action can be taken to prevent progression to arterial occlusion. Routine postangiographic monitoring if neurological signs appear will allow early detection of ischaemic complications. These should be treated by heparinisation unless precluded by the danger of haemorrhage.

In general, the incidence of severe complications from diagnostic neuroradiological procedures is sufficiently low to require only a brief comment when obtaining consent for justification of a study which is clinically indicated.

The fatality rate from angiography is in the region of 0.03%. This is usually caused by technical complications, in particular embolisation or obstruction of the artery being catheterised, either by the catheter, sometimes with superadded spasm, or by dissection.

Permanent or severe neurological complications occur in 0.25% overall, but are reported to be around 0.7% in a careful prospective teaching hospital study (Stevens *et al.*, 1989), and as low as 0.04% in a retrospective non-teaching centre study (Mani *et al.*, 1978). The cause of stroke is embolism (Winding, 1980) in the great majority of cases. Emboli have been visualised during angiography

(Olivecrona, 1977). New peripheral middle cerebral infarcts have been shown on CT in patients developing neurological deficits during angiography (Stevens *et al.*, 1989), or the infarcts have been 'silent'. Infarcts have been shown on MRI after both carotid and vertebral angiography (Mamourian and Drayer, 1990). The risk of embolic stroke is as great with aortic arch injection (0.7%) as with selective catheterisation (0.8%) (Stevens *et al.* 1989), again suggesting that thrombus in or around the catheter tip is the usual source of emboli. Severe and distressing deficit may be motor, with or without aphasia, sensory or visual, or there may be amnesia or seizures.

Because of the unstable condition of many patients, the incidence of procedure-induced transient neurological defects is difficult to assess, especially in retrospective surveys, but it is probably about 1%, and possibly less with the newer non-ionic contrast media. However, angiography on elderly and arteriopathic subjects carries an incidence of ischaemic events sufficient to require specific mention of the possibility of stroke when obtaining consent, and consideration of the possibility of using non-invasive methods (ultrasound, MRI) or less neurologically invasive methods such as intravenous digital subtraction angiography. Thus, the incidence of neurological complications is higher in the following circumstances:

(1) In the presence of cerebrovascular disease, in elderly patients suffering from severe systolic hypertension and in younger patients with fibromuscular hyperplasia (Huckman *et al.*, 1979). Permanent complications in patients with symptomatic cerebrovascular disease are usually recorded at between 0.5% (Huckman *et al.* 1979) and 0.63% of examinations (Earnest *et al.*, 1983). However, in a recent prospective study confined to patients with cerebrovascular disease, ischaemic events occurred in the unusually high proportion of 11%, and persistent neurological deficit was present after one month in 5% (McIvor *et al.*, 1987).

    There is no additional increase in risk in cases with a history of recent stroke or transient ischaemic attacks (Caplan and Wolpert, 1991), but in such cases spontaneous clinical deterioration is frequent (Baum *et al.*, 1966) and should be mentioned.

(2) In the presence of severe extracranial vessel stenosis (Faught *et al.*, 1979), especially if the catheter is passed through the stenotic region (Eisenberg *et al.*, 1980), which should be avoided.

(3) In patients with gross vertebrobasilar ectasia undergoing vertebral angiography (Smoker *et al.*, 1986).

(4) Spinal angiography may be required for elucidation of fistulas or angiomatous malformations draining to the perimedullary venous plexus, or for vascular metastases or angiomatous malformations involving the vertebrae. Transient deterioration in neurological symptoms occurred in 7.7% of

patients with spinal arterio-venous fistulae examined using an ionic contrast medium; these were probably owing to the vasodilator effects of the contrast medium causing increase in blood flow through the justamedullary venous plexus. No deterioration has occurred following injection of iohexol; this is presumably because the systemic vasodilator effects of this contrast medium are less than those of the ionic media (Kendall, 1986).

In conclusion, any complication, avoidable or unavoidable, is ultimately the responsibility of the radiologist performing or supervising an angiogram. If the radiologist instructs another doctor to obtain consent, he or she must be sure that appropriate warnings regarding potential complications have been explained in the context of benefits to be obtained from the study.

Neurointerventional procedures

More exact emphasis on specific complications is necessary in consenting patients for neurointerventional angiographic procedures. The risks of interventional procedures should be explained by the doctor performing the procedure. Care must be taken to discuss the relative merits of any other method of treatment, including both surgical and conservative approaches.

Access to intensive care facilities must be available for all cases. For procedures carrying a risk of haemorrhage, liason with a neurosurgeon with operating theatre access is essential. Embolisation, angioplasty and thrombolysis are only parts of the overall therapy and they require a co-ordinated team approach. The clinical team monitoring the procedure should be involved in preoperative assessment and postinterventional care. Associated procedures such as postembolisation surgery or radiotherapy should be planned and co-ordinated before the event.

Embolisation

Embolisation is subject to all the complications of selective angiography and to additional, more specific complications, including:

(1) Aberrant embolisation – brain tissue is most likely to be involved during superselective embolisation of brain arterio-venous malformations, but even in high-risk cases the incidence should be no more than 5% (Picard *et al.*, 1985).

In systemic embolisations, cerebral embolisation can occur by reflux of emboli back to the origins of cerebral vessels, or through anastomoses between a vessel supplying the brain and one being embolised (Lasjaunias, 1980). Scrutiny of preliminary angiograms for connections between the external carotid or subclavian branches and the vertebral, internal carotid or ophthalmic circulations is essential. Flow towards the brain through such anastomoses may increase during embolisation and should be sought on each control angiogram made during the course of embolisation.

Spinal embolisation may be a definitive procedure or a prelude to surgical excision. Embolisation is more likely to be complicated by neurological deficit in dural fistulae and spinal cord aterio-venous malformations, usually owing to progressive venous thrombosis, and the patient should be warned of this possibility. Deficit can also be caused by inadvertent embolisation of a segmental artery supplying a vessel feeding the anterior spinal artery. Great care should be given to identifying the major vessels supplying the anterior spinal artery prior to any embolisation procedure.

Ischaemic events are treated symptomatically, using control of systemic blood pressure, aspirin, anticoagulants and steroids, as indicated.

Emboli passing through systemic arterio-venous shunts may cause pulmonary infarcts. When particles are failing to produce the expected degree of diminution in arterio-venous shunting, a more appropriate larger size of embolus should be substituted.

(2) Displacement of balloons or coils during treatment of a fistula or aneurysm. If a balloon or coil is carried to the venous side, the fistula may reopen but pulmonary infarction is rare. Proximal dislodgement may encroach into the parent artery, causing narrowing or occlusion, with or without reopening of the fistula, or may cause a distal embolus. If the balloon or coil is noted to be unstable as the detachment manoeuvre is commenced, it may be maintained in position by introducing a balloon in tandem. This balloon is inflated in the lumen of the artery to prevent proximal displacement of the definitive occluding balloon or coil during detachment. Retrieval devices should be available and used as indicated.

(3) A microcatheter being used to inject polymerising substances may become stuck into a vessel. No attempt should be made to extract it by forceful traction. It should be put under slight tension, cut at the skin surface and allowed to retract. No complication has been recorded from an adherent microcatheter.

(4) Nerve palsies – paralysis of cranial nerves, brachial and sacral plexuses has been observed. These are unusual even with enthusiastic particulate embolisation, since the blood supply of the nerves is segmental and the main vessels join an anastomosing perineural plexus. It is more frequent when using fluid embolic materials which may penetrate into the vascular plexus and into end arterioles of the nerves.

(5) Critical blood flow reduction in superficial vessels may cause poor wound healing (Chan and Thompson, 1984).

(6) Bleeding – embolization of subarachnoid aneurysms which have recently ruptured may precipitate further haemorrhage. This possibility is kept to a minimum by avoiding distension of the sac, particularly at the fundus. Rupture of intracranial vessels causing subdural, subarachnoid or parenchymal haemorrhage occasionally occurs during catheter manipulation. If the catheter is suitably placed, bleeding may be controlled by embolisation. Otherwise reversal of anticoagulants and conservative measures are usually adequate; surgery is rarely necessary. Some authorities use systemic hypotension as routine after brain embolisations, for prophylaxis against both bleeding and brain swelling.

(7) False aneurysms may be caused by damage to small vessels, but these rarely produce any clinical abnormality. False aneurysms may form or enlarge at the site of a traumatic fistula following balloon occlusion. They are not infrequent after closure of caroticocavernous fistulae but only occasionally become symptomatic. Intractable trigeminal pain or a progressive cavernous sinus syndrome may necessitate treatment by aneurysm or carotid occlusion.

Angioplasty

Angioplasty (Higashida *et al.*, 1987; Vitek, 1989) may be the most appropriate method of relieving stenosis in the following circumstances:

(1) In intracranial vessels for intractable spasm.
(2) Due to atheroma in surgically inaccessible regions, e.g. carotid siphon, high cervical, basilar (Sundt *et al.*, 1980).
(3) Due to pathologies in which surgical results are poor, e.g. postsurgical fibrosis, fibromuscular hyperplasia.

Angioplasty is also used for surgical amenable atheromatous stenosis. The complication rate is surprisingly low, but has not been clearly established for routine practice and this requires discussion prior to intervention. Surgical or interventional relief of stenosis more severe than 70% is currently considered to be beneficial, but the overall risk of precipitating stroke in the group undergoing screening and during intervention has to be minimal to justify this conclusion.

Thrombolysis of cerebral vessels

Facilities for thrombolysis should be available and it should be used immediately if thrombosis of a critical vessel is precipitated during embolotherapy. It is also used to lyse a recent clot that is causing ischaemic symptoms of under six hours' duration in which computed imaging has excluded a major haemorrhagic component. The risk of precipitating haemorrhage has to be balanced against limitation of the extent of infarction.

Conclusion

In all neurointerventional cases, it is the duty of the radiologist to discuss with the patient and a near relative in simple terms the commoner and the significant potential complications. These must be considered in relation to potential benefits of the procedure and the advantages and disadvantages of any alternative types of therapy, including conservative treatment.

Myelography

Myelography, with the attendant danger of puncture of the spinal theca, should no longer be necessary in those hazardous situations which were responsible for most of the rare catastrophes that were associated with the method. These included:

(1) Increased neurological defect in patients with spinal block.
(2) Puncture at the site of pathology causing bleeding or dissemination of infection.
(3) Puncture in the presence of a bleeding diathesis which could result in epidural or subdural bleeding and rapid neurological deterioration.

Cervical puncture carries the additional danger of direct needle damage to the cervical spinal cord, of which the radiologist should be aware. It is only necessary in cases in which myelography is essential and where lumbar puncture is inappropriate or unlikely to allow successful examination of the cervical theca, because of dorsal subarachnoid block or any contraindication (such as orthopnoea) to positioning to permit transfer of contrast medium from the lumbar theca.

Myelograms continue to be necessary in cases in which MRI is not tolerated or contraindicated by the presence of ferromagnetic or radiosensitive implants or strategically sited ferromagnetic foreign bodies. A few are still performed when MRI proves inconclusive. Most myelograms which are necessary after MRI are for the detection of subtle intrathecal pathology, such as congested juxtamedullary veins in cases of dural fistulae. It is essential that they are of excellent quality and generally are followed by computed myelography.

Discography

Clear indications for discography are rare, although it is still used, in particular, as a prelude to nucleolysis and for the assessment of pain induction by the procedure. This subjective assessment is considered to be justifiable provided that interpretation is cautious.

The procedure should be performed by a route which avoids puncture of the theca. The pain induced may be very severe: it usually abates very rapidly but, rarely, it has persisted to some degree and has been the cause of litigation. The possibility of postdiscographic pain and infection, though rare, should be mentioned to the patient.

Errors in intracranial diagnosis

For many conditions the essential function of radiology is to localise pathology regionally and to determine whether it is extra-axial – displacing or minimally invading the brain substance – or intra-axial. The diagnosis may be clarified by the age of the patient, the history and the appearance of the images, and confirmed by histology, serology, cerebrospinal fluid (CSF) analysis or culture of CSF or other body fluids. There are, however, important exceptions in which such confirmatory studies are not helpful and a mistaken radiological diagnosis can be life-threatening. Examples include:

(1) Occasional confusion of a subarachnoid aneurysm for a tumour, or an angiomatous malformation for an enhancing infarct.
(2) Failure to recognise a blood clot on CT or MRI.
(3) Failure to recognise intracranial subdural or extradural abscess.
(4) Errors in differentiating between neoplasm, inflammatory and vascular lesions.

(1) Occasional confusion of a subarachnoid aneurysm for a tumour or an angiomatous malformation for an enhancing infarct

In both these situations, flow void is generally sufficient to show the abnormal blood vessels, but some form of angiography may be indicated for specific diagnosis.

(2) Failure to recognise the presence of a blood clot on CT or MRI

This is most serious when the failure dispels the urgency to search for an aneurysm or arterio-venous malformation. Subarachnoid blood is visible on imaging in 80% of cases of subarachnoid haemorrhage during the first week after a bleed. In the other 20% and after the first week, hydrocephalus (often of minor degree) recognised by dilation of the temporal horns is a valuable supplementary sign.

Recognition of the haemorrhage may lead to a modification of anticoagulant treatment for ischaemic lesions or to monitoring of small extra-axial bleeds for progression.

Factors contributing to failure to recognise blood clots or blood in the CSF are:

- Time from haemorrhage; volume of haemorrhage.
- Incorrect MRI and CT techniques (e.g. using enhanced CT alone).

Biochemical changes occur in haematoma with the passage if time. These cause typical appearances on imaging and the constituents which can be recognised on MRI allow some estimation of the time since the haemorrhage. This is not of particular significance when the history is reliable, but there are cases, such as non-accidental injury in which indirect evidence of the timing of an incident may have medico-legal implications.

The density of blood and clot on CT is proportional mainly to the protein concentration and is highest in a recent, fully contracted clot, diminishing as the clot is denatured. Small haemorrhages, anaemia, admixture with CSF and defective clot contraction may reduce the initial density of the blood and/or clot. Imaging may provide evidence of failure of the blood to clot: cells will precipitate, producing a fluid level with the denser part dependant.

Time to denature varies with the size of the clot, but CT isodensity generally occurs between 14 and 28 days after bleeding and hypodensity beyond these periods.

Chronic subdural haematomas

These are of lower density on CT than grey matter and are biconvex in configuration. Post-traumatic headaches, other symptoms of raised intracranial pressure, or recurrent subdural bleeding may be present.

Chronic subdural haematoma in infants includes many cases of so-called external hydrocephalus: it presents generally at between two and six months of age, more often in boys. It is usually bilateral, with fluid extending into the interhemispheric fissure. It may follow known head injury with previously documented high-density subdural haematoma; more often, a history of trauma is lacking and the aetiology is uncertain, although non-accidental injury may be suspected. Encephalomalacia and/or focal atrophy more frequent in the parieto-occipital region(s), or evidence of systemic injury, may support this premise. Presentation is usually with an enlarging or large head without focal signs, although retinal haemorrhages or CSF xanthochromia may be present.

The extracerebral fluid tends to be of slightly higher CT density and T_2 signal than CSF. The underlying subarachnoid space may be visible or even dilated and the brain may be compressed away from the vault.

Haemosiderin tends to be present within subdural membranes only when haemorrhage is recurrent. Meningeal haemosiderosis is rare and is usually restricted to cases of chronic or recurrent subarachnoid haemorrhage, which may complicate vascular abnormalities and tumours, but it has been described as a complication of antiocoagulant therapy and should be emphasised as a sign of bleeding which may lead to irreversible neurological deficits.

(3) Failure to recognise intracranial subdural or extradural abscess

This can be a difficult problem for the radiologist but it should be anticipated in appropriate clinical situations, for example the presence of acute paranasal sinusitis or meningitis associated with localised headache, diminished consciousness level or convulsions or acute backache with ascending paresis. Even though no abnormality is evident on plain MRI or CT, epidural enhancement is often present and diagnostic. Therefore, imaging with and without contrast enhancement is obligatory.

(4) Errors in differentiating between neoplasm, inflammatory and vascular lesions

When biopsy is considered to be inappropriate, weight may be placed on the degree of probability of radiological abnormalities being specific for a particular pathology, and the focus in imaging studies should reflect this. Many 'typical' appearances are not in fact unique and care should be taken in reporting to avoid being misleadingly specific. For example, although an intrinsic tumour almost always produces mass effect, other pathologies, such as inflammatory, acute ischaemic and demyelinating lesions, also may do so. Biopsy of a plaque causing spinal cord swelling may be associated with permanent neurological deficit and has been the subject of litigation.

A nodular or irregular ring-enhancing intrinsic mass with adjacent vasogenic oedema is often considered to be a glioma (if single) or metastases or lymphoma (if multiple). However, granulomas or abscesses, particularly those due to poorly invasive organisms, infarcts, resolving haematomas, multiple sclerosis plaques and radiation necrosis, can all simulate tumour and should be specifically considered and mentioned when the diagnosis may not be confirmed by other methods. Avoidable pain and suffering, disability or premature death may be claimed to be due to negligent misdiagnosis.

Multifocal white matter foci without additional features frequently lack significance in the elderly and form the background against which important disease processes are diagnosed (Hunt *et al.*, 1989).

Encephalitis

Herpes simplex type 1 encephalitis often begins with a non-specific clinical state which includes fever, headache and alteration in consciousness. Early treatment to limit brain damage is very important at a stage when neuroimaging may be normal. Neuroimaging may show little in the early stages, MRI becoming abnormal before CT, within three or four days of clinical onset. The inflammatory changes characteristically involve the temporal and inferior parts of the frontal lobes, extending to the insular cortex but sparing the basal ganglia. Diffuse disease approximating to this distribution should be reported as suggestive of this diagnosis. Haemorrhagic changes are common and contrast enhancement occurs in more advanced disease. In some cases, the radiological appearances may be similar to those caused by the early stages of a cerebral pyogenic infection, of which the radiologist should alert the clinician.

Skull fractures

A skull fracture is present in about 75% of severe head injuries, and even a simple linear vault fracture in a conscious patient increases the likelihood of intracranial haematoma by a factor of 400, and of the need for craniotomy by a factor of 20 (Jennet and Teasdale, 1981; Dacey *et al.*, 1986). However, intracranial bleeding not infrequently occurs in the absence of skull fracture; a fracture was absent in 44% of cases requiring craniotomy in one large series (Masters *et al.*, 1987), and the demonstration of a fracture provides inadequate information about intracranial damage. If there is clinical suspicion of intracranial haemorrhage or of a skull-base fracture, or when clinical assessment is complicated by alcohol or drug abuse, a CT scan gives much more useful information than a skull X-ray. Skull X-rays are not a routine requirement in the management of head trauma (Rosenarn *et al.*, 1991) and failure to perform any imaging is not negligent if a clinical indication is lacking.

X-rays or other studies should not be performed solely for medico-legal purposes unless non-accidental injury is suspected, and then a full skeletal X-ray study is indicated for potential evidence both to confirm and document the effects of trauma. Skull X-rays are not commonly necessary for the elucidation of complications of fractures. Depression is more conveniently shown by CT than on tangential plain X-ray projections. Post-traumatic epilepsy occurs much more frequently after depressed fractures with underlying cerebral laceration than with simple contusion. Skull X-rays are indicated in patients who have had CSF diversion procedures in order to verify the possibility of post-traumatic shunt disconnection.

When computed imaging is not available, skull X-ray studies are appropriate but are limited by the guidelines of the Royal College of Radiologists (Clarke and Adams, 1990). Of much greater significance than the method of study is the immediate availability of competent assessment of appropriate images, which is the responsibility of the radiology department. Skull X-rays have often been made prior to referral and correct interpretation is essential, because they provide a permanent record on which a relationship of abnormalities to the severity of the injury and potential complications may be based.

Failure to recognise a skull fracture in a patient who developed an intracranial complication may be a major issue in medio-legal proceedings. Failure to emphasise inadequacy of imaging studies for diagnosis or exclusion of a significant abnormality may also assume importance.

Skull fractures are often evident on CT scans, particularly when using bone windowing, and should be documented. High-resolution CT is the optimum procedure for the diagnosis of skull-base fractures. A fracture line extends through both tables of the skull so that it appears darker than vascular grooves and diploic channels. When the X-ray beam is oblique to the fracture line, breaks in the inner and outer tables may appear as overlapping lines. In a recent fracture the margins are parallel and clearly defined, particularly when the fracture is on the side of the skull adjacent to the film, but they are not corticated. This feature is helpful in distinguishing between unusually placed sutures and congenital cranial defects. The latter more commonly occur with neurofibromatosis type 1 but are occasionally seen as isolated anomalies. Fractures usually extend into and frequently across sutures. In children in particular, this may be accompanied by diastasis of the suture.

As healing commences, the edges of the fracture are eroded and by about two weeks after the injury the fracture line tends to become more ill-defined. Fractures usually heal completely within six months in adults, and within as little as eight weeks in young children.

Particular attention should be paid to any sign which may be indicative of:

(1) A compound fracture.
(2) A foreign body, particularly a metallic foreign body within the cranium, orbit or spinal canal which may be a contraindication to MRI.
(3) A fracture of the maxilla or mandible which may be associated with airway obstruction or cosmetic disfigurement.

It is of particular importance to recognise compound fractures as avenues for infection, which may facilitate meningitis or abscess formation. Some are evident on clinical inspection, for example a depressed vault fracture with overlying laceration of the scalp or CSF leakage or bleeding. Radiological features indicative of compound fractures include:

(1) Gas in the tissues near the fracture line or within the cranium. It may remain extradural, lifting dural attachments, or extend into the subdural

space, along the falx or tentorium. It may become subarachnoid or intraventricular, with fluid levels in appropriate positions. The possibility that air may have entered the CSF by diagnostic needle puncture should be noted. Finally air may be driven into brain substance. Air under tension (aerocoele) may displace intracranial structures. This may be sufficient to require urgent drainage to avoid brain damage from vascular compression secondary to transfalcine or tentorial herniation.

(2) Extension of a fracture into air-containing structures such as paranasal sinuses, nasal cavity, middle ears or mastoids.
(3) Any intracranial foreign body.
(4) Intracranial abscess – intracranial sepsis is usually suspected clinically from fever, systemic upset and intracranial mass signs. Intraparenchymal abscess usually shows on imaging as a thin-walled, ring-enhancing mass with surrounding oedema.

Extracerebral abscesses, particularly extradural pus, may be difficult to detect: a thin layer of pus can be associated with considerable clinical disturbance, and even when a plain scan is completely normal, in appropriate clinical situations a post-contrast medium study should be performed to seek an enhancing membrane.

Some accidental and many non-accidental injuries may be unsuspected from the history. The accidental situations in which this occurs are birth injury and pathological fractures.

Birth injury

Birth injury fractures are usually associated with the use of forceps and may or may not be accompanied by bruising, a cephalhaematoma or obvious depression. Their significance lies in the possibility of underlying intracranial haemorrhage, especially subdural and extradural haematoma above the tentorium or in the posterior fossa, which may require evacuation.

Rarely, fractures may be caused in a narrow pelvis, usually due to pressure by the sacral promontory, or by a benign tumour such as an osteochondroma. If these fractures are not recognised they may later cause confusion, and may even lead to consideration of the possibility of non-accidental injury.

Penetrating injury

Metallic fragments due to a gun-shot injury may pass through the skull or spine; entry and exit wounds will be evident, the latter being larger. Low-velocity missiles tend to be retained. When examined by CT, they cause considerable artefact which may obscure adjacent damage. Metallic fragments are potentially mobile and ferromagnetic fragments are a contraindication to MRI. Other metallic objects such as knives and arrows may be extracted following the injury, but the possibility of retained fragments should always be considered and MRI is contraindicated until these have been excluded. The metallic fragments may lie within a fluid-filled cavity and may move under the influence of gravity. Many metallic foreign bodies and bone fragments are sterile, but particles of skin and clothing are not, so that infection may occur and this may be suggested by increasing oedema adjacent to the foreign body, abscess formation is confirmed by thin-walled ring enhancement.

Erosion of a foreign body into the CSF or damage to an adjacent blood vessel may be precipitated. For these reasons, carefully planned extraction of the metal through a non-evocative region of the brain should be considered.

Penetrating trauma is not always associated with an obvious entry wound. Particularly in children, self-inflicted accidental damage by a sharp object entering the eye or mouth may be associated with only superficial trauma or with asymptomatic deep penetration into brain substance. The object may be radiopaque, but wooden skewers and pencils are usually of low density on CT and reflect little signal on MRI, on which they are visible as linear, low-intensity structures on all sequences.

As well as infection, penetrating trauma may cause damage to blood vessels, producing haematoma, aneurysm, dissection or arterio-venous fistulae. Percutaneous needling for treatment of trigeminal neuralgia (caroticocavernous fistula), percutaneous transjugular catheterisation (vertebro-vertebral fistula) and direct puncture of cervical vessels for angiography (vertebro-vertebral and carotid jugular fistula) are well-recorded, uncommon complications which should be recognised and should not lead to successful litigation, provided that the procedure was clinically indicated and that informed consent was obtained.

A rare form of penetrating trauma may involve the fetal head during amniocentesis. This may cause damage to the developing brain either directly from intracranial haemorrhage, which may also result in hydrocephalus, or indirectly due to arterial damage, causing infarction. A history of difficulty with the amniocentesis, withdrawal of fetal blood or tissue, fetal disturbance and/or, after birth, the presence of a scar in the superficial tissues overlying the brain damage, may be helpful in diagnosis (Youroukos *et al.*, 1980; Chong *et al.*, 1989; Naylor *et al.*, 1990).

Brain damage and intracranial haematoma

The combination of CT (or MRI) and clinical observation provides the basis for decisions on whether medical management of head injury should be supplemented by intensive care or surgical intervention. Imaging may show:

(1) A normal CT – in a patient with a depressed conscious level, this may occur with:

  (a) diffuse axonal injury which may be revealed by MRI;
  (b) early contusions and hypoxic ischaemic lesions which will become evident on delayed CT or on MRI;
  (c) epilepsy;
  (d) intoxication by alcohol, drugs or metabolic disturbances.

(2) Diffuse lesions which in a comatose patient require immediate intensive care management in order to prevent secondary brain damage due to hypoxia, hypercarbia, hypotension, brain swelling with herniation, seizures or metabolic imbalance, all of which may have medico-legal implications.

(3) Focal lesions which are potentially correctable by surgery aimed at relief of raised intracranial pressure. Generally speaking, focal intracerebral haemorrhages or haemorrhagic contusions causing mass effect and sited in non-evocative regions should be considered for surgery in appropriate clinical circumstances if their volume exceeds about 25 ml in the supratentorial compartment, but less in the intratentorial compartment.

Extradural bleeding is usually arterial, classically from the middle meningeal artery and often associated with skull fractures crossing arterial grooves. Binding of the dura to the skull tends to restrict the haematoma and results in a biconvex configuration. Rapid accumulation of the haematoma is associated with progressive neurological deficit, responding to early surgery. Basal and vertex haematomas are best shown on coronal sections and therefore by MRI, being more easily overlooked on axial CT. The latter usually originate in a torn venous sinus which is displaced from the vault by a haematoma crossing the midline. Similarly, transtentorial extradural haematomas separate the transverse sinus from the bone.

Urgent drainage of extracerebral blood may be life-saving. Primary brain injury is not usually present and the prognosis for full recovery is good. When the clinical diagnosis is evident, the delays for confirmatory radiological studies, such as may occur outside normal working hours and with inexperienced staff, should be avoided in rapidly deteriorating patients.

Acute subdural haemorrhage is from the surface of injured brain substance and is one component of severe primary brain injury. The extracerebral clot frequently extends widely over the surface of a damaged lobe or hemisphere and conforms in shape to the convexity. The damaged brain contributes to the mass effect and displacement and it may be the predominant factor in cases with a shallow but diffuse subdural haemorrhage. The radiologist should estimate and record the relative contribution of each component, since unnecessary or aggressive surgery may have medico-legal implications. Contralateral or, in the case of posterior fossa subdural haemorrhage, third-ventricular hydrocephalus are poor prognostic signs, treated by urgent surgical relief of the swelling. In general, the prognosis for good clinical recovery is poor.

As haematomas become subacute in 7–21 days after bleeding, they tend to isodensity with grey matter and may be difficult to visualise directly with CT. Displacement from the surface of the cerebral white matter and compression of the ventricle(s) are important diagnostic features generally visible on imaging, even in bilateral cases without midline shift. With MRI, altered signal in the haematoma is always evident.

Cerebrospinal fluid fistula: recurrent meningitis or abscess

Most CSF leaks occur soon after accidental trauma and cease spontaneously, but some persist. Leaks are also caused by surgical trauma or by erosion of the skull base due to local pathology or chronic hydrocephalus; developmental defects may also be the site of leakage. All types of leaks are a cause of recurrent intracranial sepsis. Failure to test for persistant CSF leakage or to recognise clinical or radiological signs suggesting a persistent leak may be liability issues. In such cases, the site of a fistula should be suggested by:

- Demonstration of watery fluid localised, for example, to one middle ear or a paranasal sinus at the skull base; or
- demonstration of a bony defect extending through the wall of an air cavity, particularly if there is herniation of intracranial contents.

In the absence of such signs, or with complex basal fractures, the actual fistula may be outlined by intrathecal non-ionic contrast medium manipulated along the cranial base, followed by CT scanning. If the leakage of CSF ceases during the procedure, it may be induced by causing an increase of CSF secretion by jugular compression or by raising CSF pressure using a Valsalva manoeuvre.

Sequelae of head injury

The phase of recovery of physiological processes following head injury is generally defined as extending to the end of the period of post-traumatic amnesia (Symonds, 1962). Post-traumatic symptoms, including paresis, involuntary movements, sensory changes, central pain and defective memory, intellect and emotional control, may occur in the presence of major brain destruction leading to encephalomalacic cystic changes ('porencephalic cysts'), gliosis and atrophy.

However, they are often associated with diffuse axonal injury or small brain stem haemorrhages caused by tearing of basal perforating arteries. In such cases, assessment of end-stage damage requires high-resolution T_2-weighted MRI (Gentry *et al.*, 1988a, b) to search for small high-intensity gliotic or low-intensity lesions due to the presence of haemosiderin. These are not infrequently demonstrated in the corpus callosum and fornices as well as in the cerebral white matter. It should be noted that even with high-field, high-resolution MRI taken to assess the degree of residual brain damage, only a minority of diffuse axonal injuries are shown. Some of these are the residua of larger haemorrhagic lesions visible in the acute phase, but in the acute phase of those cases of major shearing injuries who survive, CT is often normal. Acute cases with haematoma in the septum pellucidum corpus callosum, fornix or upper brain stem and blood within the lateral ventricles evident on CT (Kido *et al.*, 1992), often remain unconscious from the moment of impact until death.

After minor head trauma, post-traumatic behaviour disorders and the postconcussion syndrome have, in some cases, been shown on high-field MRI to be associated with similar residua of axonal shearing in the white matter of the cerebral hemispheres (Mittl *et al.*, 1994).

Hydrocephalus/atrophy

Communicating hydrocephalus related to bleeding into the CSF and blockage of Pacchionian granulations may be a significant feature in the radiological diagnosis of subarachnoid haemorrhage. When mild, the temporal horns alone may be enlarged and this sign must be sought and its significance emphasised. Intraventricular masses or clot occluding the aqueduct or other narrow parts of the ventricular system are best shown by MRI.

Unilateral hydrocephalus may occur on the side opposite a cerebral hemisphere mass lesion causing compression of the third ventricle. In such cases, an acute increase in intracranial pressure may be fatal unless attention is focused onto surgical relief of the mass lesion if possible.

Hydrocephalus in infections may be related to obstruction of CSF pathways or Pacchionian granulations by exudate or fibrosis.

Hydrocephalus associated with raised intracranial pressure can generally be recognised and distinguished from atrophy both clinically and on imaging. It usually occurs within a month of bleeding into the CSF, but occasionally as late as three months, and may be suspected if there is a failure to improve clinically to the expected degree.

All parts of the ventricular system above the obstructed region are distended with a tendency to rounding of their contours. The restraining effect of the septum pellucidum and/or falx cerebri results in a diminished angle between the ventricular roofs and enlargement of the temporal horn(s) tends to be relatively pronounced; in early hydrocephalus, the temporal horns alone may be distended and are an important diagnostic feature. The ventricular distention tends to be more marked in regions where the brain is damaged and compliance thereby is diminished. Communicating intracerebral cysts may also become distended. Regions of the ventricular system supported by only a thin layer of nervous tissue are particularly prone to become distended during hydrocephalus. These regions, which are not affected in atrophic conditions, include the anterior and posterior recesses of the third ventricle and the roof of the fourth ventricle.

Fluid distention of interstitial spaces may be present and is most marked close to the lateral ventricles in the acute phase. The hydrocephalus may resolve spontaneously or become balanced to a state of 'normal pressure hydrocephalus' or may persist at high pressure. Then, if the hydrocephalus is not relieved, the distension may persist and be associated with chronic periventricular gliosis and central atrophy.

It should be clearly understood that in chronic hydrocephalus, and particularly in hydrocephalus relieved by shunting procedures, recurrence of high intraventricular pressure may produce slight or even no increase in ventricular size, probably owing to decreased compliance of the brain tissue. The radiologist cannot exclude increase in intracranial pressure or shunt blockage from this lack of change in ventricular size: failure to diagnose elevated intracranial pressure on the basis of clinical features may become a liability issue if, for example, permanent diminution in visual acuity is a result. Focal and/or generalised atrophy causing ventricular and sulcal dilatation may be present within three months of head injury and may progress. It may be accompanied by Wallerian degeneration of descending tracts which return T_2-high signal and show loss of volume.

Cerebral infarction and ischaemia

Errors in diagnosis are infrequent but can usually be avoided if both clinical and radiological features are considered in isolation and then in combination. Infarction and/or ischaemia may result from:

(1) Systemic conditions which reduce the flow of oxygen and nutrients or metabolites to and from central nervous tissue.
(2) Local disruption of the circulation.
(3) A combination of (1) and (2).

Strokes are diagnosed clinically and their nature is confirmed by imaging. Non-contrast-enhanced imaging is essential to distinguish tumours (Weisberg and Nice, 1977) and haemorrhage. A haemorrhagic stroke can generally be distinguished using CT and MRI, and this may be of particular significance if thrombolysis and/or anticoagulation are to be considered on the one hand, or if elucidation of an underlying source of haemorrhage is necessary on the other.

Acute infarction may produce a local mass effect with solid or ring enhancement and vasogenic oedema simulating a neoplastic or inflammatory lesion. Provided the diagnosis has been considered, an unnecessary biopsy is unlikely to be performed: short-term follow-up will show the evolution of the infarct. There may be progression to a typical appearance and distribution and/or resolution or regression to encephalomalacia and/or atrophy. Even in the unusual case where an infarct complicates a tumour, the situation will usually be resolved by a short period of observation.

Infantile hemiplegia may be an issue in litigation. In such cases, a focal lesion occurring before or at the time of birth may not present clinical signs until after six months of age. End-stage brain damage is usually best shown by MRI, although CT also may reveal calcification and atrophy in addition to low density within old haematomas and some infarcts. Infarction in middle or posterior cerebral distribution is often a spontaneous event, although it can occur as a complication of hypoxic-ischaemic encephalopathy. It can also be a complication of birth injury related to over-vigorous forceps or ventouse extraction. This may be owing to:

(1) Marked distortion of the skull.
(2) A basal subdural haematoma causing compression of the middle cerebral artery.
(3) Subarachnoid bleeding causing arterial spasm.

MRI should be performed for the distinction of encephalomalacia from malformations, germinal matrix damage with schizencephaly, porencephaly or hydranencephaly which may be associated with adjacent neuronal migration defects.

Since the central nervous system is dependent entirely on the aerobic metabolism of glucose, the effects of generalised anoxia are manifest on the brain before other organ systems.

Generalised hypoxic ischaemia can occur by two very different mechanisms which need to be distinguished. Either or both of these may occur in a medico-legal setting:

(1) Profound hypoxic ischaemia
(2) Arterial hypotension

(1) Profound hypoxic ischaemia

This can occur due to total loss of perfusion, as in circulatory arrest, or complete loss of oxygenation, as for example in failure of the oxygen supply during anaesthesia, gas exchange in the lungs, placental separation (which will soon result in circulatory arrest or respiratory obstruction) or paralysis by disease or drugs.

Cessation of neural function may take place within a few minutes and may be reversible when it lasts for under ten minutes without additional protective measures. The tissues with the most active metabolism are the first to develop irreversible damage and this produces typical end-stage patterns detectable on MRI. In general, mature grey matter has about three times the metabolic activity and oxygen consumption of white matter. Metabolism is also particularly high in myelinating tissues, and this has a particular significance in the likely timing of an insult in relation to obstetric malpractice. Myelination commences in the thalami at about 25 weeks, in the lentiform nuclei at about 35 weeks, in the perirolandic white matter at 36–38 weeks, in the caudate nuclei at 44 weeks and in the cerebral white matter other than the perirolandic region during the first year of life.

End-stage damage from profound hypoxic ischaemia reflects this myelination pattern. For example, perinatal asphyxia at term will cause symmetrical gliosis and/or necrosis involving the postero-lateral thalami, the posterior thirds of the lentiform nuclei and the perirolandic white matter. In the fully myelinated brain, necrosis of the lentiform nuclei, caudate heads and cerebral cortex occur, progressing to atrophy. Diffuse white matter swelling or demyelination occur with more prolonged anoxic episodes.

Metabolic abnormalities may be associated with tissue necrosis. These should be considered in differential diagnosis. With supportive and/or specific therapy the permanent damage can be limited. Imaging features may be useful in differential diagnosis in both a clinical and medico-legal context. These conditions include:

- Hypoglycaemia – the grey matter is most vulnerable, especially the third and fourth layers of the cortex and the hippocampi. The occipital and posterior parietal lobes are particularly vulnerable to this condition in the neonatal period.
- Mitochondrial cytopathies in which there are inherited defects in respiratory enzymes controlling tissue metabolism. These again tend to affect different parts of the nervous system in various age groups, partly dependent on metabolic activity. The basal ganglia and subthalamic structures tend to be involved in infants, and the brain stem in children and adolescents. The cerebral white matter and cortex may also be affected.
- Other inherited defects of metabolism; these may occur at different times of development and their effects are again related to the activity of metabolic processes at the time of onset. Examples include maple syrup urine disease, which tends to occur in the first few months of life and affects the

myelinating brain stem; urea cycle disorders are usually later in onset and tend to affect the myelinating hemispheres, often asymmetrically or even unilaterally. Consideration of the possibility of metabolic disorders should help to distinguish these conditions from encephalitis and ischaemic infarction.

Poisoning by carbon monoxide and by cyanide, which inhibit tissue oxygen exchange, and by methyl alcohol and ethylene glycol, which cause metabolic acidosis, results in necrosis particularly affecting the basal ganglia.

(2) Arterial hypotension

The second mechanism is arterial hypotension of a degree sufficient to overcome the autoregulation capacity of the arterioles of the brain, leading to distal perfusion failure resulting in border zone infarctions.

Inadequacy of treatment or failure to prevent anoxia during the perinatal period, resulting in cardiac insufficiency with secondary cerebral perfusion failure, is a common medico-legal issue in cases of cerebral palsy. Less frequently it is an issue after any form of profound circulatory collapse. At all ages, from the mature fetus throughout life, the ischaemic changes are in the border zones at the periphery of the distributions of the major cortical arteries. These may be modified by anatomical variants and superimposed vascular disease. In this condition also there is a vulnerability factor depending on metabolic activity.

In premature infants where the germinal matrix adjacent to the ventricular system is active in cell production, it is particularly vulnerable to hypoperfusion, and ischaemia results in infarction causing periventricular leucomalacia. The fragile capillaries within the plexus are liable to haemorrhage and even more so when it has been damaged by asphyxia; haemorrhage may be precipitated by elevation of the venous pressure, which is liable to occur with cardiopulmonary pressure changes related to pulmonary immaturity.

Calcification in necrotic tissue is generally more frequent in children, particularly in the newborn period. In an infarct, it tends to occur in the deeper layers of the cortex and may simulate Sturge–Weber syndrome. However, the ishcaemic calcification tends to absorb, whereas in Sturge–Weber syndrome it is progressive and the affected region enhances. Both conditions are associated with hemiatrophy.

The spine

Provided that the appropriate part of the spine has been covered by modern MRI, it is unlikely that spinal cord or nerve root compression will not be appreciated. However, the significance of chronic spondylotic cord compression may be over-emphasised on modern cross-sectional imaging. Spondylosis is an almost universal accompaniment of aging, and degrees of encroachment on the spinal canal causing up to 50% narrowing of the sagittal diameter of the spinal cord may fail to produce significant symptoms. The danger of assuming that symptoms are caused by such chronic cord compression is that it may divert attention from a significant but less obvious lesion, such as a dural arterio-venous fistula or a tumour. On the other hand, the incidental detection of spondylotic cord compression may have considerable significance in that a sudden hyperextension or whiplash type of trauma, in which the ligamenta flava are buckled into the spinal canal, may precipitate cord contusion and paralysis; in relatively young persons, a discussion of prophylactic decompression may be appropriate.

Spinal injuries

In the conscious patient, attention is generally drawn to injury by pain, and adequate plain X-rays to show the whole of the potentially affected region of the spine are made, supplemented as necessary by CT. In patients with reduced levels of consciousness following a head injury, it is the responsibility of the admitting team to exclude cervical instability. A good-quality lateral X-ray of the whole length of the cervical spine is necessary to show an unstable fracture or a fracture-dislocation, from which damage to the cervical spinal cord could occur with even gentle passive movement during diagnostic imaging or active movement during recovery from head injury. In all cases, the CT scout view should cover the upper cervical spine and it should be carefully assessed.

It is now well-established that the cross-table, lateral, cervical X-ray and the standard three-film trauma series are considerably less accurate than CT (Streitweiser *et al.*, 1983), and even more so when spiral CT is available. However, the majority of lesions which are potentially significant in terms of spinal cord compression will show some abnormality on X-ray. Important abnormalities such as rotatory dislocations missed due to lack of adequately skilled interpretation of X-rays cannot be defended.

In practice, with displaced fractures and dislocations the degree of encroachment into the spinal canal is a significant feature in the determination of spinal cord compression and damage. In severe flexion, vertical compression and torsion injuries, bone and disc fragments may occlude the canal at the time of impact, causing damage to the spinal cord followed by realignment, relieving the neural compression but leaving an unstable situation. The presence or absence of instability is determined by demonstrating disruption of the anterior and posterior osseous–ligamentous complexes constituting the vertebral column (McAfee *et al.*, 1983), and not by subjecting the patient to potentially harmful trial movements. The integrity of the longitudinal ligament complexes should be specifically sought on MRI because of their significance in the prevention of shearing injuries (Magerl *et al.*, 1994). In normal cases, the anterior complex (anterior longitudinal ligament and annulus fibrosus) and posterior complex (ligamentum flava, supra- and interspinous posterior and capsular ligaments of the facet joints) are visible as continuous black lines anterior and posterior to the vertebrae on sagittal sequences. Discontinuity of the complexes is usually associated with focal high-T_2 signal and often with extradural and/or para- or antevertebral haematoma.

Encroachment on the spinal canal can be by bone, which is best shown by CT, or by disc material, haemorrhage or ligaments, which is better shown by MRI. Partial volume in any form of computed imaging and metal-induced phase shift in particular on MRI may give a false or exaggerated impression of diminished canal size. The degree of neural compression is best assessed by the relation of canal encroachment to congruous distortion of the spinal cord.

The spinal cord should be examined by T_1- and T_2-weighted imaging for:

(1) Disruption in which the ends of the cord, shown best on T_1-weighted images, are discontinuous (Mathis *et al.*, 1988). In such cases, there can of course be no possibility of a return of voluntary control of body and limb functions below the break.
(2) Contusion, haemorrhage or infarction in which blood breakdown products are visible with signal changes, depending on the chemical state, within the spinal cord which is usually swollen.
(3) Myelomalacia in which the cord substance returns a T_1-low, T_2-high signal. A T_2-high signal with a normal T_1 signal may be due to oedema or non-haemorrhagic contusion or even petechial haemorrhages without coalescence, and may be reversible.
(4) Cystic change, with a well-defined focal region of T_1-low, T_2-high signal.
(5) Syrinx formation in which a similar, well-defined region which extends longitudinally for a varying distance beyond the site of the trauma. The size of the syrinx may vary with posture and it may increase in extent with time.
(6) The degree of compression and/or angulation of the cord at the site of injury to the spinal column. If there has been immediate loss of function, and particularly if the cord itself has been affected by marked haemorrhagic contusion or disruption, correction of the compression or angulation is unlikely to result in recovery of function, although it may be necessary in order to stabilise the vertebral column.

Baseline images are of importance for future assessment of progressive or delayed myelopathy which may be related to atrophy of, or cystic extension within, the spinal cord.

In conclusion, non-penetrating spinal injuries should be assessed clinically without moving the spine. Plain X-rays should be studied by experienced radiologists and supplemented by CT, particularly to show the degree of any canal encroachment. MRI is necessary to assess neural involvement when this is clinically indicated in both adults (Sato *et al.*, 1994) and children (Davis *et al.*, 1991).

Penetrating injuries

Penetrating injuries, though uncommon in civilian practice, constitute 85% of war injuries. Neural tissue may be injured by the missile, by displaced bone fragments or by the 'shock waves' induced by a near miss. MRI may still allow the best assessment of the pathological anatomy. However, it may (1) be contraindicated if plain X-rays show metal fragments of knives or bullets close to the cord; (2) be rendered less effective or uninterpretable by artefacts: these are generally less evident on spin echo than gradient echo sequences.

In such cases, non-ionic contrast myelography may be necessary to assess neural encroachment.

In injury to the cervical spine, the possibility of vertebral artery dissection should be considered when interpreting MRI, particularly in uni- or bilateral facet joint displacements. Dissections may result in infarction affecting the cerebrum, cerebellum or brain stem as well as the spinal cord, in which the upper thoracic watershed may be involved.

Scoliosis

Painful scoliosis of acute onset is often related to mechanical derangement that requires clinical management without radiological study. Should it become chronic, local back pain plus a minor scoliosis does require imaging because of the possibility of an intraspinal tumour, or tumours of the spine, such as osteoid osteoma or osteoblastoma, as well as disc protrusion. Because of the possibility of revealing soft tissue lesions as well as bony abnormalities and the capacity for longitudinal imaging, MRI is the procedure of choice. It is indicated also for the elucidation of progressive scoliosis, often diagnosed as idiopathic but in which both tumour and syrinx are not uncommon underlying abnormalities requiring investigation by MRI, in any case with atypical features and especially prior to any surgery.

Back pain

Recurrent or continuing back pain, sometimes extending into the legs and with or without neurological signs, may suggest arachnoiditis, particularly if myodil myelography has been used in the past, with or without subsequent surgery. Gross arachnoiditis is generally evident on MRI of reasonable quality, particularly if there is construction, thickening or obliteration of the theca. However, in order to diagnose lesser degrees of arachnoiditis it is essential that image quality is high and such that the nerve roots within the theca and root pouches can routinely be demonstrated in the absence of arachnoiditis. Images that do not achieve this quality cannot be used to exclude lesser degrees of arachnoiditis, and this fact should be stated clearly in medico-legal reports. High-resolution fast-spin echo images are currently the most appropriate for establishing this diagnosis.

The distinction between inflammatory and mechanical discogenic disease is usually evident and should be suggested using computed imaging before plain X-rays show any diagnostic features. Clinical suspicion and disc space narrowing and paravertebral swelling should lead to computed imaging followed, if necessary, by aspiration of the disc space. In mechanical disease, there is preservation of the vertebral end plates, whereas in inflammatory disease, reactive granulation tissue tends to destroy the end plates and extend into the adjacent bone in which there may be T_1-low, T_2-high signal inflammatory tissue. Enhancing soft tissue masses adjacent to the bony disease or fluid-containing abscesses with surrounding ring enhancement may be present in the adjacent paravertebral region or within the spinal canal. Some difficulty with diagnosis is possible when granulation tissue is associated with local exudation of serum or blood products.

The distinction between residual or recurrent disc protrusion and post-operative granulation tissue usually requires gadolinium enhancement. It should be noted that reactive tissue along the operative approach and around the dura is commonly present even in asymptomatic patients for some weeks following disc surgery.

The decision to reoperate should be based mainly on clinical rather than radiological features, unless there is evidence in addition of fluid collections requiring drainage.

Spinal tumour

Commonly, tumours present with progressive neurological deficit. The likely diagnosis and the differential diagnosis – from demyelination and angiomatous malformation and/or fistula – are elucidated by MRI.

Tumours, particularly in the lumbar or sacral region, may present with pain and only slowly progressive and relatively inconspicuous neurological deficits, a syndrome which may be mistaken for a mechanical problem. In such cases, plain X-rays of the spine may be the only study made, and corticated erosion of the margins of the spinal canal resulting in enlargement of the canal or intervertebral foramina have been overlooked but have provided important medico-legal evidence. The slightest suspicion of any erosion should be elucidated by MRI.

References

Baum, S., Stern, G.N. and Kuroda, K.K. (1966) Complications of 'no arteriography'. *Radiology* **86**, 835–8.

Caplan, L.R. and Wolpert, S.M. (1991) Angiography in patients with occlusive cerebrovascular disease. *American Journal of Neuroradiology* **12**, 593–601.

Chan, R.C. and Thompson, G.B. (1984) Ischaemic necrosis of the scalp after preoperative embolisation of meningeal tumours. *Neurosurgery* **15**, 76–81.

Chong, S.K.F., Levitt, G.A., Lawson, J., Lloyd, U. and, Newman, C.G.H. (1989) Subarachnoid cysts with hydrocephalus; a complication of mid-trimester amniocentesis. *Prenatal Diagnosis* **9**, 677–9.

Clarke, J.A. and Adams, J.E. (1990) The application of clinical guidelines for skull radiography in accident and emergency departments; theory and practice. *Clinical Radiology* **41**, 152–5.

Dacey, R.G., Alves, W.M., Rimel, R.W., Winn, H.R. and Jane, J.A. (1986) Neurosurgical complications after apparently minor head injury – assessment of risk in a series of 610 patients. *Journal of Neurosurgery* **65**, 203–10.

Davis, P.C., Reisner, A., Hudgins, P.A., Davis, W.E. and O'Brien, M.S. (1991) Spinal injuries in children: role of MR. *American Journal of Neuroradiology* **14**, 607–17.

Earnest, F., Forbes, G., Sandok, B.A., Piepgras, D.B., Faust, R.J., Instrup, D.M. and Arndt, L.J. (1983) Complications of cerebral angiography: prospective assessment of risk. *American Journal of Neuroradiology* **4**, 1191–7.

Eisenberg, R.L., Bank, W.O. and Hedgcock, M.W. (1980) Neurologic complication of angiography in patients with critical stenosis of the carotid artery. *Neurology* **30**, 892–5.

Faught, E., Trader, S.D. and Hanna, G.R. (1979) Cerebral complications of angiography for transient ischaemia and stroke. Predication of risk. *Neurology* **29**, 4–15.

Gentry, L.R., Godersky, J.C. and Thompson, B. (1988) MR imaging of head trauma: review of the distribution of radiopathologic features of traumatic lesions. *American Journal of Neuroradiology* **150**, 663–72.

Gentry, L.R., Godersky, G.C., Thompson, B. and Dunn, V.D. (1988) Prospective comparative study of intermediate-field MR and CT in the evaluation of closed head trauma. *American Journal of Neuroradiology* **150**, 673–82.

Higashida, R.T., Hieshima, G.B., Tsai, F.Y., Halbach, V.V., Norman, D. and Newton, T.H. (1987) Transluminal angioplasty of the vertebral and basilar artery. *American Journal of Neuroradiology* **8**, 745–9.

Huckman, M.S., Shenk, G.L., Neems, R.L. and Tinor, T. (1979) Transfemoral cerebral arteriography versus direct percutaneous carotid and brachial arteriography. A comparison of complication rates. *Radiology* **132**, 93–7.

Hunt, A.L., Orrison, W.W., Yeo, R.A., Haaland, K.Y., Rhyne, R.L., Garry, P.J. and Rosenberg, G.A. (1989) Clinical significance of MRI white matter in the elderly. *Neurology* **39**, 1470–74.

Jennett, B. and Teasdale, G. (1981) Early assessment of the head-injured patient. In *Management of Head Injury*, pp. 77–93. F.A. Davis, Philadelphia.

Kendall, B. (1986) Spinal angiography with iohexol. *Neuroradiology* **28**, 72–3.

Kido, D.K., Cox, C., Hamill, R.W., Rothenberg, B.M. and Woolf, P.D. (1992) Traumatic brain injuries: predictive usefulness of CT. *Radiology* **182**, 777–81.

Klueznik, R.P., Carrier, D.A., Pyka, R. and Haid, R.W. (1993) Placement of a ferromagnetic intracerebral aneurysm clip in a magnetic field with fatal outcome. *Radiology* **187**, 855–6.

Lasjaunias, P. (1980) Nasopharyngeal angiofibromas: hazards of embolisation. *Radiology* **136**, 119–23.

Magerl, F., Aebi, M., Gertzbein, S.D., Harms, J. and Nazarian, S. (1994) A comprehensive classification of thoracic and lumbar injuries. *European Spine Journal* **3**, 184–201.

Mamourian, A. and Drayer, B.P. (1990) Clinically silent angiography. *Neuroradiology* **14**, 1084.

Mani, R.L., Eisenberg, R.L., McDonald, J.R., Pollack, J.A. and Mani, J.R. (1978) Complications of catheter cerebral arteriography I–III. *American Journal of Radiology* **131**, 861–74.

Masters, S.J., McClean, P.M. Arcarese, J.S., Brown, R.F., Campbell, J.A., Freed, H.A., Hess, G.H., Hoff, J.T., Korrine, A., Koziol, D.F., Marasco, J.A., Marten, D.F., Metcalf, H., Morrison, J.L., Rachlin, J.A., Shaver, J.W. and Thornbury, J.R. (1987) Skull X-ray examinations after head trauma. *New England Journal of Medicine* **316**, 84–91.

Mathis, J.M., Wilson, J.T., Bernard, J.W. and Zelenik, M.E. (1988) MR imaging of spinal cord avulsion. *American Journal of Neuroradiology* **9**, 1232–3.

McAfee, P.C., Yuan, H.A., Fredrickson, B.E. and Lubicky, J.P. (1983) The value of CT in thoracolumbar fractures. *Journal of Bone and Joint Surgery (America)* **65**, 461–79.

McIvor, J., Steiner, T.J., Perkin, G.D., Greenhalgh, R.M., and Clifford Rose, F. (1987) Neurological morbidity of arch and carotid arteriography in cerebrovascular disease. *British Journal of Radiology* **60**, 117–22.

Mittl, R.L., Grossman, R.I., Hiehle, J.F., Hurst, R.W , Kauder, D.R., Gennarelli, T.A. and Alburger, G.W. (1994) Prevalence of MR evidence of diffuse axonal injury in patients with mild head injury and normal head CT findings. *American Journal of Neuroradiology* **15**, 1583–9.

Naylor, G., Roper, J.P. and Willshaw, H.E. (1990) Ophthalmic complications of amniocentesis. *Eye* **4**, 845–59.

Olivecrona, H. (1977) Complications of cerebral angiography. *Neuroradiology* **14**, 175–81.

Picard, L., Moret, J. and Lepoire, J. (1985) Traitement endovasculaire des angiomes arterio-veineux, intracerebraux. *Bulletin et memoires de l'Academie Royale de Medicine de Belgique* **140**, 419–31.

Rosenarn, J., Duus, B., Nielsen, K., Kruse, K. and Boesen, T. (1991) Is a skull X-ray necessary after milder head trauma? *British Journal of Radiology* **5**(2), 135–9.

Sato, T., Kokubun, S., Rijal, K.P., Ojima, T., Mordai, N., Hashimoto, M., Hyodo, H. and Oonuma, H. (1994) Prognosis of spinal cord injury in correlation with magnetic resonance imaging. *Paraplegia* **32**, 81–5.

Smoker, W.R.K., Corbett, J.J., Gentry, L.R., Keyes, W.D., Price, M.J. and McKusker, S. (1986) High resolution computed tomography of the basilar artery: 2. Vertebrobasilar dolichoectasia: clinical-pathological correlation and review. *American Journal of Neuroradiology* **7**, 61–72.

Stevens, J.M., Barter, S., Kerslake, R., Schneidau, A., Barber, C. and Thomas, D.J. (1989) Relative safety of intravenous digital subtraction angiography over other methods of carotid angiography and impact on clinical management of cerebrovascular disease. *British Journal of Radiology* **62**, 813–16.

Streitweiser, D.R., Knopp, R., Wales, L.R., Williams. J.L. and Tonnemacher, K. (1983) Accuracy of standard radiographic views in detecting cervical spine fractures. *Annals of Emergency Medicine* **12**, 538–42.

Sundt, T.M., Smith, H.C., Campbell, J.K., Cucchiara, R.F. and Stanson, A.W. (1980) Transluminal angioplasty for basilar artery stenosis. *Mayo Clinic Proceedings* **55**, 673–80.

Symonds, C. (1962) Concussion and its sequelae. *Lancet* **1**, 1–5.

Vitek, J.J. (1989) Subclavian artery angioplasty and the origin of the vertebral artery. *Radiology* **170**, 407–9.

Weisberg, L.A. and Nice, C.N. (1977) Intracranial tumours simulating the presentation of cerebrovascular syndromes. *American Journal of Medicine* **63**, 517–24.

Winding, O. (1980) Intrinsic particles in angiographic contrast media. *Radiology* **134**, 317–20.

Youroukos, S., Papdelis, F. and Matsanoitis, N. (1980) Porencephalic cyst after amniocentesis. *Archives of Diseases of Childhood* **55**, 814–15.

Chapter 17

Epilepsy

C.J. Earl

Introduction

The diagnosis of epilepsy may have serious consequences for a patient in terms of his or her employment or way of life. It may influence decisions about a future career, marriage or starting a family. It is therefore very important that a diagnosis of epilepsy should be made on proper evidence. It is not appropriate in a chapter of this sort to discuss the details of diagnosis and management, but it is important for medical men and women to remember that the diagnosis itself, or the failure to make the diagnosis, may have various legal implications. Thus, a patient in whom a diagnosis of epilepsy was wrongly made might well call the doctor to account if, for example, the consequence was that the patient could no longer be employed, because he or she could not legally drive a car. Similarly a patient who develops epilepsy, and as a result of the epilepsy has a serious accident while driving, might in some circumstances hold his or her doctor responsible for failing to make the diagnosis or, having made the diagnosis, for failing to give clear advice (which he or she certainly should have given) that the patient should not drive.

The commonest legal issue that a doctor encounters in dealing with patients with epilepsy, once the diagnosis has been made, concerns driving. Patients must be advised to report their disability to the licensing authorities. Some may fail to do so, and where this happens, and where the doctor is aware of it and is concerned that the patient is a serious risk to himself or herself or others, the doctor is obliged personally to report the case to the Driver and Vehicle Licensing Agency (DVLA). Of course, the doctor must if necessary be prepared to defend such action later, but this breach of confidentiality would be in keeping with the guidelines laid down by the General Medical Council.

It is important to be quite certain that the patient understands what the law requires, and before taking the decision to report the case to the DVLA the doctor would be wise to inform the patient in writing of his or her intentions, and make clear notes in the patient's records that he or she has done so. Minor attacks of epilepsy are no less significant than major attacks with complete loss of consciousness; experiences sometimes referred to as 'auras' are, in fact, minor epileptic seizures, and from the point of view of fitness to drive, must be regarded as such. In this respect the law makes no distinction between severe (major) and minor attacks.

Failure of the doctor to warn a patient with epilepsy that he or she must not drive may certainly lead to litigation if the patient has a seizure while driving and causes injury to himself or herself or a third party.

A case of this sort concerned a lorry driver who developed attacks of epilepsy with loss of consciousness. He had appropriate investigations carried out and was prescribed regular antiepileptic medication. After he had started taking the drug his doctor, who had not properly understood the regulations, told him that he could return to his work as a driver. Soon afterwards he suffered another attack while driving his lorry. The lorry went out of control, ran down a hill and virtually demolished a small house, fortunately unoccupied at the time. It had to be agreed with the insurance company concerned that the advice given was negligent, and financial responsibility for the consequences of the accident lay with the doctor.

Drug therapy

Modern drug regimes used in the treatment of epilepsy rarely give rise to serious disability. In the past, drowsiness was not uncommon from the use of high doses of anticonvulsants with sedative side-effects. With modern drug regimes this is much less frequent, but warnings about side-effects are still important. Some are particularly likely to occur when a drug is first taken and will pass after a few days (e.g. dizziness and ataxia with carbamazepine or primidone). It is important to warn patients of the possibility of such side-effects, so that during the first few days of treatment they do not put themselves in situations where there would be a risk to themselves or others.

There are more serious, though fortunately rare, early complications such as bone marrow damage with carbamazepine. Other unwanted side-effects from long-continued treatment with phenytoin and phenobarbitone are related to induced folate and vitamin B_{12} deficiency which may lead to macrocytic anaemia. In addition, phenytoin after many years may cause impairment of absorption of vitamin D, which may lead in turn to osteomalacia and muscular weakness. Both are readily treatable if recognised. Phenytoin may rarely induce lupus erythematosus with clinical manifestations.

Some important serious side-effects are listed under the appropriate heading in the *British National Formulary* (*BNF*) and any doctors prescribing medication for the first time are well-advised to spend a few minutes familiarising themselves with the appropriate entry. Failure to act in accordance with advice given in the *BNF* is frequently used as a powerful argument in allegations of negligence.

Some anticonvulsants have serious side-effects which may indirectly give rise to legal problems. Barbiturates, carbamazepine and phenytoin all increase the activity of liver enzymes. This increased enzyme activity has the effect of increasing the rate of metabolism of some other forms of medication and consequently may reduce their clinical effectiveness.

A special and potentially serious problem to which this may give rise is the effect of anticonvulsants on the activity of oral contraceptives. When a patient already taking anticonvulsant medication starts to take an oral contraceptive preparation, the fact that she is taking anticonvulsants must be taken into account in deciding the dose of the oral contraceptive necessary for the drug to be effective. Similarly, when a patient is already taking oral contraceptives, a decision that she should take anticonvulsants will mean that the dose of the oral contraceptive will need to be increased. The relevant detailed recommendations can be found in the information provided by the drug manufacturers of particular anticonvulsants.

Failure to consider this possibility has led to litigation following unplanned pregnancy. In such cases, there may be a dispute about the responsibility for failure to give an appropriate dose of the oral contraceptive. Does this lie with the general practitioner (GP) or the consultant? It seems reasonable in most cases that the responsibility should rest on the doctor who first *prescribes* the second drug, that is, the doctor who prescribes the oral contraceptive for a patient already taking a relevant anticonvulsant medication, or who first prescribes the anticonvulsant for a patient who is taking an oral contraceptive.

The other, and even more serious, effect of anticonvulsants in pregnancy lies in their effects on the fetus. Fetal abnormalities, particularly spina bifida and cleft palate, have a higher than expected incidence in patients taking any form of anticonvulsant medication, and an appropriate warning should be given to women of child-bearing age. The decision whether or not to stop anticonvulsants, if such a patient decides to become pregnant, must be discussed; in some instances, the risk to the fetus from the recurrence of frequent epileptic seizures may outweigh that of continuing the medication. A patient who becomes pregnant while taking anticonvulsants should be informed of the risks of fetal malformation and may decide not to continue with the pregnancy.

Changes in medication

Any sudden reduction in the dose of anticonvulsants may lead to a dangerous increase in the frequency of seizures, and in some cases may lead to the condition known as status epilepticus. This is a highly dangerous condition that may be fatal in which major seizures follow one another without the patient regaining consciousness. The change in medication may be accidental, e.g. a pharmacist may misread a prescription, or a patient may see a new doctor who does not have the information in his or her records. In other cases, a change of medication may be made quite deliberately, involving the substitution of a drug with less powerful anticonvulsant activity for one which is more potent. A reduction in the dose or cessation of treatment with phenobarbitone is thought to be particularly dangerous in this respect. Sometimes doctors in hospitals may be involved, because when a patient is admitted they may not realise and therefore not prescribe anticonvulsant medication which the patient has been taking under the direction of the family doctor. In a case of this sort, any harm which might result from loss of seizure control could be held to be the responsibility of the hospital doctor.

Symptomatic epilepsy

Epilepsy beginning in childhood is unlikely to be a symptom of some serious progressive cerebral disorder. When epilepsy develops later in life, it is much more likely to be caused by some acquired disease of the brain. The disease may be static (e.g. brain damage owing to head injury) or it may be progressive (e.g. cerebral glioma or intracranial meningioma).

In adults, the occurrence of epileptic attacks for the first time must always be fully investigated to exclude some serious underlying cause. Failure to carry out appropriate investigations may be the cause of an action for negligence by the patient, who has subsequently suffered damage as a result of the delay in detection of some remediable cause. Investigations to exclude intracranial tumours are now much easier to arrange than in past years, with the introduction of scanning in place of invasive and potentially dangerous investigations by air encephalography and arteriography.

Failure to detect a treatable metabolic cause for seizures may also give rise to litigation. Hypocalcaemia and hypoglycaemia, although both uncommon as causes of epilepsy, do give rise to seizures, and in the author's experience both have led to claims against doctors who had failed to make the correct diagnosis.

In one such case, a patient complained of episodes of dizziness and feelings of mental dullness, particularly in the morning but also at other times during the day. These were thought at first to be minor epileptic attacks, but their timing suggested the possibility of hypoglycaemia. This was investigated by admitting the patient to hospital for a prolonged fast. His blood sugar did not fall to abnormally low levels and he was discharged. His symptoms continued and he was admitted again for prolonged electroencephalographic studies. On the day after admission he insisted on discharging himself early in the morning before blood samples were taken. He was admitted for a third time some months later, and on this occasion low blood sugar levels were confirmed and insulin levels were abnormally high. A pancreatic insulinoma was found and removed. He later claimed that he had suffered unnecessarily over the two years during which the diagnosis had been missed. Examination of the notes revealed a report of high plasma insulin levels estimated at his first admission. This report had been returned long after his discharge and filed in his notes without being brought to the consultant's attention. Liability had to be admitted.

A common cause of epilepsy is head injury. With penetrating head injuries the incidence of epilepsy is very high. After closed head injuries, epilepsy occurs much less frequently, but it is important that doctors, in providing reports on prognosis for patients who have suffered head injuries, should make it clear that there is a risk that post-traumatic epilepsy may develop. It may develop even many years after the original trauma and the possibility of a long delay must be taken into account when advising solicitors about the settlement of claims. Failure to give this advice to solicitors would lay the doctor who provides the report open to a claim for negligence, should epilepsy develop later.

Chapter 18

Adverse Effects of Medication on the Nervous System

C.J. Earl

Peripheral nervous system

There are many different drugs which are well-recognised as causes of peripheral neuropathy. This means that practitioners may be held responsible for any disabilities arising from the use of these drugs if there has been any deviation from a pattern of practice ordinarily regarded as safe.

Gold

Gold was recognised as a cause of neuropathy as long ago as 1936. It is frequently used in the treatment of rheumatoid arthritis and the development of neuropathy appears to be rare (Katrak *et al.*, 1980). The earliest symptoms may be mild peripheral paraesthesiae in the hands and feet, associated with widespread muscle fasciculations. These mild symptoms may precede the development of muscle weakness, which may increase rapidly from the time it first appears. Once treatment is stopped the neuropathy begins to recover; it may do so completely, or leave some residual symptoms. It is essential that treatment with gold should be stopped if symptoms of neuropathy develop, even though they may be mild; therefore, patients should be advised to watch for the appropriate symptoms, and they should be observed carefully. Failure to stop treatment at the earliest sign of toxicity could be considered negligent.

Isoniazid

Soon after the introduction of isoniazid in the treatment of tuberculosis it was realised that it might cause a peripheral neuropathy. The neuropathy is caused by the inactivation of pyridoxal phosphate (the biochemically active form of pyridoxine), with which the isoniazid combines. Neuropathy can be avoided by concomitant administration of pyridoxine in an appropriate dose. As with gold neuropathy, early sensory symptoms may respond rapidly to cessation of medication or pyridoxine administration, while motor weakness, once present, may take many months to recover. For this reason, slow recovery and prolonged disability can be claimed to be the responsibility of the prescribing doctor if the early symptoms had not led to appropriate action.

Nitrofurantoin (furadantin)

This drug is used for the treatment of urinary infections. The development of a neuropathy usually begins after prolonged use, such as in the treatment of chronic urinary tract infections which are not uncommon. The development of neuropathy is also related to the presence of abnormally high plasma levels of the drug. Chronic urinary infection may be complicated by impairment of renal function. This reduces the excretion of the drug with consequent elevation of plasma levels to the toxic range. Physicians should be aware of this and should ensure that renal function is normal before embarking on a long course of treatment, and they may need to reassess renal function from time to time. As with drugs already considered, the rate of recovery from neuropathy depends upon the period during which the drug was administered after the first symptoms (usually paraesthesiae in the feet) appeared.

Phenytoin

Phenytoin has been used as an anticonvulsant for about 60 years. In 1968, Lovelace and Horwitz (1968) described a very mild neuropathy manifested clinically by no more than loss of ankle jerks and, in even fewer patients, by very mild sensory changes. The main abnormalities were found on electrophysiological examination in about 50% of patients who had been taking phenytoin for over 15 years. It is very unlikely that these effects would cause clinical manifestations that would lead to litigation. Phenytoin may also cause persistent lesions of the central nervous system, which are referred to below.

Cytotoxic drugs

Cisplatin will produce clinical symptoms of sensory neuropathy in about 50% of those who receive it, but there is no known way of avoiding this complication. However, it is important to explain the risk of neuropathy to the patient before treatment is started and when consent to treatment is obtained. The vinca alkaloids (vinblastine, vincristine and vindesine) all produce a neuropathy of a mixed type with sensory and motor symptoms. The neuropathy may be severe but, as is the case with cisplatin, may be unavoidable. The doctor ordering the treatment could be criticised only for failing to warn the patient of the likely side effects of this medication which, in any case, is given only for very serious and life-threatening disease.

Central nervous system

Phenothiazines

The clinical features of parkinsonism are often observed in patients taking drugs of the phenothiazine group in the high doses which may be needed to control severe manifestations of psychotic illness. It is particularly interesting that some of the features associated in the past specifically with post-encephalitic parkinsonism, such as akathisia (restless inability to sit still) and oculogyric crises, occur also as a result of treatment with phenothiazines. All these reactions are dose dependent and generally disappear when the dose is reduced. If it is necessary to continue with a high dosage, the symptoms may be controlled with antiparkinsonian medication of the standard sort. Patients who have been taking phenothiazines or related antipsychotic drugs for long periods (usually for some years) may develop quite a different type of movement disorder, first described 40 years ago (Hunter *et al.*, 1964). The patient develops abnormal movements affecting the limbs and the trunk and, most distressingly, the face, lips and tongue. This dyskinesia (as it is called) may persist for many months or sometimes indefinitely even after medication is stopped. Not only do patients find this very distressing but their family and friends find them distressing to watch.

When these drugs have been needed for the treatment of severe and prolonged psychotic illness, such symptoms cannot altogether be avoided, and on balance the risk of their developing must be regarded as acceptable in view of the importance of controlling the severe and perhaps dangerous manifestations of a chronic psychotic illness. Unfortunately, this syndrome of abnormal movements, which may be very distressing, is sometimes seen in patients who have been given phenothiazines, perhaps in small or moderate doses, over many years for symptoms which do not really justify the risk of this complication. In these circumstances, it is very difficult to defend the actions of a doctor who has continued the medication unnecessarily, especially when the drug has been continued even when the abnormal movements have begun. In one case, perphenazine had been prescribed over many years for the treatment of mild vertigo; in another, chlorpromazine had been given simply for mild anxiety. Persistent abnormal movements of this sort are particularly likely to occur in the elderly, or in those who already suffer from some other disturbance of cerebral function.

Lithium carbonate

Lithium carbonate is used commonly and very successfully for the treatment of manic–depressive disease. Lithium has very clear toxic effects on the nervous system which are dependent on the concentration of lithium in the brain, which in turn depends on the level of lithium in the plasma. It is very important that the level of lithium should be measured regularly to make certain that it is not too high. Where the level is higher than is safe the drug should be temporarily discontinued. It is also important to remember that metabolic disturbances involving changes in electrolyte balance may affect the levels of lithium in the plasma and in the nervous system. When such metabolic disturbances have occurred (for example, with severe vomiting and diarrhoea, or the concomitant administration of a diuretic), the levels should be checked frequently. Many patients in whom the level of plasma lithium is well within the therapeutic range have a mild tremor and no more. More serious neurological side-effects are ataxia, dysarthria, a confusional state and seizures. In severe cases the patient may die, or the clinical picture may not be wholly reversible. In cases where the diagnosis has not been made and there is persistent disability, patients have been successful in litigation against the prescribing doctor.

In some patients with severe mental disease, the behavioural disturbances that are associated with the illness itself may make an assessment of physical disease very difficult, but doctors who prescribe the drug should be aware of the possibility of serious organic neurological disease resulting from lithium therapy.

Phenytoin

Phenytoin in high doses produces a syndrome of nystagmus, dysarthria, incoordination of limb movement and loss of balance. The syndrome resembles that produced by acute alcoholic intoxication or cerebellar disease. With a reduction in the dose of phenytoin these signs usually disappear; but there are cases in which a high dose of phenytoin has been continued, despite the presence of such signs, where a persistent cerebellar syndrome has developed. Clearly, in such a case the prescribing doctor could be held responsible for the patient's continuing disabilities. The important subject of the teratogenic effects of phenytoin is considered in Chapter 17.

Aminoglycoside antibiotics

Deafness may complicate treatment with antibiotics of this group. Gentamycin is the one used most frequently. It is given intravenously or intramuscularly and the dose should be adjusted by monitoring of plasma levels, since the occurrence of deafness is related to levels of the drug in the plasma and the duration of the course of treatment. When careful monitoring of the plasma levels has not been carried out, the prescribing doctor could certainly be held responsible for the development of deafness, which in most instances is irreversible. A number of children suffered from deafness as a result of absorption of neomycin applied to extensive skin burns before this route of absorption was recognised. Now that this hazard is known, patients should not be put at risk in this way.

Vestibular damage may follow treatment with streptomycin. In some patients this occurs only after treatment for many weeks, but some patients appear to be highly sensitive to the drug and symptoms may appear soon after the course of treatment has begun. When symptoms first appear the situation is usually reversible if the drug is stopped, but if the drug is continued severe and persistent loss of balance may result. This is particularly likely to occur and to be disabling in the elderly. It is important, therefore, to recognise the earliest symptoms which may indicate vestibular damage. Classical vertigo should be readily recognised, but some patients complain of oscillopsia (a sensation that objects around them are moving up and down, or from side to side when the head is moved). This may be disregarded by doctors who are unfamiliar with its significance, but a failure to recognise it as the earliest symptom of vestibular damage would clearly be criticised.

In elderly patients, the loss of vestibular function may be devastating, and the use of streptomycin in the elderly for anything but dangerous infections which cannot be treated otherwise would be difficult to justify should treatment be followed by persistent symptoms in an elderly patient.

Oxytocin

Synthetic preparations of oxytocin are used to stimulate uterine contractions and induce the onset of labour, and in the management of incomplete abortion. The drug is given usually in a solution of 5% dextrose and the combination of the drug, with its antidiuretic properties, and a large volume of fluid may produce the syndrome of 'water intoxication' with hyponatraemia and consequent cerebral oedema, convulsions, confusion, coma and death. Such cases have occurred in obstetric practice, and although in mild cases the patient's state will become normal with simple fluid restriction, in others there may be severe and persistent impairment of intellectual function. Obstetricians should be aware of the risk and be prepared to deal appropriately with this emergency. There is some evidence that in such cases gradual correction of hyponatraemia is preferable to rapid change, which may give rise to a serious and usually fatal condition known as central pontine myelinolysis (Laureno, 1983).

Example

A woman of 35 was given oxytocin for induction of labour. After delivery she suffered a number of convulsions, was confused and lapsed into a coma before it was realised that the cause of this clinical picture was 'water intoxication'. Her serum sodium level was low, as was her serum osmolality. She improved when these abnormalities were corrected, but remained severely demented and quite unable to care for herself and her family. A claim for damages was settled before the case came to trial.

Ergotamine

Cases have occurred in which allegations of negligence are made in connection with the use of ergotamine in the treatment of migraine. This may happen either as the result of prescription of an excessive dose, or as the result of the patient taking an excessive dose on his or her own initiative. In either case, a doctor may be held responsible.

Where the patient has taken a higher dose than was ordered it may be important for the doctor to be able to satisfy a court that an adequate warning was given when the drug was prescribed. The known effects on the peripheral circulation, where ergotamine may cause severe arterial spasm in the limbs, are well-recognised and usually reversible in the early stages if the drug is stopped. If the drug is not stopped peripheral gangrene leading to amputation may result. In such cases there can be little dispute about causation. In other cases it is claimed that cerebral infarction has occurred as a result of the use of ergotamine in migraine, when the question of causation is much less easily decided. Migrainous attacks themselves, whether treated or not, may give rise to cerebral infarction, and unless the dose of ergotamine is grossly excessive it will be difficult for a plaintiff to prove a causative link (Broderick and Swanson, 1987).

Visual failure from medication

There are a number of drugs which may cause visual failure. In some cases the visual problems are rare, sporadic and apparently unpredictable. Quinine, for example, may cause loss of vision when given in ordinary therapeutic doses to individuals who appear to suffer from a unusual susceptibility to its toxic effects. Visual loss is rapid and, although there may be some recovery, acuity often remains impaired. It is clear that in this situation the doctor prescribing the drug could not reasonably be blamed.

Other drugs may cause a slowly progressive loss of visual function, and if treatment is stopped when symptoms first appear recovery may follow. When drugs that fall into this category cause persistent loss of vision the prescriber may be held responsible.

Ethambutol

Ethambutol is widely used in the treatment of tuberculosis and it has been recognised for many years that visual failure may result from its use (Citron,

1969). The visual impairment develops gradually with loss of visual acuity, and patients themselves should be asked to report any change in their visual acuity to the doctor. Before starting on a long course of ethambutol, visual function should be assessed carefully. In some cases, the disorder seems to have developed very rapidly when, presumably, there is some idiosyncratic hypersensitivity to the toxic effects of the drug. In the more usual cases, careful observation of visual acuity by the patient and his or her medical advisors should lead to early cessation of treatment and prompt recovery.

Chloroquine

Retinopathy and a reduction in visual acuity may occur with treatment with chloroquine, an antimalarial drug which is also used in the treatment of rheumatoid arthritis. Routine ophthalmic examination should be done before long-term treatment is started and patients should be told to report any change in vision to their doctor. If this warning is not given and serious visual loss occurs, it is likely that the doctor will be held responsible.

References

Broderick, J.P. and Swanson, J.W. (1987) Migraine-related strokes. *Archives of Neurology* **44**, 868–71.

Citron, K.M. (1969) Ethambutol: a review with special reference to ethambutol toxicity. *Tubercle* **50** (Suppl.), 32–6.

Hunter, R.A., Earl, C.J. and Janz, D. (1964) A syndrome of abnormal movements and dementia in leucotomised patients treated with phenothiazines. *Journal of Neurology, Neurosurgery and Psychiatry* **27**, 219–23.

Katrak, S.M., Pollock, M., O'Brien, C.P., Nukada, H., Allpress, S., Calder, C., Palmer, D.G., Grennan, D.M., McCormack, P.L. and Lavrent, M.R. (1980) Clinical and morphological features of gold neuropathy. *Brain* **103**, 671–93.

Laureno, R. (1983) Central pontine myelinolysis following rapid correction of hyponatraemia. *Annals of Neurology* **13**, 232–42.

Lovelace, R.E. and Horwitz, S.J. (1968) Peripheral neuropathy in long-term diphenylhydantoin therapy. *Archives of Neurology* **18**, 69–77.

Chapter 19

Psychosurgery

J.R. Bartlett

Introduction

For the purposes of this review, psychosurgery is defined as: 'a neurosurgical intervention to sever fibres connecting one part of the brain with another, or destroy part of the brain with the intent of modifying or correcting severe disturbances of mood, or particular thought contents (obsessional disorders).'

Concepts in psychiatry

Psychiatry – the treatment of disorders of the mind – raises many philosophical problems which are not easily tackled because they are not well-understood. The physical sciences, until comparatively recently, have had little to offer. The clinical classification proposed by Kraepelin, based on his study of several hundred patients in a German psychiatric hospital, has proved remarkably robust, while the analytical concepts of Jung and Freud have progressively lost validity. Kraepelin's classification of mental illness involved three diagnostic groups: (1) manic depression, now usually called affective disorders; (2) dementia praecox, now called schizophrenia; and (3) the organic psychoses. This last group in Kraepelin's time was largely due to neurosyphilis. The neuroses were described by Freud and his followers.

A particular problem is that the words used to describe mental illnesses are the same as are used to describe the normal mental experiences resulting from life's stresses. For example, people feel sad when someone close to them dies, anxious before testing situations, and elated or depressed depending on the outcome. However, a patient may complain of being depressed when he or she has a profound depressive illness which may in fact to be due to a metabolic fault in the brain that has no relationship to simple adversity. It is not always possible to distinguish between these two mechanisms but, of course, in many patients both mechanisms may play a part.

The first major advance in understanding, and with it the foundation of a scientific explanation for certain psychiatric illnesses, was the discovery, in the 1950s, of the neuroleptic drugs, the first being chlorpromazine. The formula of chlorpromazine was subsequently modified and this produced the first antidepressant, imipramine. From an entirely different direction came the monoamine oxidase inhibitors. The antituberculous drug, isoniazid, was modified to iproniazid, which was found to have antidepressant properties. Up to this time all psychiatric treatments had been empirical. Nonetheless, because a treatment is empirical does not necessarily imply that it is inappropriate. The test must be one of utility. The first half of the twentieth century saw major advances in medicine and surgery, but the huge problems faced by psychiatrists seemed to be intractable. It should, therefore, come as no surprise that many measures, even some extreme ones, were tried in the search for treatment of chronically distressed patients, but most measures were quickly abandoned.

The original psychosurgical operation, prefrontal leucotomy, was specifically intended to help patients with schizophrenia. Commonly, these patients suffered from an illness with an onset in their early twenties, and with a very long natural history. Despite the major side-effects of prefrontal leucotomy, one in five patients were discharged from hospital (Tooth and Newton, 1961). When chlorpromazine became available, schizophrenia was no longer an indication for psychosurgery. However, although there were fewer cases undergoing prefrontal leucotomy for affective disorders, as many as 50% of these cases could be discharged.

Therefore, after the advent of chlorpromazine, the aim of psychosurgery was to refine operations in order to reduce side-effects and to target affective disorders. It became clear that a lesion in the ventromedial segment of the frontal lobe (part of the limbic system) produced the best results with little risk of side-effects when accurately placed. These indications and the lesion have stood the test of time.

However, the 1950s and 1960s saw a number of attempts to tackle other difficult problems; for example, hypersexuality, outbursts of uncontrollable violent behaviour (sometimes in children), drug addiction and anorexia nervosa. A great variety of brain sites were used, as if each 'diagnosis' was clearly linked to a specific site which, if destroyed, would cure the condition. The risks were considerable and benefits at the best very uncertain. By the mid-1970s, most of these procedures had been abandoned. The stories made for a good press and found a public ready to get involved. Modern psychosurgery, more than any other psychiatric treatment, suffered for a long time from the legacy of its crude predecessors and long-abandoned procedures.

Public perception and knowledge

There is a social view that all psychiatric illnesses are caused by deprivations and social stresses of one form or another; they should be soluble by counselling and behaviour therapy. The use of medication, electroconvulsive therapy (ECT) or psychosurgery, all with possible irreversible side-effects, is considered an unwarranted invasion. The alternative opinion asserts that there are instances where the primary fault is in the brain and no amount of counselling or psychotherapy will be of the slightest use. For many, anything done to the brain is a threat to the autonomy of the person, and herein lies an explanation and important reason for public concern.

With the advent of effective medication and a better understanding of its use, the number of patients to whom psychosurgery is now offered is small. Few people will have first-hand knowledge of these patients or the results of treatment. Nonetheless there are a number of, in many respects, well-informed experts who unfortunately often have not had the opportunity to make any first-hand assessment of current practice, and yet are prepared to present a firm point of view to the public. Present practice is judged by results of the abandoned procedures of bygone years. Historical scholarship demands that the historian must marshall the facts and place himself or herself in the context of the time before passing any judgement. Information and data increase daily but the understanding and interpretation of the data is more elusive. Not surprisingly the medical profession, general public and politicians misunderstand one another from time to time. When a controlled trial for psychosurgery was proposed, a protocol was produced under the auspices of the Royal College of Psychiatrists (Research Committee of the Royal College of Psychiatrists, 1977) but it could not be funded. The debate that surrounded the issues highlighted a number of public concerns creating pressure for regulation of psychosurgery (and ECT). It was argued that:

- Alternative management regimes are not adequately used.
- Psychosurgery had no reasoned scientific basis.
- Its efficacy was in doubt.
- Regulation was necessary for proper and reliable assessment of its utility.
- The possible consequences of operations on behaviour and personality are matters of public concern.
- Doctors do not take adequate account of ethical issues.

The introduction and origin of regulation

The discovery of the first effective medications for psychiatric illnesses in the early 1950s, offering a solution to many hitherto intractable problems, occurred at a time when increasing energy was being put into medical research. It was a time with new hope for those with mental illness. The discovery that people with Parkinson's disease could be relieved with a small, precisely placed lesion in the brain gave some hope that certain psychiatric problems might be similarly treated. The short-lived International Society for Psychiatric Surgery did much to promote a rapid dissemination of information and understanding, and the demise of operations of doubtful efficacy. As a general principle the clinical practice of medicine has not been subject to formal external regulation. However, operations on, for example, violent prisoners, children and sexual deviants attracted much adverse attention, particularly in the USA. Arguments concerned:

- The autonomy of the individual.
- The distortion of a person's judgement and understanding by mental illness.
- Voluntary consent.
- Possible coercion of minors and prisoners.
- Diagnostic uncertainty in psychiatry.
- Unproven therapeutic efficacy of physical treatments including ECT.
- Irreversibility of psychosurgery.
- The fear that it might be used as an instrument of social control.

These arguments contributed to a haphazard introduction of regulation and case law. In 1973, the State of Oregon, and California the following year, produced legislation which effectively stopped psychosurgery. The method laid down for ensuring informed consent was so complex that it became virtually impossible to treat a patient without breaking the law. These events were to have influence far beyond the boundaries of the USA. Having raised reasons for concern, the debate has led to more measured proposals for regulating medical activity. These now include peer review (considered to be professionally biased) and committees, either local (parochial) or national (costly and difficult to administer). A balance of lay persons and professionals is required to ensure one section cannot intimidate a minority view. An independent psychiatrist is necessary to ensure that the diagnosis is correct, that the operation is indicated and that all other less-invasive and appropriate treatments have been properly tried. Many physicians believe regulation is a threat to their professional relationship with their patients.

The Mental Health Act 1983

Section 57 of the Mental Health Act is concerned with psychosurgery, defined as:

'(a) any surgical operation for destroying brain tissue or for destroying the function of brain tissue; and
(b) such other forms of treatment as may be specified for the purposes of the section by regulations made by the Secretary of State.'

The Act defines the commissioners, their responsibilities and gives certain powers to the Secretary of State. The full text is set out in Appendix 1.

The UK Mental Health Act Commission

The UK Parliament decided in 1983 that there should be a new Mental Health Act. This has proved to be a very forward-looking piece of legislation. It involved the setting up of the Mental Health Act Commission, a large council with psychiatrists, solicitors, social workers, psychologists and lay members. It is almost exclusively concerned with the civil rights and legal protection of patients compulsorily detained in hospital. In the circumstances it would, of course, be especially concerned with patients compulsorily admitted who accept psychosurgery. However, in practice, at the Geoffrey Knight Unit for Affective Disorders at London's Brook Hospital, very few patients who were compulsorily detained were admitted, and then only to prevent suicide.

There is no question at all that psychosurgery should be carried out on a compulsory basis. But the UK Parliament, during the time that it was debating the details of the Mental Health Act 1983, came to the conclusion that psychosurgery, in particular, required the Mental Health Act Commission to ensure that the patient had given fully informed consent, and that the operation was correctly recommended, with both sectioned patients and patients not at all detained. This was an extraordinary development because it meant that people who are entirely free, in relation to the 1983 Act, must compulsorily see members of the Commission and not their own consultant, in order to agree that psychosurgery may be carried out. For a council especially concerned with the human rights of detained patients, it is remarkable that they would wish to deprive patients, who are not detained, of their own human rights to agree or otherwise to a particular treatment. Furthermore, this legal process requires the final decision as to whether a patient has psychosurgery or not to depend upon a psychiatrist, appointed by the Mental Health Act Commission, whose experience of psychosurgery is likely to be very limited. Occasionally, the patient and family pay a heavy price as the following two cases illustrate.

First, a patient accepted for psychosurgery by the Geoffrey Knight Unit was not approved by the Commission's visitors and subsequently committed suicide (Bridges, 1984a, b). A second patient in depressive stupor, who could not give informed consent, was not seen by the Commission's visitors because she could not communicate (Bridges, 1992). She died in stupor of bronchopneumonia. Her husband had demanded that she should be treated in the unit because the unit had offered and accepted her for psychosurgery.

Judicial review is not a certain solution as these two cases illustrate. Section 57 of the Act is concerned with psychosurgery and also:

> 'such other forms of treatments as may be specified for the purposes of this Section by regulations made by the Secretary of State'.

The other form of treatment available at present consists of surgical implants. There has been a case of a paedophile for whom other forms of treatment had not sufficiently reduced his sexual drive, and so he had been imprisoned on a number of occasions. The patient was, therefore, much in favour of an implant of goserelin, but this was refused by a doctor appointed by the Mental Health Act Commission on the grounds that the patient did not understand how goserelin was effective. At a judicial review (Dyer, 1988) it was discovered that the patient thought that, as the goserelin is implanted into the lower abdomen, it had direct effects on the sexual organs. Of course, goserelin has a central effect. The judge dismissed the case because it was unreasonable to expect the patient to know the precise action of the drug he was given. Such is the effect of involving the law in specifically medical matters.

The Geoffrey Knight Unit also offered surgery for a lady in her early thirties. She undoubtedly had a bipolar affective disorder, as did her brother. The importance of psychosurgery was that, although she tolerated her illness unusually well, it was clear that her work record had gradually deteriorated over the years. From being an Oxford graduate, she then became a personal secretary. As the years went by she took secretarial work when she felt well enough, and for a period of some years was unable to work at all and had difficulty getting out of bed each day. The Mental Health Act Commission declined to agree to psychosurgery. The lady instructed a solicitor to go to a judicial review but the solicitor felt that this would not succeed because, in effect, it was the opinion of one consultant psychiatrist against another. However, the consultant psychiatrist supporting her had an experience of hundreds of psychosurgical operations which the Commission's psychiatrist did not have. This seems to be a particular legal difficulty in these circumstances, where the Mental Health Act Commission has an entirely autocratic role based on the law and not based on medical principles.

Informed consent

> 'Every human being of adult years, with sound mind, has a right to determine what shall be done with his own body.' (Justice Cardozo 1914)

This quotation encapsulates the legal and ethical principles which determine the relationship between physician and patient.

The right to autonomy of one's body and informed consent are closely related topics. If there is an inalienable right to autonomy (self-determination), it follows that a person from whom consent is obtained must be informed of any consequences of the treatment that might influence his or her decision. The process of obtaining informed consent attempts to make the physician and patient equal bargaining partners (if this were possible). It is much easier to state the principles than to find universal rules for their application, particularly where psychiatric illness is concerned. To this end, there are three fundamental questions (embodied in the Nuremberg Code) which should be considered:

- Competence.
- Knowledge.
- Whether or not the patient is able to accept treatment voluntarily.

Competence

Competence to give consent implies that the person is of sound mind and of sufficient maturity to understand the nature and purpose of treatment. Psychiatric patients may be incompetent to give informed consent as a result of their illness, which may distort a person's perceptions and understanding. The Mental Health Act places constraints on the management of these patients. Nonetheless, the criteria for assessing competence are not entirely clear and remain to an extent subjective without universal applicability.

The competence of persons detained under the Mental Health Act remains contentious. Some depressed patients with a very high suicidal risk may require the force of law to keep them in hospital for their own safety. In these circumstances, a patient may be treated with psychosurgery while detained, as one patient who was admitted to the Geoffrey Knight Unit explained. She instructed that she be kept on an order for her own safety, as without it she would leave hospital to kill herself and knew without the order the unit would not have the authority to stop her. Fortunately, the majority of patients lose their intense suicidal drive very soon after psychosurgery, a curious outcome that we always notice – early resolution of suicidal drive and anorexia, later resolution of depression, etc.

Psychosurgery is not an appropriate treatment for severe antisocial behaviour of the kind that may lead to imprisonment. The treatment of prisoners with personality and behaviour disorders which was much discussed in early literature is only of historical interest. There were serious doubts (mainly in the USA) about the competence of any prisoner to give consent. Legal competence should be separated from informed consent. 'Imprisoning' *per se* does not necessarily render a patient incompetent.

Knowledge

The provision of sufficient and relevant information about the operation to the patient, and ensuring his or her understanding, makes demands on the patient, the patient's relatives and the physician. The issues are listed below:

- Is the diagnosis correct taking into account the difficulties in psychiatric taxonomy?
- How clear are the reasons for supposing the treatment will achieve the therapeutic goals?
- Have all the relevant alternatives been tried and tested?
- To what extent will the education and intellectual endowments of each patient affect their ability to understand the nature and purpose of the proposed treatment?

The physician must, of course, be aware of the alternative methods of treatment. Referrals for psychosurgery to the Geoffrey Knight Unit demonstrate that this is not always the case. Giving guidance on the alternatives to psychosurgery in the management of severe affective disorders has become a major role for the team of this psychosurgical unit (Bridges *et al.*, 1994).

Despite every endeavour, it may remain extremely difficult to determine if a patient has gained a clear and balanced understanding of the potential benefits and the risks of treatment. Within the medical profession there used to be, and perhaps still is, a paternalistic approach to the patient, believing that the physician, acting altruistically, can make a sound judgement of what the patient needs to know; an opinion supported by *Sidaway* v. *Board of Governors of the Bethlem Royal Hospital and the Maudlsey Hospital* (1985). On the other hand, 'informed' consent is increasingly an instrument used to ensure improved communication between physician and patient. Many patients wish to be active participants in the decision-making process. There is an increasing body of opinion that considers that a lay person is best equipped to assess a patient's understanding of the illness and proposed treatment. If the assessor has no professional knowledge, it is difficult to understand how the interrogation could be carried out in a meaningful manner. A mixed body like the Commissioners appointed under the 1983 Act probably offers as good a safeguard as is possible.

Voluntary

There are people who believe that all mental illnesses distort intellectual faculties and rational judgement to such a degree that informed consent is impossible. It is now established that psychosurgery is not indicated for those mental disorders where severe delusions are the major feature, for example schizophrenia. Severely depressed patients often believe, at times with delusional intensity, that there is no hope of recovery and hence may refuse treatment on the grounds that it is a waste of time. Some patients with relapsing illnesses have expressed the wish that they are to be treated in the event of a relapse. Severe depression to the point of stupor make it impossible to obtain consent from the patient. A caring family may be able to express a view of what they believe the patient would wish in the circumstances, but it is unlikely that psychosurgery as opposed to, for example, ECT could be used. It is difficult to conceive a legal framework that deals with this situation satisfactorily. It also begs the question, should a patient be denied essential treatment because he or she is unable to understand what is at stake?

It is prudent to obtain consent within a short time before psychosurgery (or for that matter any major elective procedure) and a period of reflection prior to surgery has much to commend it. The waiting list and the machinations of the Mental Health Act Commission serves this function. It is always emphasised that the patient must make the final decision after hearing the evidence. Because of the nature of psychiatric illness, it was the Geoffrey Knight Unit's practice to bring patients into hospital at least a week before the operation to provide them with an opportunity to discuss the operation and perhaps change their mind. The medical team need to be sure that psychosurgery is the correct course of action. Many patients find the extra days in hospital tedious. On a rare occasion, this process provides the opportunity for a patient to decline the previously accepted offer of psychosurgery. There is also the very rare patient who, having been offered operative treatment, feels that in the event of refusal, he or she would lose all support from the local psychiatric services. It is important that these patients are detected and reassured accordingly.

Malpractice

Clearly, it is not appropriate for a neurosurgeon to be wholly responsible for the psychiatric assessment or to have a detailed knowledge of all possibly relevant treatments. Similarly is it impossible for the psychiatrist to fully understand the intricacies of the surgical procedure. However, each should be satisfied that the other has carried out or will carry out his or her task to the standard required. Working together during the preoperative assessment and early postoperative course is important. It is prudent for anyone involved in uncommon treatments to have a protocol; for example, that used by the Geoffrey Knight Unit (Bridges *et al.*, 1995; Bowskill & Bridges, 1997) or that used in the Netherlands (Cosyns *et al.*, 1994) (see Appendix 2). It is necessary to record reasons for any variations which on occasion may be justified. Clear documentation is mandatory and could be used to guide the court in its judicial function if it were ever necessary. So few people are now involved in psychosurgery that to find a body of informed opinion would be difficult. In England and Wales this issue will also be covered by the Mental Health Act Commissioners.

Ethical issues

Society has yet to produce a satisfactory set of universal rules which defines fully informed consent or completely copes with the issues arising from imperfectly understood treatments. Psychiatry is likely to remain a focal point for debate as illustrated by the following points:

- No person should be denied treatment because he or she is involuntarily confined or unable to understand what is at stake. However, to treat such a person is an infringement of his or her right to autonomy. Has society a solution?
- Should patients ever be treated against their expressed wishes? The conviction (without punishment) of Dr Chabot by the Dutch Supreme Court for assisting a patient, suffering from depression which was likely to be treatable, to commit suicide is interesting (Ogalvie and Potts, 1994).
- The outcome of all treatment is accompanied by a degree of uncertainty. If the treatment of the patient is the sole objective the process is regarded as therapy. If the outcome is being recorded for the purpose of accumulation of knowledge the treatment is, at least in part, research and the physician's motives may be questioned. The dividing line is unclear and there are implications for the methods used to obtain consent and its perceived validity.
- Rigid regulation may not be in the best interests of either the patient or the medical profession. It likely to stifle innovation, research and development. Ethical committees (with lay representation) already assist in the process of self-regulation.

Conclusion

The key issues for psychosurgery, some of which may have more general application, are as follows:

- Informed consent is a legal concept which allows no ignorance.
- Autonomy of the individual is a right which must be respected.
- The relationship between physician and patient is changing from one of paternalism to informed partner.
- The patient must be given sufficient information to maintain his or her right to self-determination.
- The physician should be properly appraised of the possible outcome and risks of the proposed treatment as well as the other options which may be relevant in the circumstances.
- The physician should be aware that a patient's illness may distort his or her judgement. When particularly risky treatments are involved, a second opinion is usually, if not always, prudent. The Mental Health Act 1983 made

an additional opinion from their appointed commissioner for psychosurgery compulsory - possibly undesirable if allowing the individual his or her personal rights.

- The position of a patient for whom a psychosurgical operation might be life-saving and who cannot consent to treatment is unclear as is the position of the medical team. The Dutch court ruling on Dr Chabot may have compounded the problem (Ogalvie and Potts, 1994).
- The motivation of the physician may be used to decide if patient management is therapeutic or experimental (audit and clinical research highlight the issues).

Case references

Sidaway v. *Board of Governors of the Bethlem Royal Hospital and the Maudsley Hospital* [1985] AC 871.

References

Bowskill, R.J. and Bridges, P.K. (1997) Treatment-resistant affective disorders. *British Journal of Hospital Medicine* **57**, 171–2.

Bridges, P.K. (1984a) Psychosurgery and Mental Health Act Commission. *Bulletin of the Royal College of Psychiatrists* **8**, 146–8.

Bridges, P.K. (1984b) Addendum to 'Psychosurgery and Mental Health Act Commission'. *Bulletin of the Royal College of Psychiatrists* **8**, 172.

Bridges, P.K. (1992) Is Psychosurgery safer than section 57? *Bulletin of the Royal College of Psychiatrists* **16**, 510.

Bridges, P.K., Bartlett, J.R., Hale, A.S., Poynton, A.M., Malizia, A.L. and Hodgkiss, A.D. (1994) Psychosurgery: stereotactic subcaudate tractotomy, an indispensable treatment. *British Journal of Psychiatry* **165**, 599–611.

Bridges, P.K., Hodgkiss, A.D. and Malizia, A.L. (1995) Practical management of treatment-resistant affective disorders. *British Journal of Hospital Medicine* **54**, 501–6.

Cosyns, P., Camaert, J., Haaijman, W., Van Veelen, C., Gybels, J., van Manen, J. and Ceha, J. (1994) Advances and functional stereotactic neurosurgery for psychiatric disorders: an experience in Belgium and the Netherlands. *Advances and Technical Standards in Neurosurgery* **21**, 239–79.

Dyer, C. (1988) Chemical castration controversy. *British Medical Journal* **297**, 640.

Ogilvie, A.D. and Potts, S.G. (1994) Assisted suicide for depression: the slippery slope in action. *British Medical Journal* **309**, 492–3.

Research Committee, Royal College of Psychiatrists (1977) Evaluation of the surgical treatment of functional mental illness: proposal for a prospective controlled trial. In *Neurosurgical Treatment in Psychiatry, Pain and Epilepsy* (W.H. Sweet, S. Obrador and J.G. Martin-Rodriguez, eds). University Park Press, Baltimore.

Tooth, G.C. and Newton, M.P. (1961) Leucotomy in England and Wales 1952–54. Reports on Public Health and Mental Subjects No. 104, Ministry of Health. HMSO, London.

Further reading

Bartlett, J.R., Bridges, P.K., Kelly, D. (1981) Contemporary indications for psychosurgery. *British Journal of Psychiatry* **38**, 507–11.

Blomquist, C.D.D. (1979) Some ethical problems in psychiatry. *Ethics in Science and Medicine* **6**, 105–14.

Boukoms, A.J. (1988) Ethics of psychosurgery. *Acta Neurochirurgica* (Suppl.) **44**, 173–8.

Bridges, P.K. and Bartlett, J.R. (1977) Psychosurgery: yesterday and today. *British Journal of Psychiatry* **131**, 249–60.

Clare, A.W. (1979) Ethical issues in psychiatry. *Practitioner* **233**, 89–96.

Dickson, D. (1979) Psychosurgery supporters sued for malpractice. *Nature* **277**, 164–5.

Dyer, C. (1994) Judge allows force feeding of mentally competent patient. *British Medical Journal* **309**, 291–2.

Field, L.H., Rollin, H. and Watts, C.A.H. (1973) New horizons in medical ethics: changing the patient's personality. *British Medical Journal* **866**(2), 594–8.

Fried, C. (1979) Experimental surgery, and predictions of outcome from severe neurological illness: legal and ethical implications (commentary). *Ciba Foundation Symposium* **69** (new series), 279–92.

Giesen, D. (1993) Legal accountability for the provision of medical care: a comparative view. *Journal of the Royal Society of Medicine* **86**, 648–52.

Gostin, L.O. (1980) Ethical considerations of psychosurgery: the unhappy legacy of prefrontal lobotomy. *Journal of Medical Ethics* **6**, 149–54.

Langley, G.E. (1998) Assessment and certification of neurosurgery for mental disorder. *Psychiatric Bulletin* **22**, 497–500.

O'Callaghan, M.A.J. and Carroll, D. (1982) *Psychosurgery: A Scientific Analysis*. M.T.P. Press, Lancaster.

Report by a Good Practice Group of the CRAG Working Group on Mental Illness (1996) Neurosurgery for Mental Disorder. Scottish Office, HMSO, London.

Sider, R.C. (1984) The ethics of therapeutic modality choice. *American Journal of Psychiatry* **141**(3), 390–94.

Stone, A.A. (1979) Informed consent: special problems for psychiatry. *Hospital and Community Psychiatry* **30**, 321–7.

Valenstien, E. (1973) *Brain Control*. John Wiley, New York.

Valenstien, E. (1980) *The Psychosurgery Debate*. W.H. Freeman, San Francisco.

APPENDIX 1
Mental Health Act 1983 (section 57)

Part IV of the Mental Health Act 1983 is concerned with consent to treatment. Section 57 applies to psychosurgery (treatment requiring consent and a second opinion) and reads as follows:

'(1) This section applies to the following forms of medical treatment for mental disorder:

(a) any surgical operation for destroying brain tissue or for destroying the function of brain tissue; and

(b) such other forms of treatment as may be specified for the purposes of the section by regulations made by the Secretary of State.

(2) Subject to section 62 below, a patient shall not be given any form of treatment to which this section applies unless he has consented to it and:
(a) a registered medical practitioner appointed for the purposes of this Act by the Secretary of State (not being the responsible medical officer) and two other persons appointed for the purpose of this paragraph by the Secretary of State (not being registered medical practitioners) have certified in writing that the patient is capable of understanding the nature, purpose and likely effects of the treatment in question and has consented to it; and
(b) the registered medical practitioner referred to in paragraph (a) above has certified in writing that, having regard to the likelihood of the treatment alleviating or preventing a deterioration of the patient's condition, the treatment should be given.

(3) Before giving a certificate under sub-section (2)(b) above, the registered medical practitioner concerned shall consult two other persons who have been professionally concerned with the patient's treatment, and of those persons one shall be a nurse and the other shall be neither a nurse nor a registered medical practitioner.

(4) Before making any regulations for the purpose of this section the Secretary of State shall consult such bodies as appear to him to be concerned.'

APPENDIX II
The Netherlands - a European example of effective self-regulation by the profession

Between 1971 and 1991, all cases offered psychosurgery in Belgium and the Netherlands have been considered by a committee, which was initially set up by a committee of psychiatrists and neurosurgeons in the Netherlands to form a review board. When a patient is accepted by this committee, the following criteria must be satisfied:

- The diagnosis is correct and appropriate.
- All other relevant treatments have been tried and failed.
- The correct operation will be carried out by a surgeon trained in the technique.
- There will be adequate follow-up and rehabilitation.
- The relatives are supportive of the procedure and adequate information has been given to the patient and the family.
- The consent of the patient is informed.

The Dutch Health Council considered that the existence of this committee on psychosurgery in Belgium and the Netherlands was a good example of self-regulation. However, they recommended that the committee should include a member with special knowledge of ethics. In many respects this committee serves a similar function to the

Commissioners who regulate psychosurgery in the UK. However, it has neither the legal status, nor does it separate those who treat the patient from those who give permission for the procedure to go ahead.

Table of cases

Index